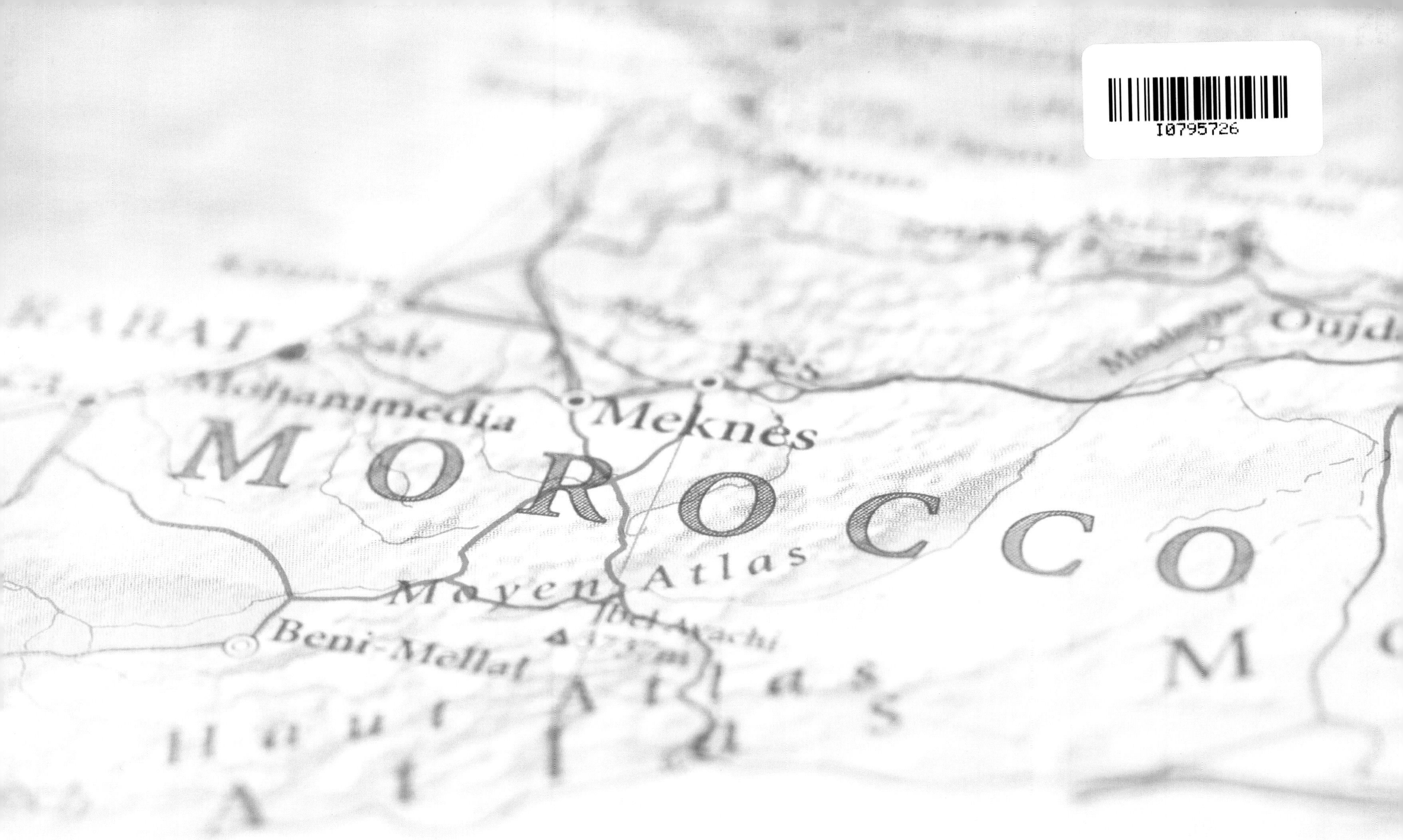
Salé
Mohammedia
Fès
Meknès
MOROCCO
Atlas
Beni-Mellal

# EPIC MOROCCO

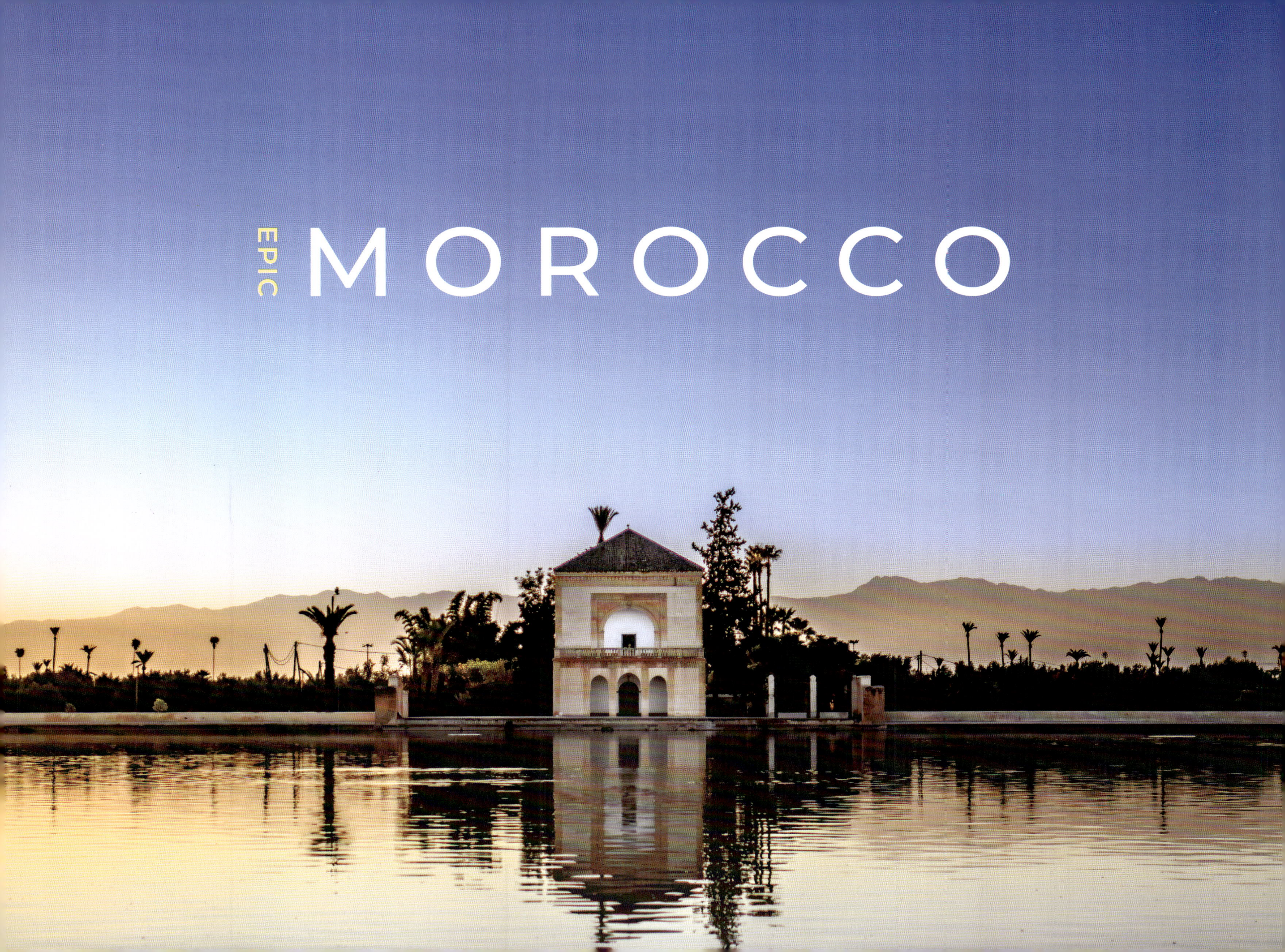

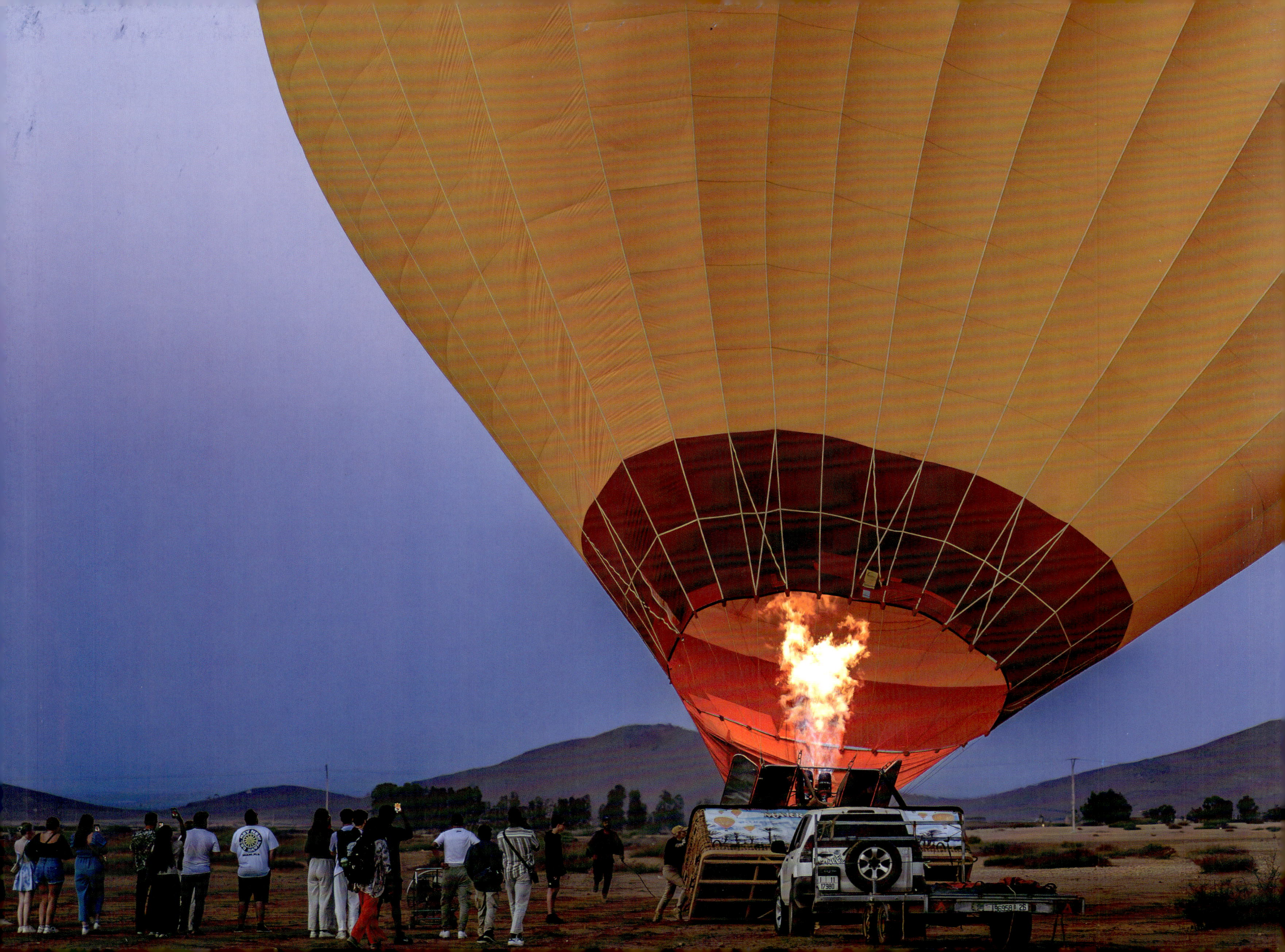

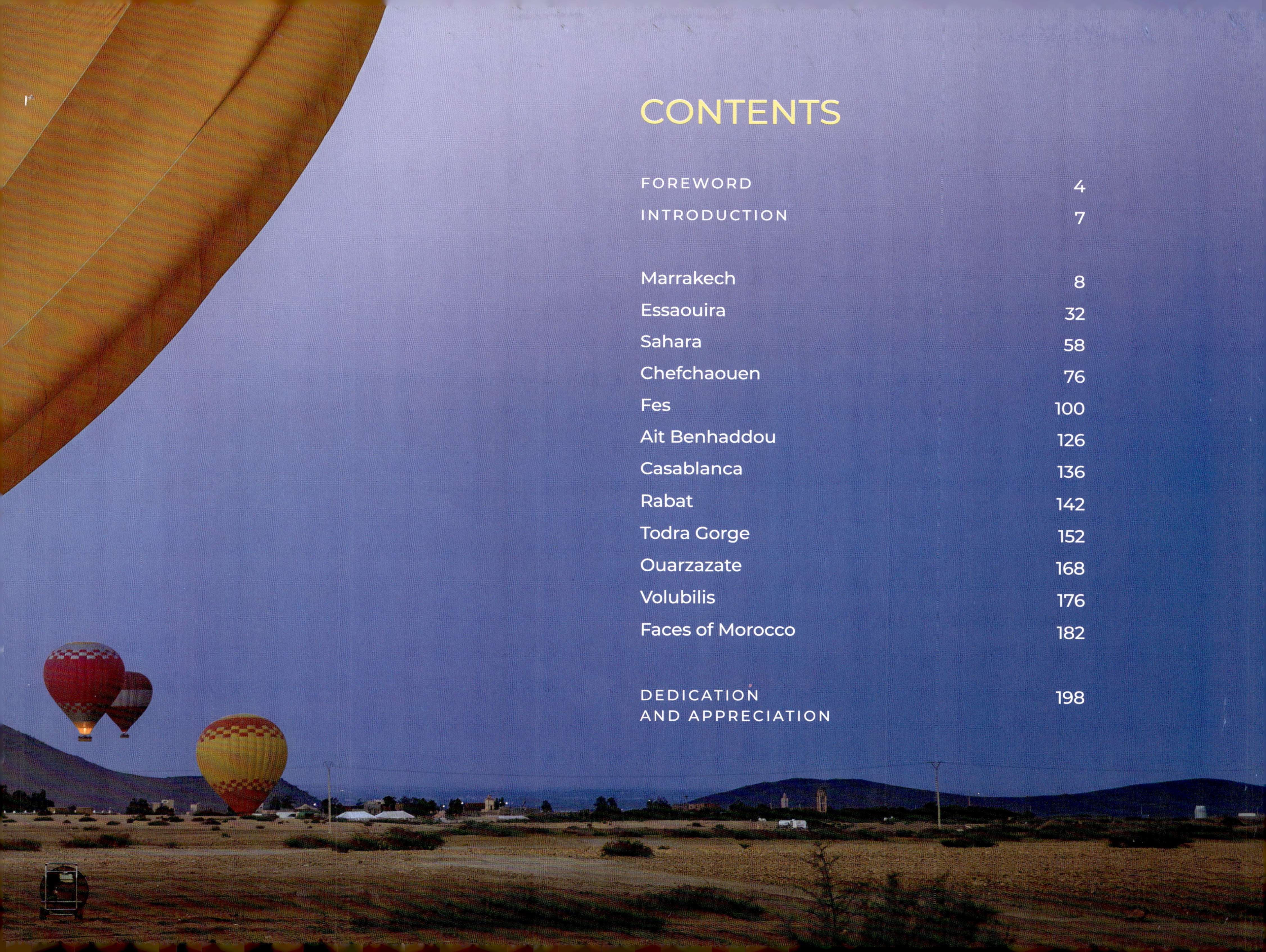

# CONTENTS

# FOREWORD—NOMADIC TOURS

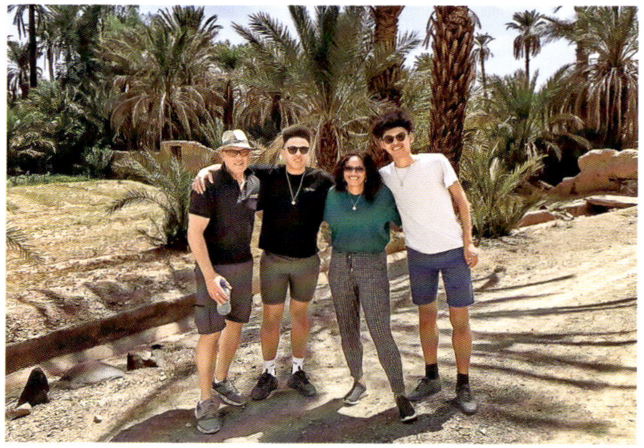

**Marhaba,**

It is with great pleasure that we introduce *Epic Morocco*, a project that holds a special place in our hearts. Our love affair with Morocco started all the way back in 1993. It was in our adventurous youth that Diana (my wife and co-owner & founder of *Nomadic Tours*) first met in the Moroccan Sahara Desert. Nomadic Tours had not even been conceived then, but all these years later, we still have a romantic and enduring connection to Morocco.

For us, Morocco became more than just a destination, it became a second home. For Diana, born in the Netherlands and later settling in the UK, it was her third. Over the years, our admiration for Morocco has only grown, as did our family when our son's Finley & Noah were born in 2001 & 2005 respectively. Beyond its breathtaking landscapes and rich diversity, what continues to captivate us is the profound cultural depth and the enduring friendships we have formed with its people. Having traveled extensively around the world, we have yet to encounter a culture as hospitable and welcoming as that of Morocco.

Our collaboration on *Epic Morocco* came about serendipitously. In November 2023, Ed and Kathy booked our 15-day Morocco Encompassed Private Tour. Their positive feedback and Kathy's enthusiastic social media updates were heartwarming, but we had no idea their journey would plant the seed for this book. Shortly after, Ed approached us with the idea of creating a visual celebration of Morocco. We didn't hesitate. Plans were soon underway for Ed's private photography trip, accompanied by our guide Khalid, to capture images that showcase the beauty and soul of this extraordinary country.

Selecting which images to include was no small task; Morocco offers an embarrassment of riches when it comes to stunning scenery and vibrant culture. While this book highlights some of the country's most iconic locations, there is so much more to discover. For those places not featured, we hope Epic Morocco inspires you to seek them out for yourself.

Ed Moran's photography captures not only the breathtaking beauty of Morocco but also its cultural depth and the genuine warmth of its people. Each image tells a story, evoking the essence of a place where history, tradition, and natural splendour come together in harmony. For me, the Sahara Desert remains a personal favorite, a place of unmatched majesty, serenity, and unforgettable sunrises and sunsets.

I hope this book inspires you to embark on your own Moroccan journey. Whether you are revisiting or discovering Morocco for the first time, you will be welcomed with open arms.

Diana and I extend our heartfelt gratitude to our incredible team here at *Nomadic Tours*, Sherrie in the UK, and our outstanding team in Marrakech, General Manager Brahim and our guides, Mustapha, Younes A, Khalid, Mohamed, El Hassan, Younes O, Lahcen, and Aissa. A special thank you goes to Ed and Kathy, whose journey with us sparked the idea for *Epic Morocco*. Your vision and collaboration have brought this stunning project to life.

We invite you to immerse yourself in the pages of this book and experience the magic of Morocco, as we have.

Shukran

*Mark Stallwood, Finley Stallwood, Diana Stallwood Codrington, and Noah Stallwood.*

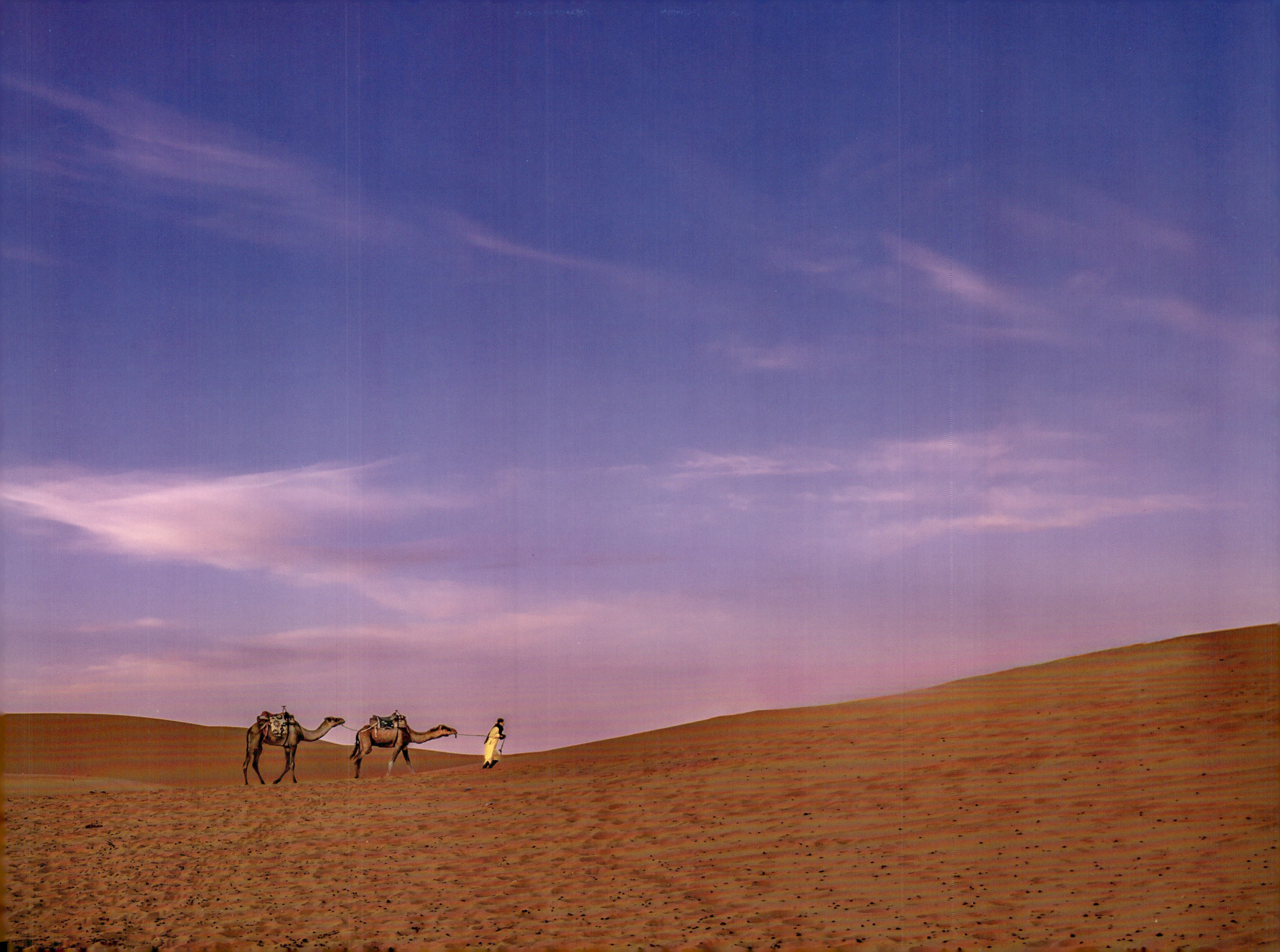

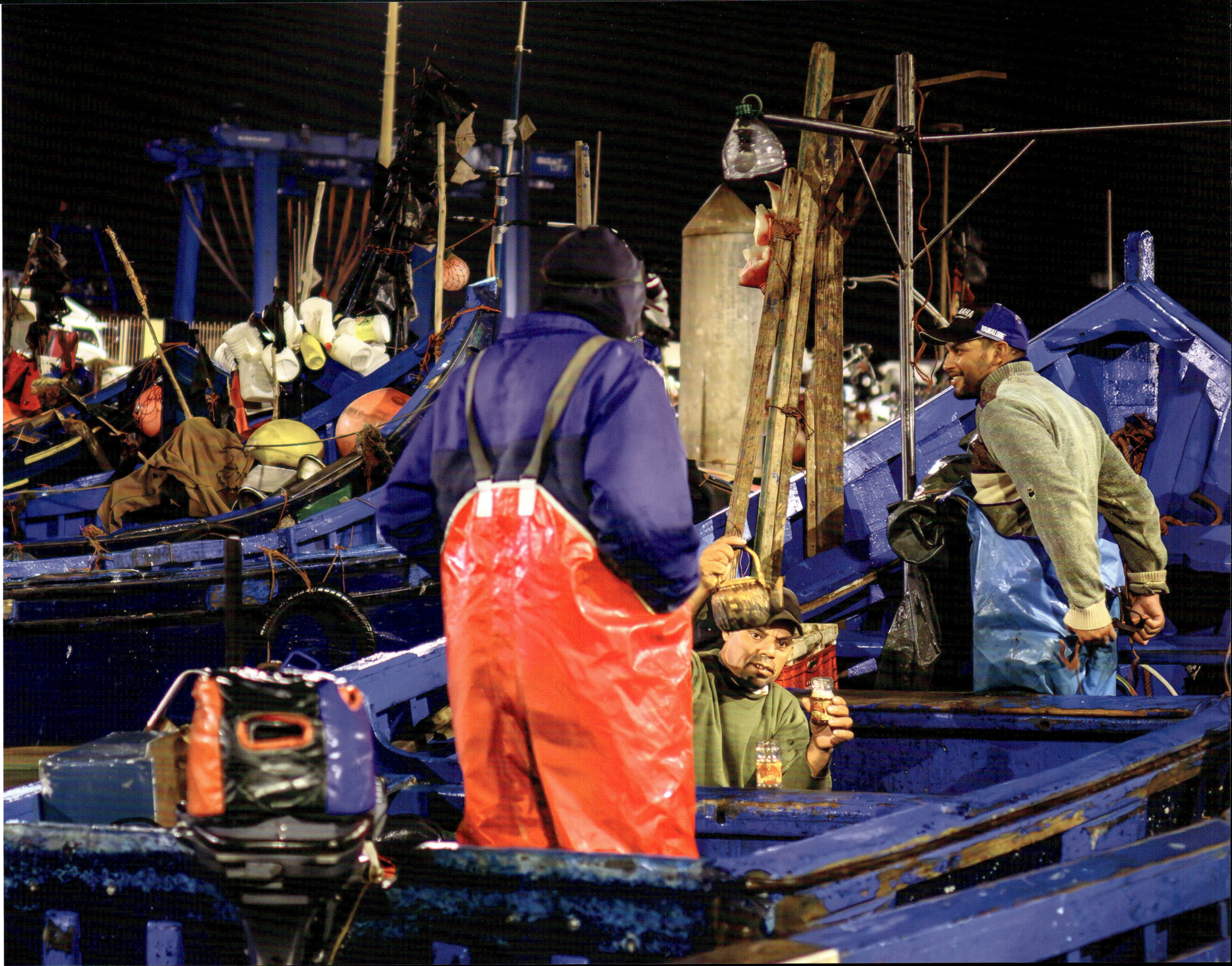

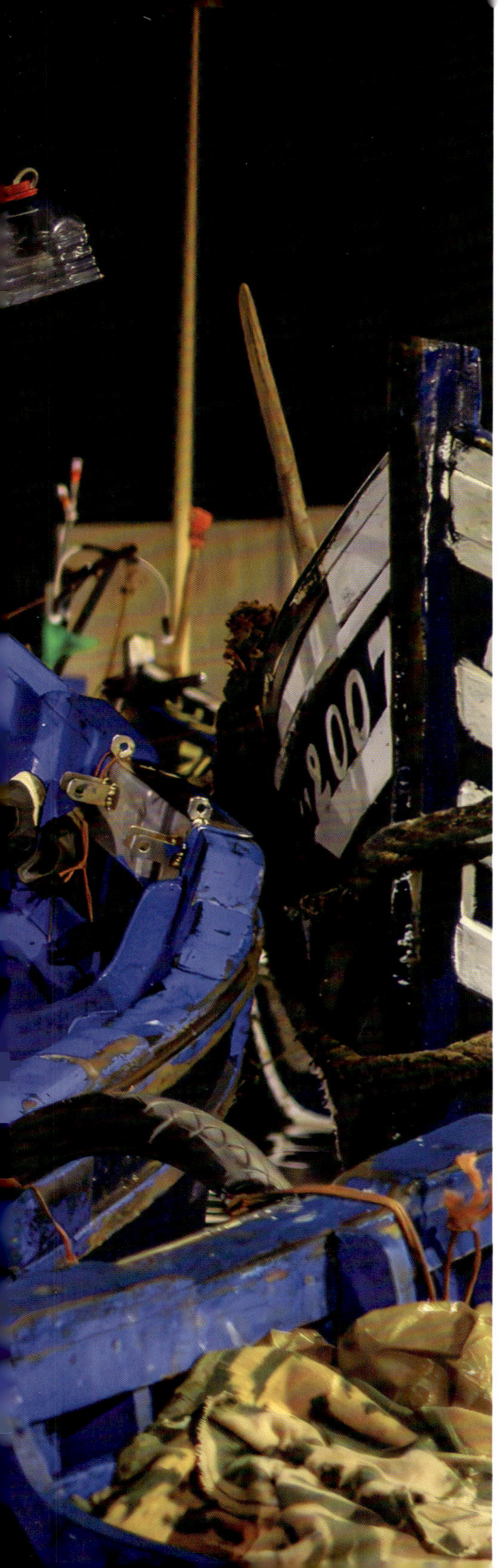

# INTRODUCTION

A pre-dawn breeze moves across the beaches and waterfront that highlight the coastal town of Essaouira. Not far from the hotels and restaurants on the main street and behind the walls of the old city, where the shops and souks were still buttoned up for the night, fishermen begin arriving and preparing for a day of labor.

The light from the just rising sun is only enough to help the men see their way down the piers and walkways to where their small boats have been buoyed for the night. They arrive quietly, and begin preparing nets, bait and gear for the long day ahead.

In many other places, the scene would be more like work, less inviting to witness.

But this is Morocco, a country where color, culture, tradition and family matter. And the approach to a day is joyful. It is when time is taken to brew Moroccan mint tea in ornate silver pots over portable stoves, to be poured into small cups in a way only a Moroccan serves tea—the pot held high above the cup and delivered in a stream down into the cup.

It's a tradition. It means the recipient is a welcomed guest.

As the sun breaks the surface of the sea, the light begins to illuminate the color surrounding the men as the melodic tones of the first call to prayer beckon the faithful to worship. Hundreds of bright blue boats, with names painted in white on their bows, bob in a packed harbor, framed by ancient walls—walls that lead to a city once named Mogador, and an Atlantic Ocean facing stone battlement of cannons, picturesque enough to be the scene of movies and episodes of television shows like *Game of Thrones*. It is breathtaking in its color and majesty.

And it is the kind of morning that is unfolding across this vast Northern African country. From the endless and timeless dunes of the Sahara Desert, above the major cities of Casablanca, Marrakech, Rabat, Fes, the Blue City of Chefchaouen, the towering walls of Todra Gorge, and ancient Ait Benhaddou, the rising sun signals the beginning of another day of stunning scenes of beauty and life that begs to be seen, experienced, and enjoyed by visitors from around the world.

The pages of this book will illustrate many of those scenes and the faces of the people who live and work here. Fishermen, yes. But also, artists, fine metal, pottery and jewel workers, shop keepers, rug and garment weavers, and the Nomad people who live in moving tent cities, tending flocks of sheep, camels, goats and living off the land, as their ancestors did before them, and their children who will follow.

This book is a love letter to Morocco, and an invitation to experience this stunning, and still largely unchanged by time, land of beauty and its welcoming joyful people. So come, turn the pages, and enjoy this through the lens look at the Kingdom of Morocco.

# HISTORY, ART AND CULTURE IN A WHIRLWIND METROPOLIS

If there is one place in Morocco that can take multiple days to explore, it's Marrakech, the fourth largest city and one of the four imperial cities of the Kingdom. Located in the South, between the Atlantic Ocean, the Sahara Desert, and the Atlas Mountains, Marrakech is a sprawling and busy cosmopolitan city centered around the Djemaa el-Fna, a vast city square packed with merchants in the shadow of the Koutoubia Mosque, which has towered over the square since it was erected in the 12th century.

Djemaa el-Fna is a vibrant, multi-staged street theater, filled with musicians, snake charmers, craftsmen, merchants and restaurants, and bursts to life after sunset. Outside of the square, and the UNESCO World Heritage Site medina, the city has a mountain backdrop, features architecture dating back to the 11th century, and breathtaking gardens. The city population is a mix of Arab, Amazigh, African and Jewish cultures, features one of the oldest Jewish quarters in Morocco, and has sites that include the Saadian Tombs, Bahia Palace, the Jardin Majorelle and Menara Gardens.

It is a city that seldom slows down and is alive with a cavalcade of buzzing traffic; all the cars, motorbikes, buses, and horse drawn carriages compete for a piece of road making crossing anywhere an adventure.

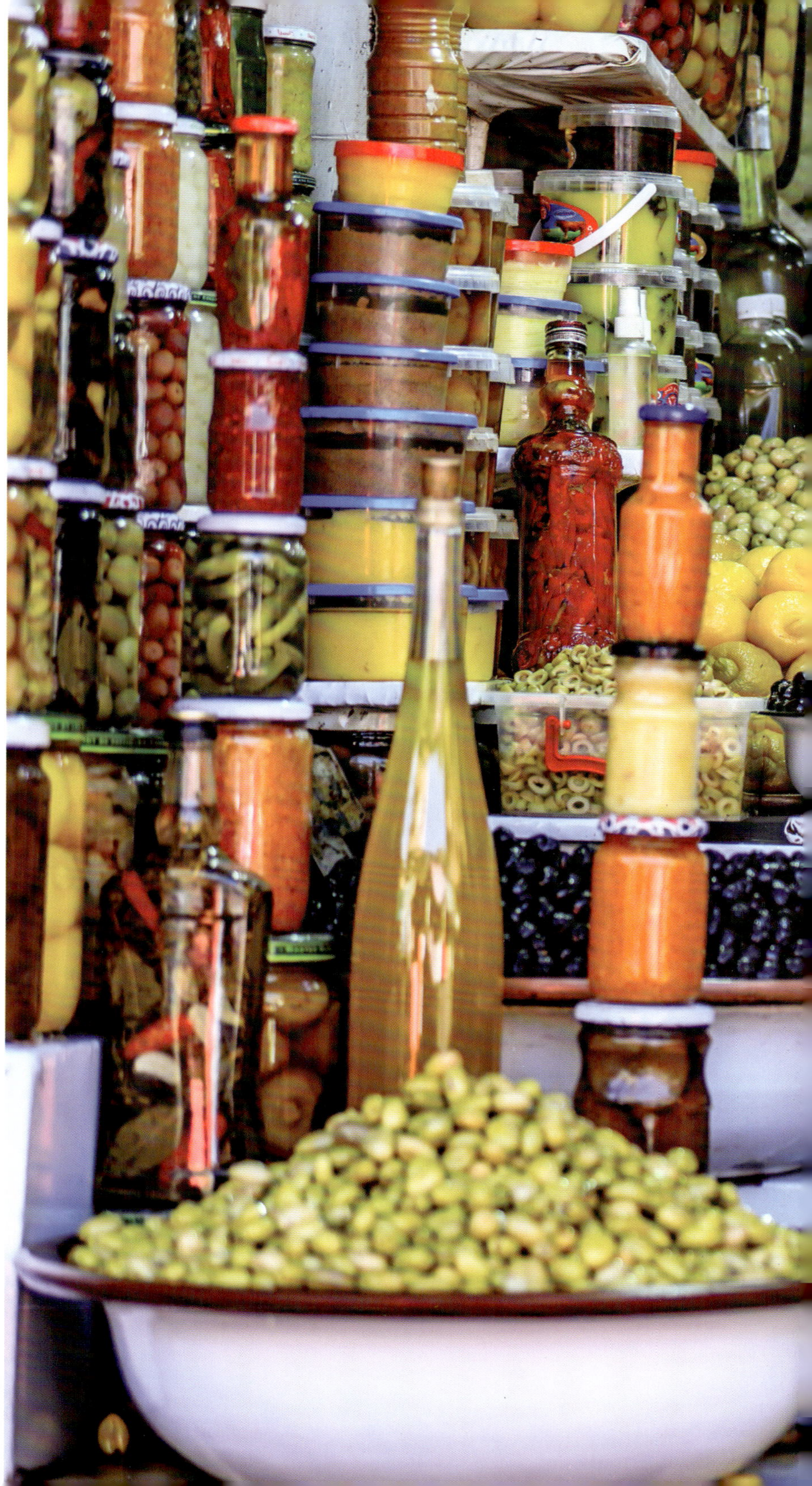

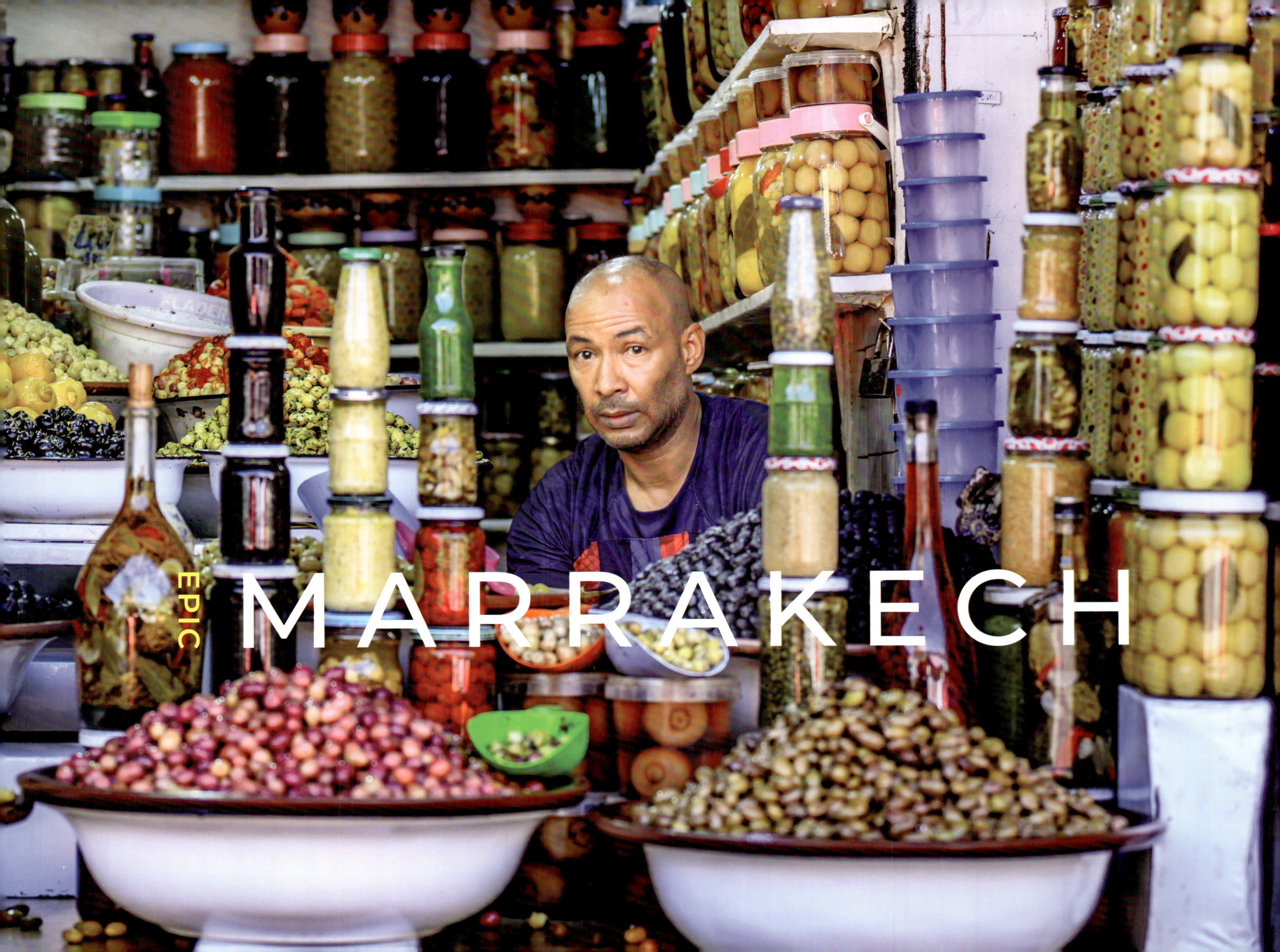
EPIC
MARRAKECH

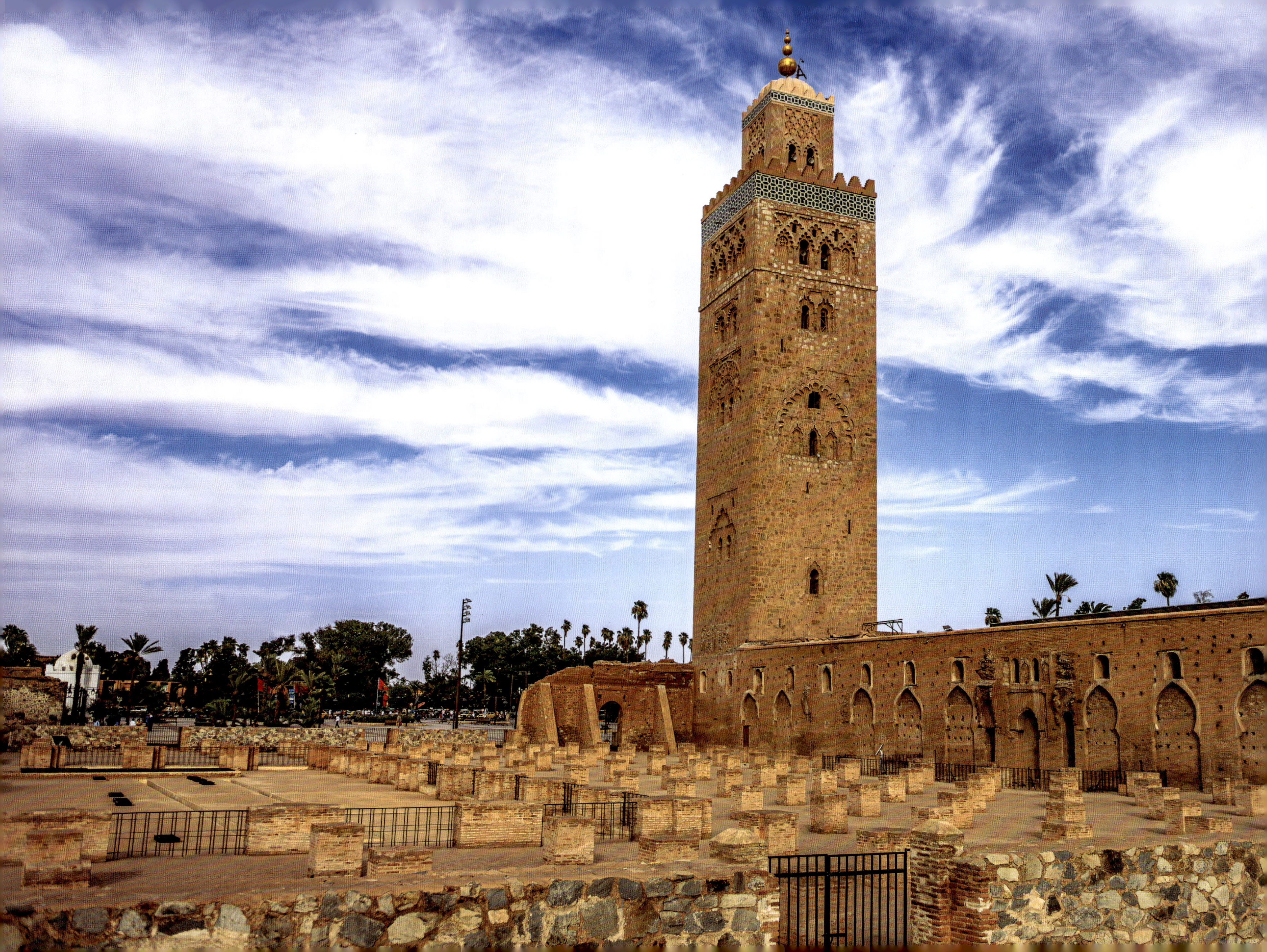

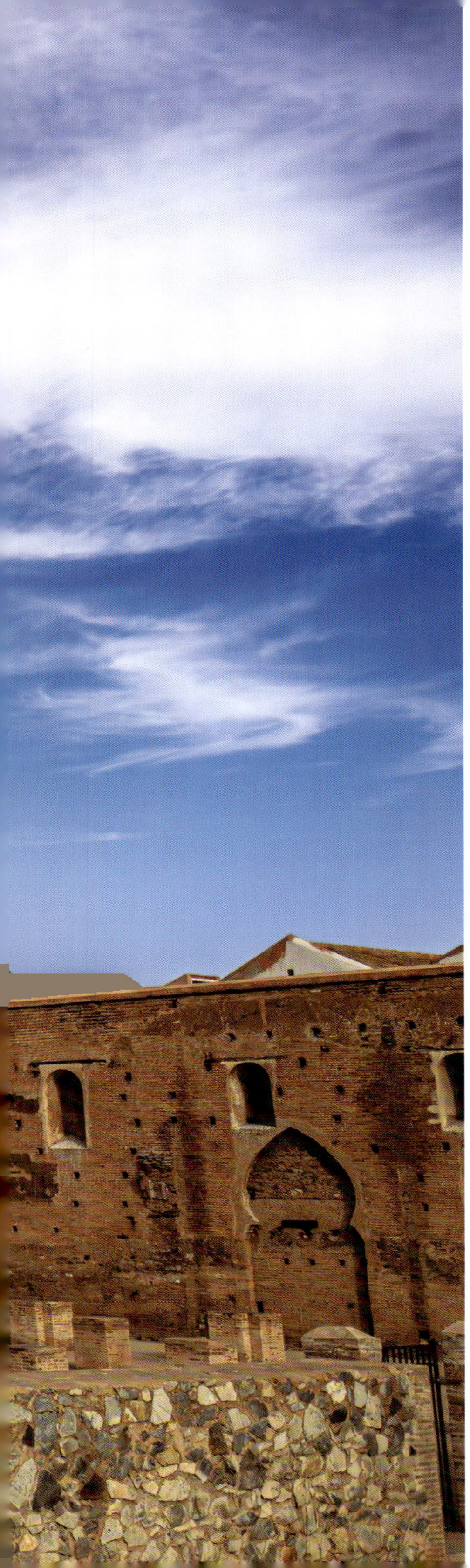

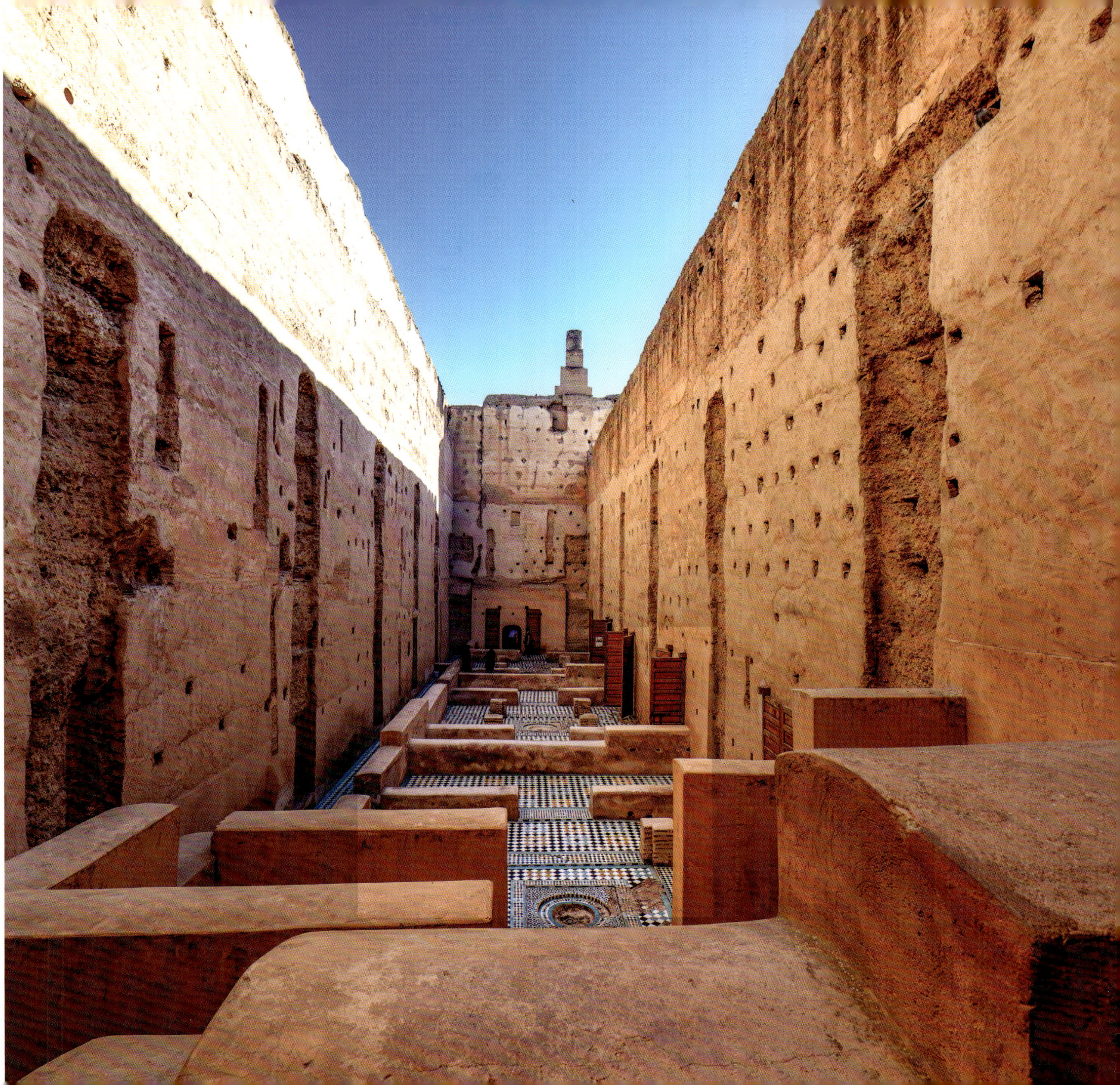

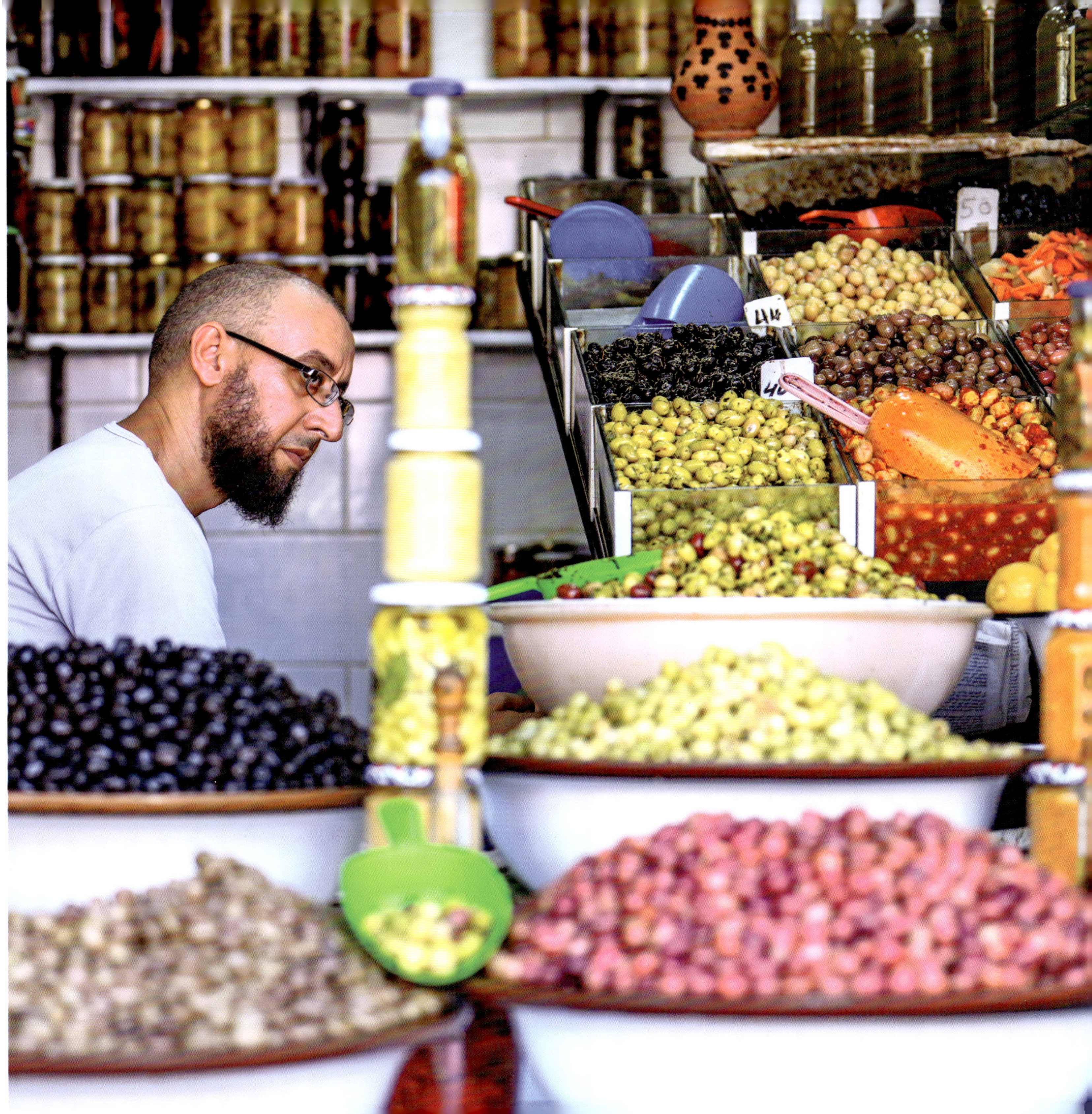

Previous page:
A side view of the Koutoubia Mosque at dusk.

Marrakech olive vendor in his souk, a stall in the market bazaar.

Medinas are the old quarters of Moroccan cities. Here, vendors display their wares in these bustling marketplaces.

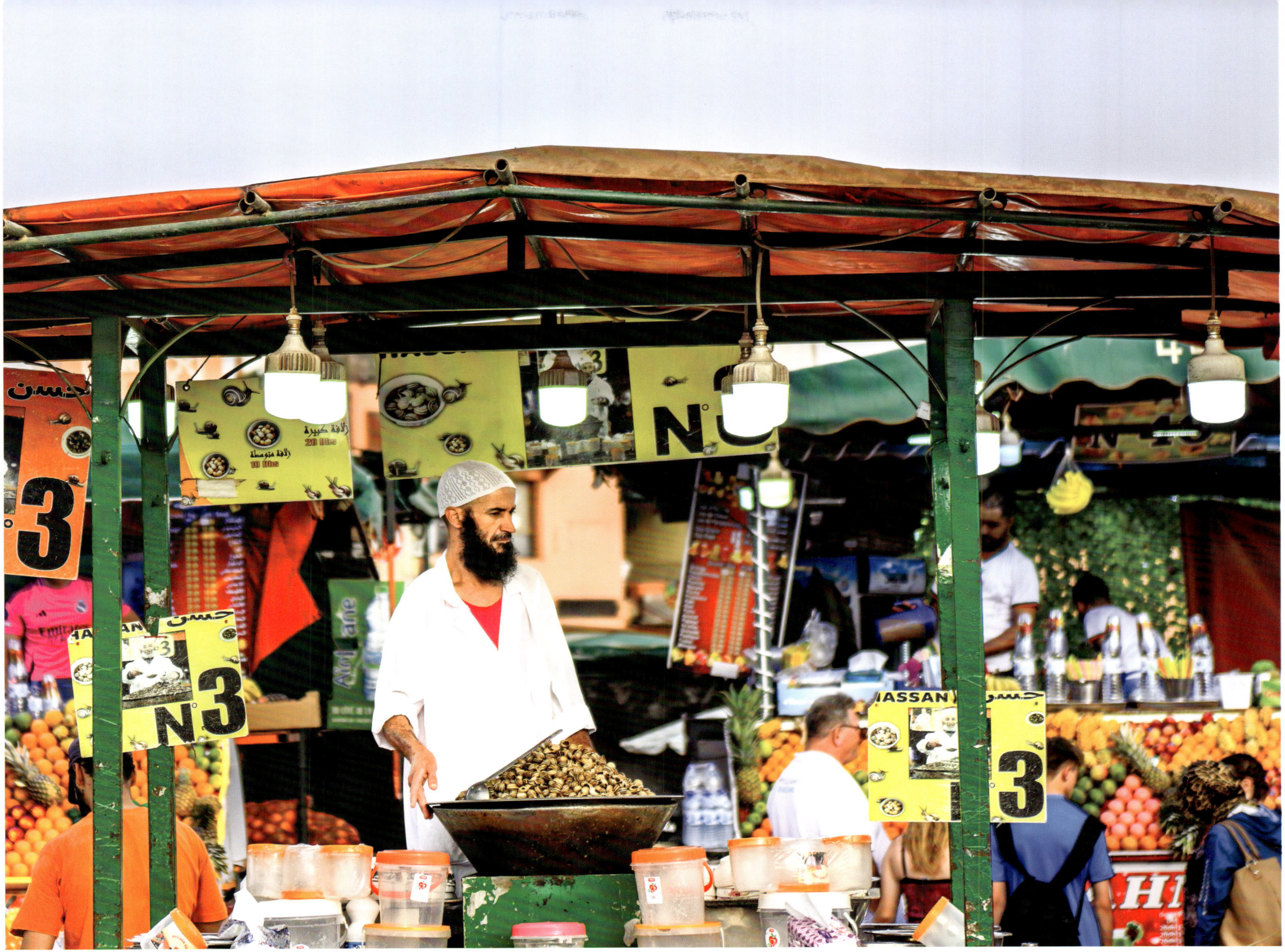
HASSAN
3

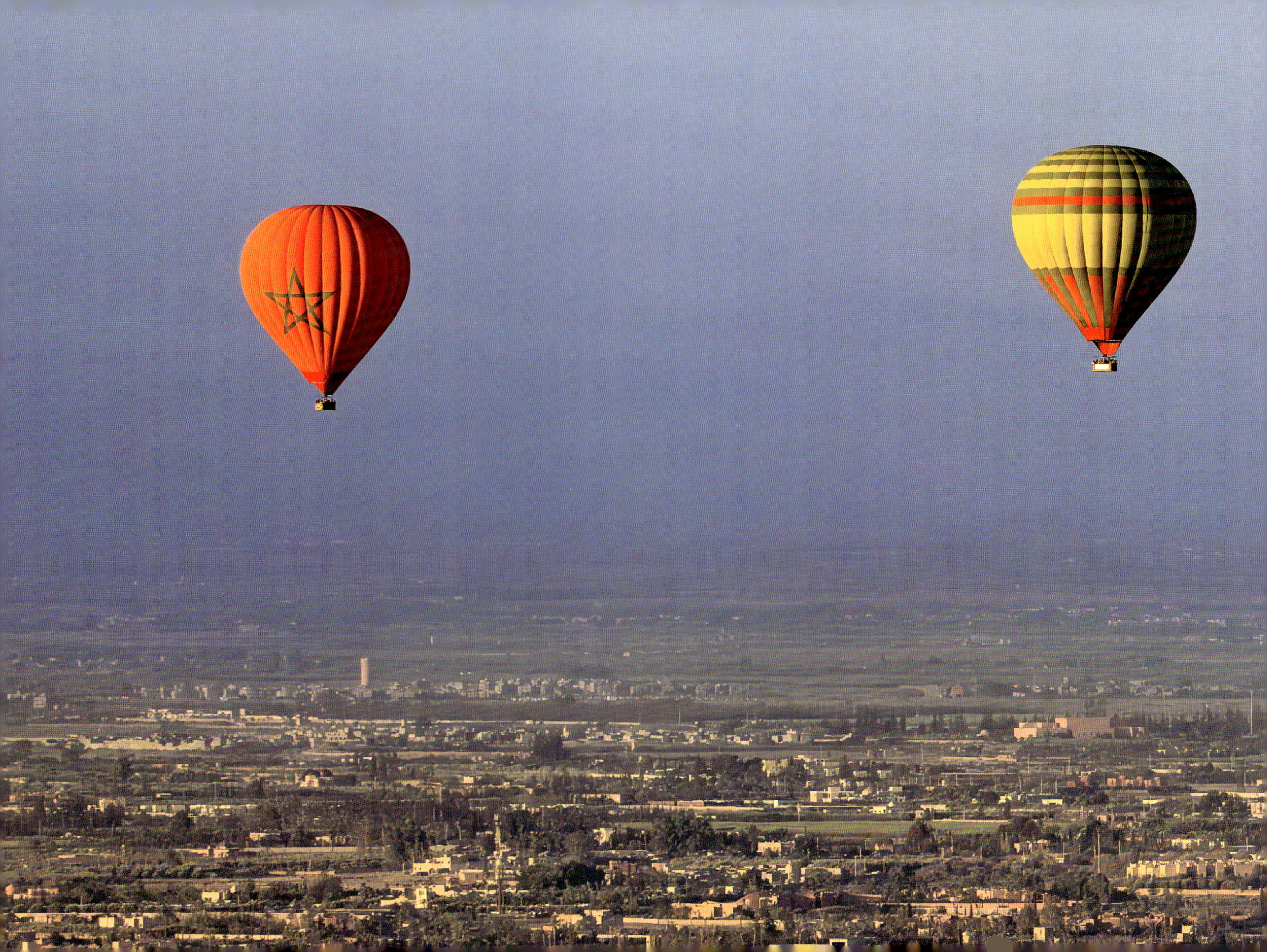

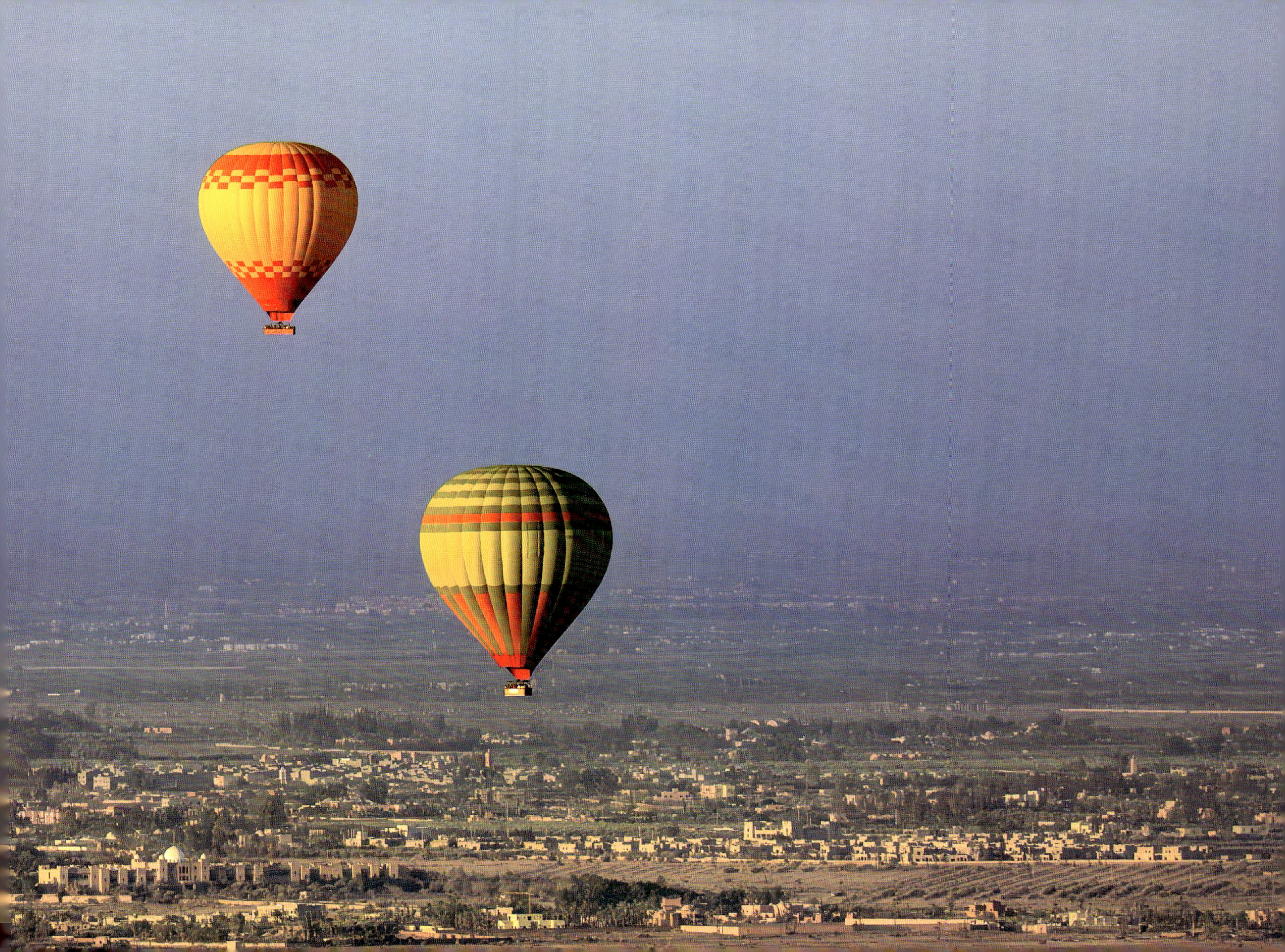

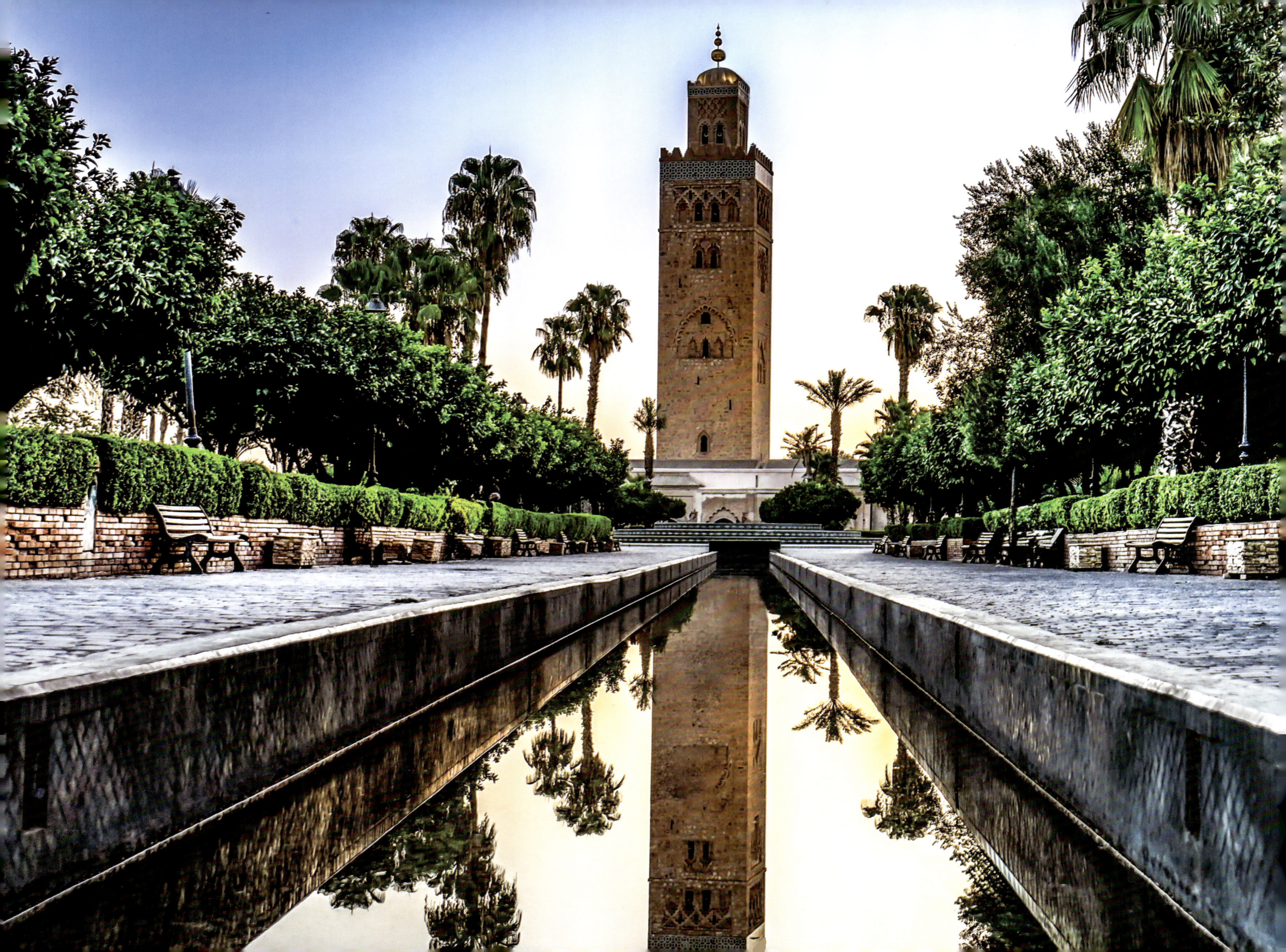

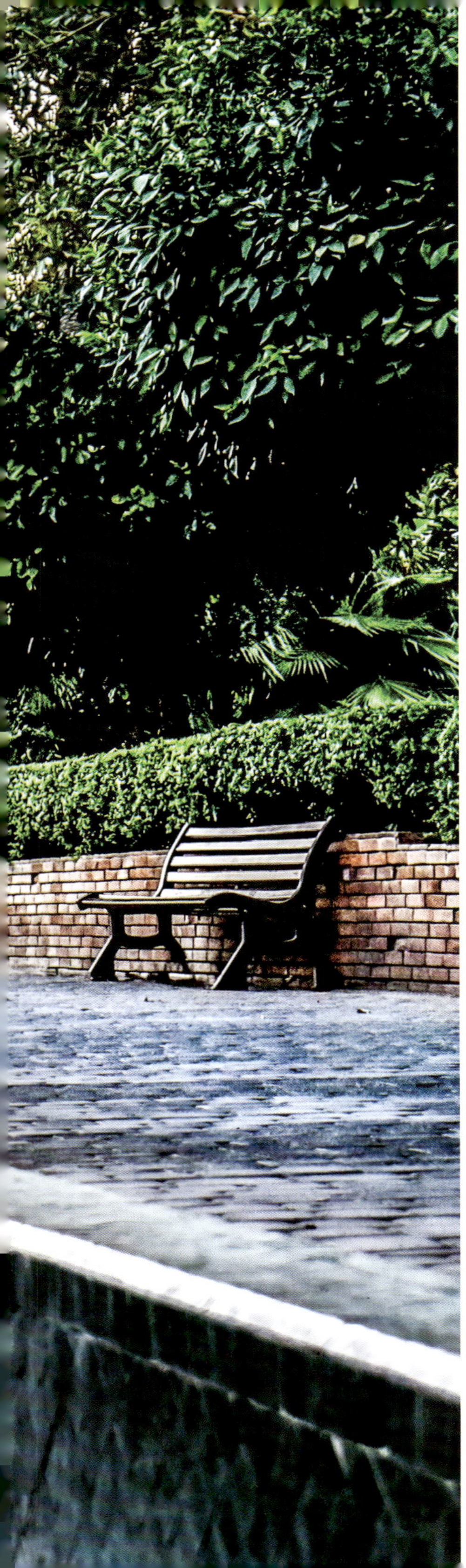

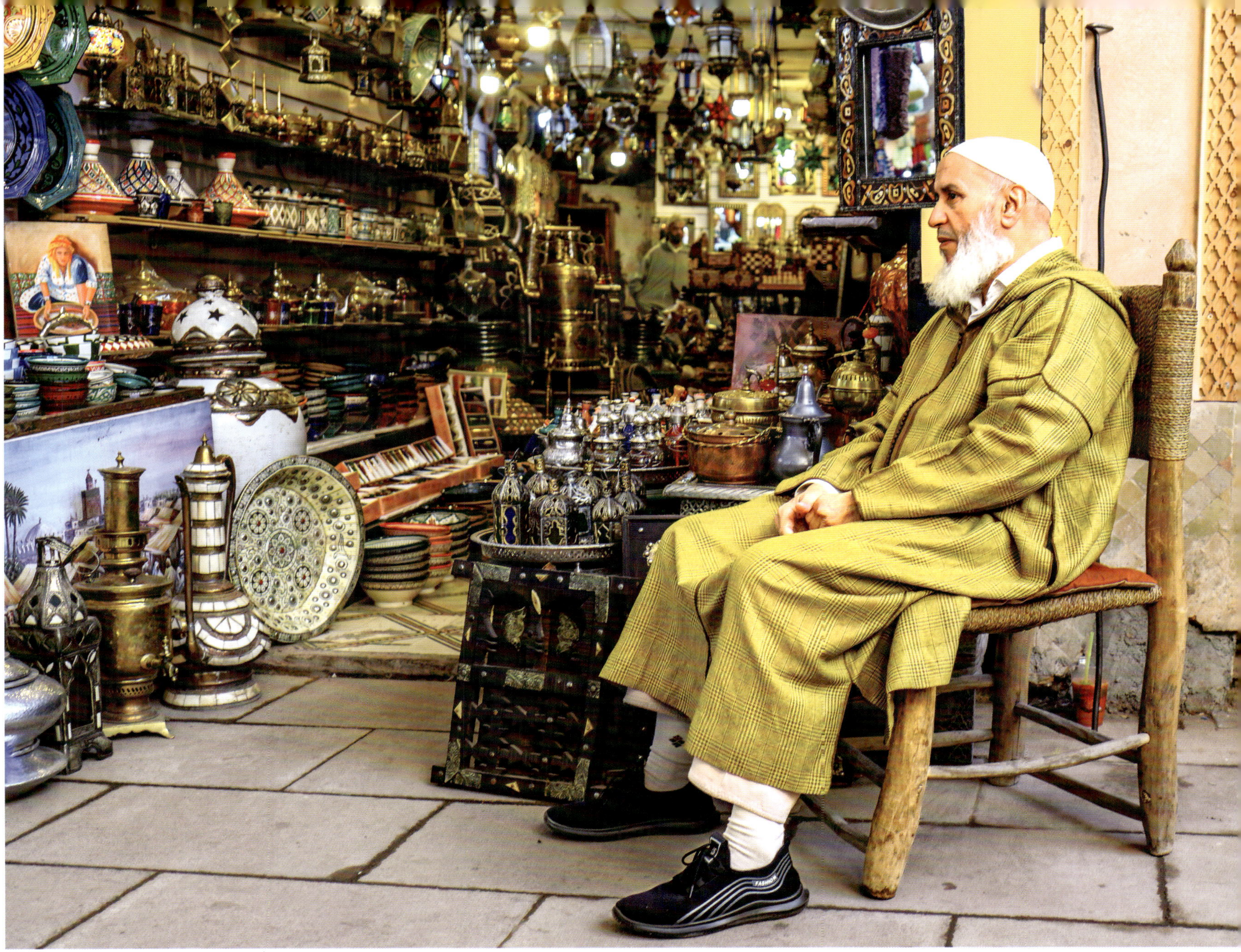

Previous page:
Hot air balloon tours over Marrakech welcome the dawn.

View of Koutoubia Mosque at dawn from gardens.

Marrakech merchant displaying handcrafted Moroccan pottery.

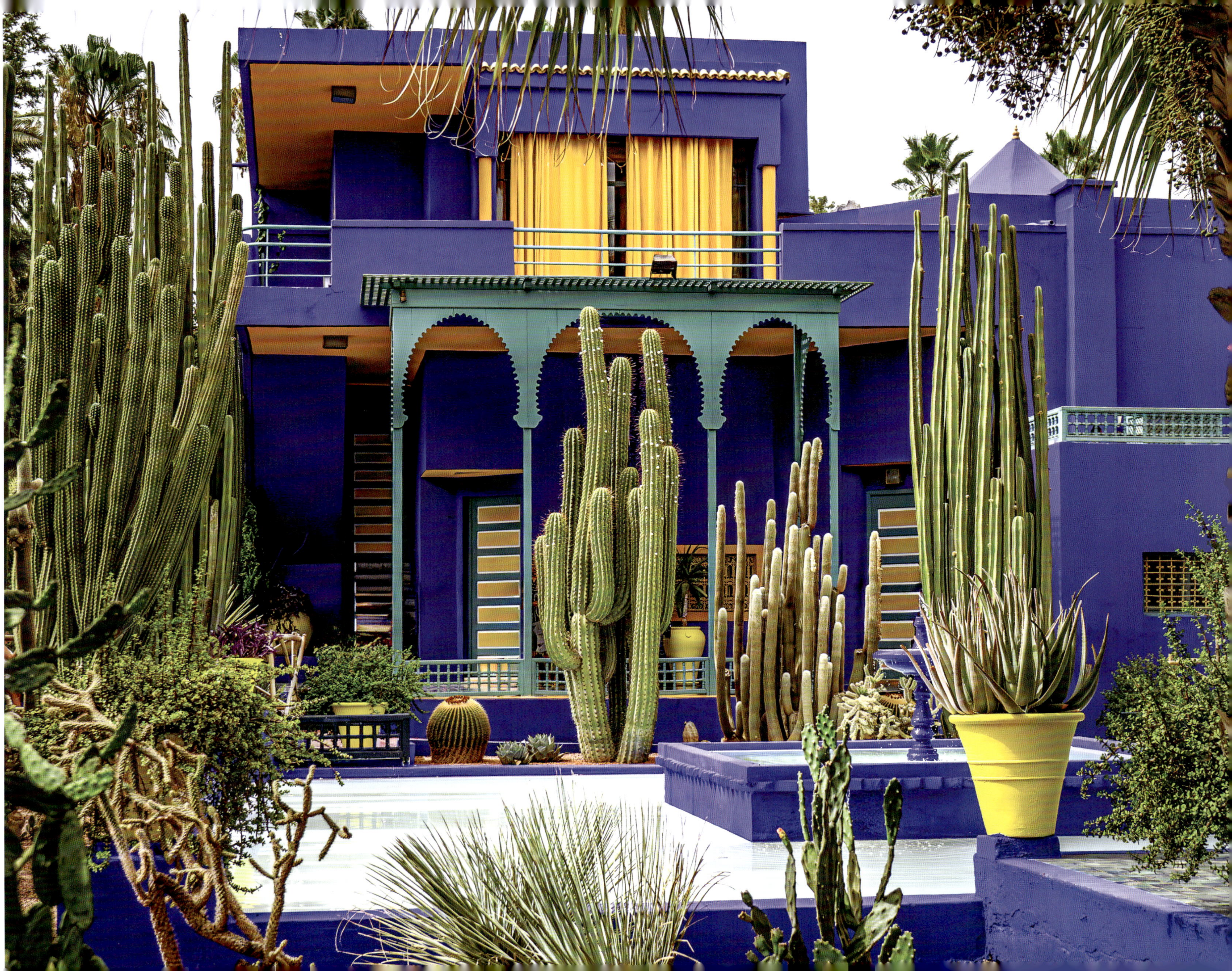

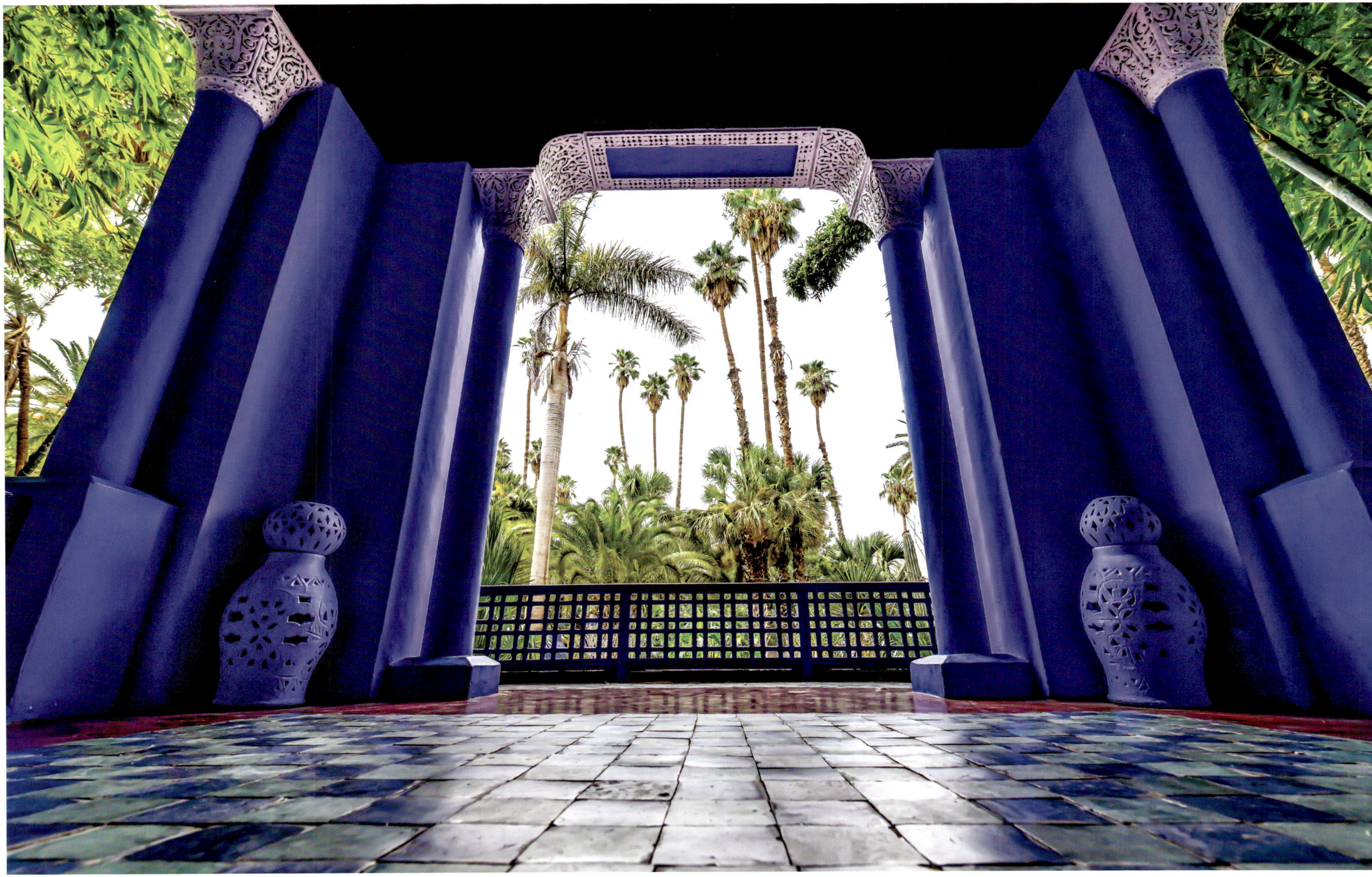

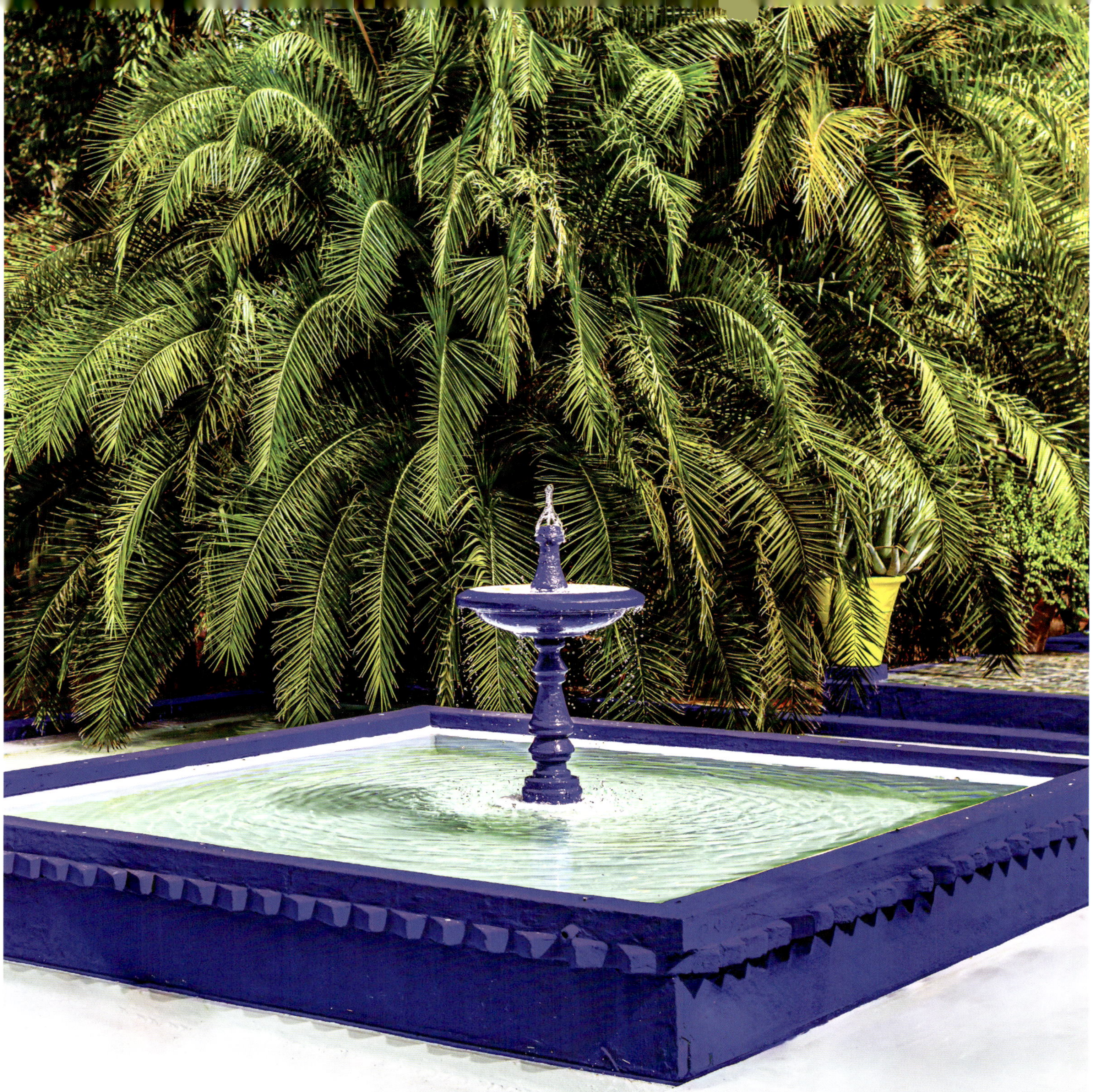

Previous and current pages: The buildings and gardens of Jardin Majorelle Garden offer a luscious feast for the senses.

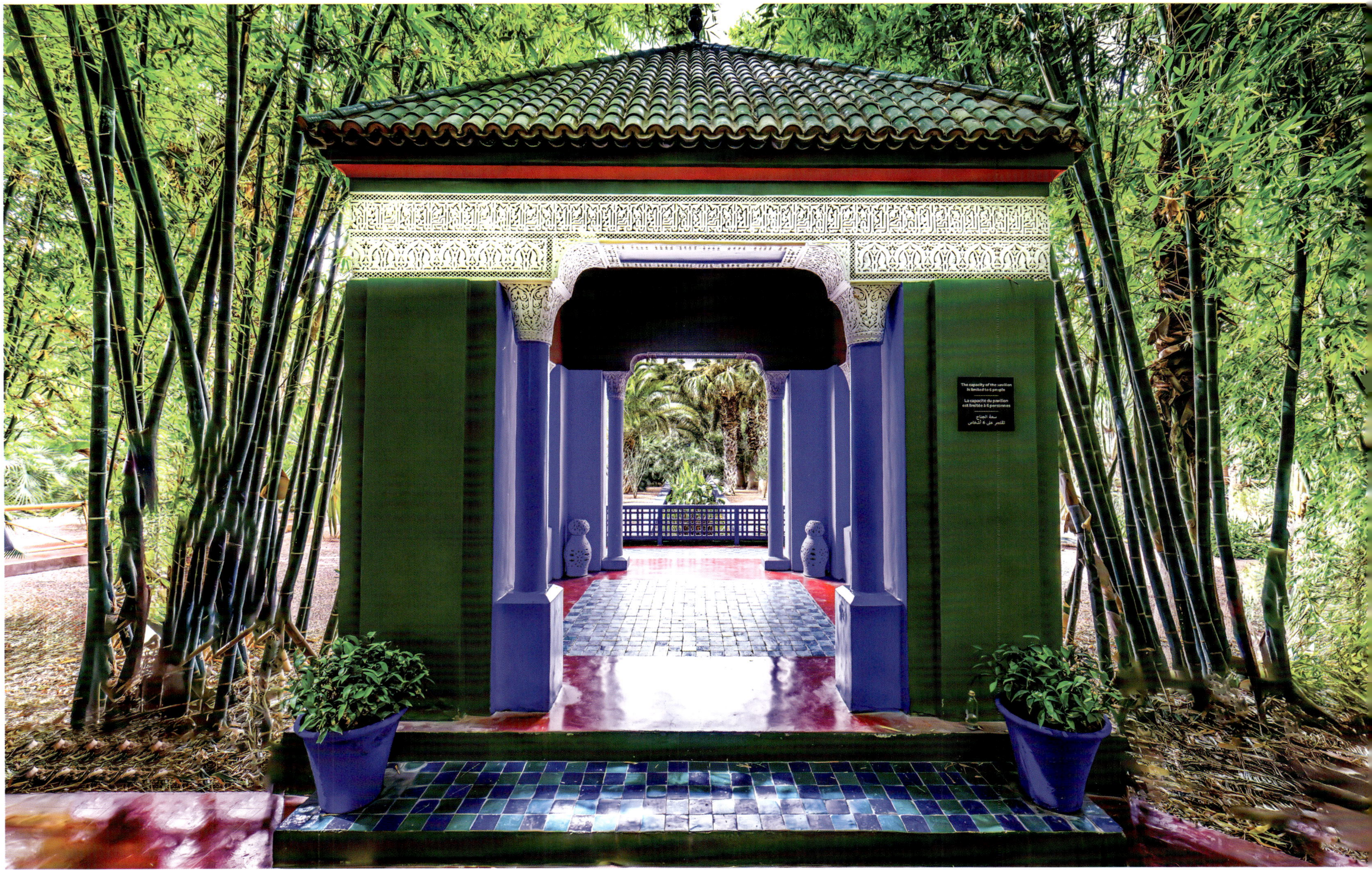
The capacity of the pavilion is limited to 6 people
La capacité du pavilion est limitée à 6 personnes
سعة الجناح
تقتصر على 6 أشخاص

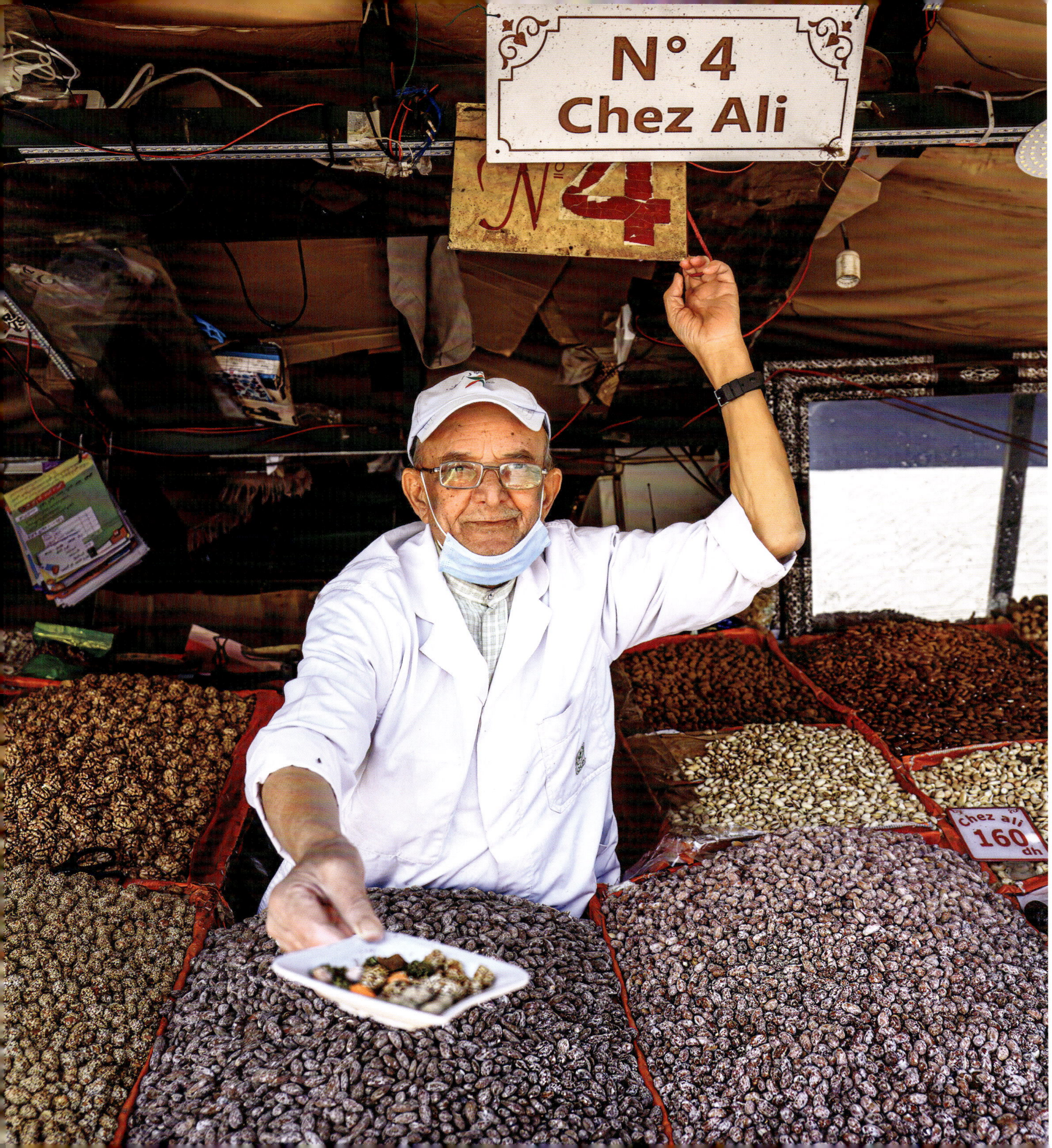
N° 4
Chez Ali
Chez ali
160
dh

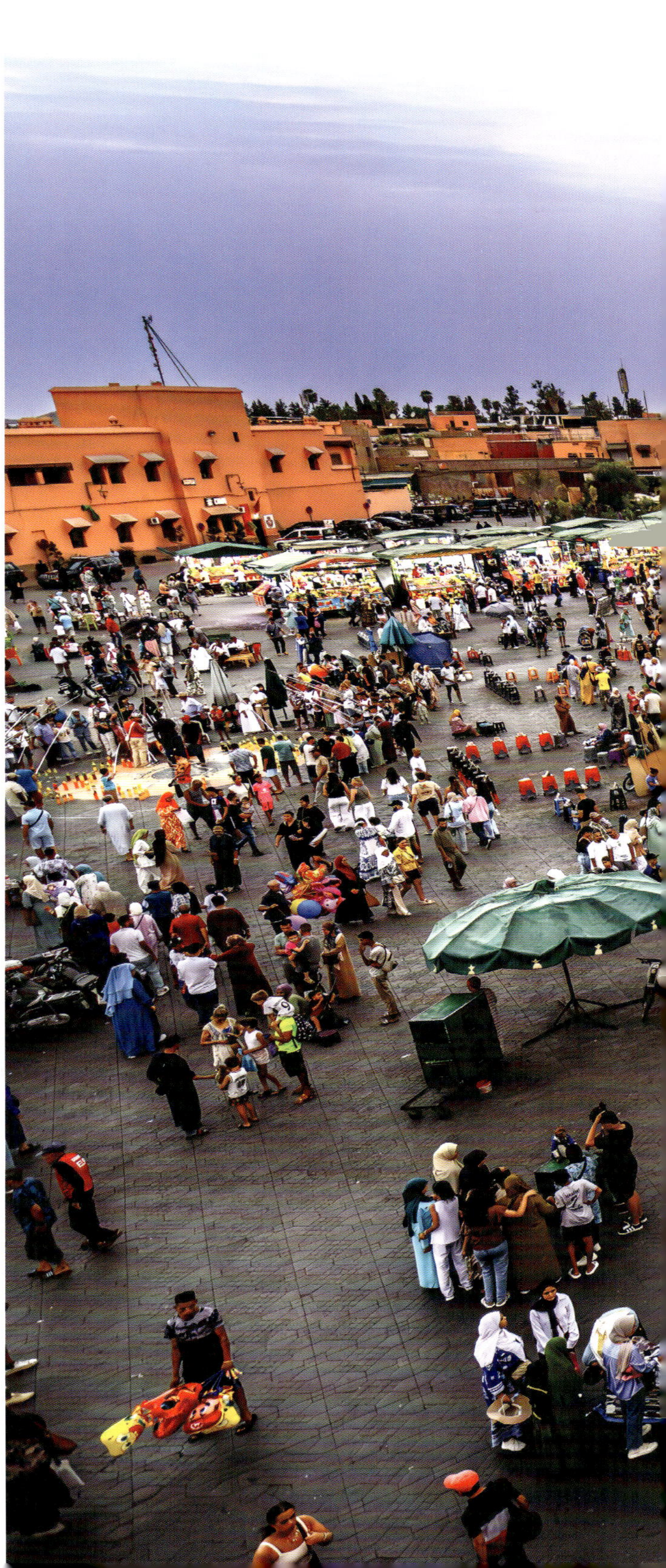

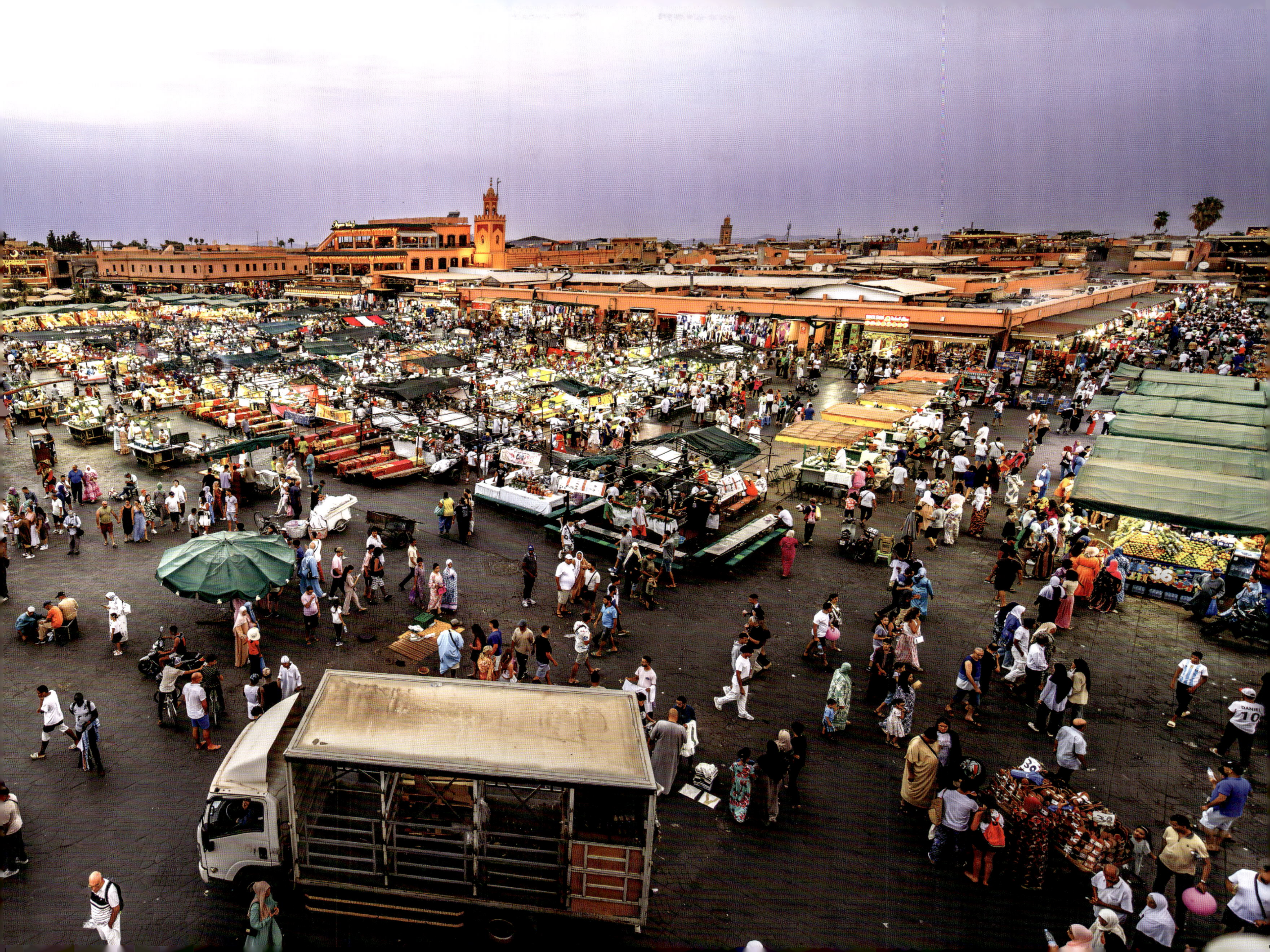

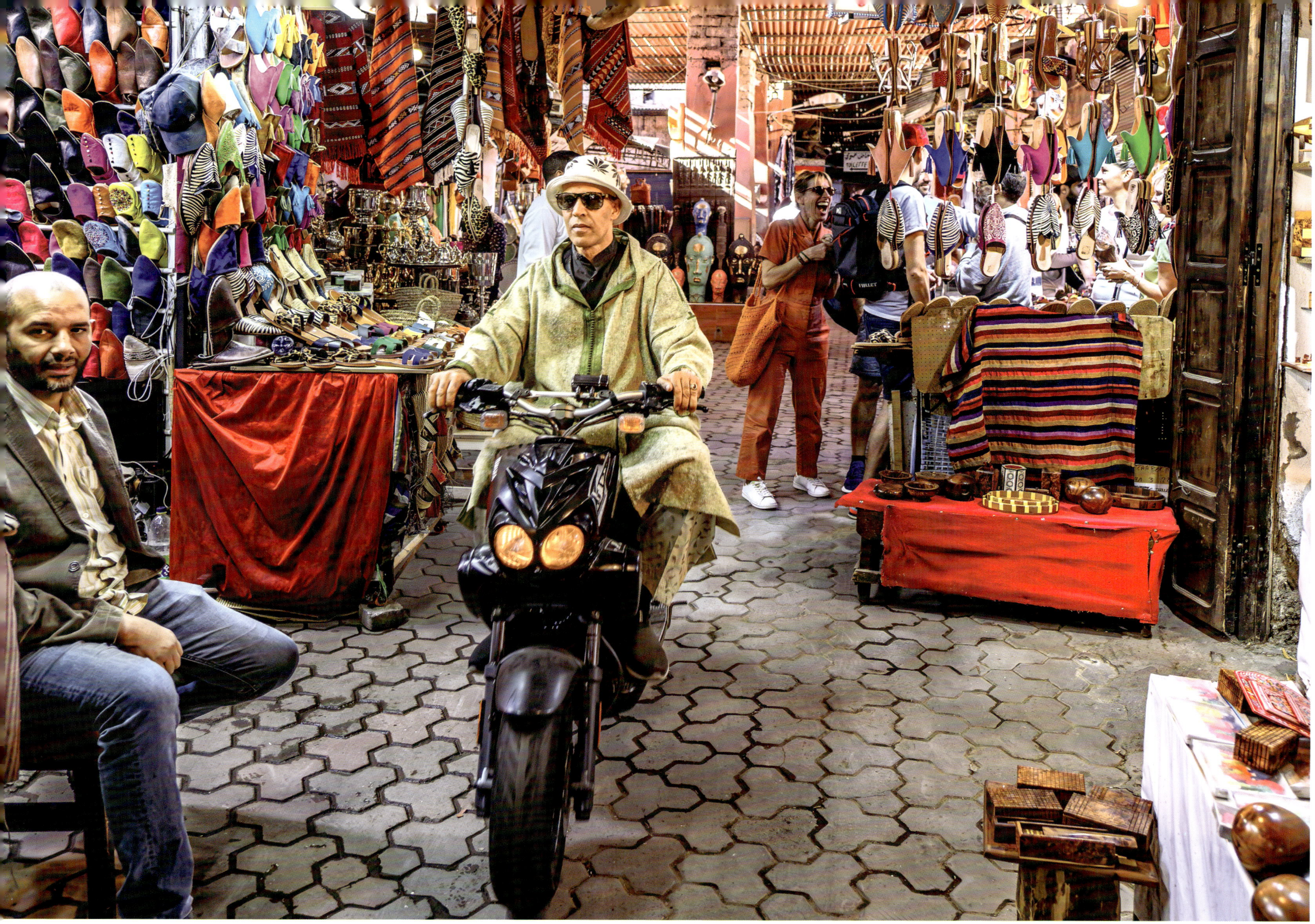

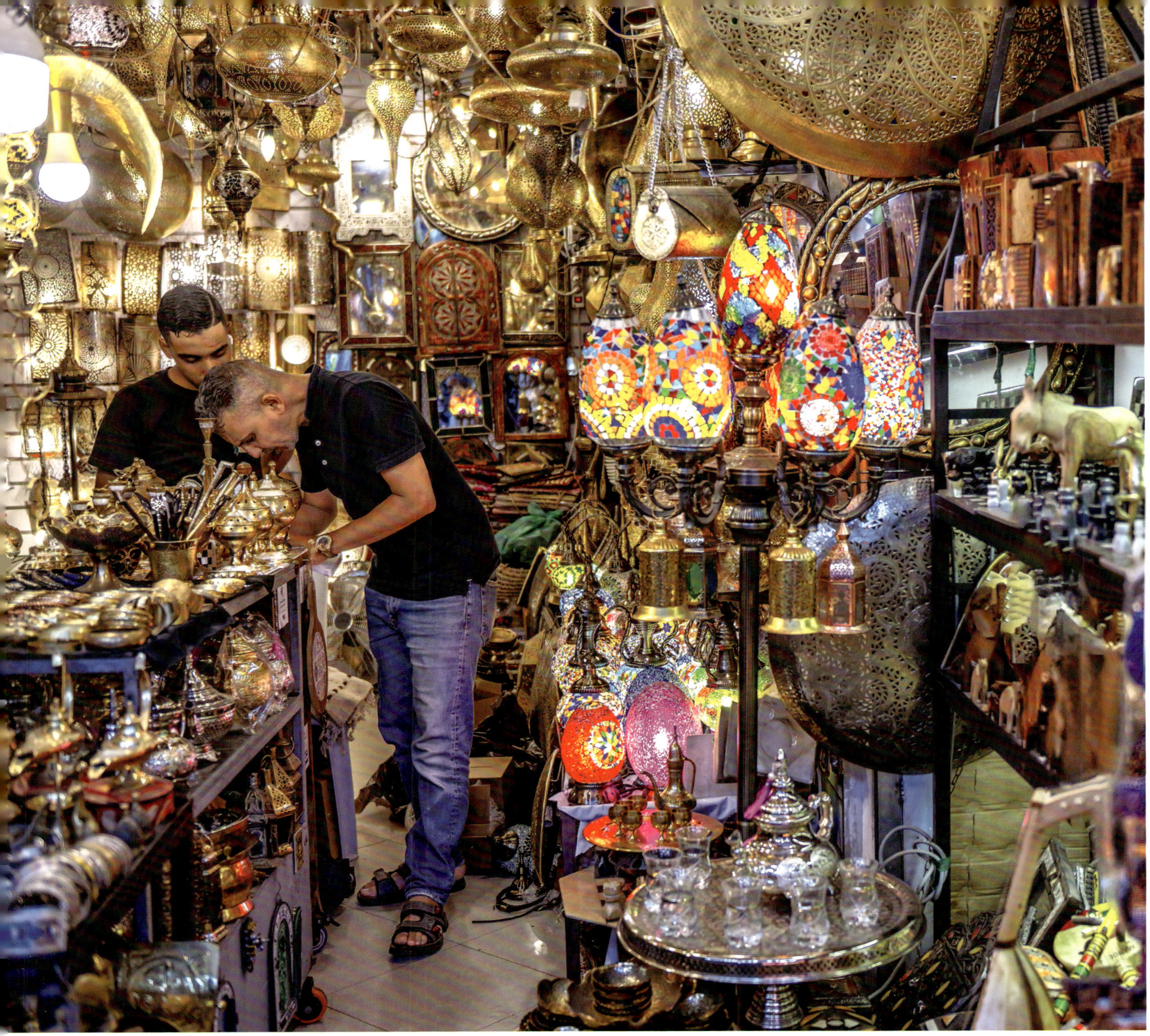

Previous page:
Marrakech merchant selling fresh nuts inside Djemaa el-Fna square.

Overhead view of the famous square at sunset.

Man on motorcycle passing through Madina. Artisans inside their souks.

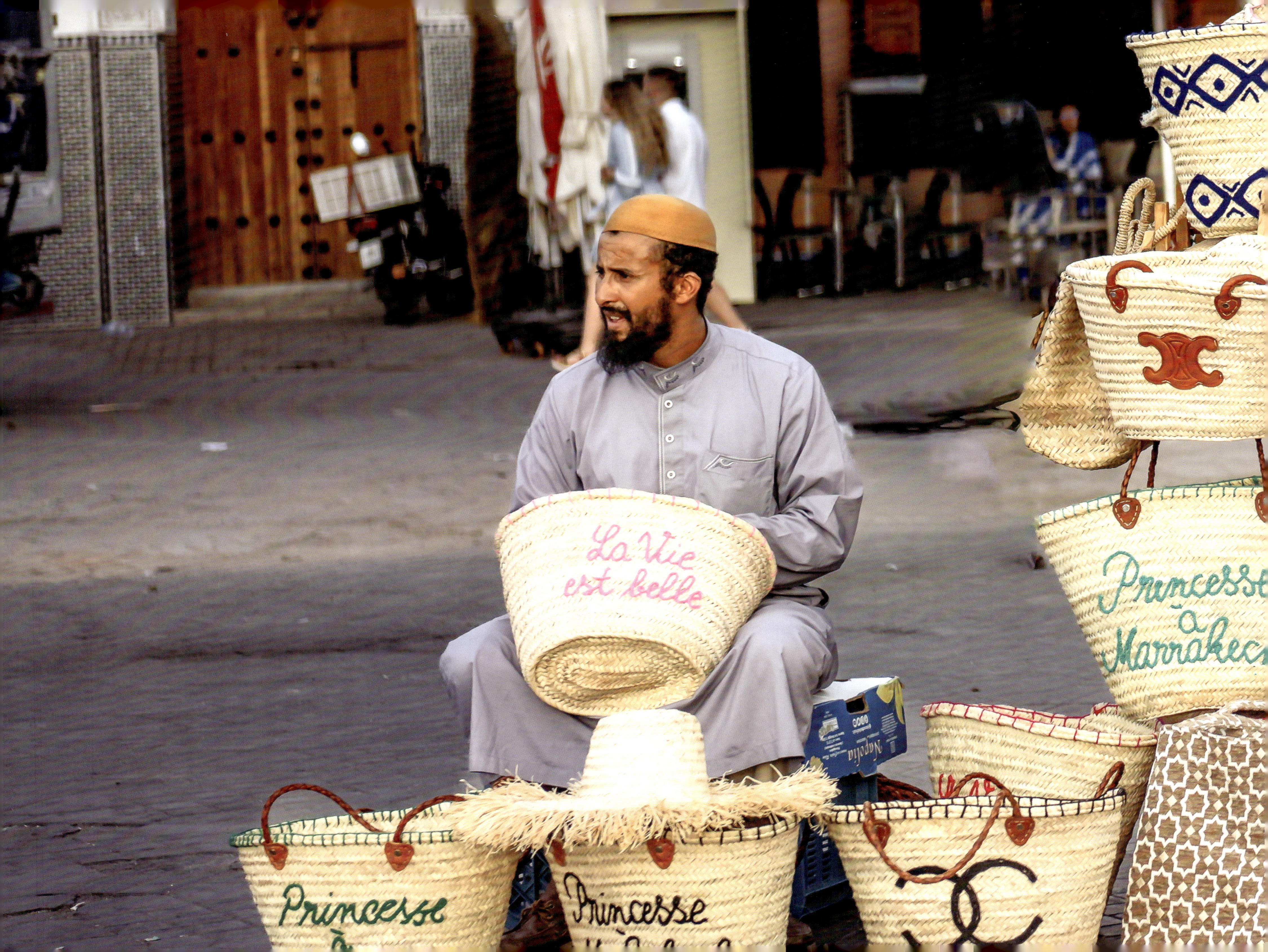
La Vie
est belle
Princesse
à
Marrakec
Princesse
Princesse

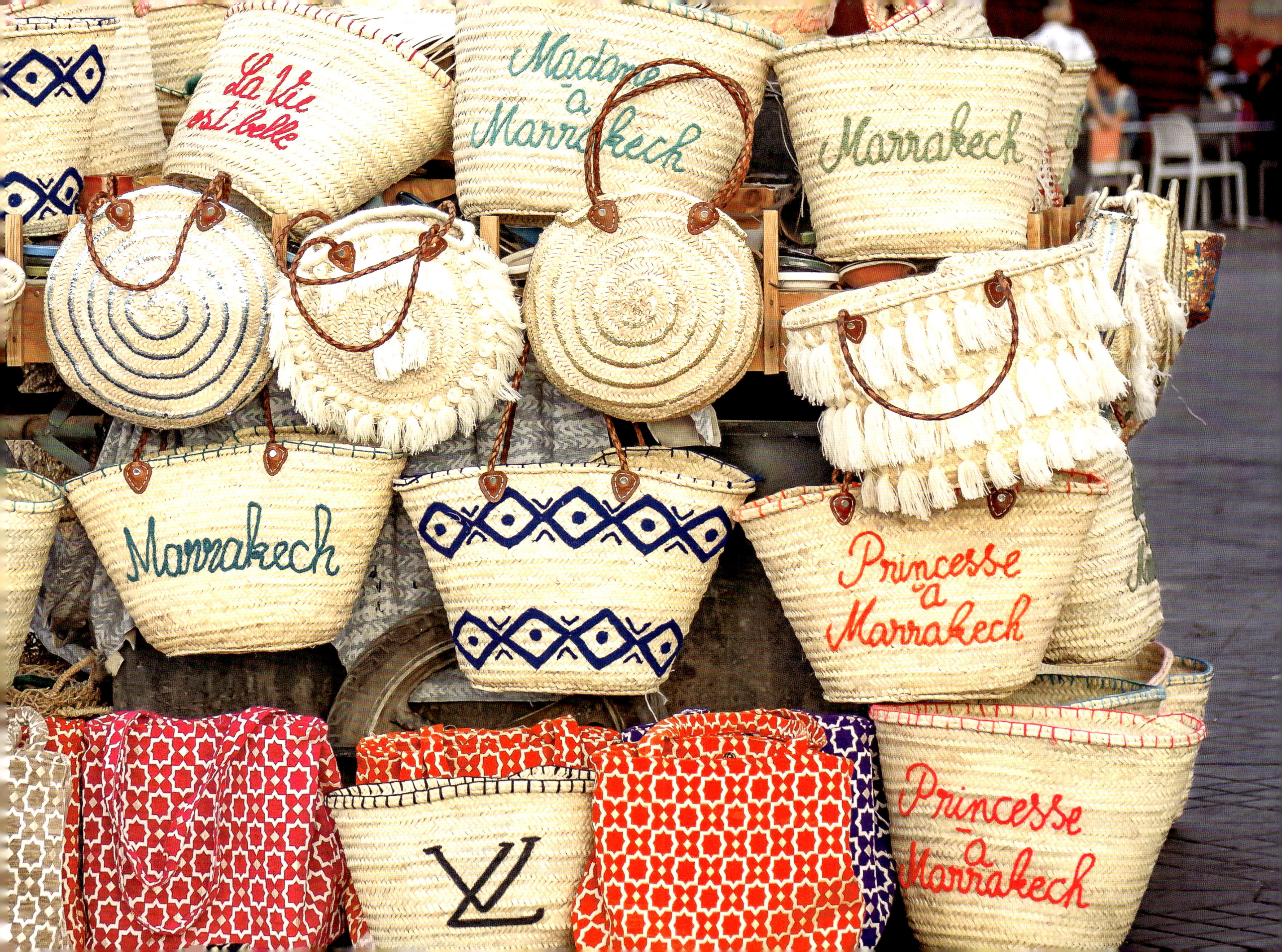
La Vie est belle
Madame à Marrakech
Marrakech
Marrakech
Princesse à Marrakech
Princesse à Marrakech

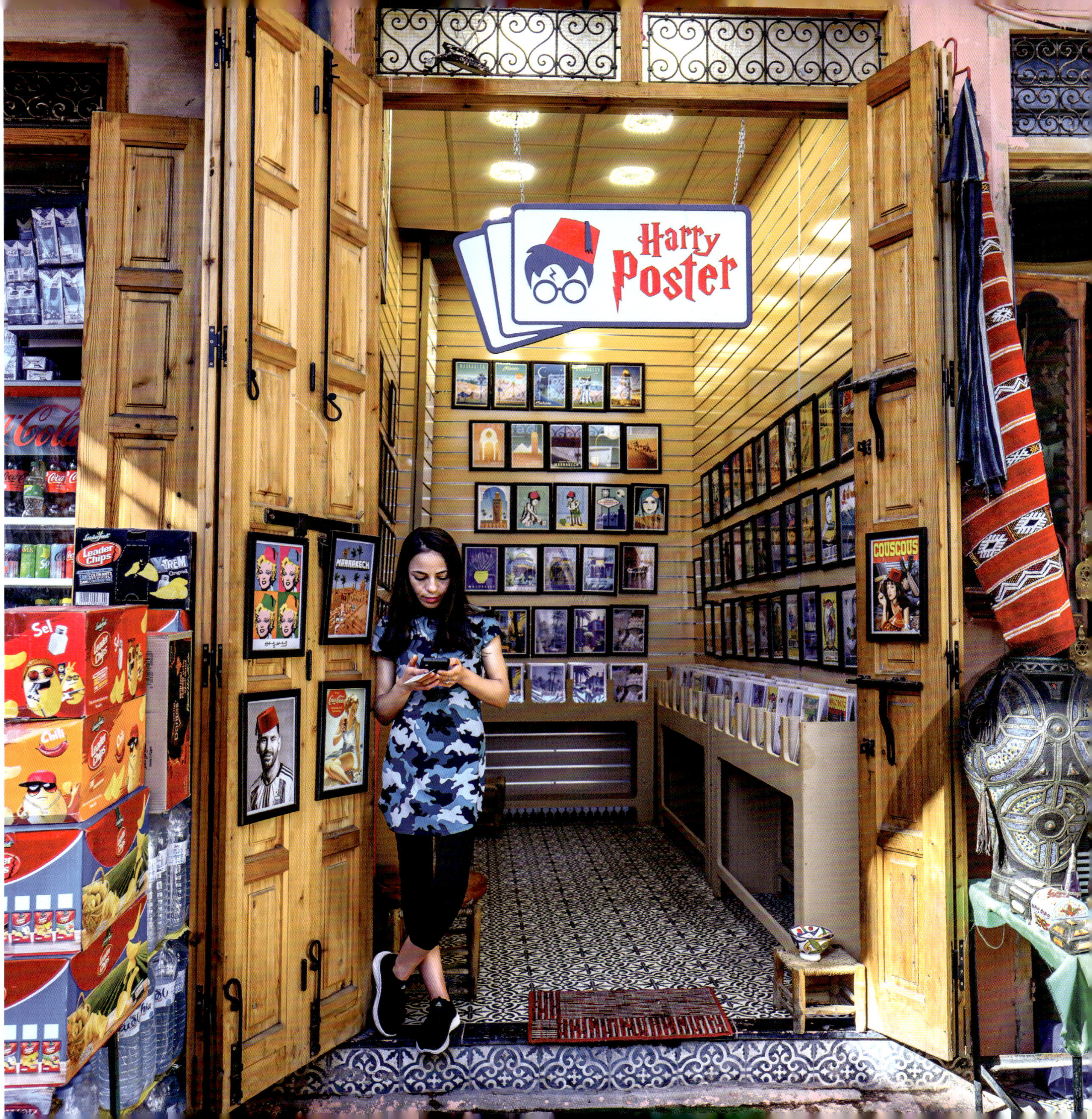


Previous page:
Merchant selling lovely, handcrafted baskets.

Vendors await customers in their souks.

Delivery man driving a donkey cart through the medina.

Next page:
Fine metal craftsman in his souk in the market.

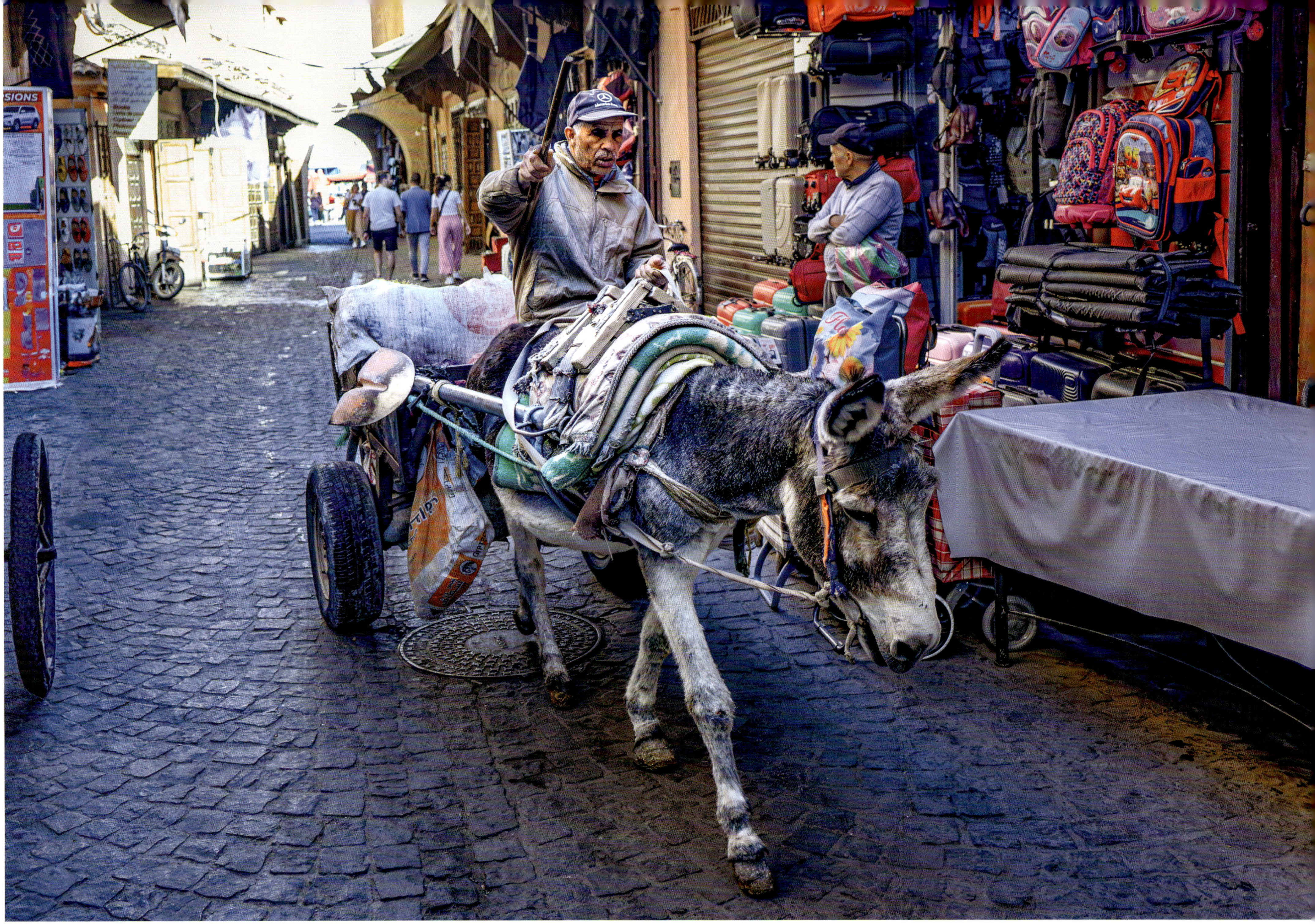

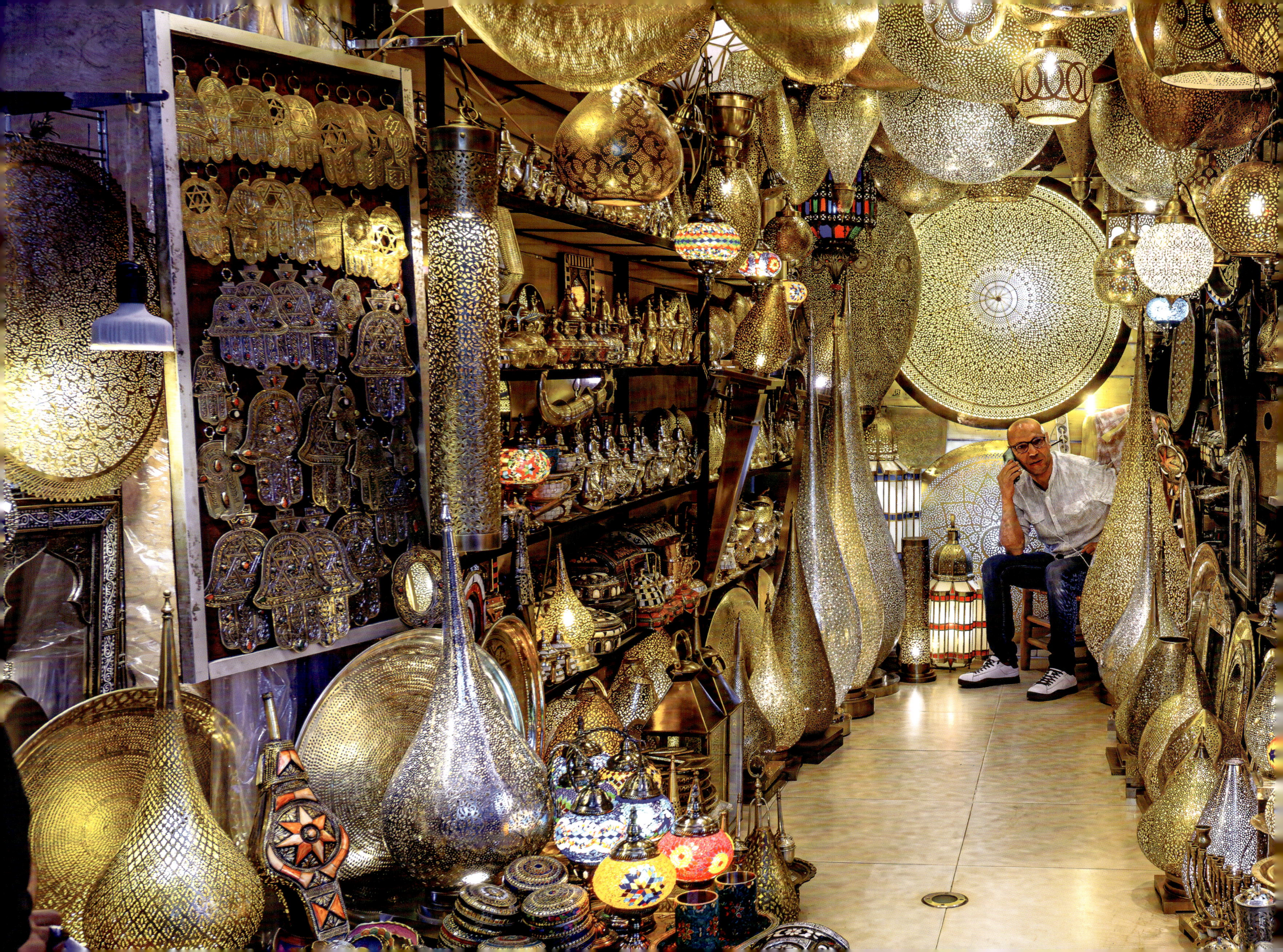

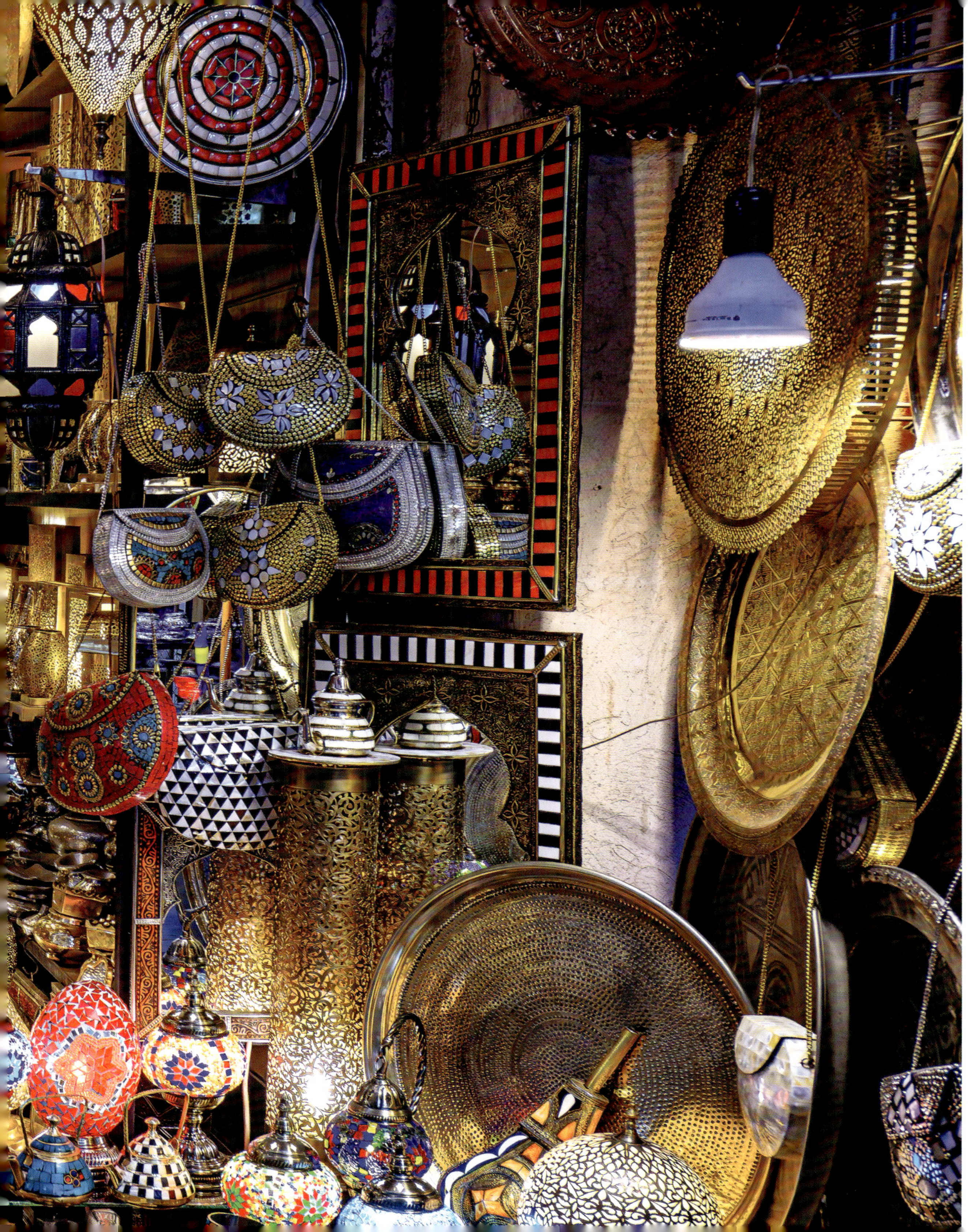

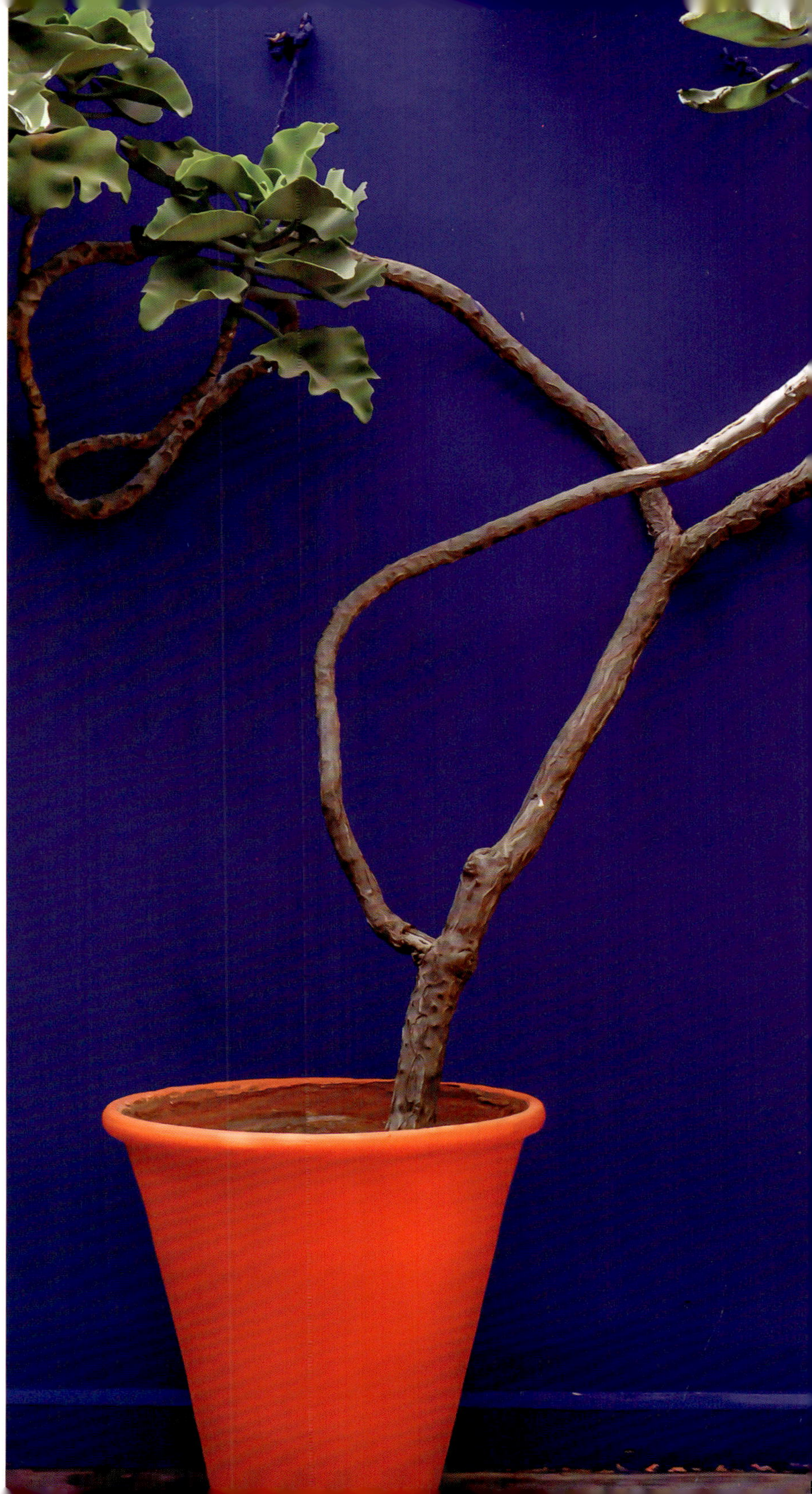

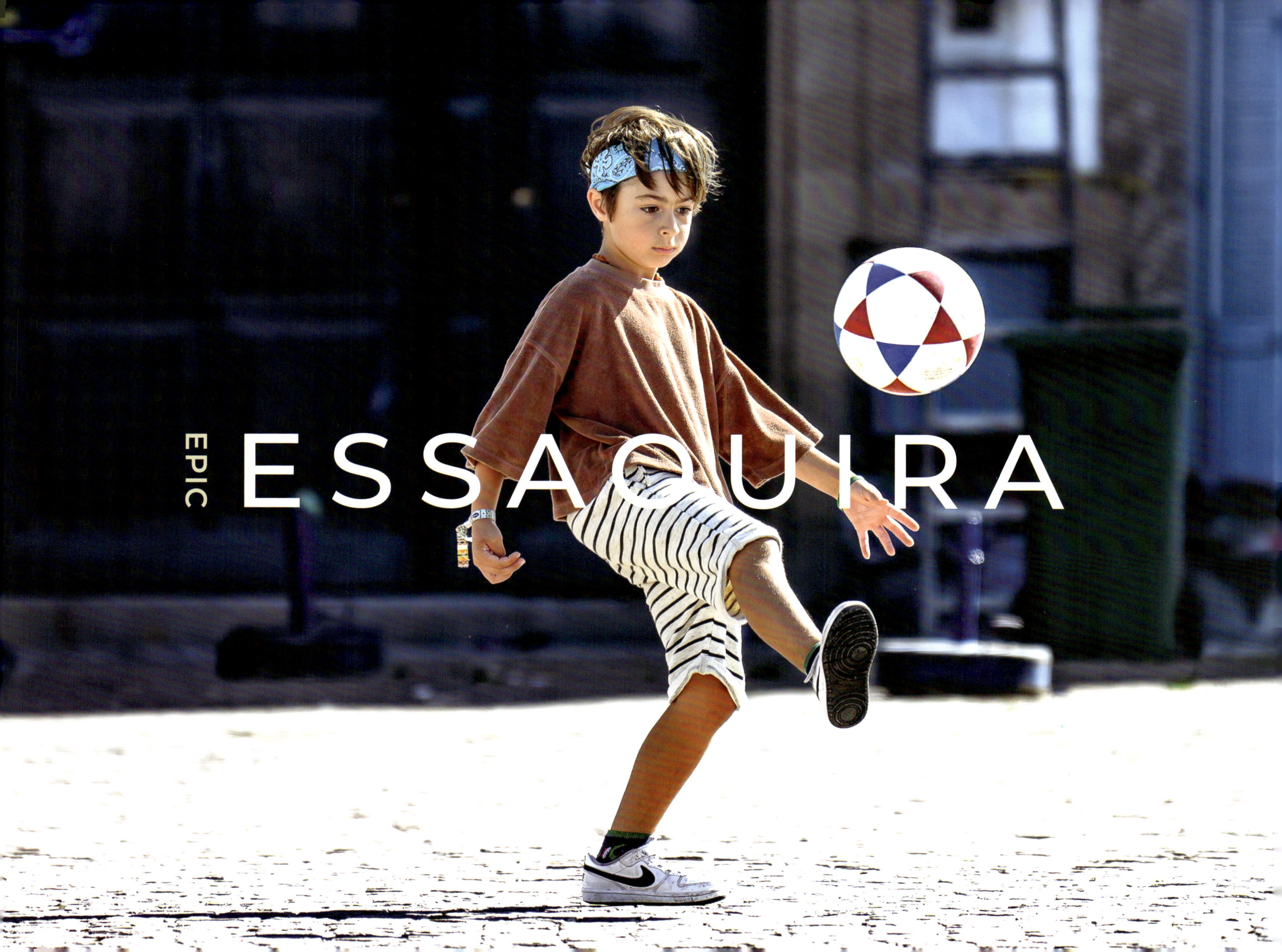
EPIC
ESSAOUIRA

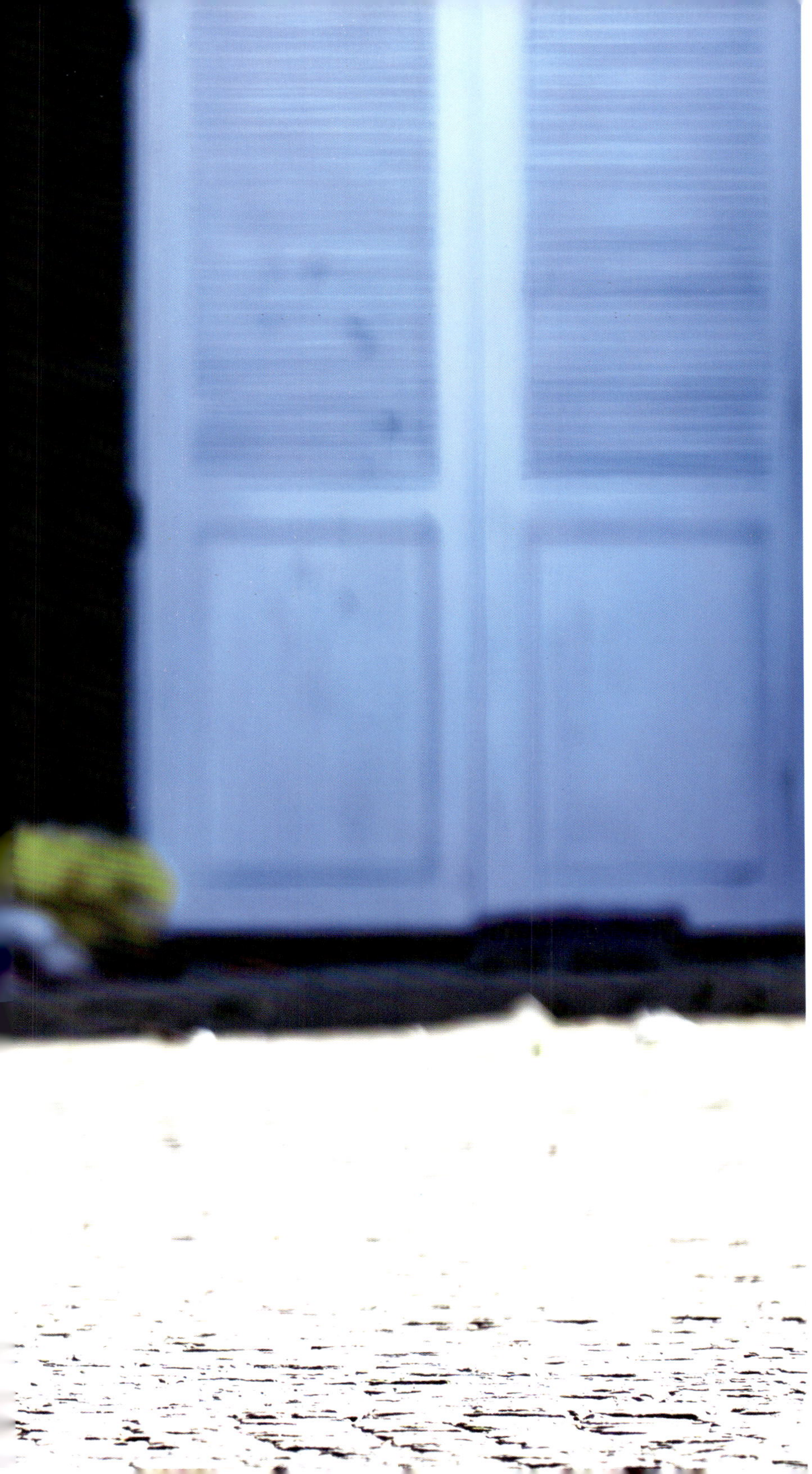

# A CITY OF COLORS AND CONTRASTS

Nestled against the North African Atlantic coast, 119 miles from Marrakech, is one of the most dazzling cities in all of Morocco. With a history that dates back more than 2500 years, Essaouira offers a bit of everything found in most other, larger, Moroccan cities—colorful souks inside a walled medina, a vibrant and active arts community that fuels multiple galleries that surround a variety of tiny restaurants, pottery and craft shops.

Yet, here is so much more. Initially named Mogador after the Muslim saint Sidi Mogdoul, Essaouria, a UNESCO World Heritage site, is both an active seaport with a bustling fleet of small bright blue fishing boats that set out from the port every morning and return late in the day loaded with fresh fish that go right to market from just behind the medina's colorful plaza—and a gathering place for musicians and people from around the world who come to watch the sun set into the sea through clouds of seagulls floating above the port, diving down trying to snatch a bite from where merchants cut and pack and sell the day's catch.

That is a scene that continues all year. But during the spring and summer months, Essaouira's ocean front transforms into a beach haven where surfers ride waves, or kite and windsurfers skip over the water and fly into the air, and where horses and camels carry riders and tourists across the sand against a backdrop of a long stretch of elegant hotels and beach front restaurants.

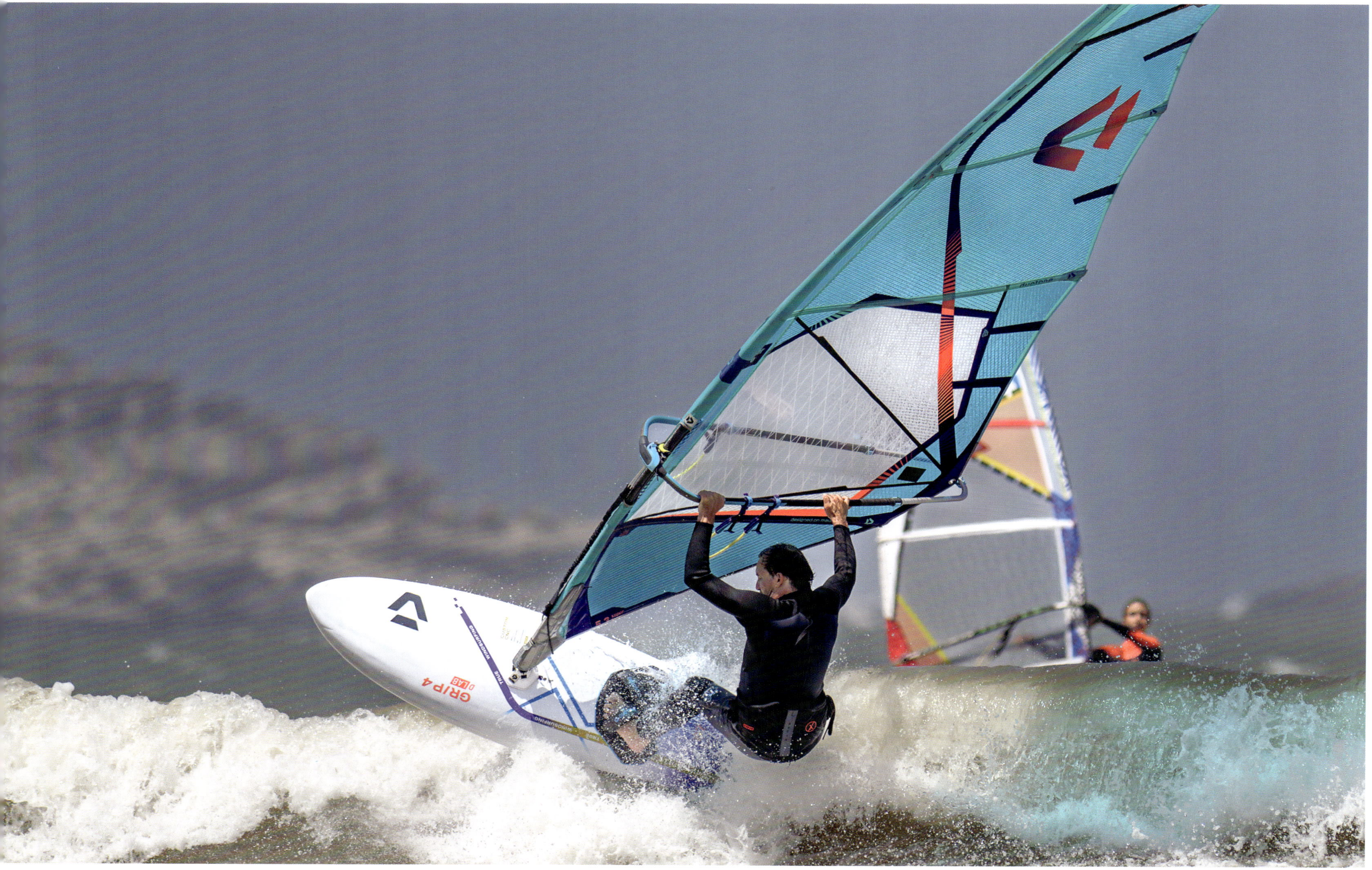

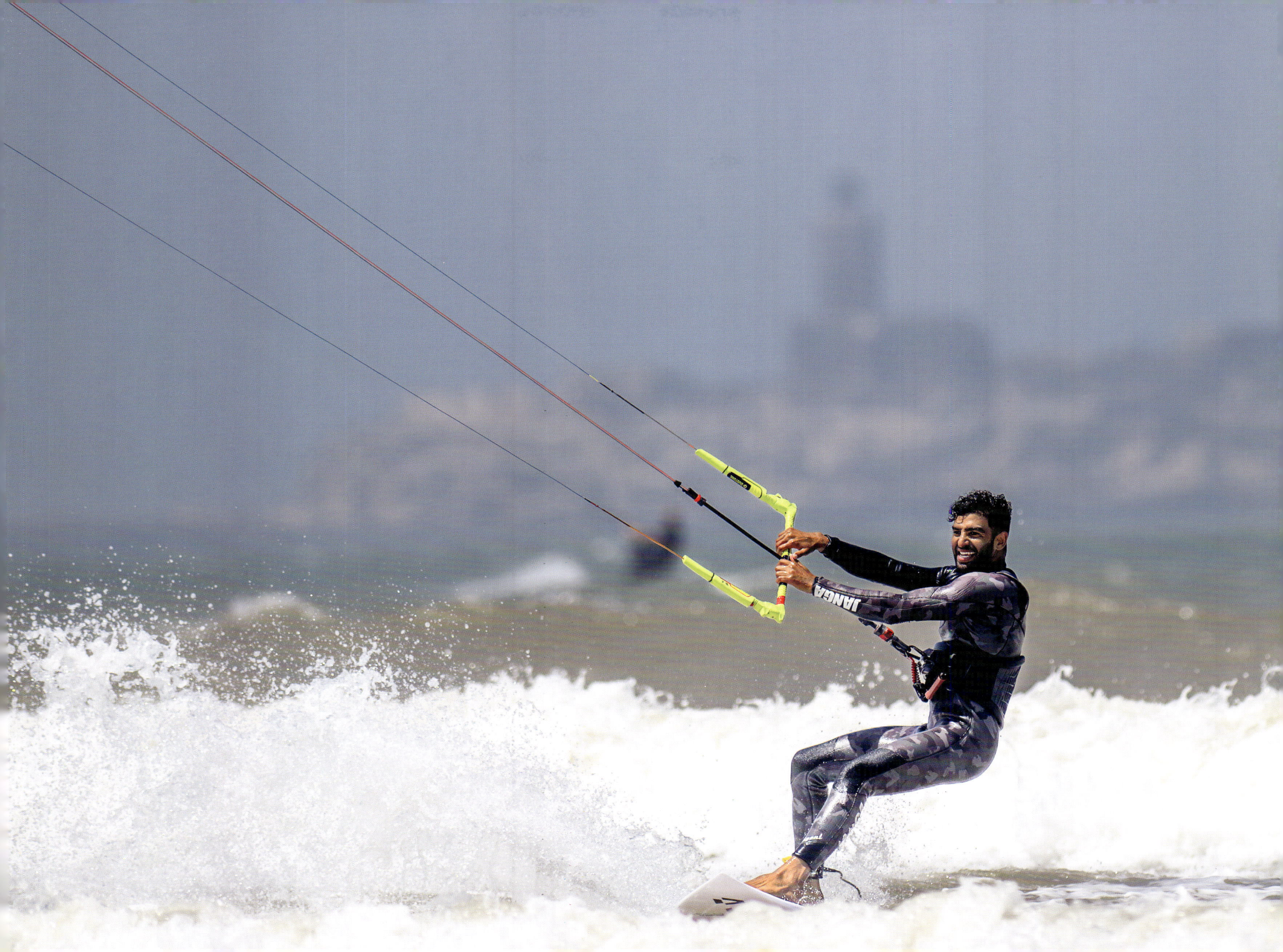
JANGA

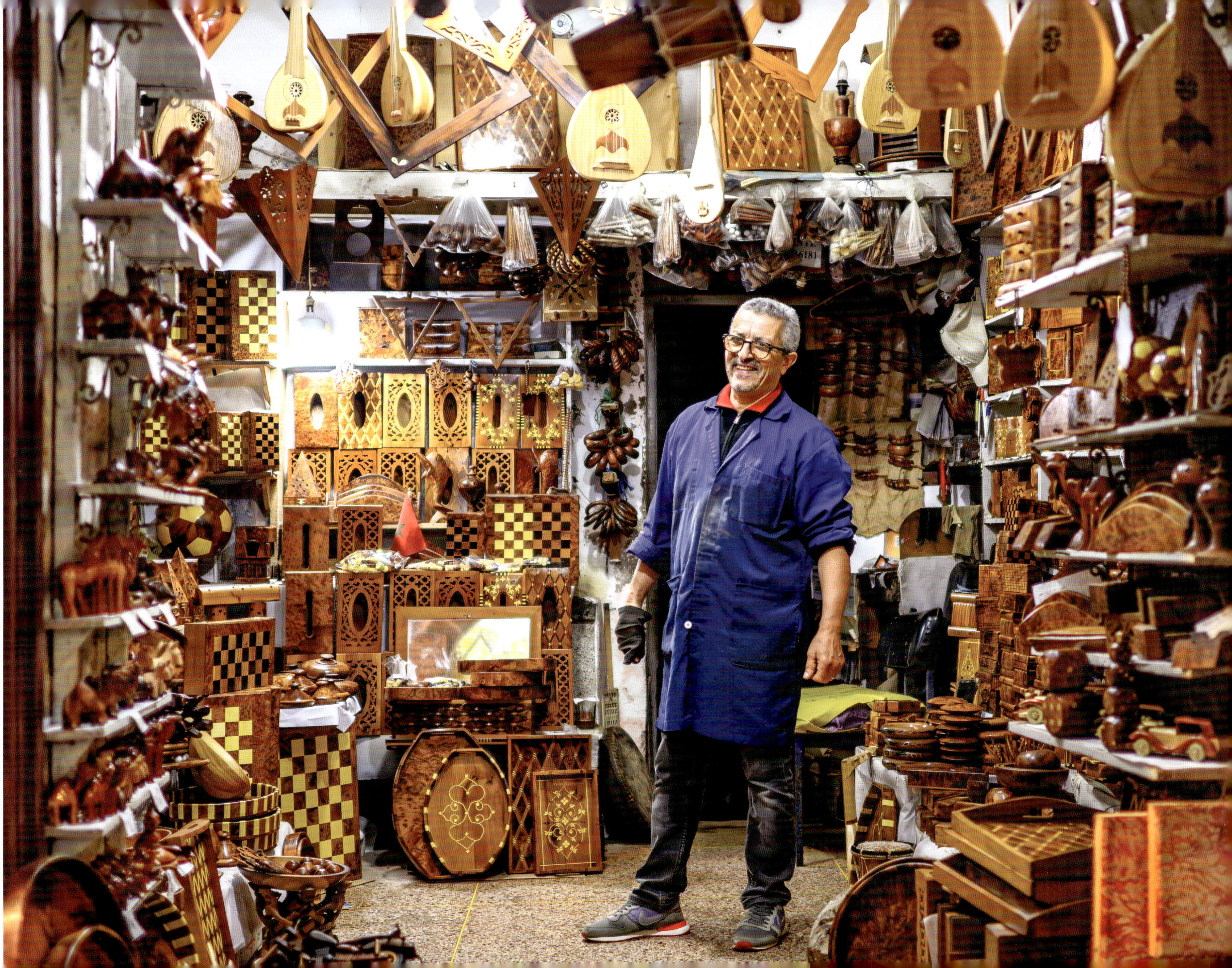

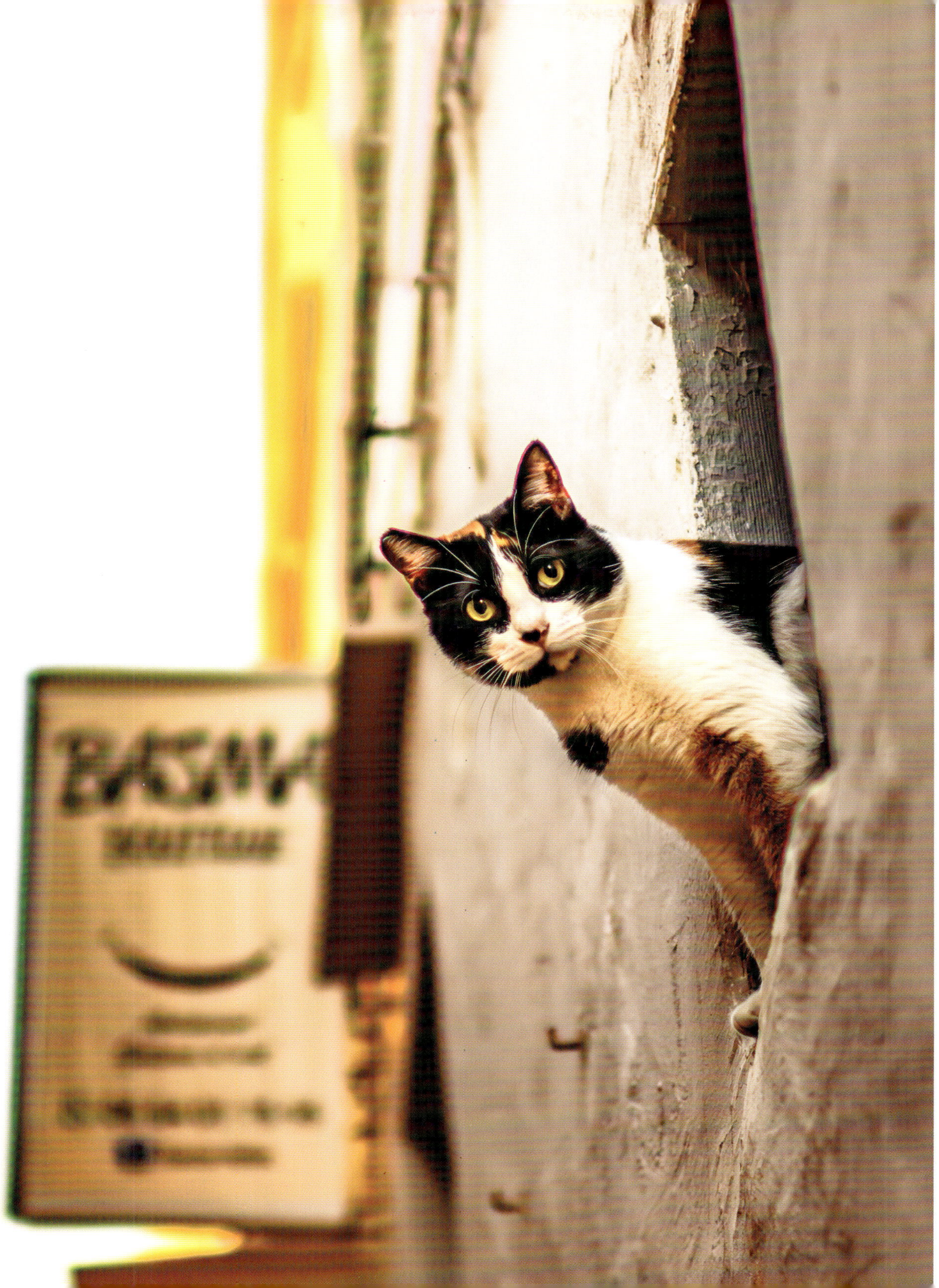

Previous page:
Kite surfers enjoying a day on the waves.

Wood craftsman is ready to greet new customers and friends.

Cat keeping an eye on passersby from an alley window in Essaouira.

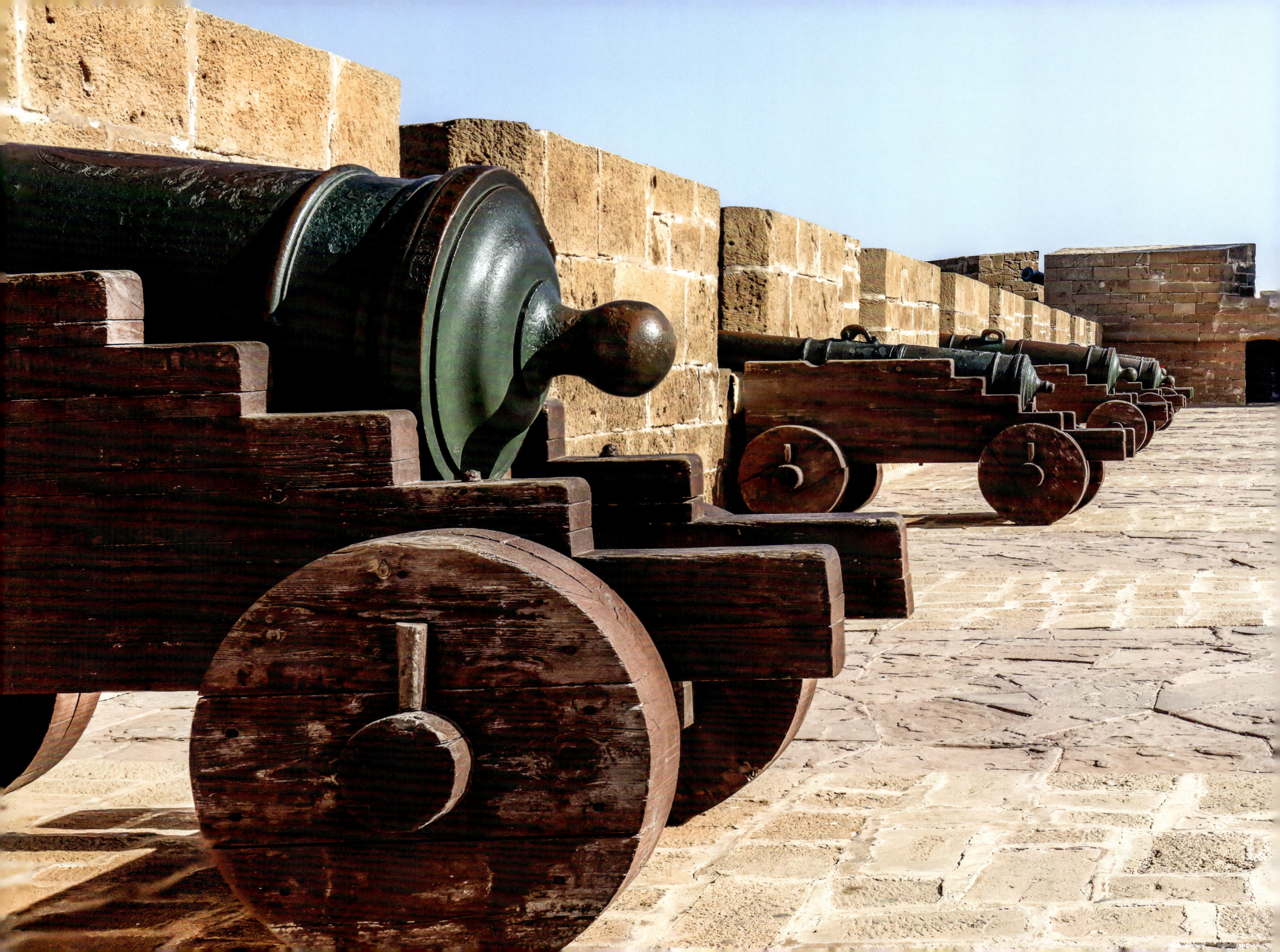

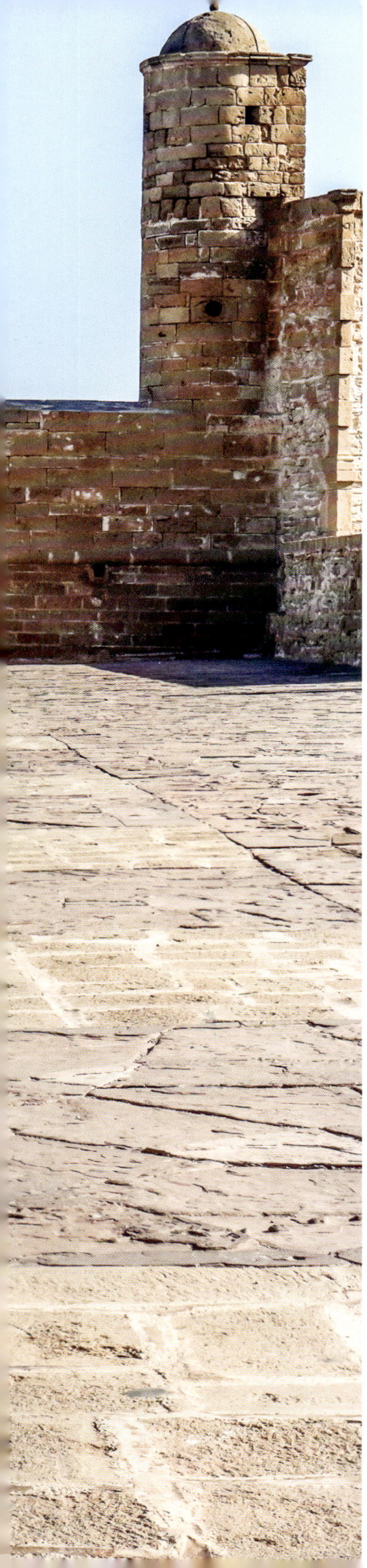
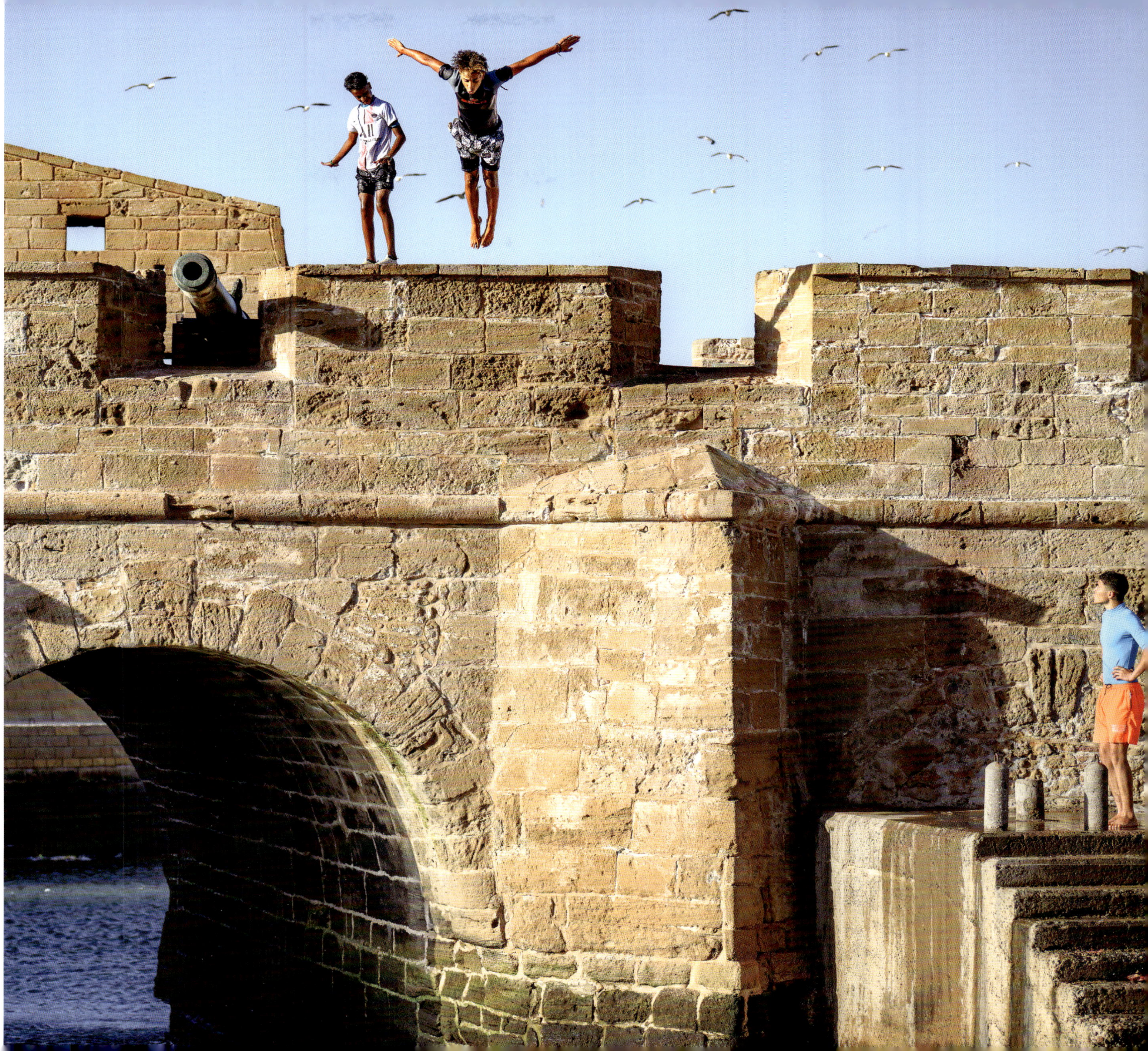

Previous page:
Cannon battlements of the port city of Essaouira.

Teenage boys diving from the battlement wall.

Locals strolling past a doorway in Moulay Hassan Square.

A fishing boat waits at sunset for its next journey.

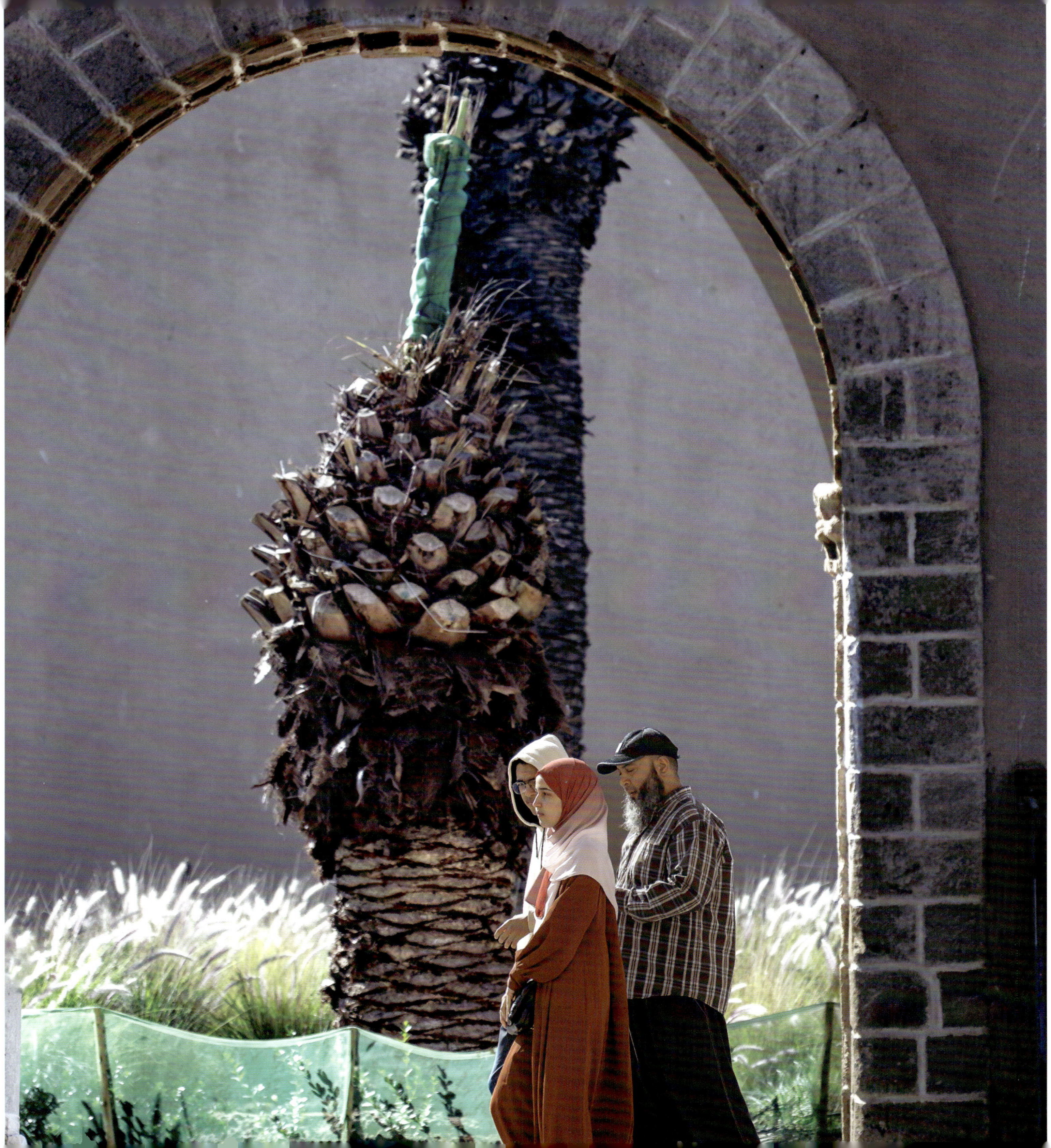

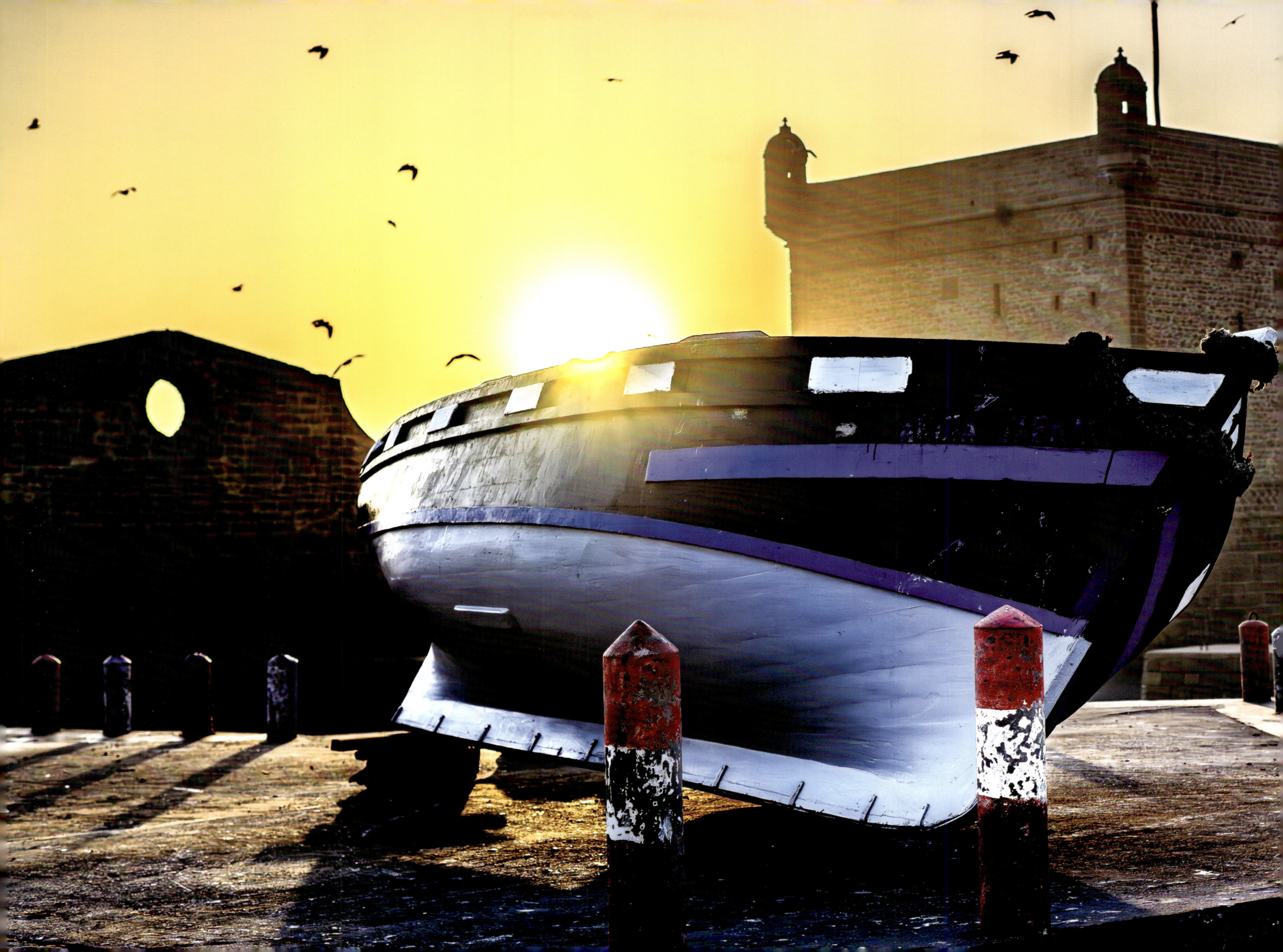

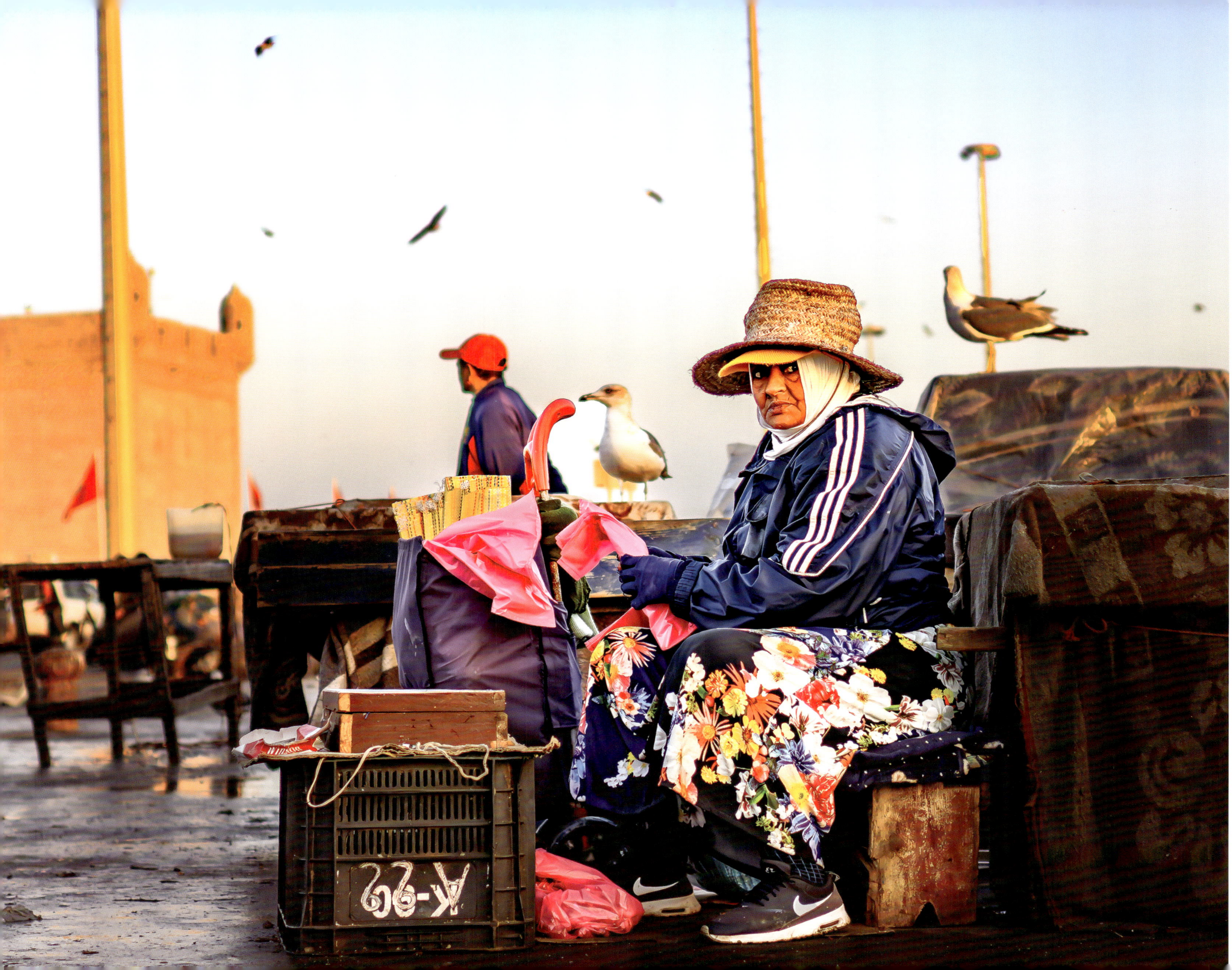

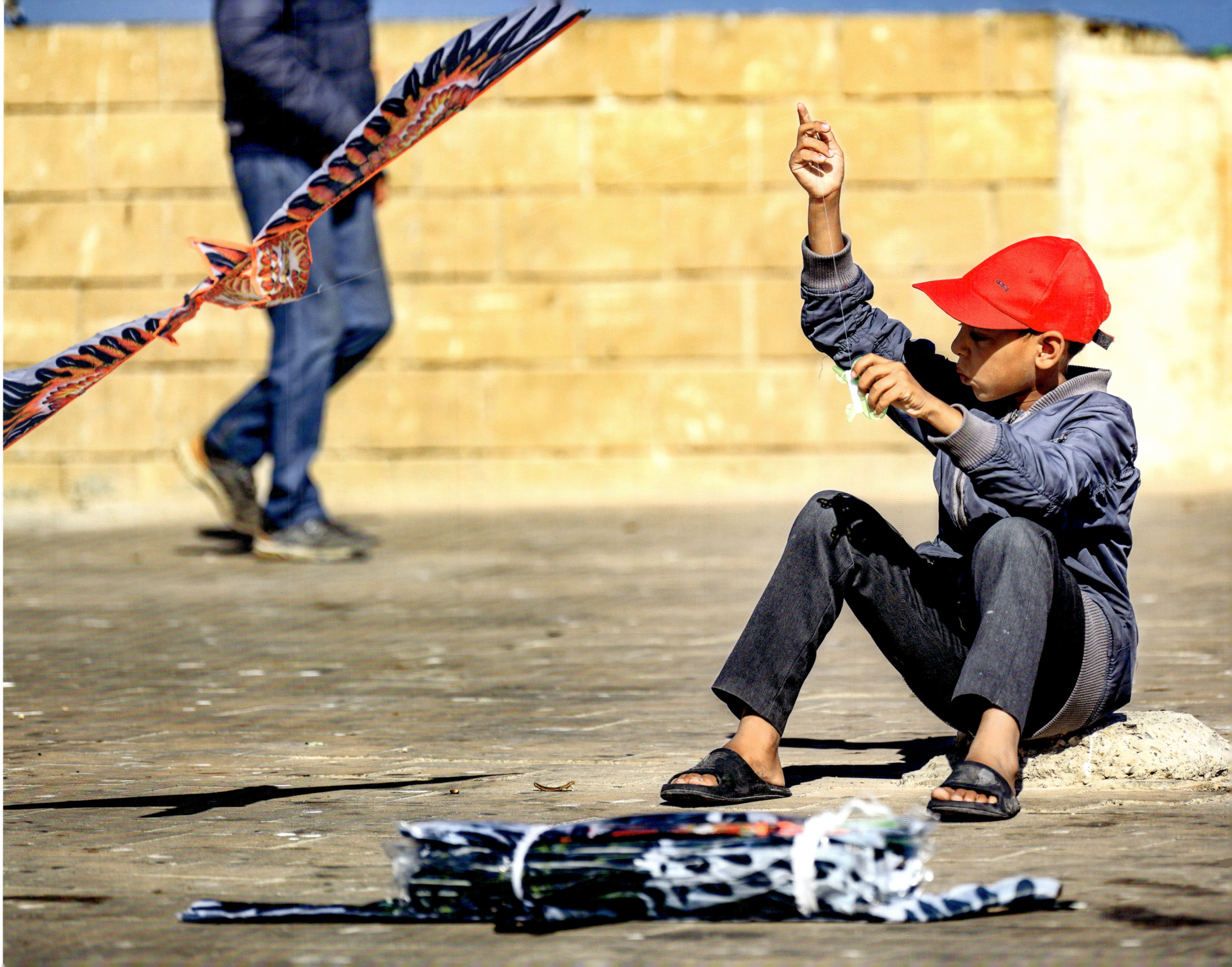

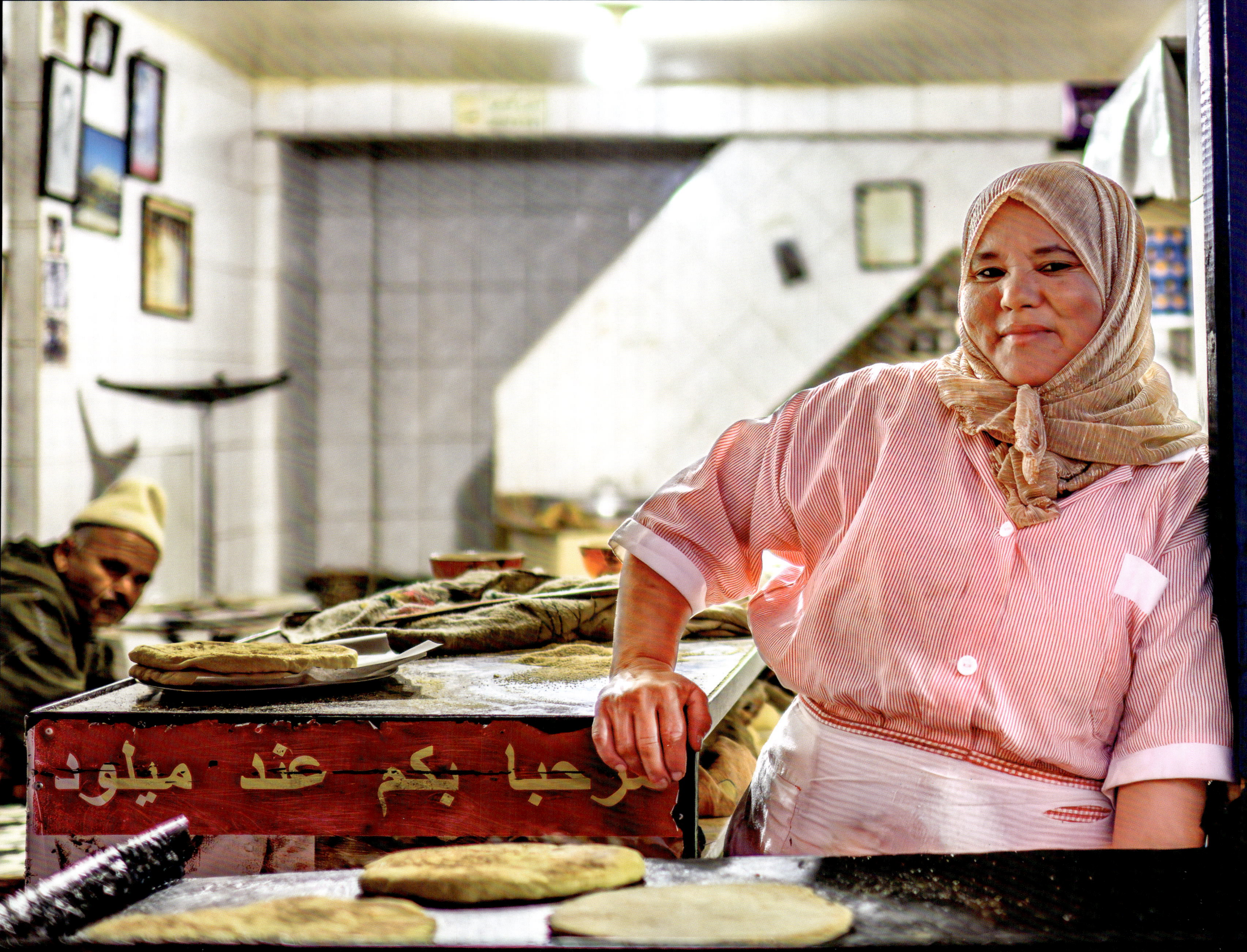
رحبا بكم عند ميلود

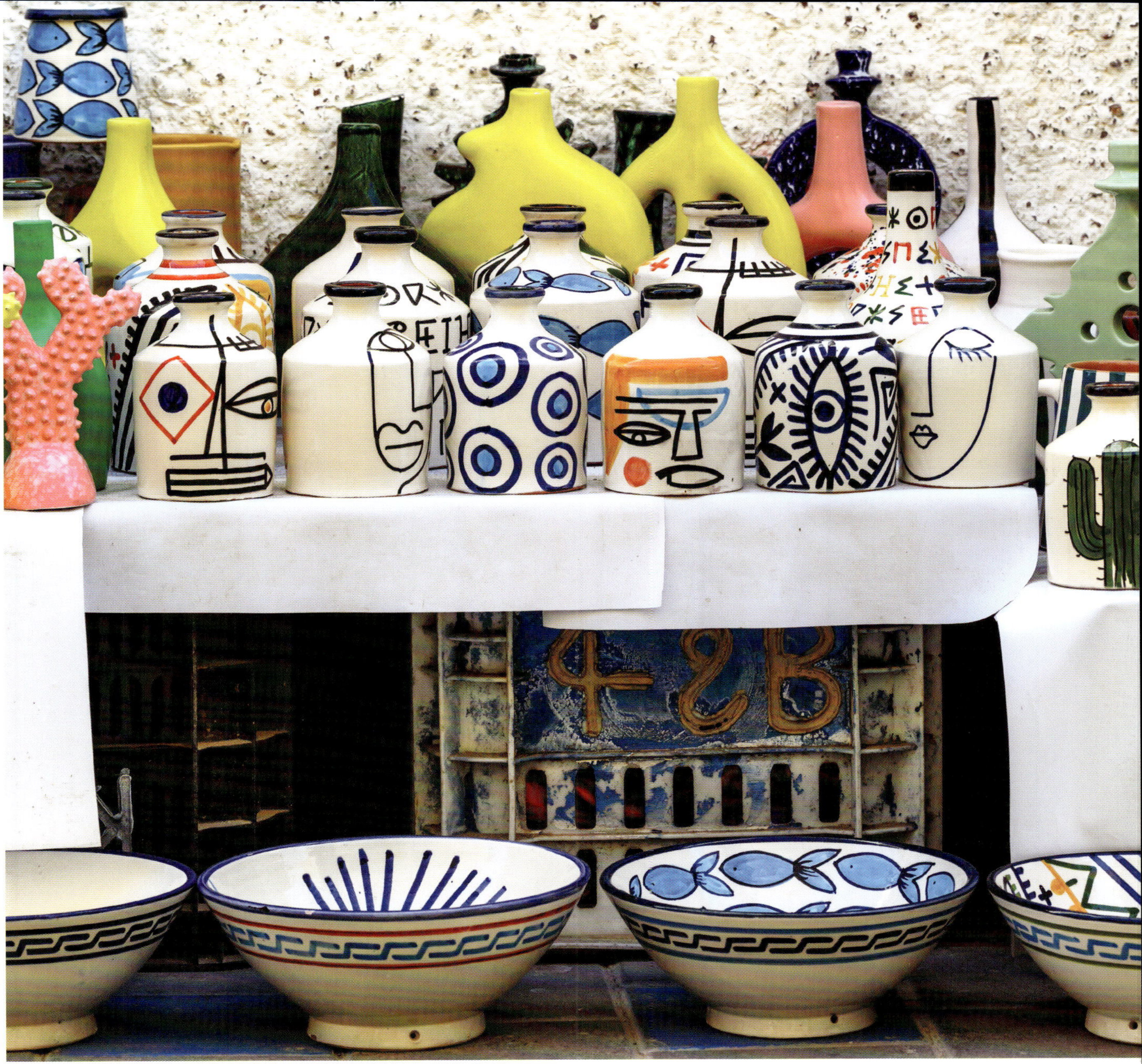

Previous page:
A woman merchant in the fish market at sunset.

A young boy selling colorful bird kites in the square.

The day starts early in souks throughout Morocco. Moroccan woman pan-frying traditional Moroccan harcha bread at dawn.

Artisan pottery for sale.

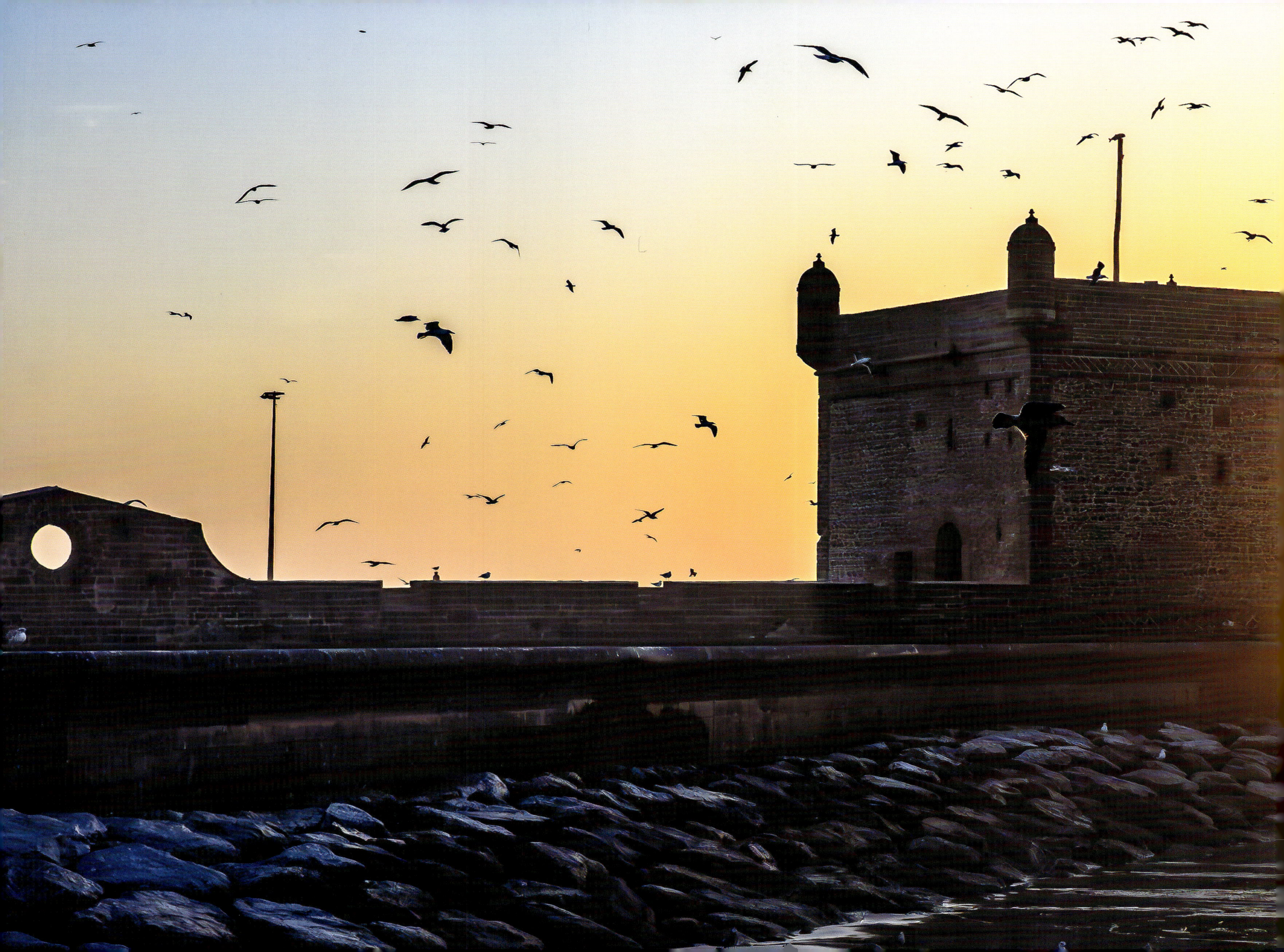

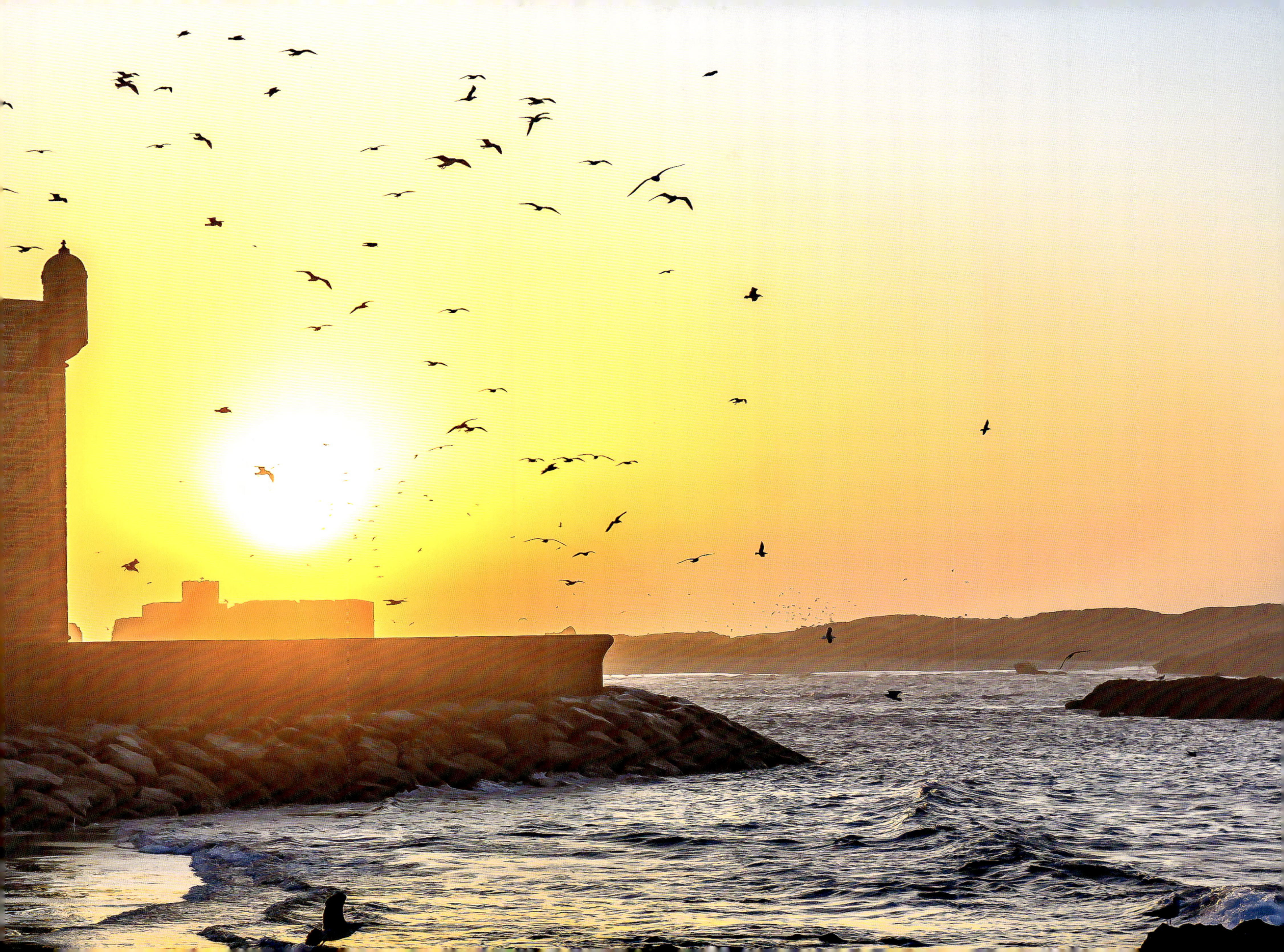

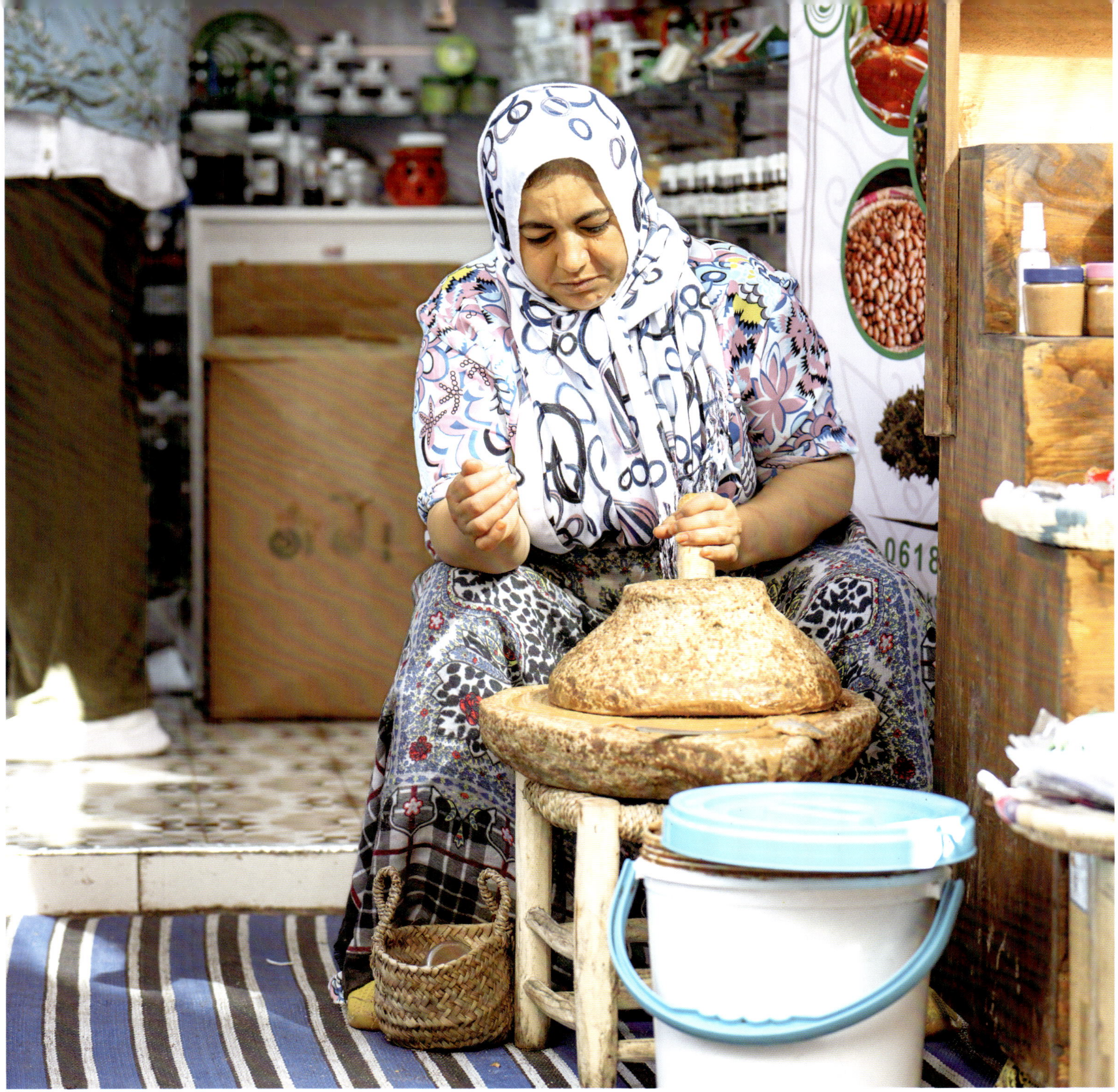

Previous page:
Seagulls dot the sky at sunset over the fish market.

Woman making argan oil, and men enjoying mint tea in their souk.

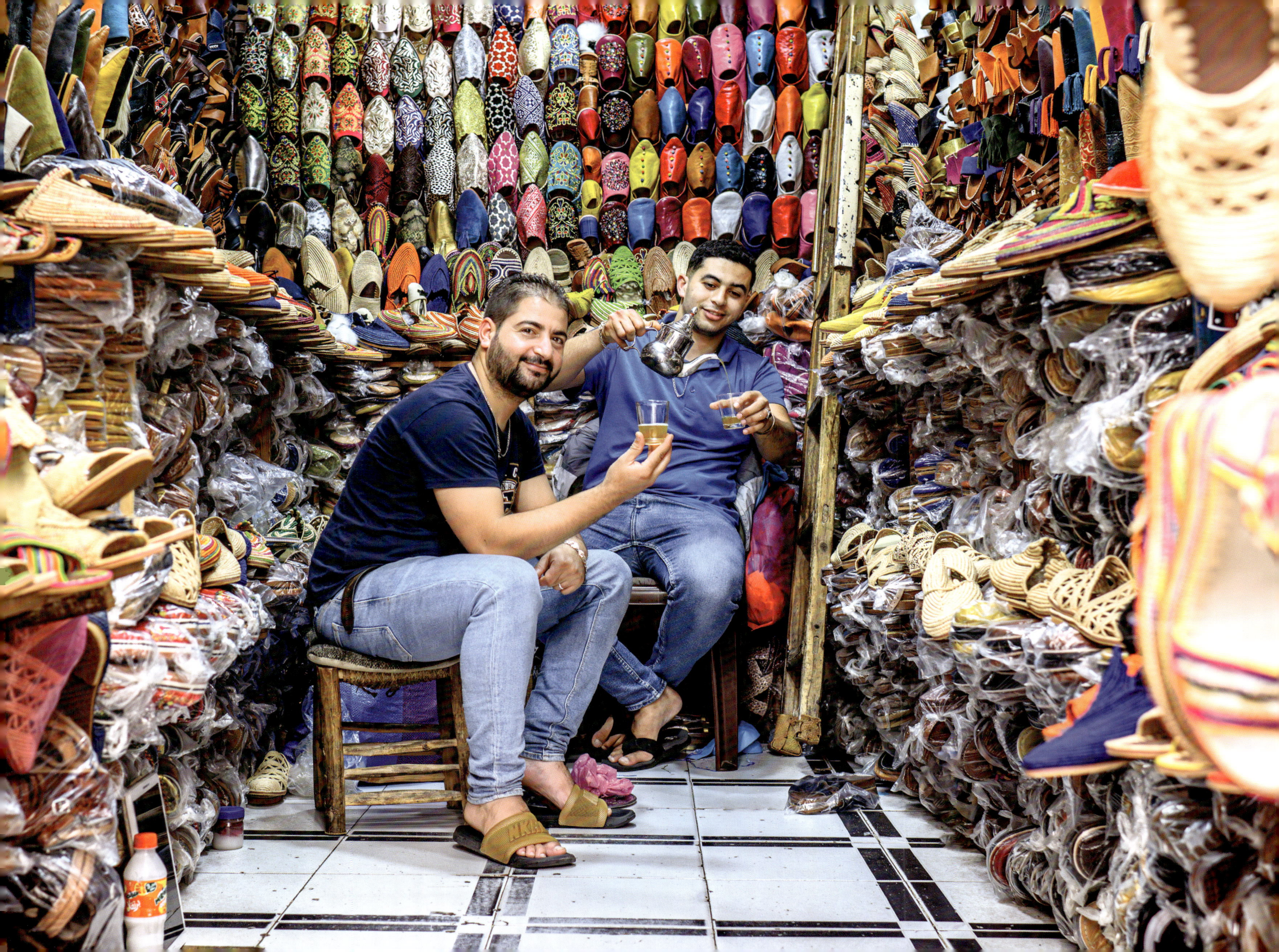

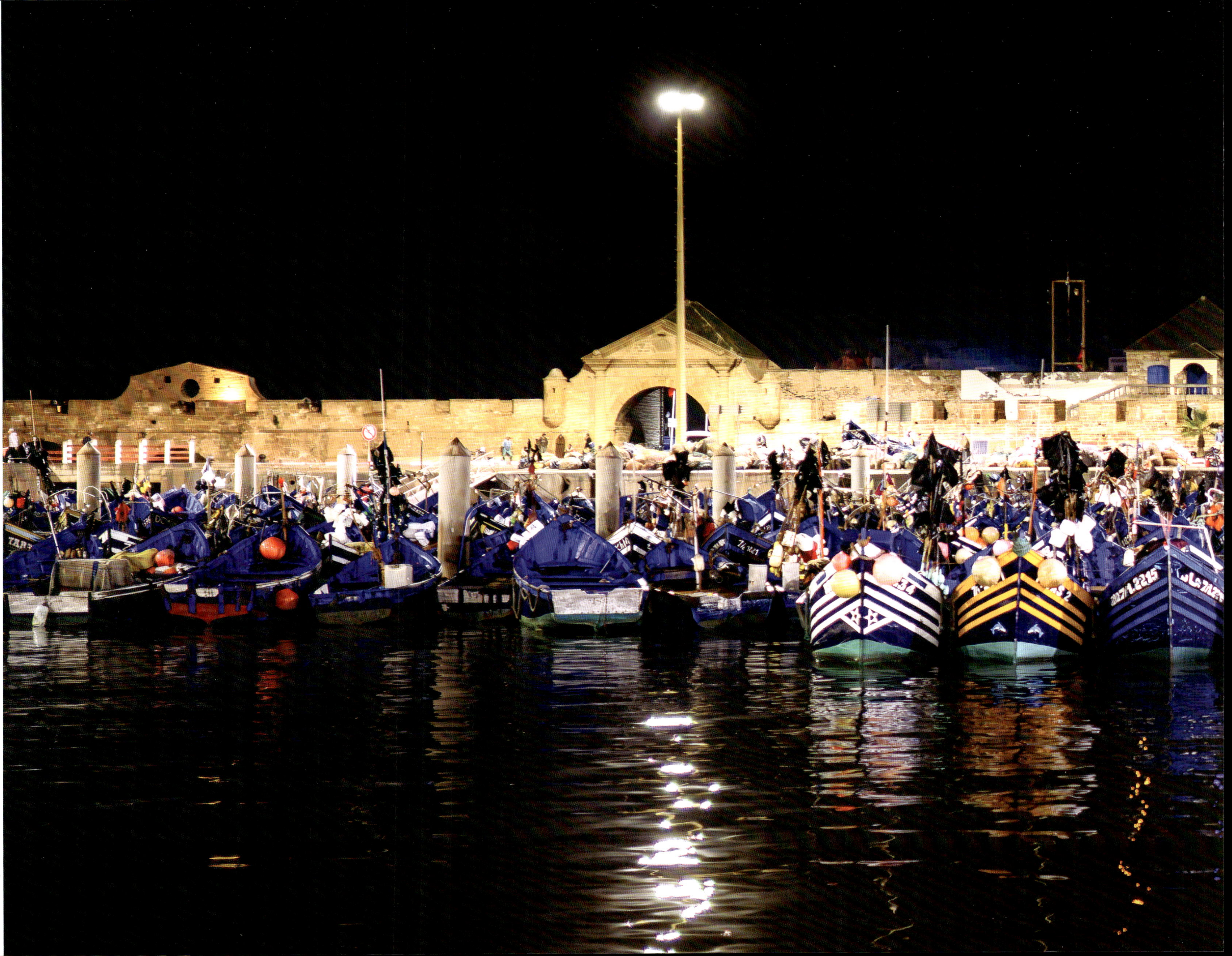

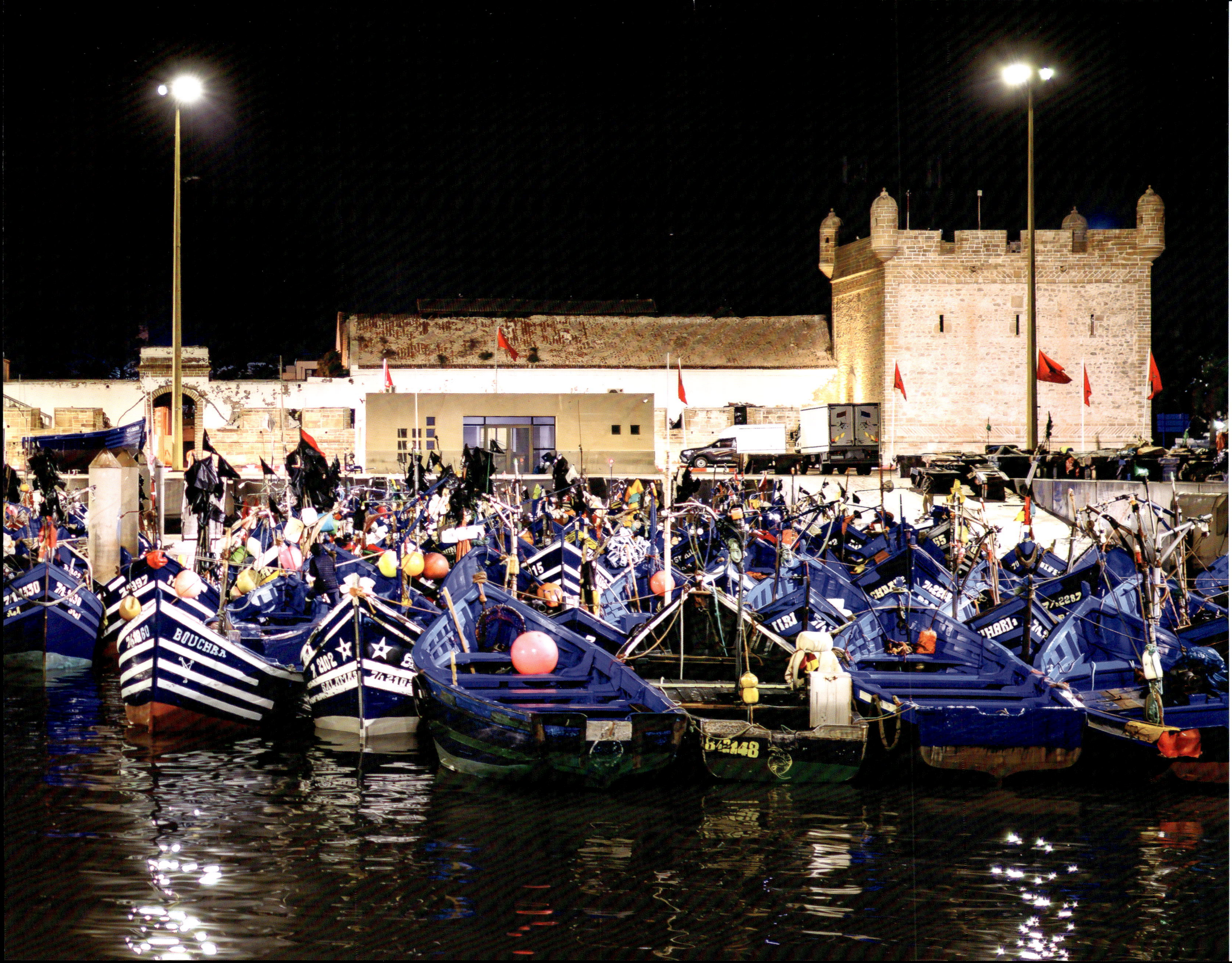
BOUCHRA

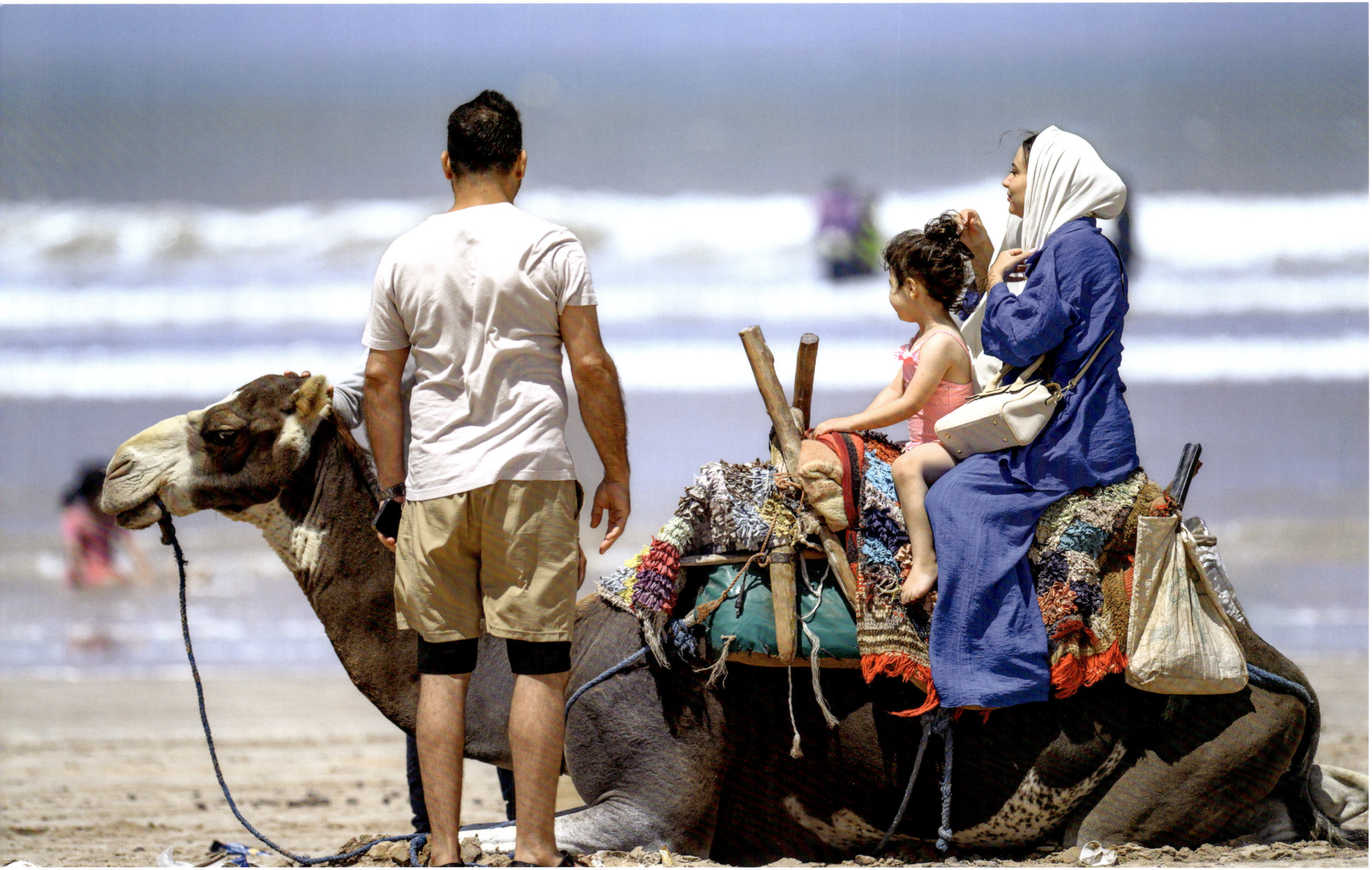

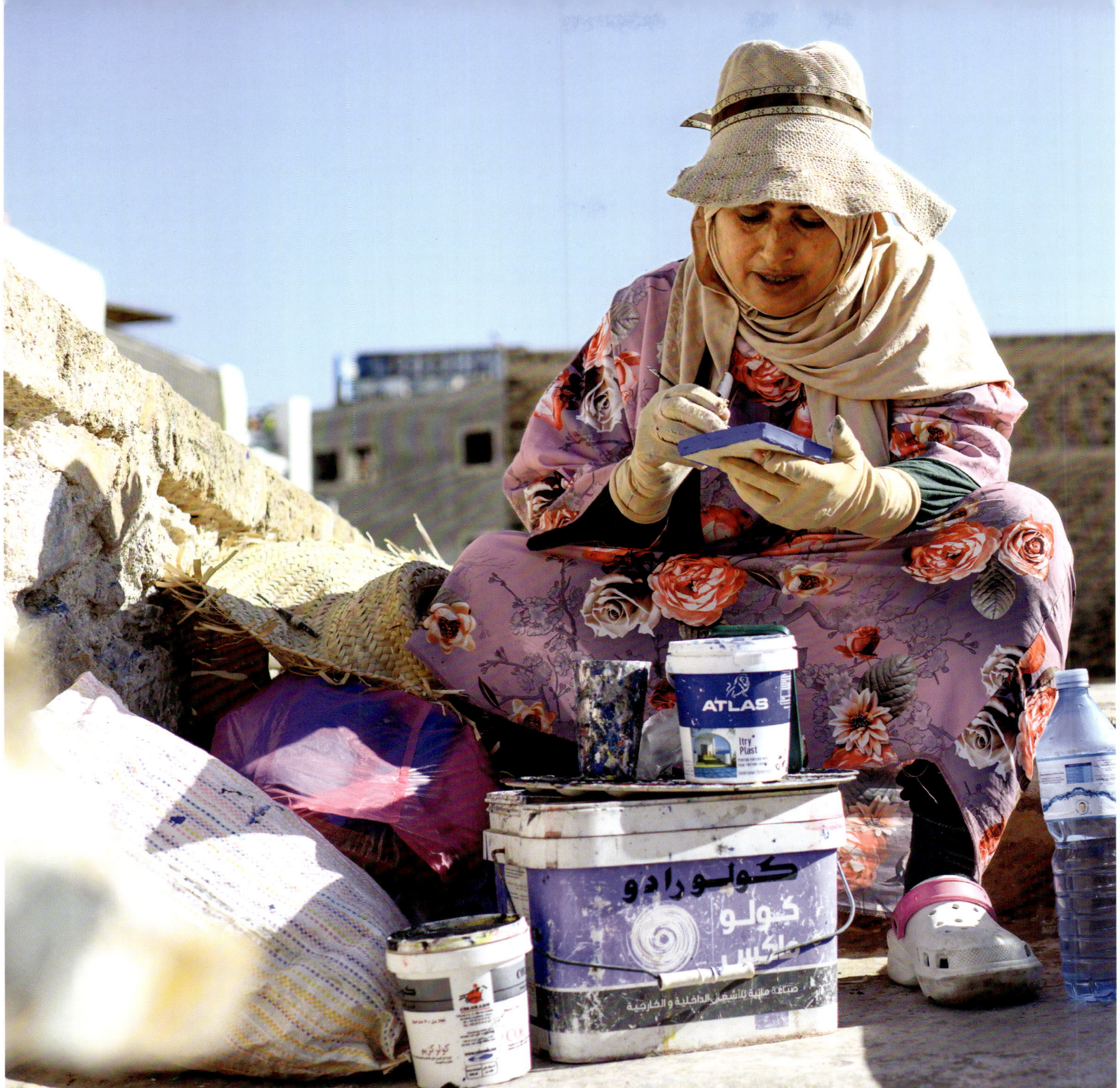


Previous page:
Myriad blue fishing boats in the fishing port at dawn.

Summer visitors take a camel ride on the beach.

An artist painting ceramic tiles on the battlement wall. Moroccan tiles are handmade using traditional techniques that have been passed down from generation to generation.

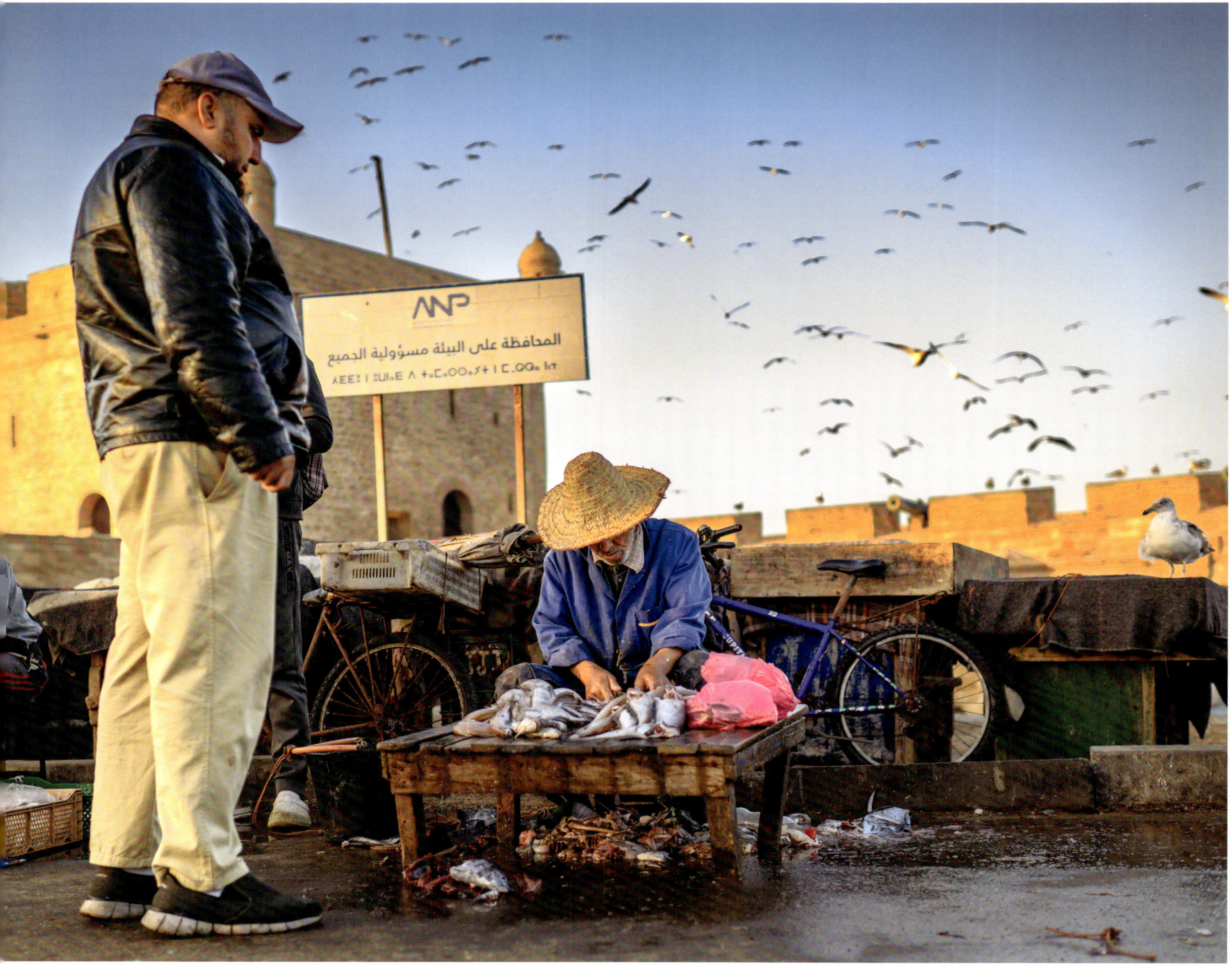
ANP
المحافظة على البيئة مسؤولية الجميع

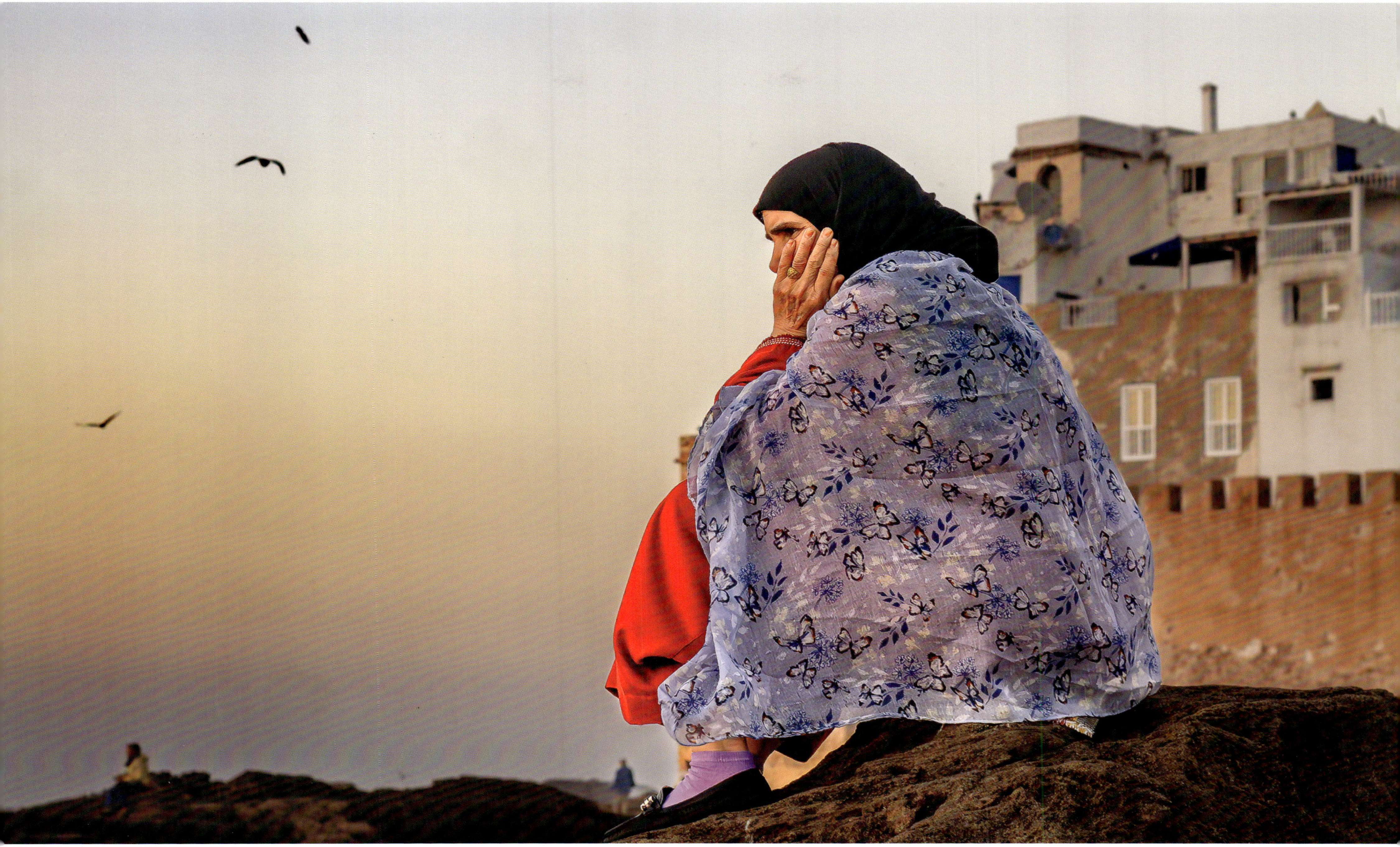

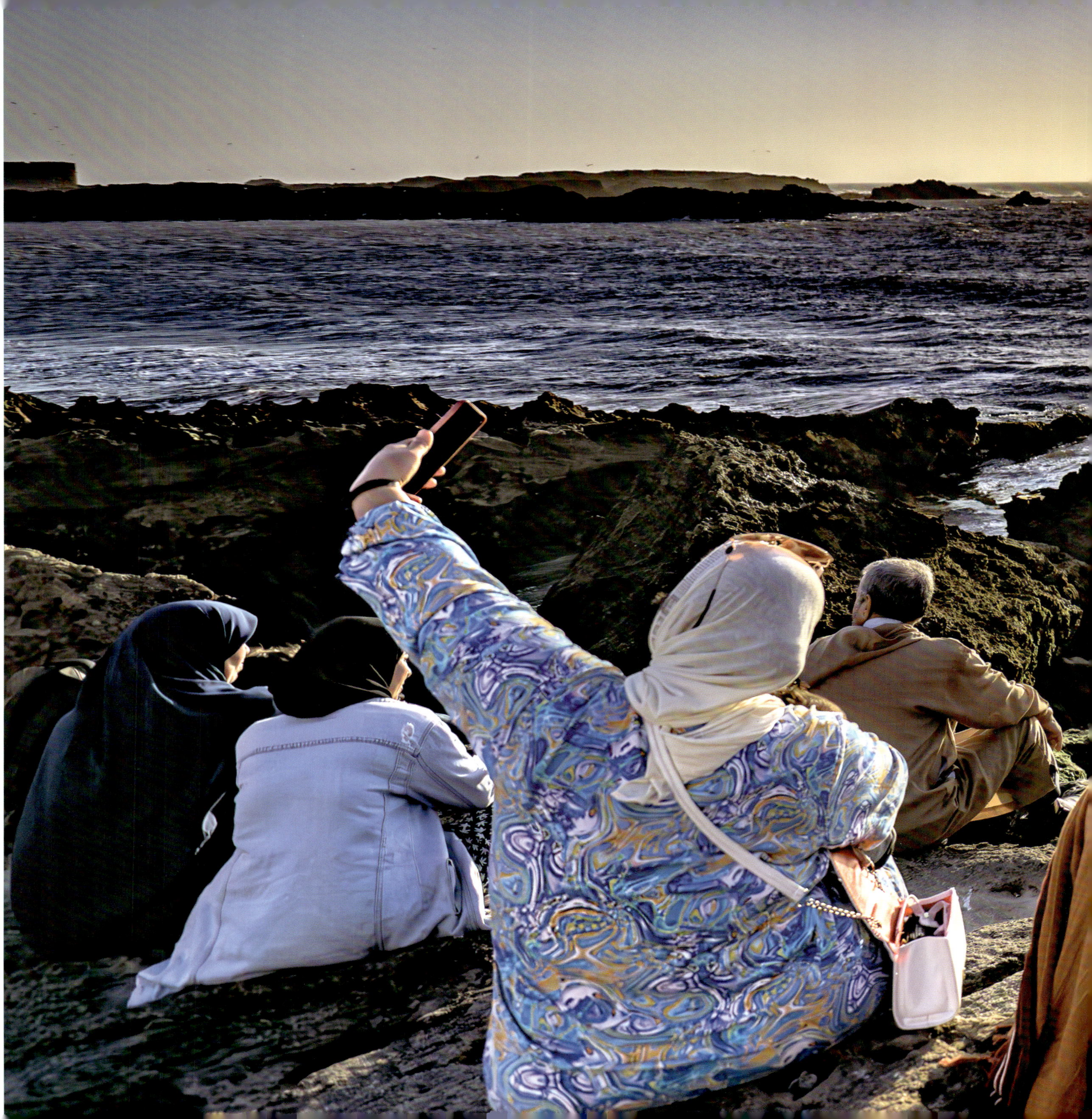

Previous page:
Merchant preparing fresh fish for sale.

Group of women taking a "selfie" as the sun sets in front of the Moulay Hassan Square.

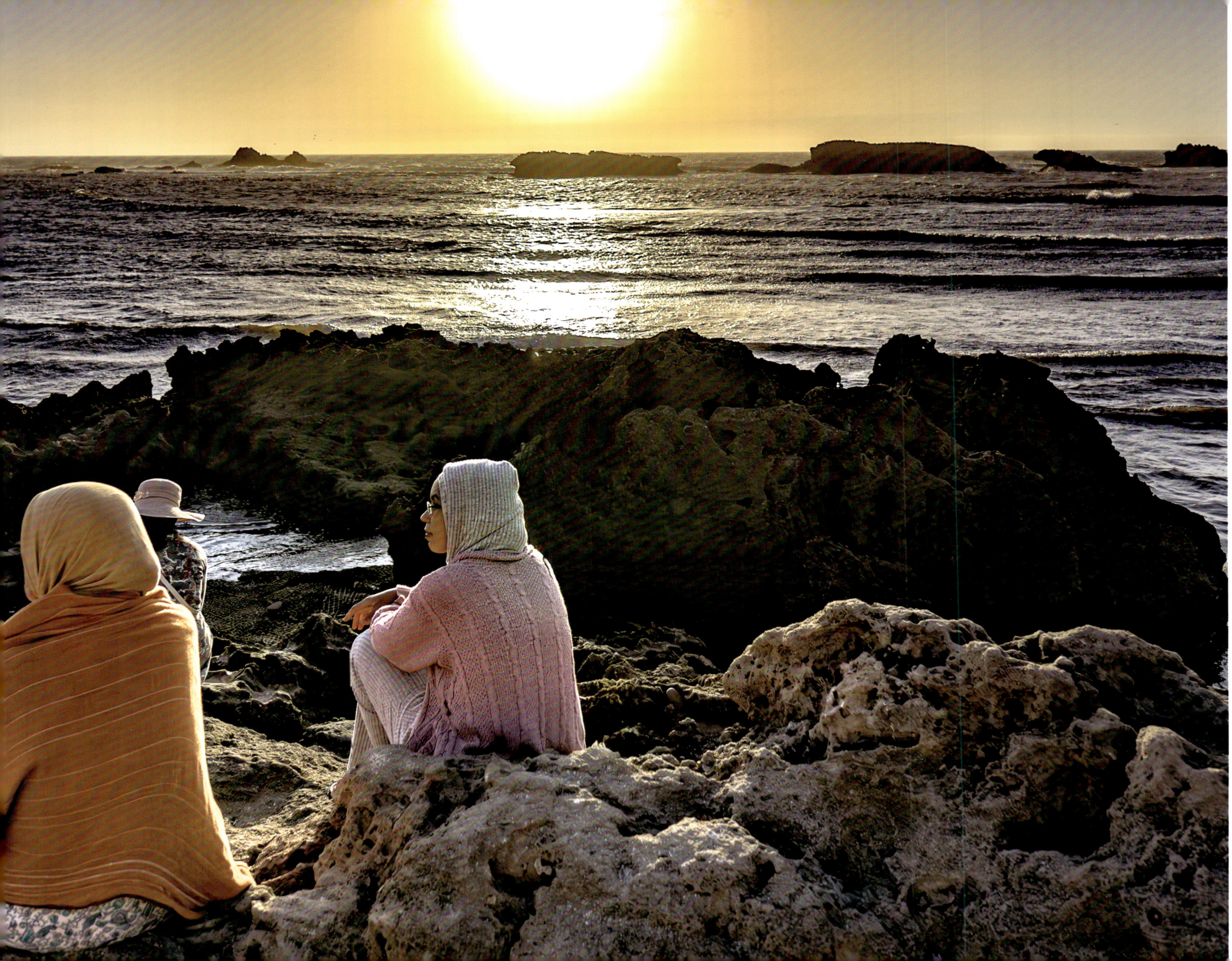

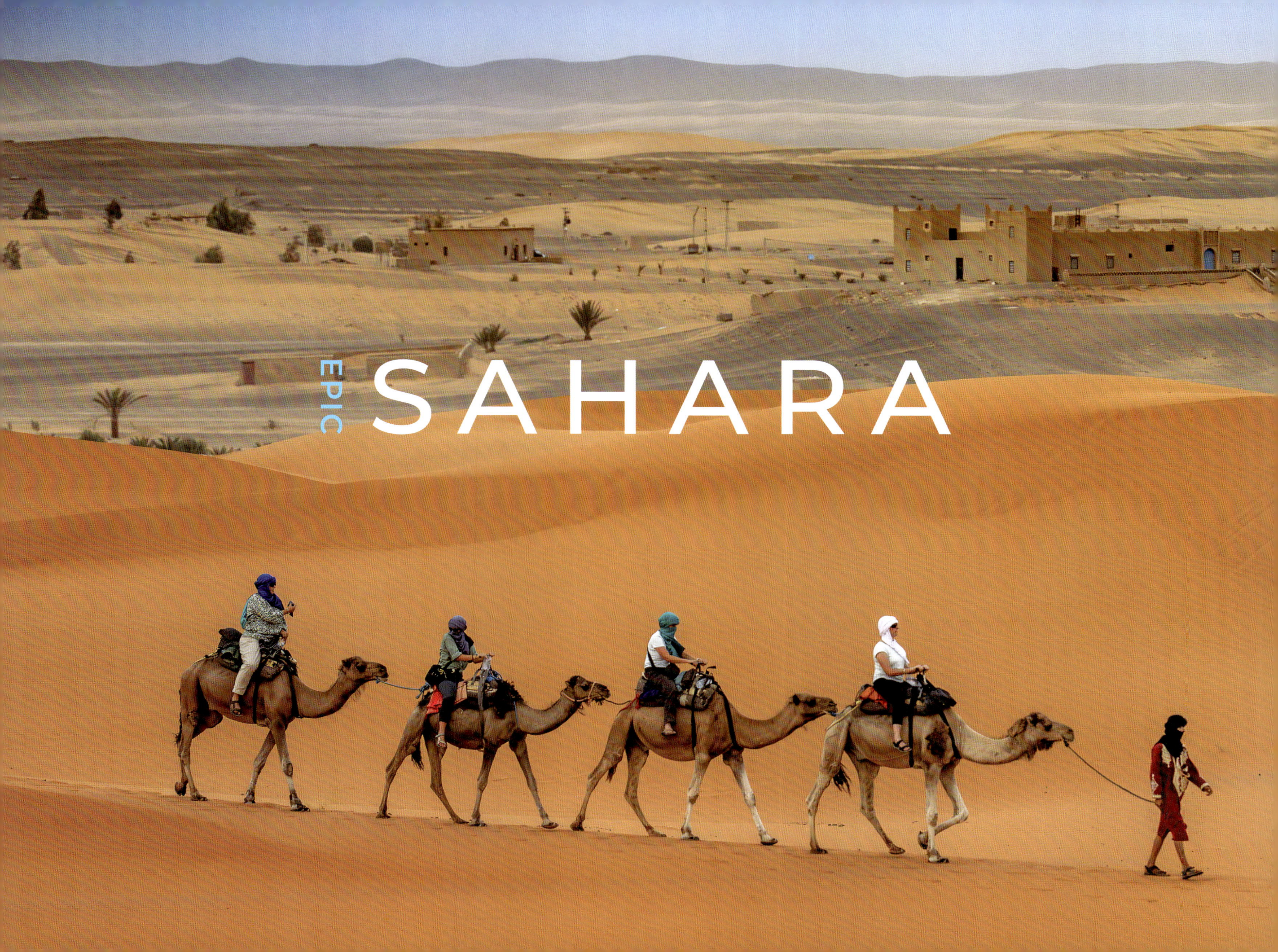
EPIC
SAHARA

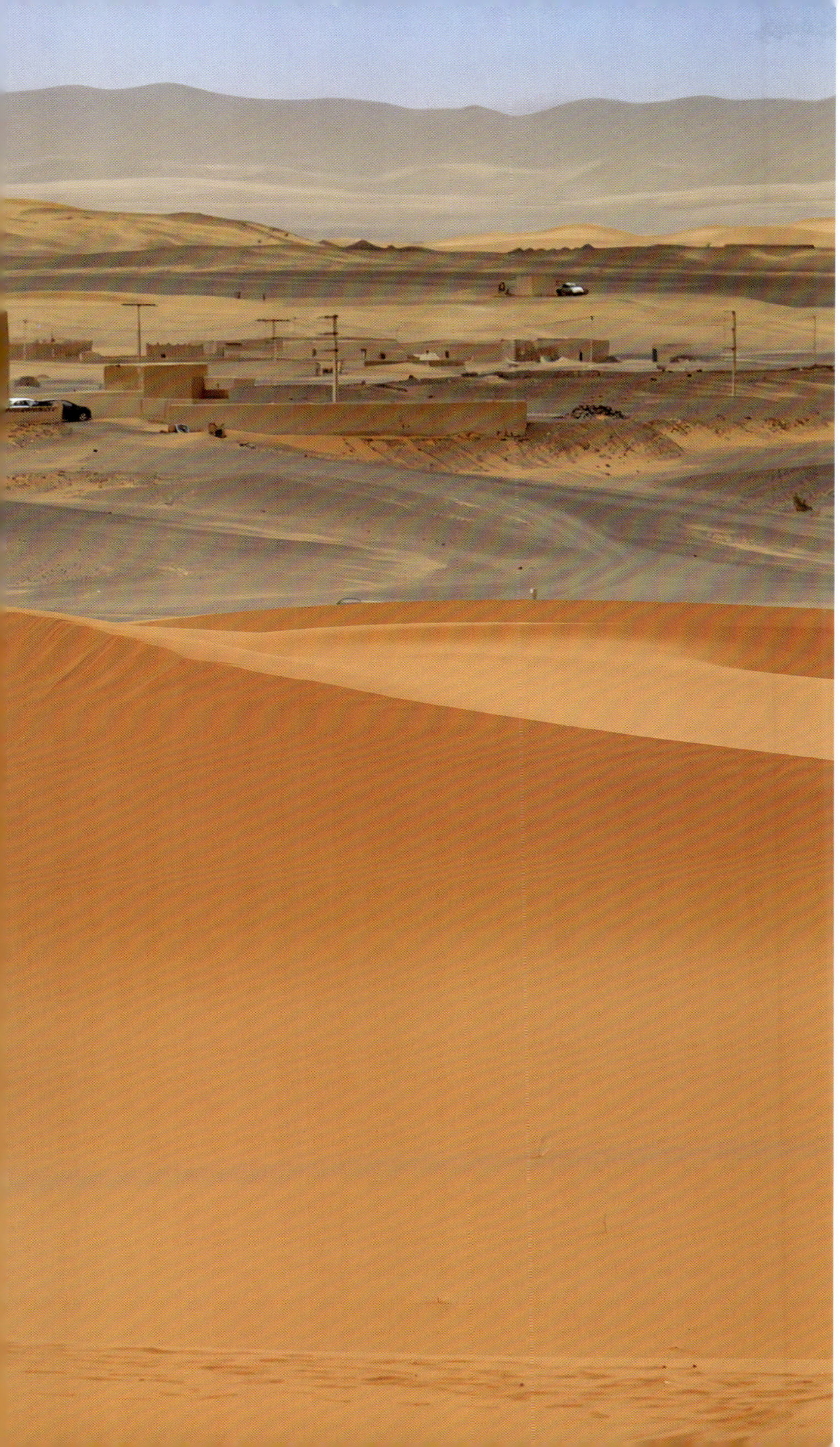

# GOLDEN DUNES, AMAZIGH NOMADS AND BREATHTAKING VIEWS

The Sahara Desert is one of largest deserts in the world, spanning over 3,000 miles across North Africa. It covers 11 African countries, including Morocco, Algeria, and Egypt. No trip to Morocco is complete without a trek across the dunes and a night spent in a traditional Amazigh tent camp. Most travelers arrive in the afternoon and meet with teams of camel guides and then ride camels or ATVs over the shifting Erg Chebbi dunes before stopping to sit and watch the sun set over the vast sea of sand that changes in hues of gold as the light drops under the horizon and gives way to an endless sea of stars hung in a jet black sky that envelops the various tent encampments.

In many of the camps, a traditional Amazigh meal is shared, followed by Amazigh music and dancing. Not to be outdone by dusk, the desert sky comes to life again in the early morning and reignites the golden sand dunes for as far as the eye can see.

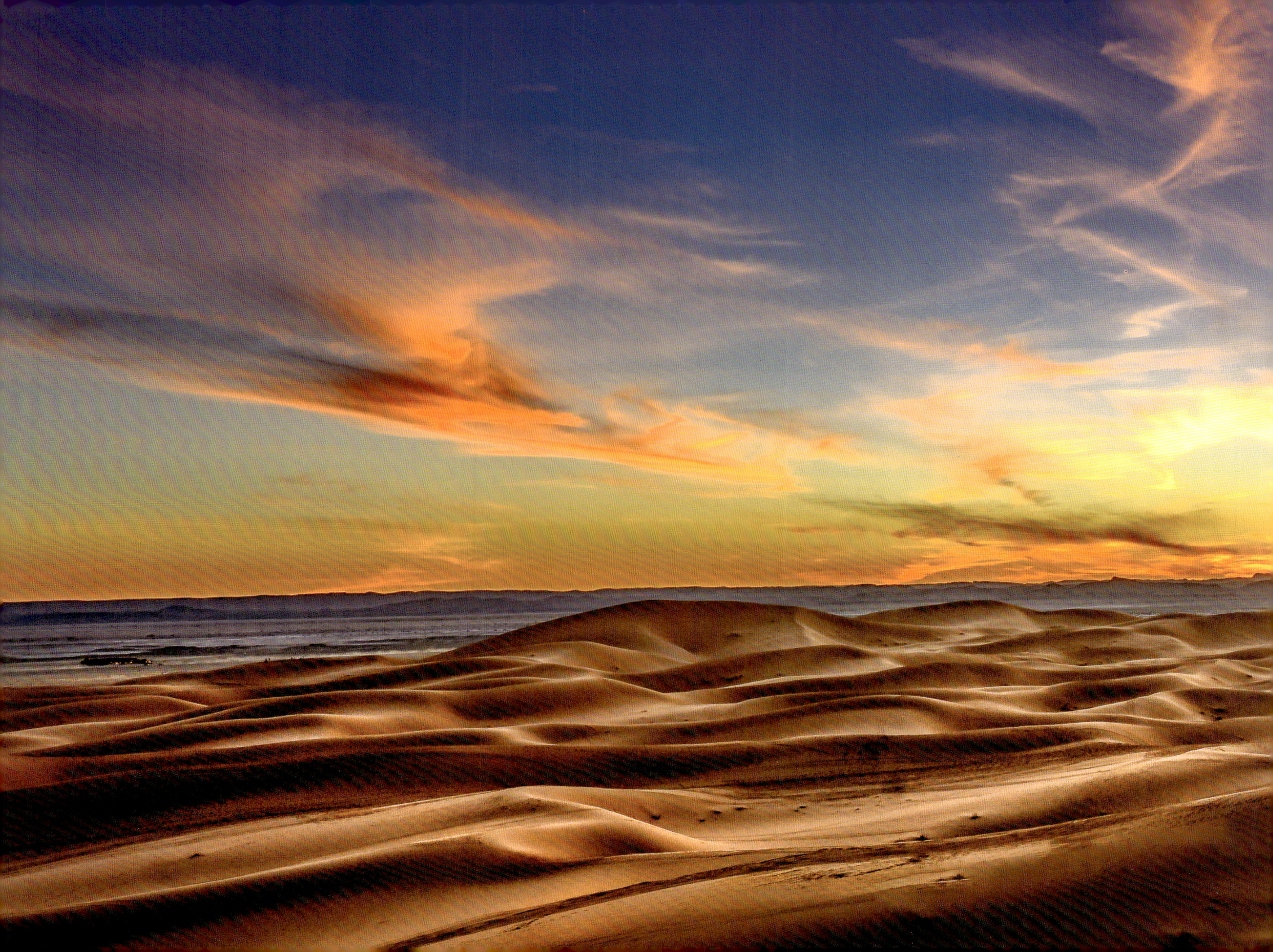

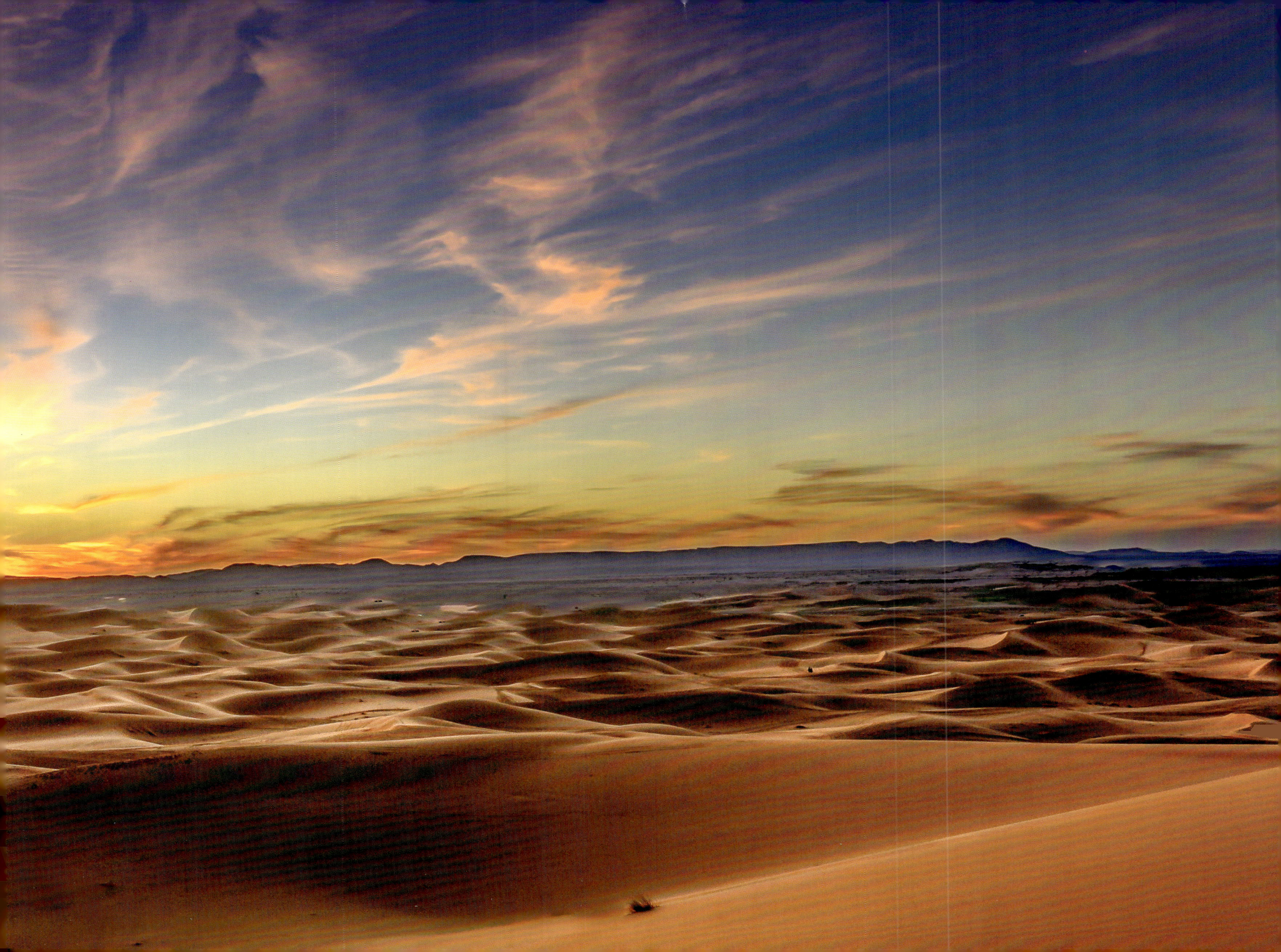

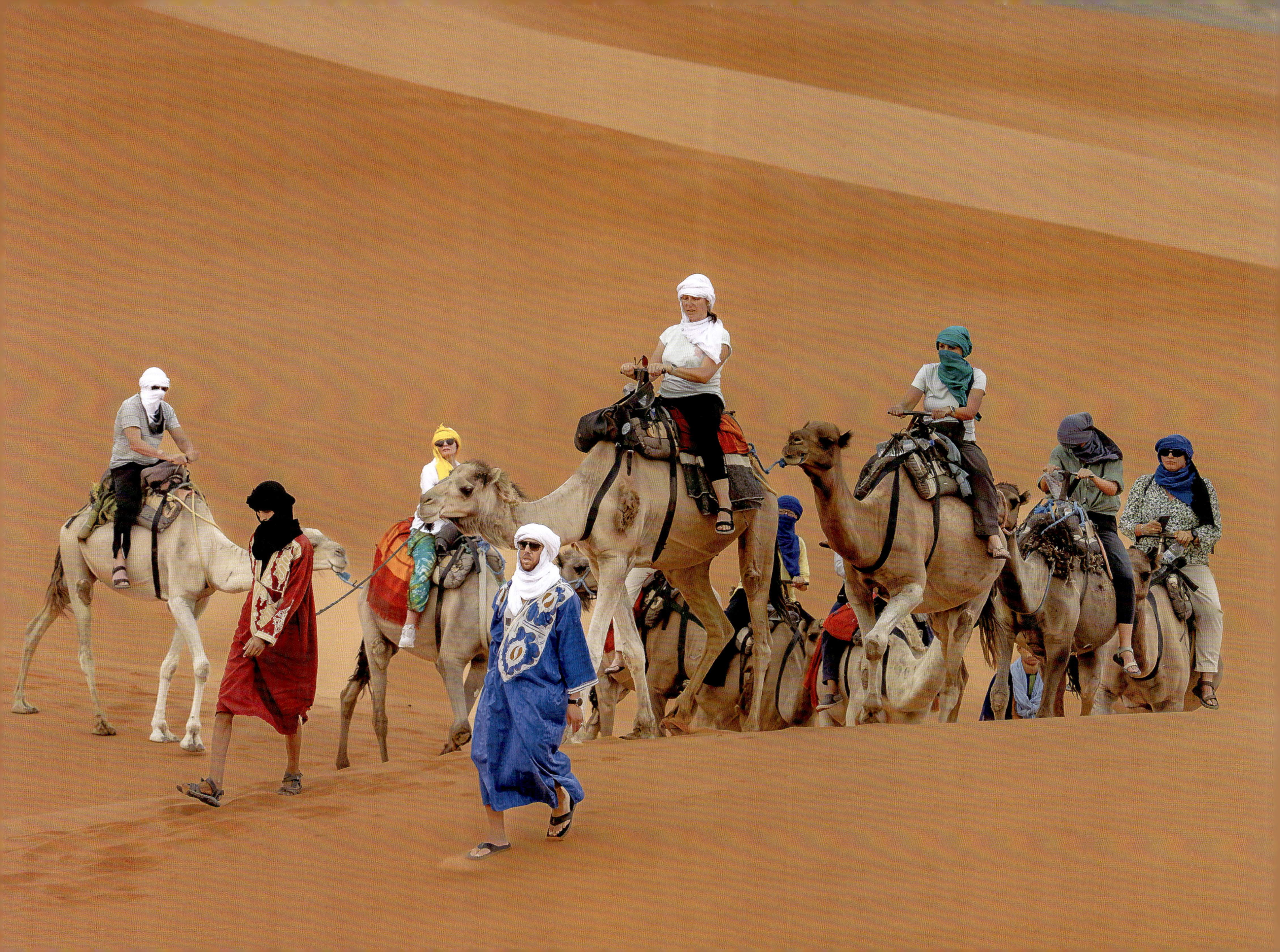

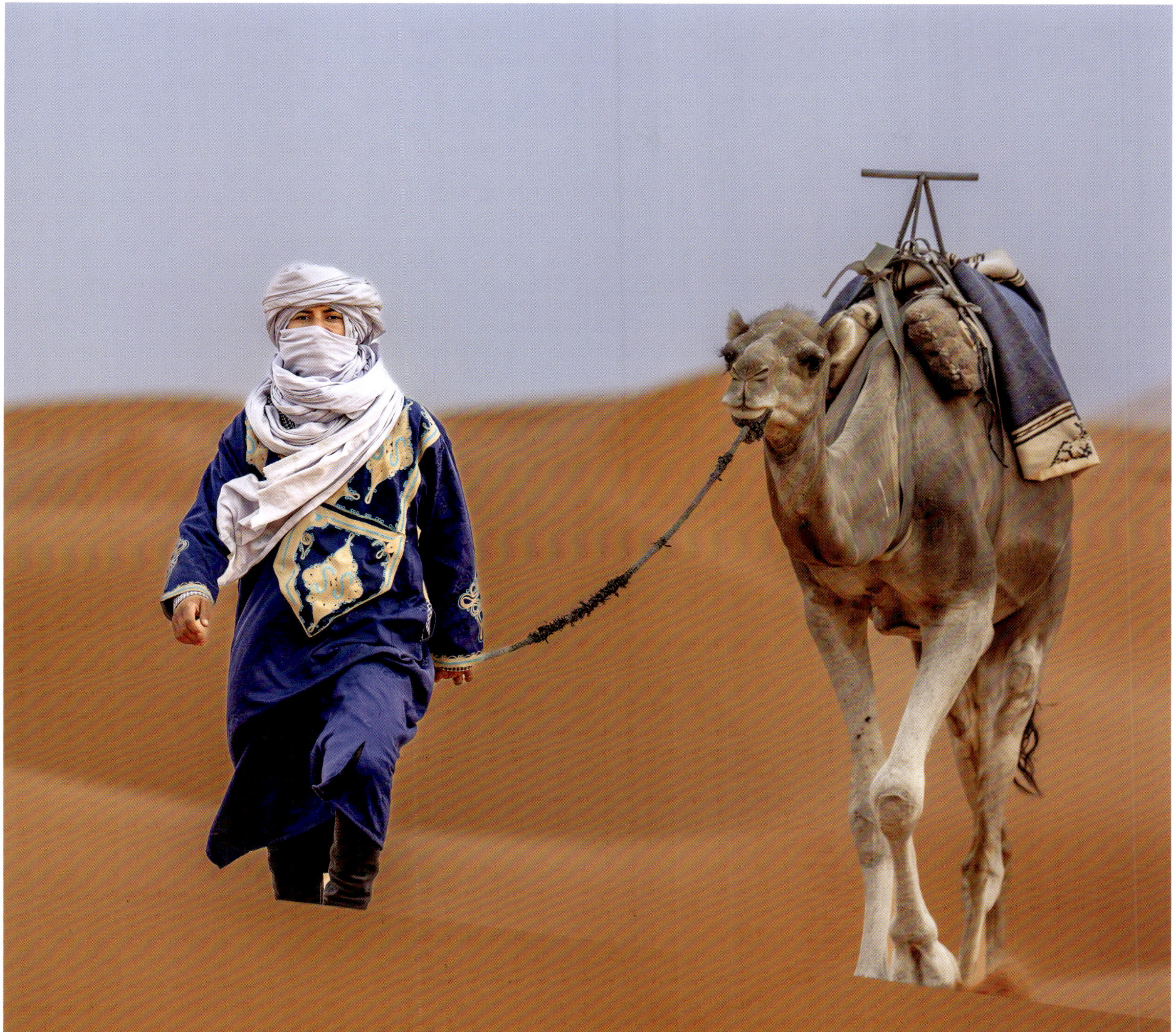

Previous page:
Saharan sunsets are known for being spectacular and often considered the most magnificent on earth. Desert sunsets are particularly breathtaking due to the dust and sand particles reflecting sunlight, which paint the sky vivid oranges, yellows and reds.

Travelers riding camels toward an Amazigh camp.

Amazigh camel driver walking a camel through the sea of dunes.

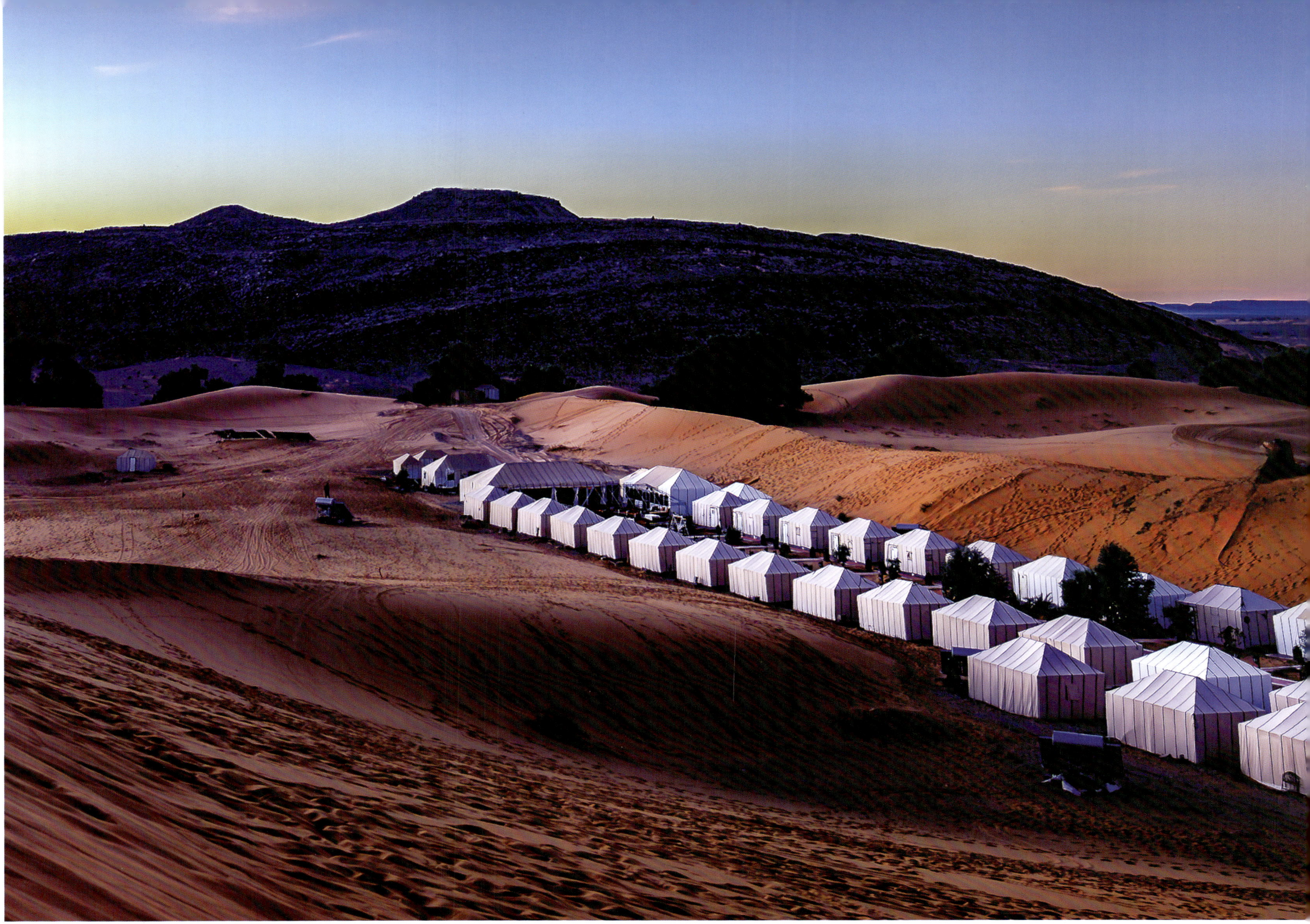

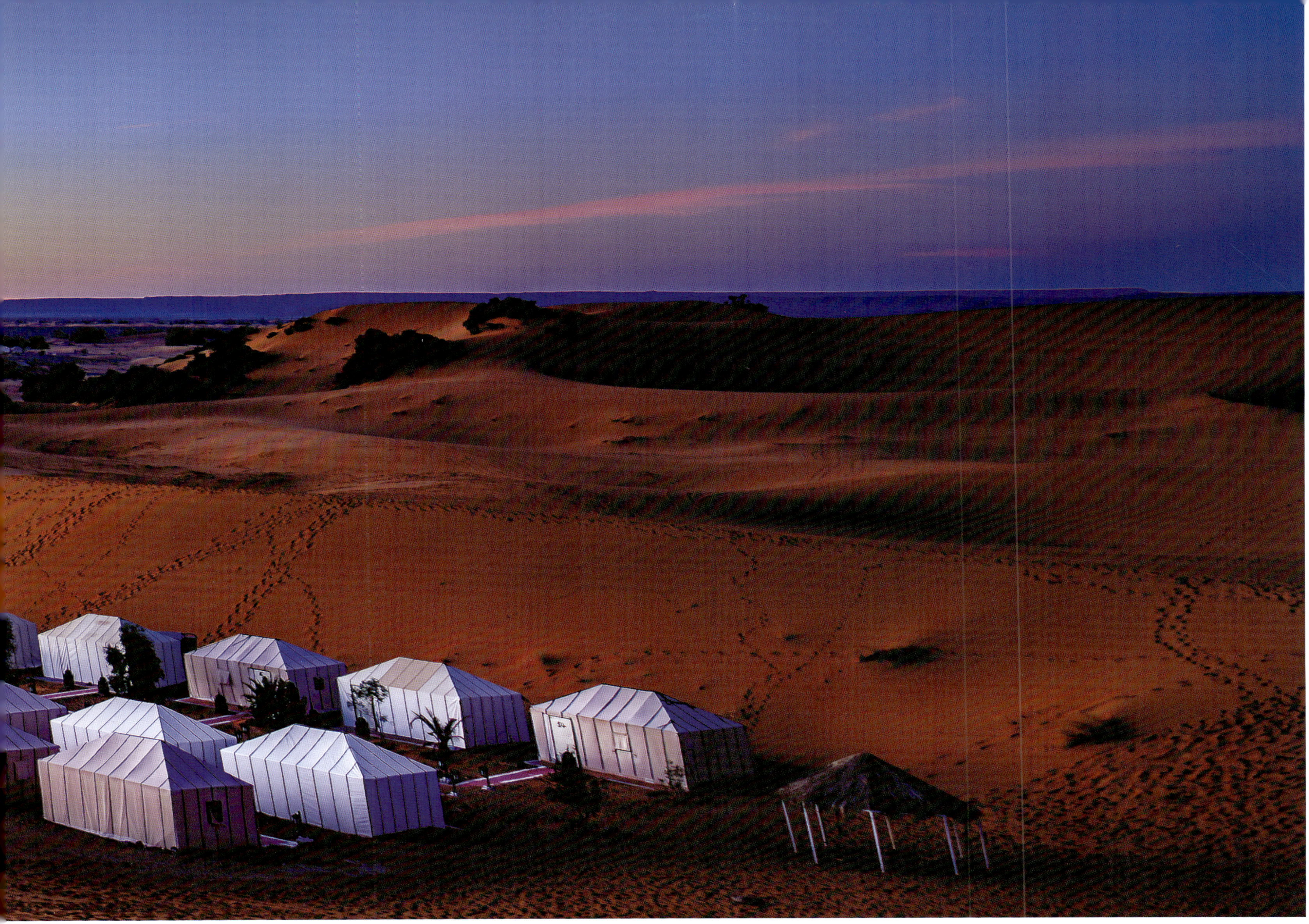

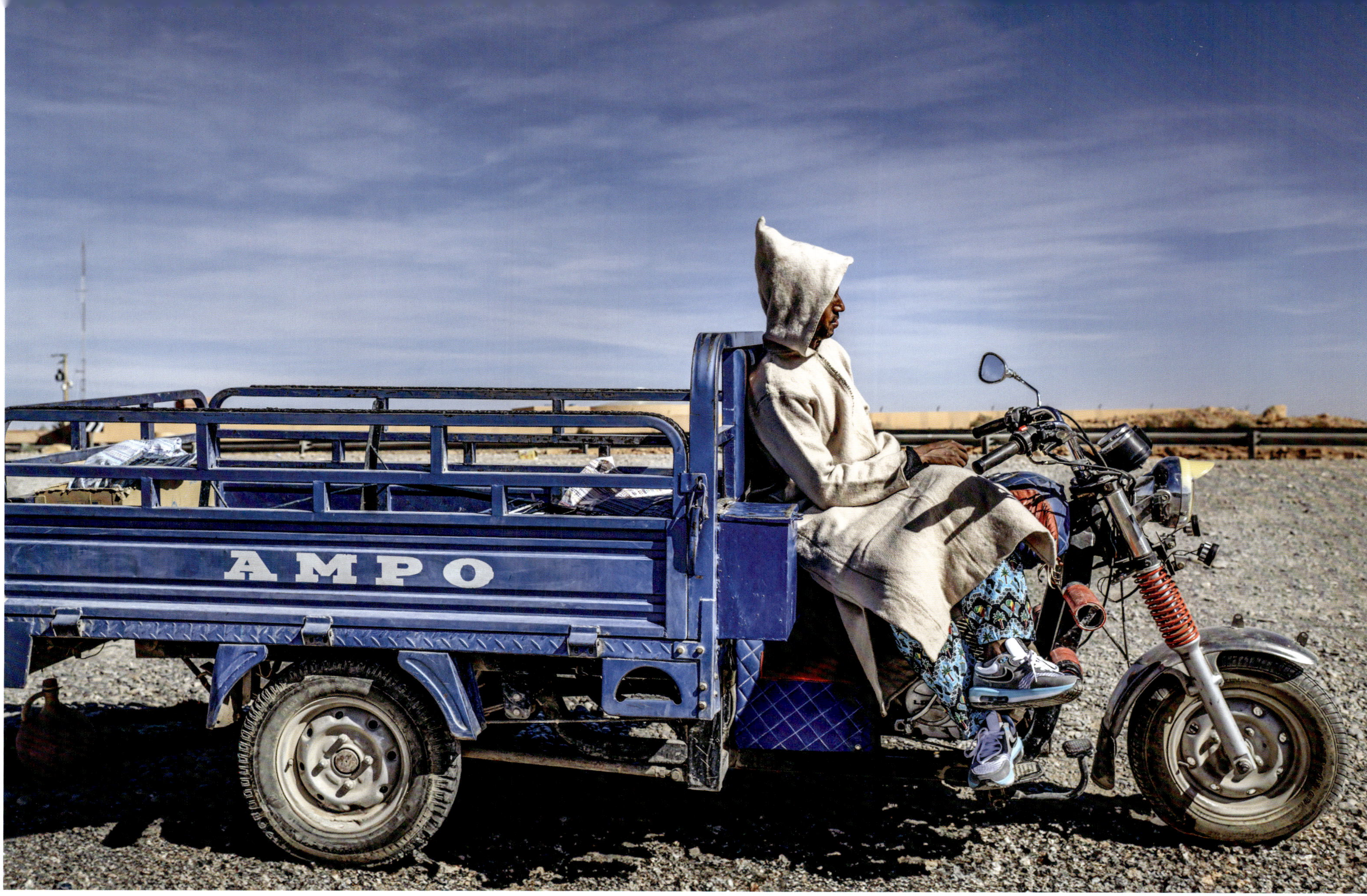


Previous page:
Luxury overnight camp coming alive at dawn in Merzouga.

Local motor trike taxi and driver outside of a tourist stop.

Merzouga camel driver awaiting guests.

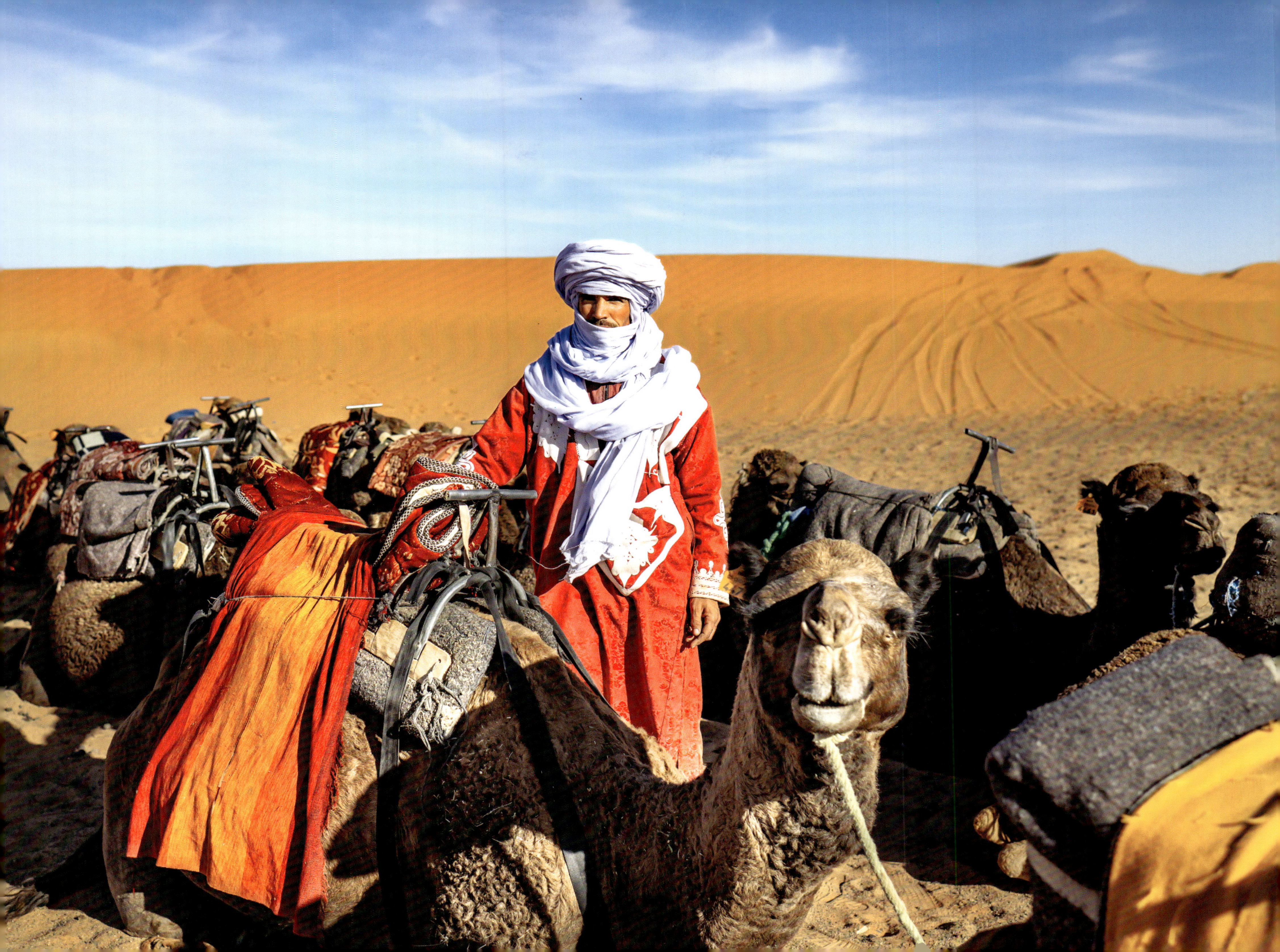

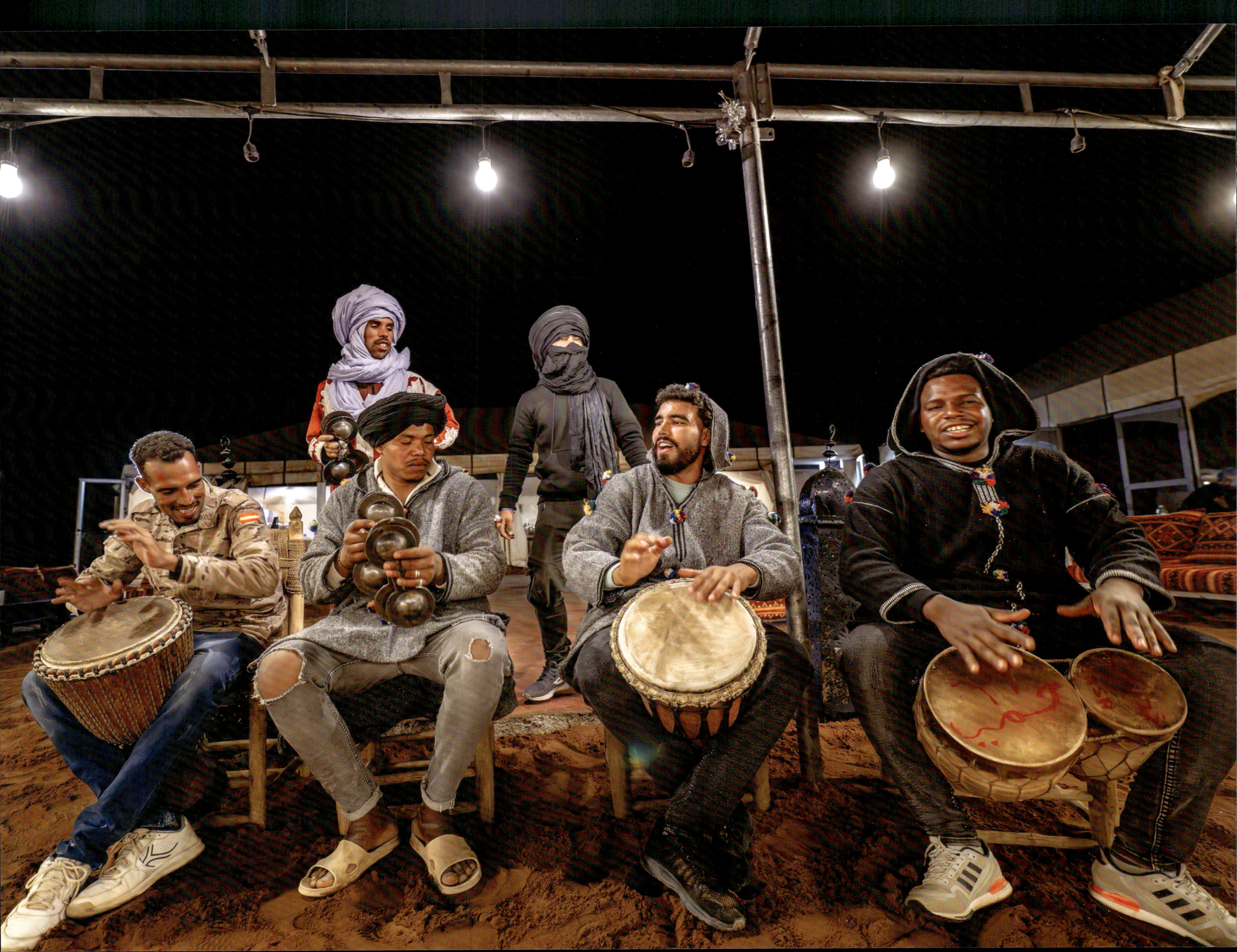

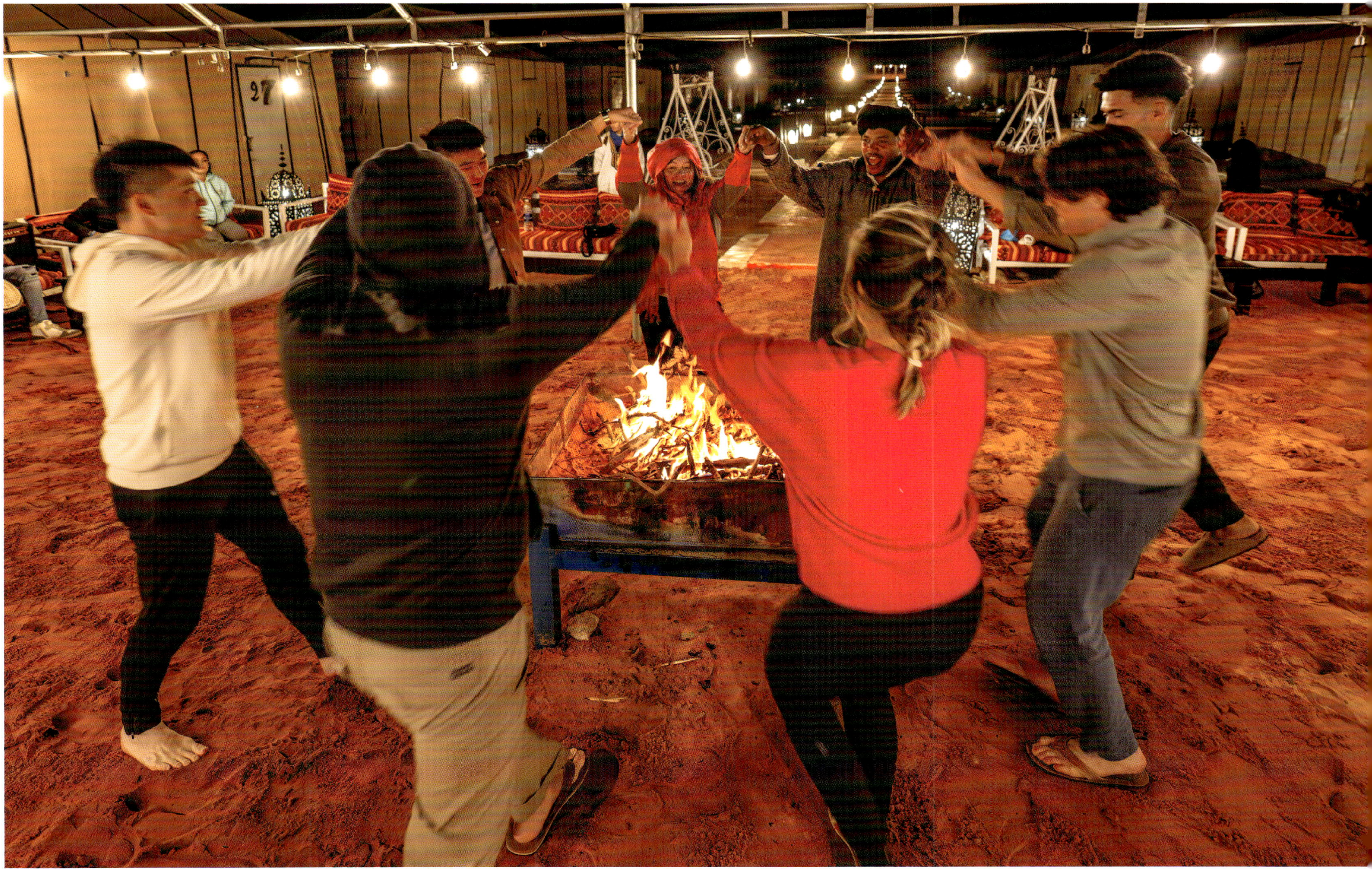

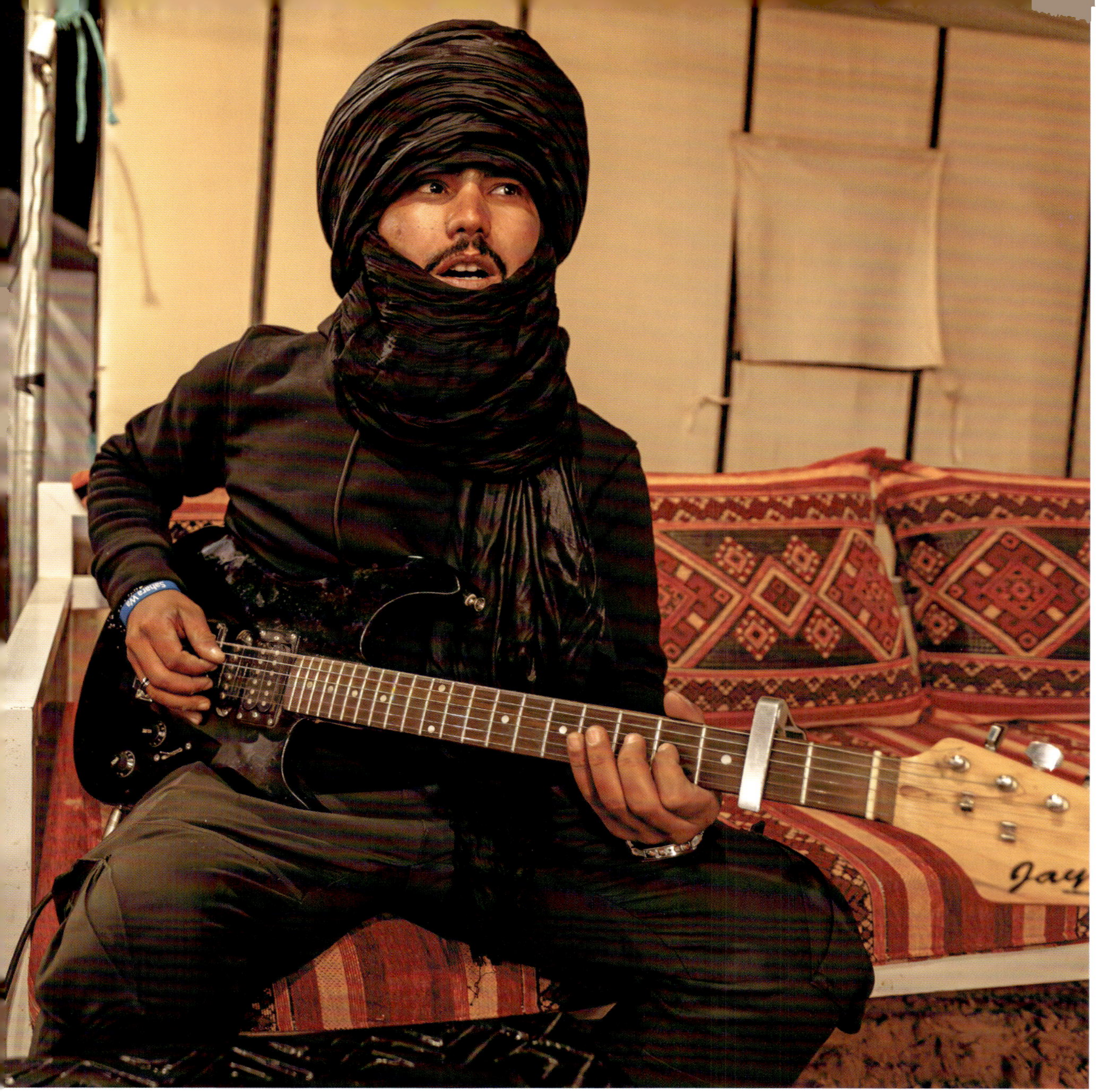

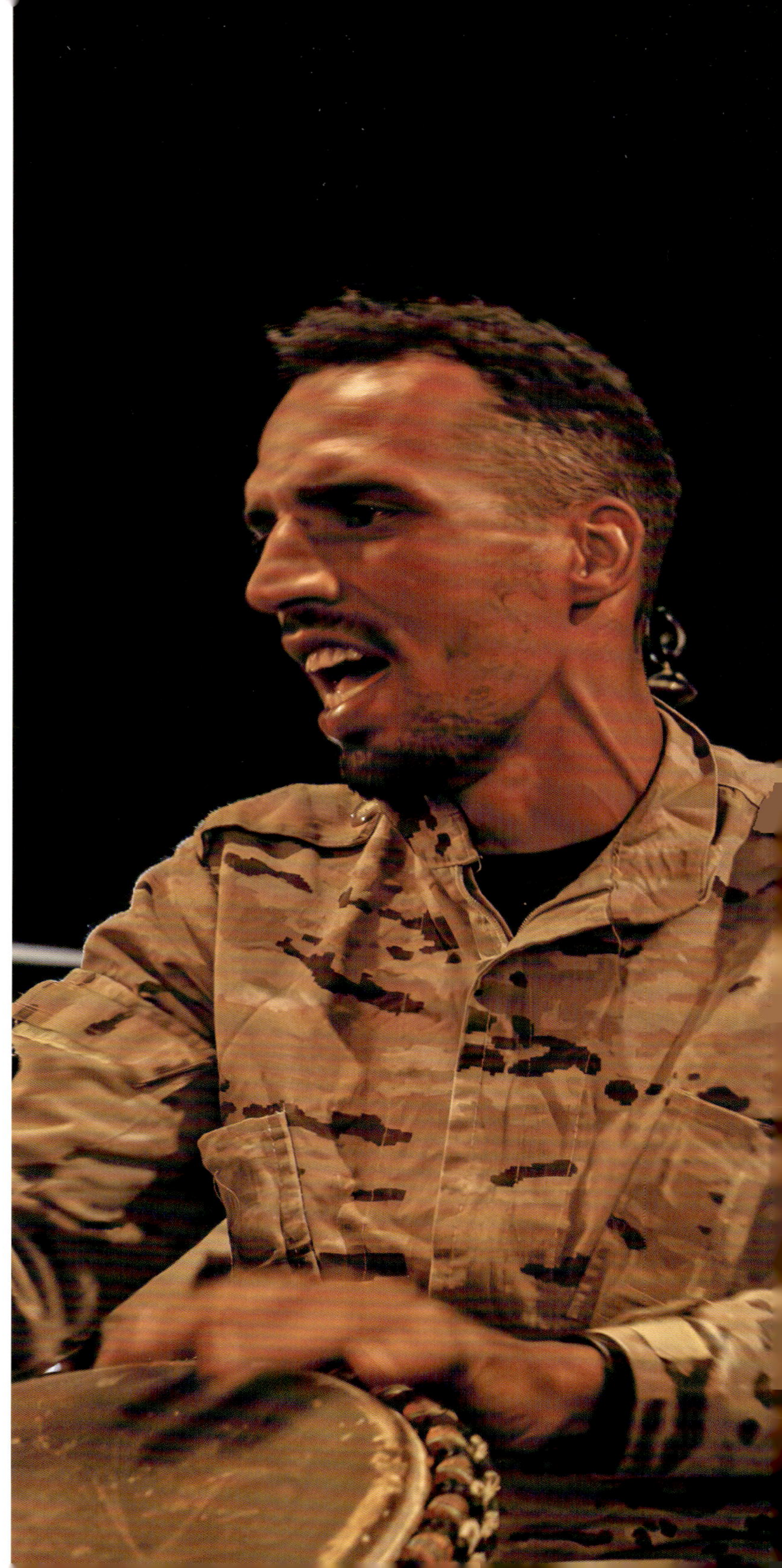

Previous and current pages:
At night in the Sahara tent camps there is a joyous celebration of traditional music and dancing around a fire pit.

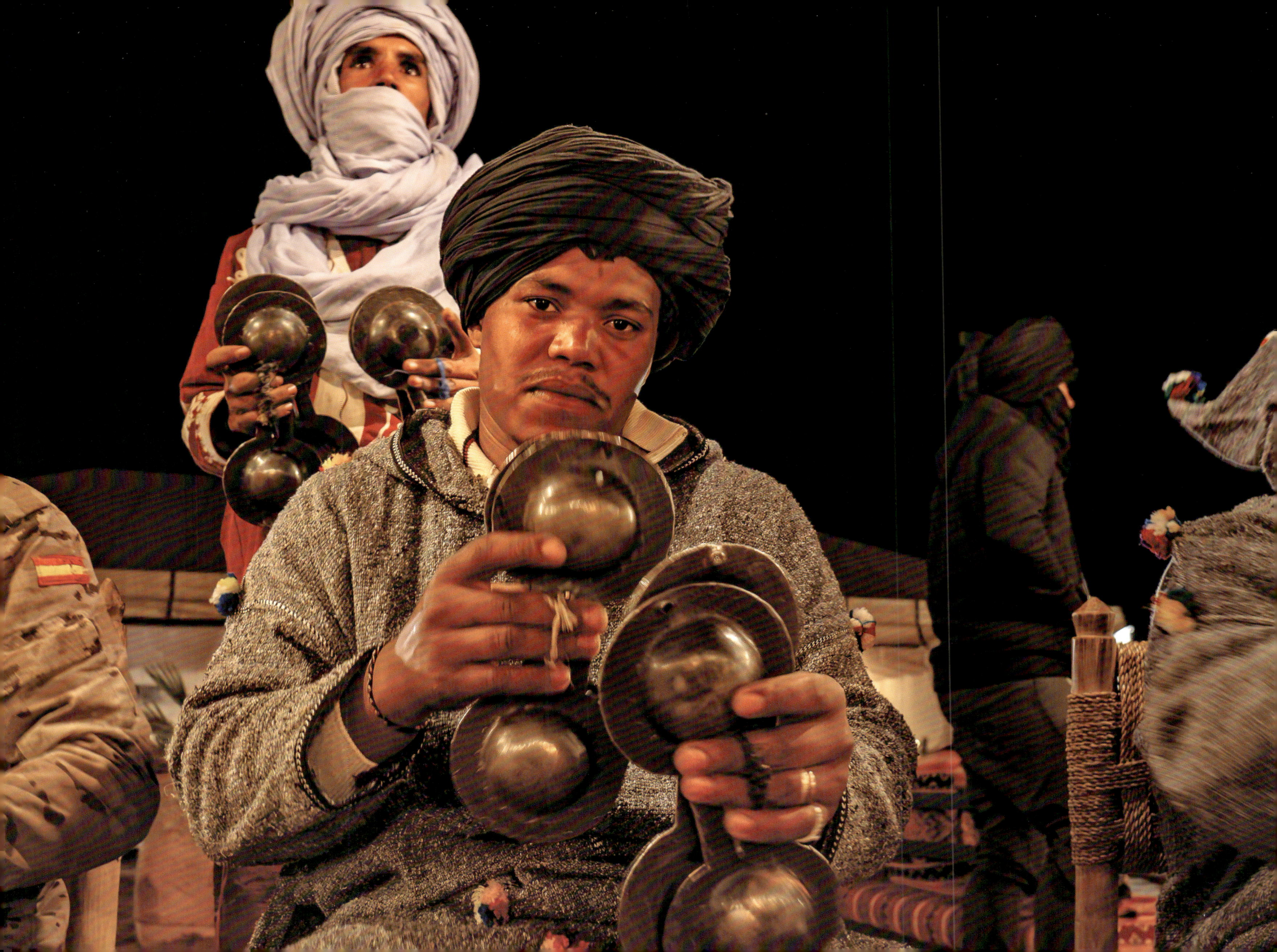

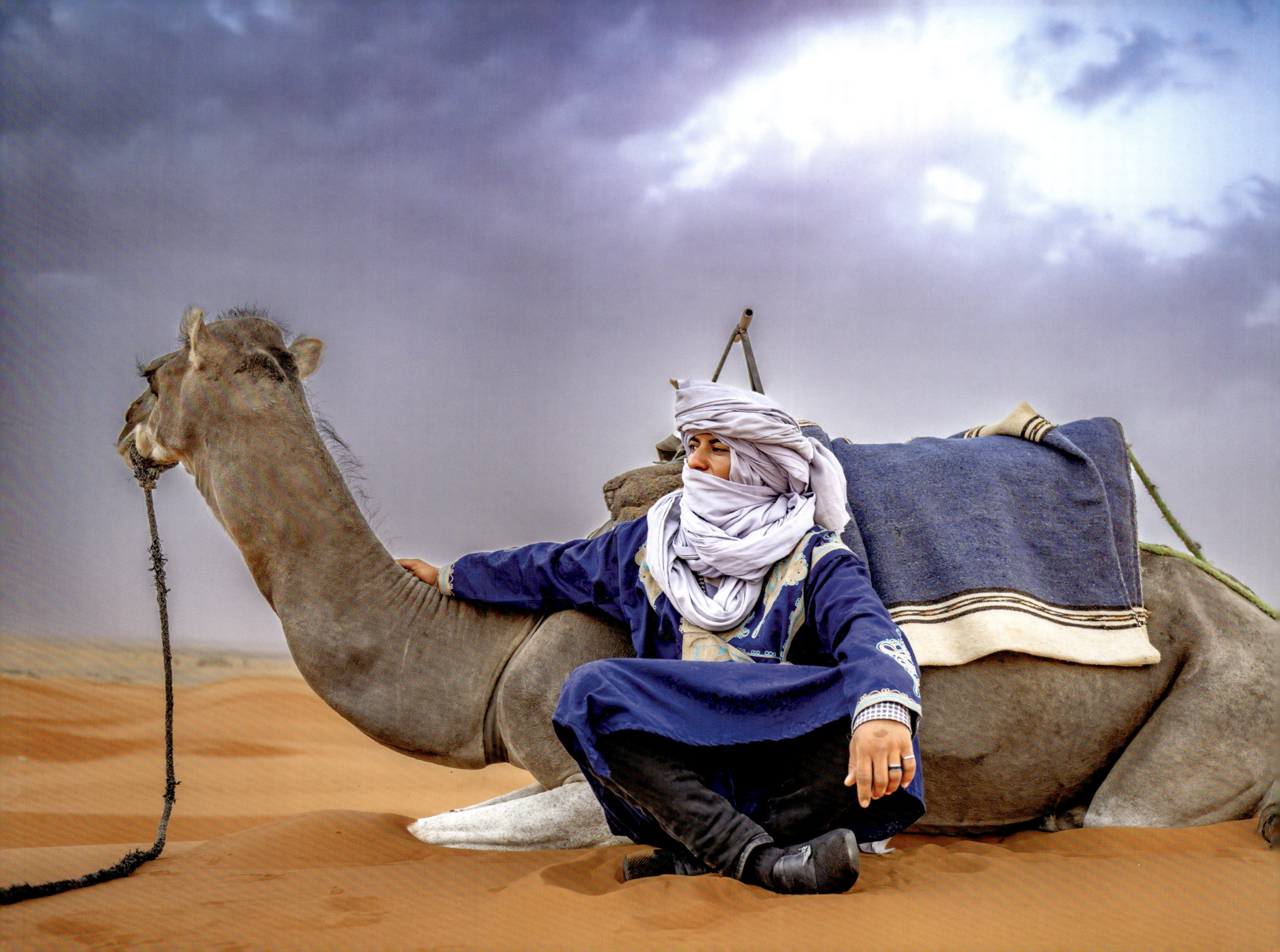

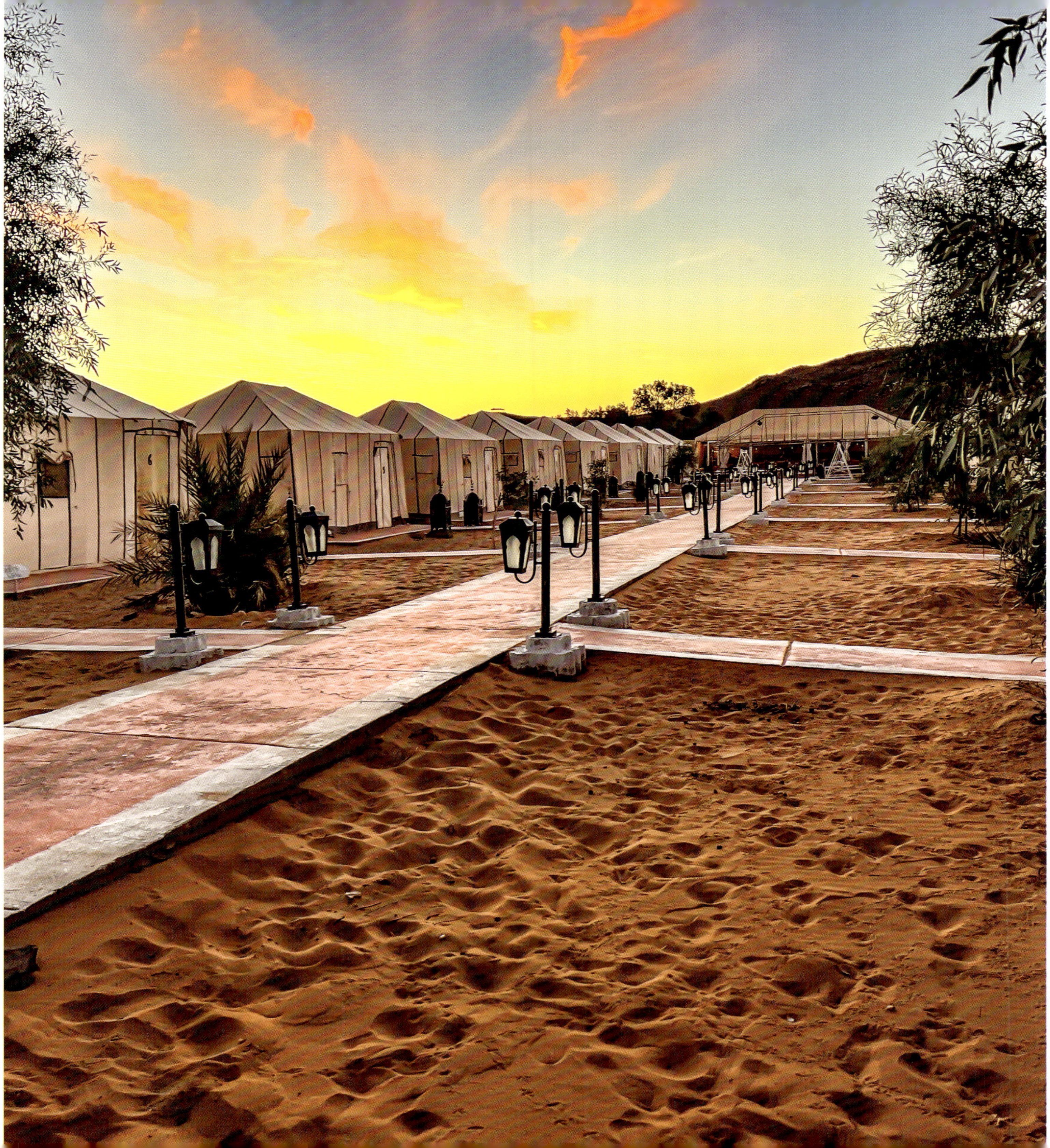

Camel driver waiting on a dune.
Inside a camp.

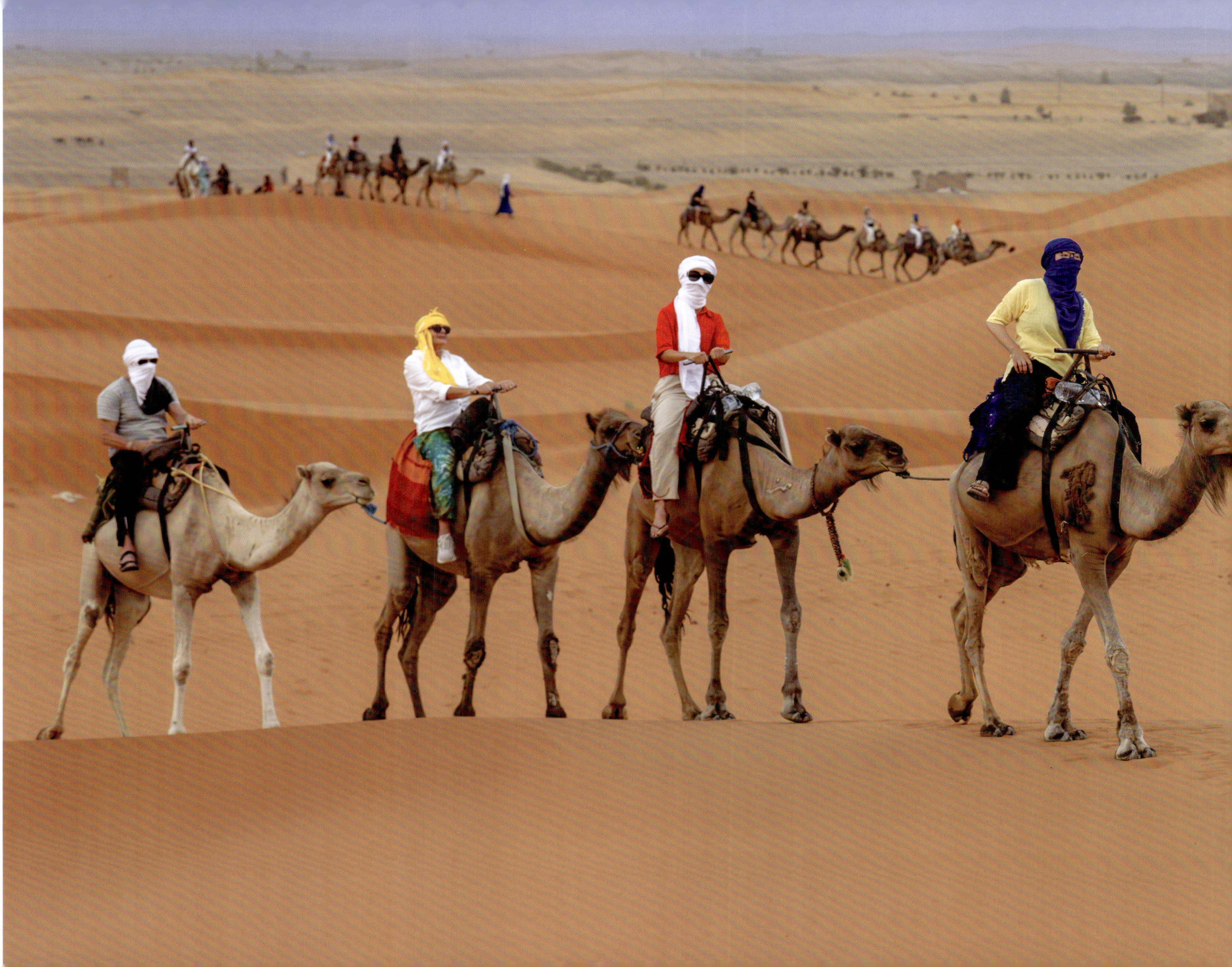

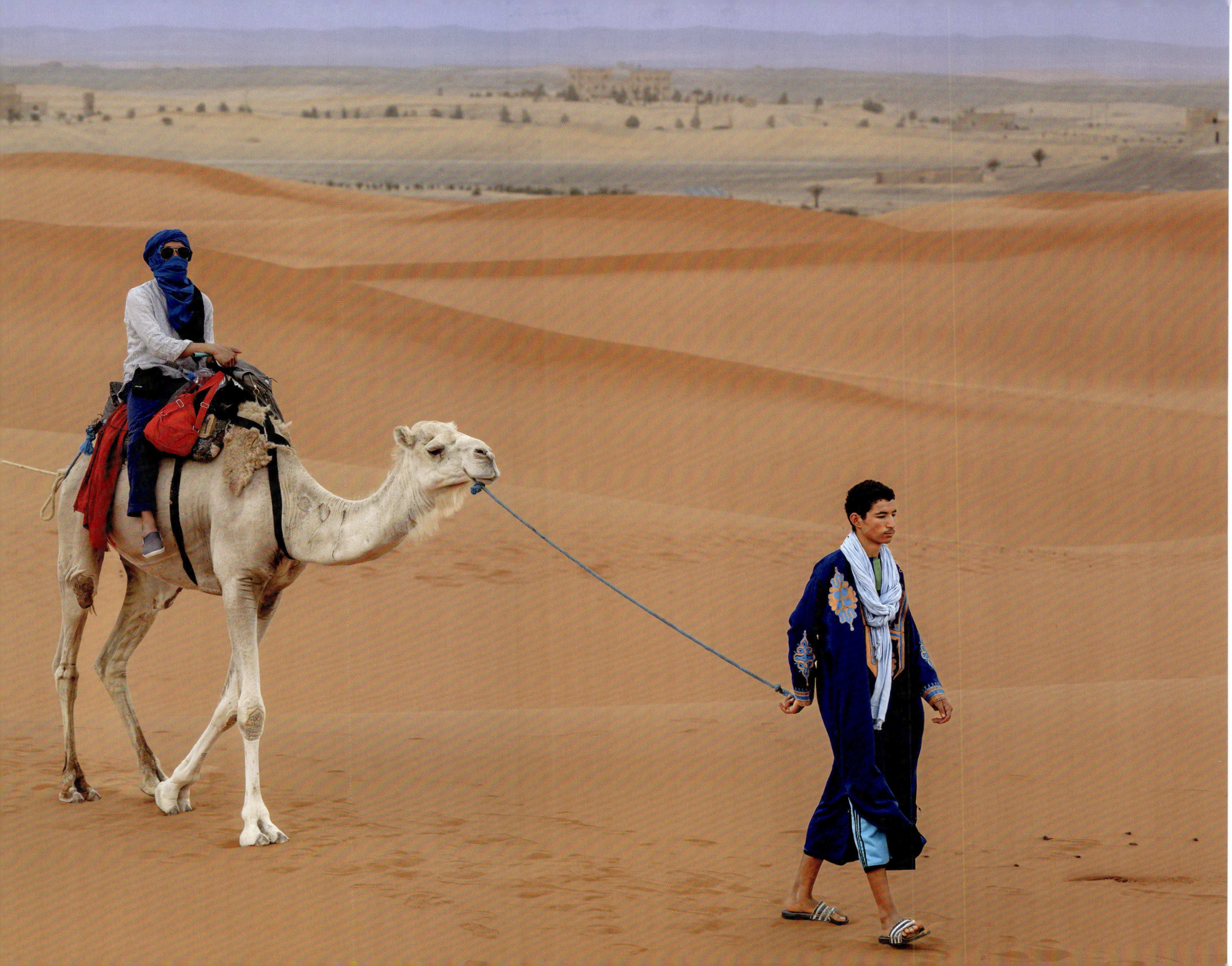

# THE BLUE PEARL CITY OF THE NORTH

Considered by many to be the most charming city in Morocco, Chefchaouen, is perched on the edge of the Rif Mountains in the country's far North. It' s a quiet village with narrow, winding alleys that offer shops, art galleries, riads, and restaurants around every corner and passage, and lots of narrow steps that lead up to the top of the hill upon which the city is perched.

But what makes this city so enchanting is that the walls and buildings are all painted various shades of vibrant blue using a talc or chalk-based, paint. The reasons for painting the city structures blue varies, according to whom you ask. Some say the practice began in the 1930s when large populations of Jewish refugees fleeing Nazi persecution painted the buildings blue because the color in Jewish religious and cultural practices represents peace, safety and heaven. Others say the blue colors deter mosquitoes.

Locals mostly say they like the calming effect and, because in Islamic culture, blue is said to be a color of happiness and optimism. Regardless of the reason, the practice continues today and makes the city one of the most unique places on Earth.

Founded in 1471 by Moulay Ali Ben Moussa Ben Rached El Alami, a distant descendant of the Islamic Prophet Muhammad, Chefchaouen was designed to be a fortress intended to defend attacks on northern Moroccan cities by Portuguese invaders.

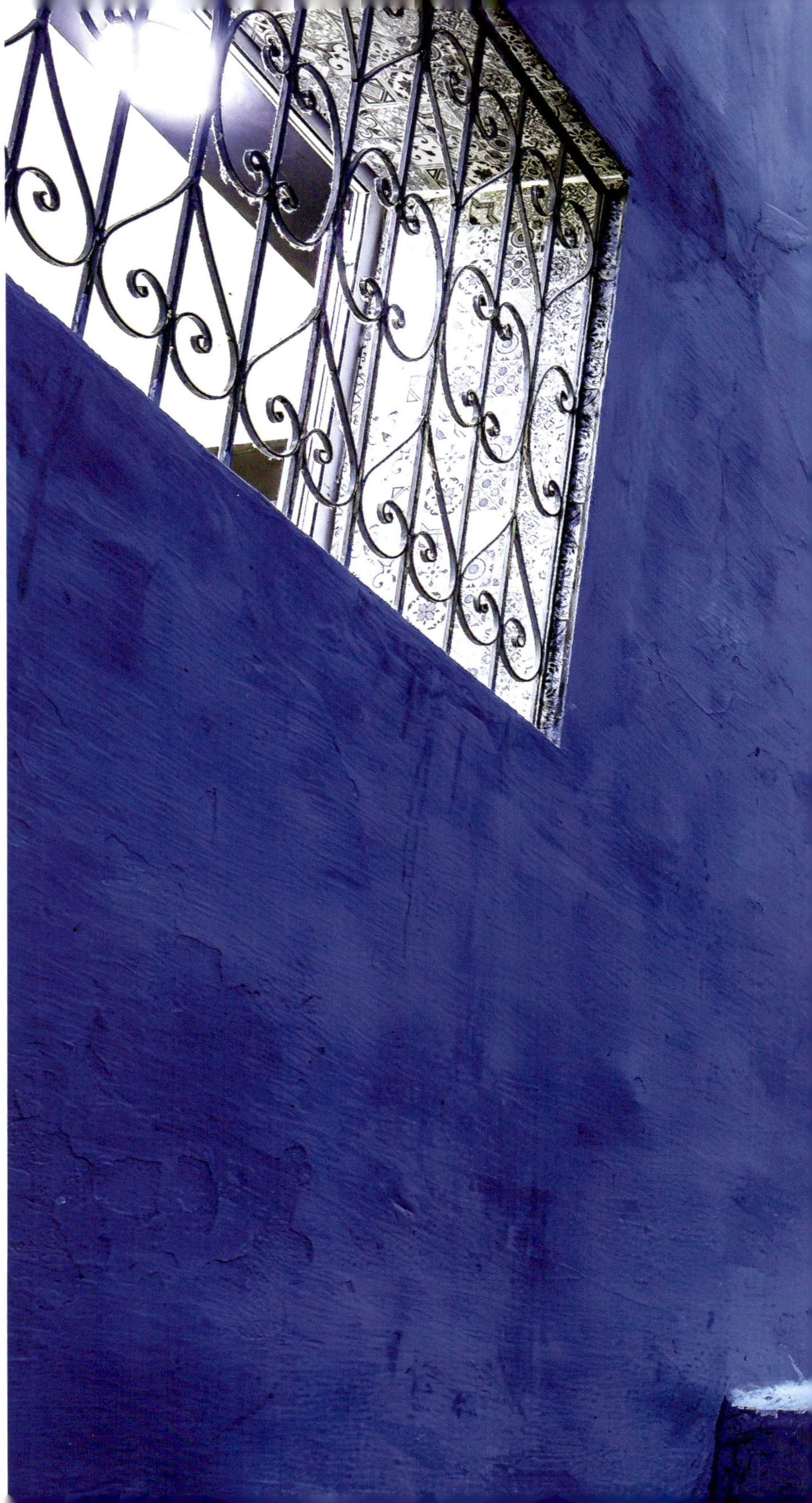

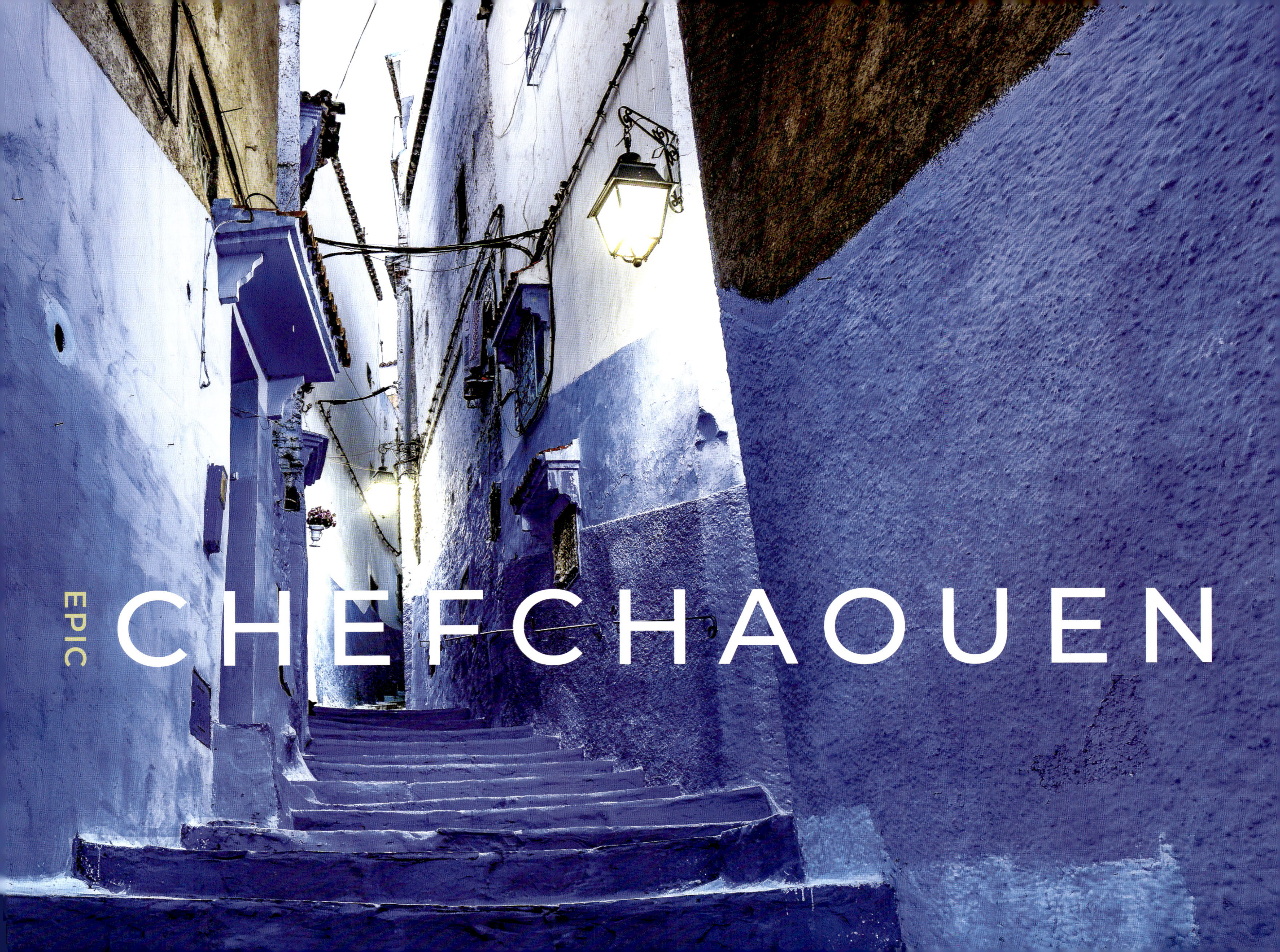
EPIC
CHEFCHAOUEN

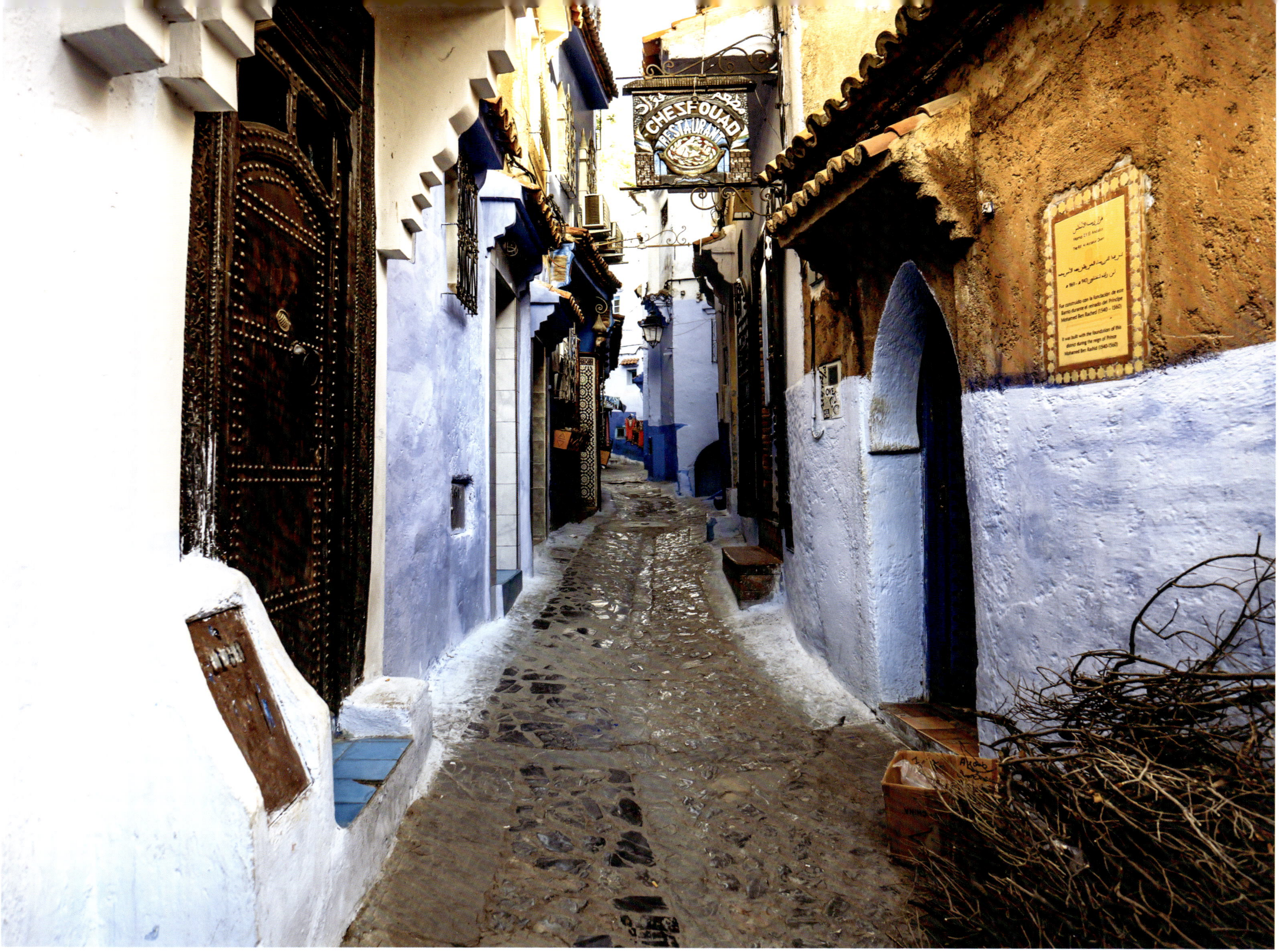
CHEZ FOUAD
RESTAURANT

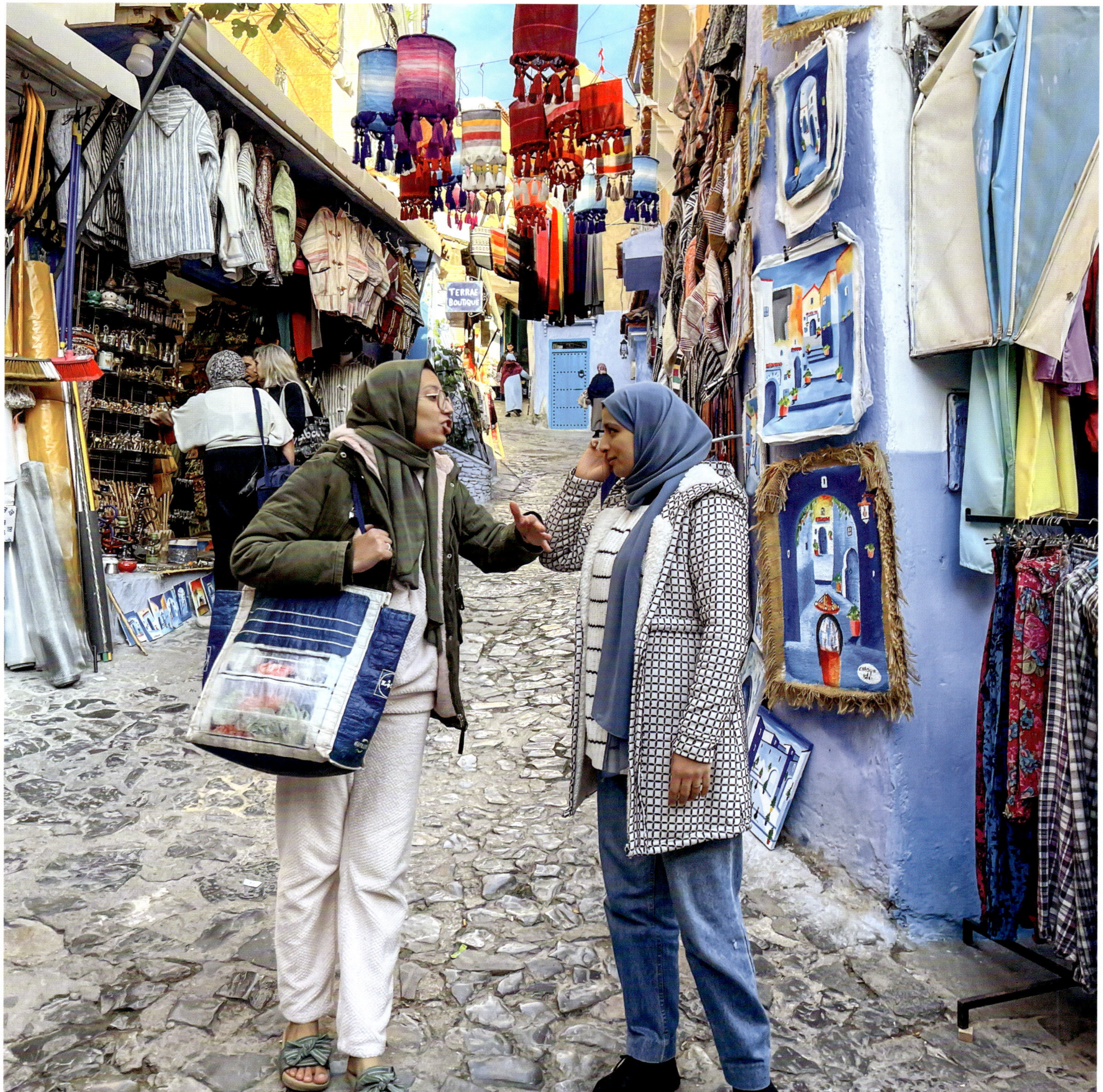


Narrow Chefchaouen ally.
Local women talking.

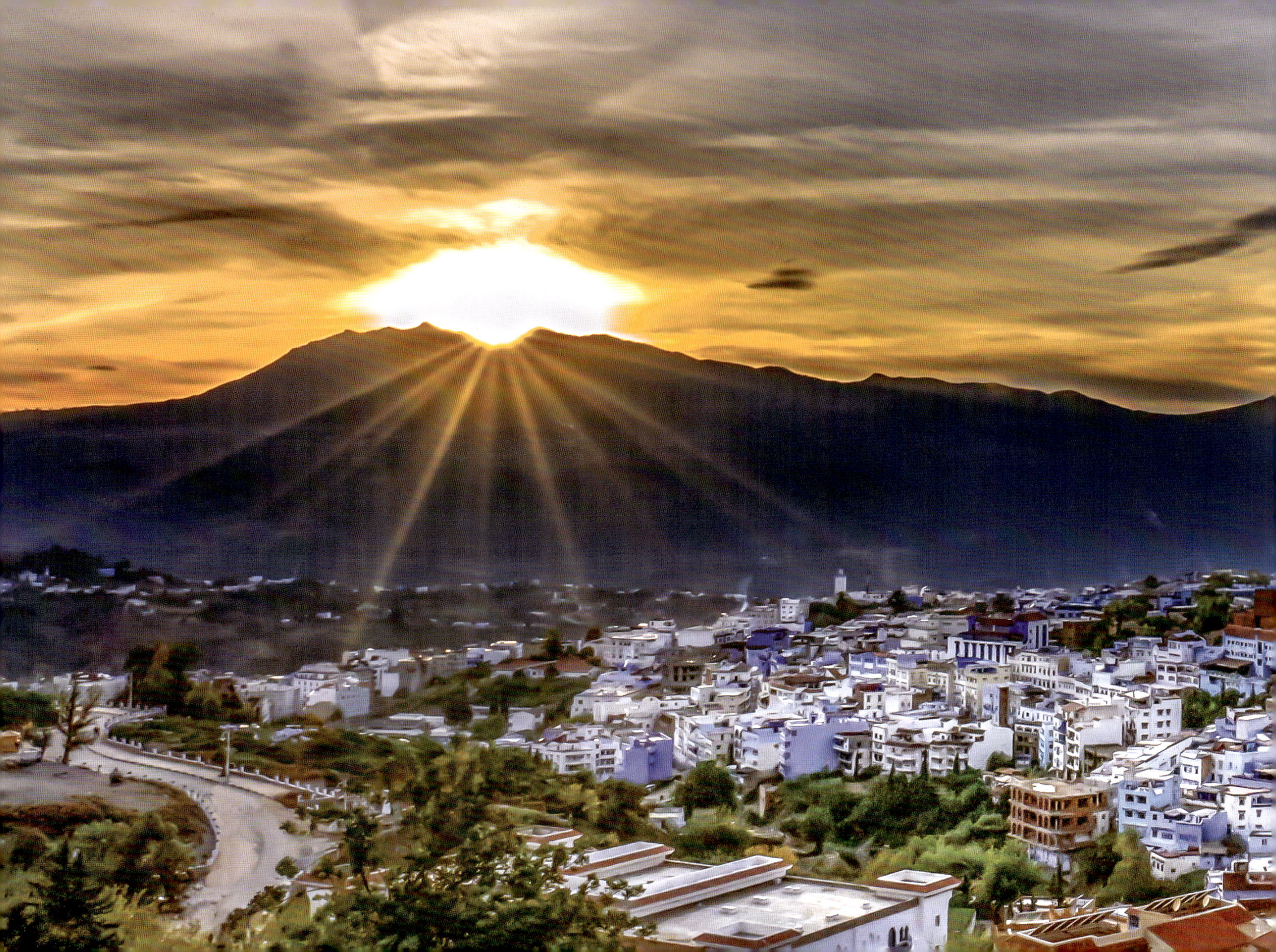

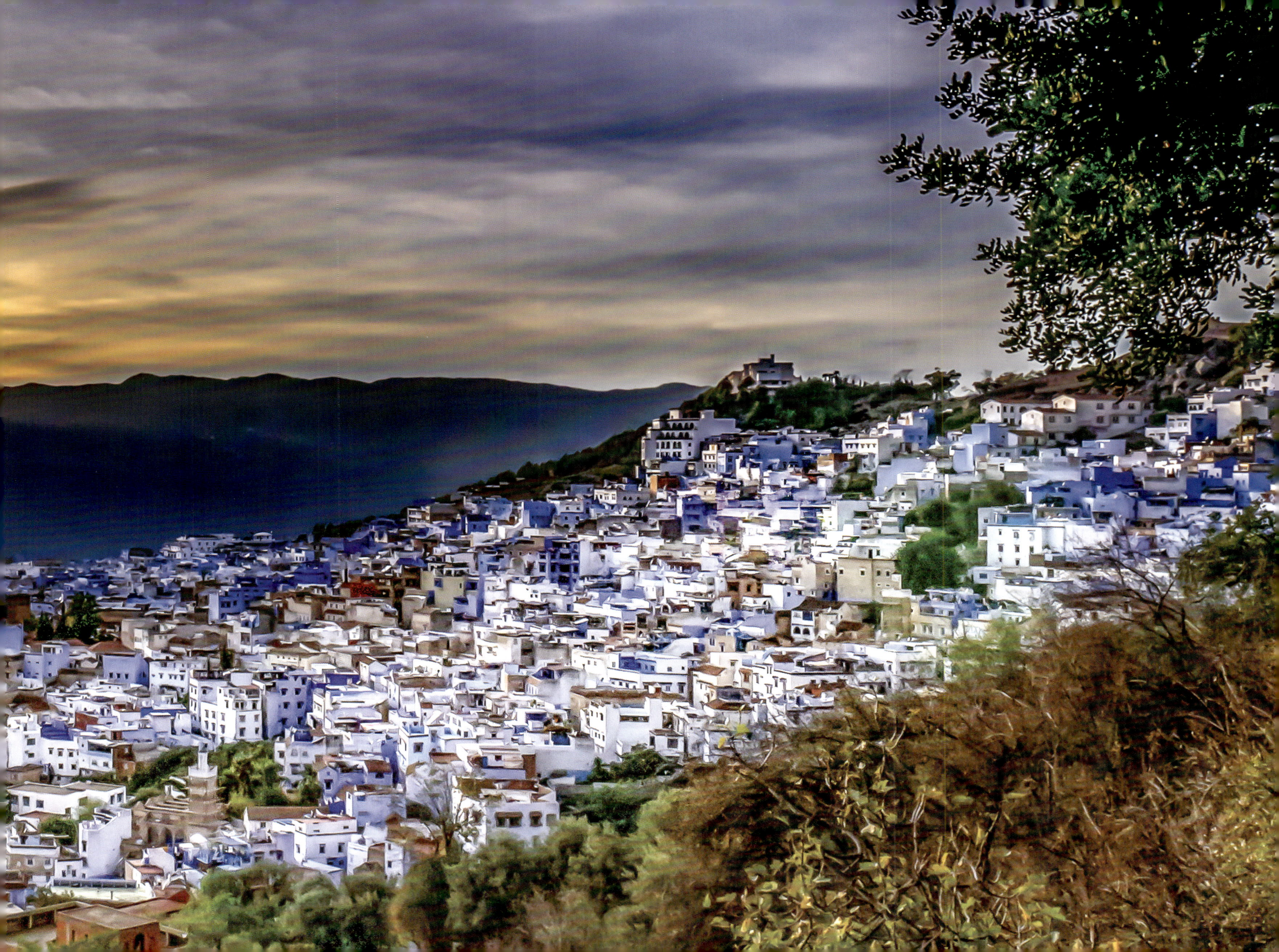

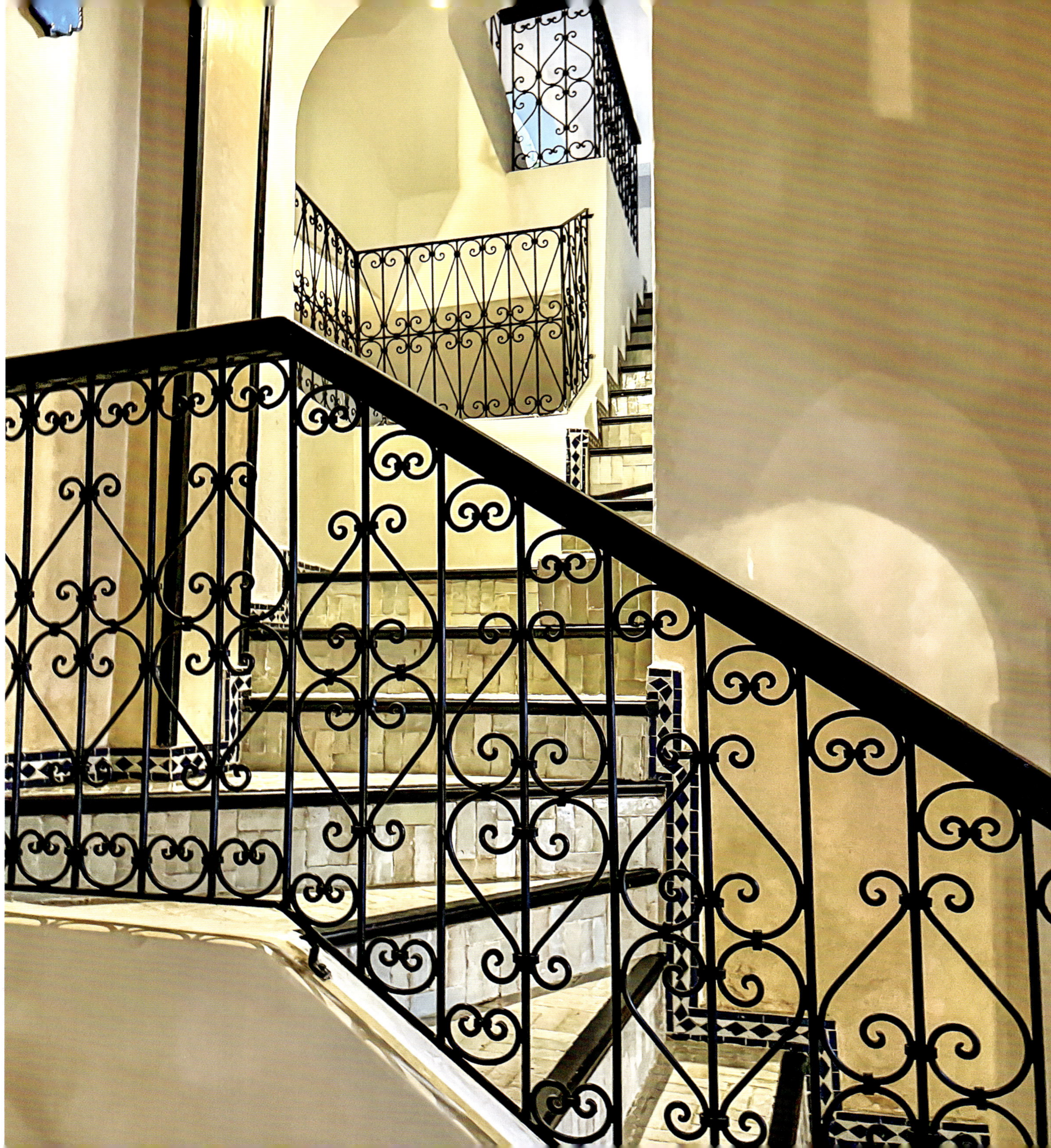

Previous page:
The sun setting behind the Rif Mountains illuminates the Blue City.

Stairway leading into a riad, a traditional Moroccan home, now often converted to serene and beautiful lodgings with above-and-beyond hospitality for guests.

Souks on a city street.

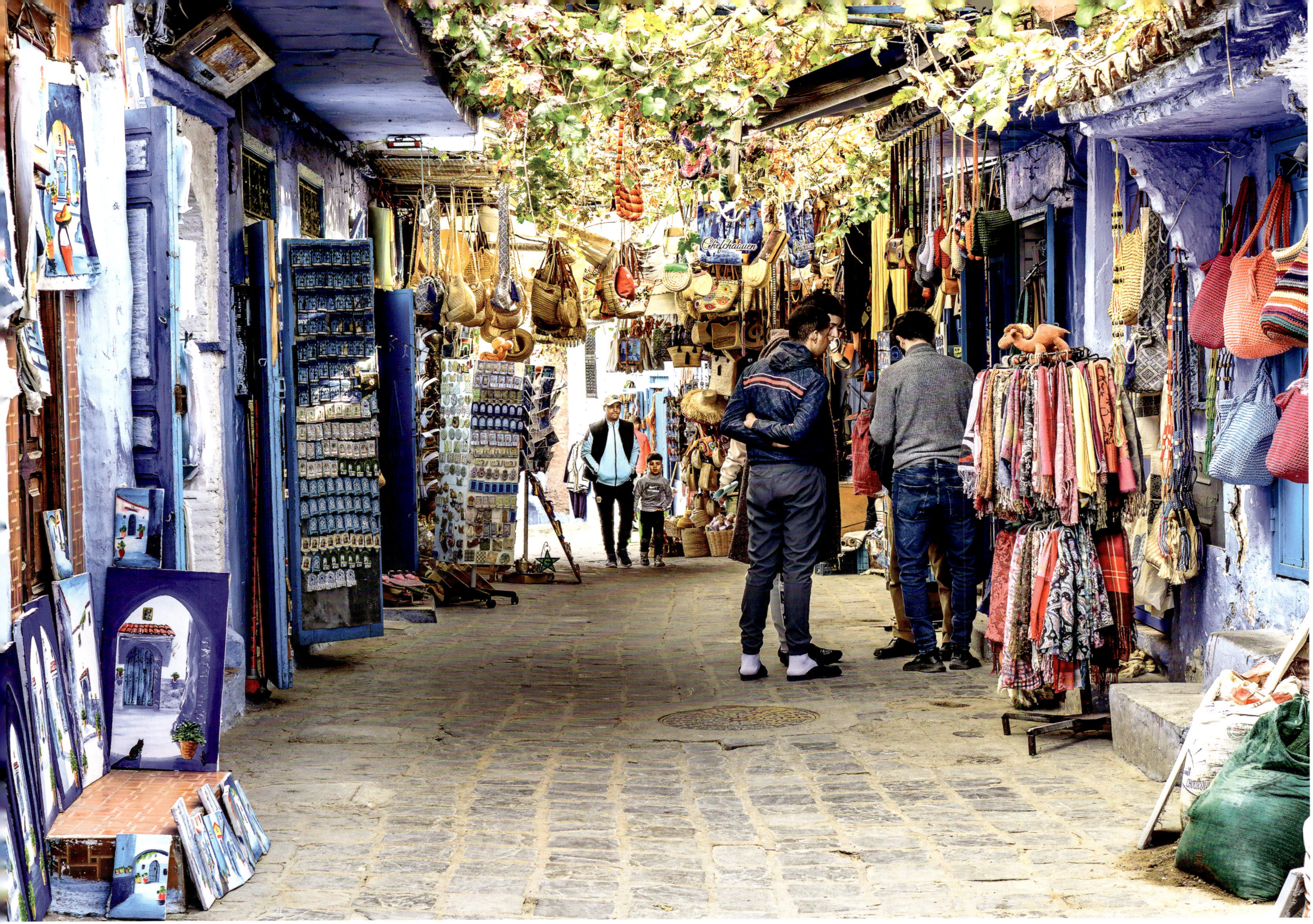
Chefchaouen

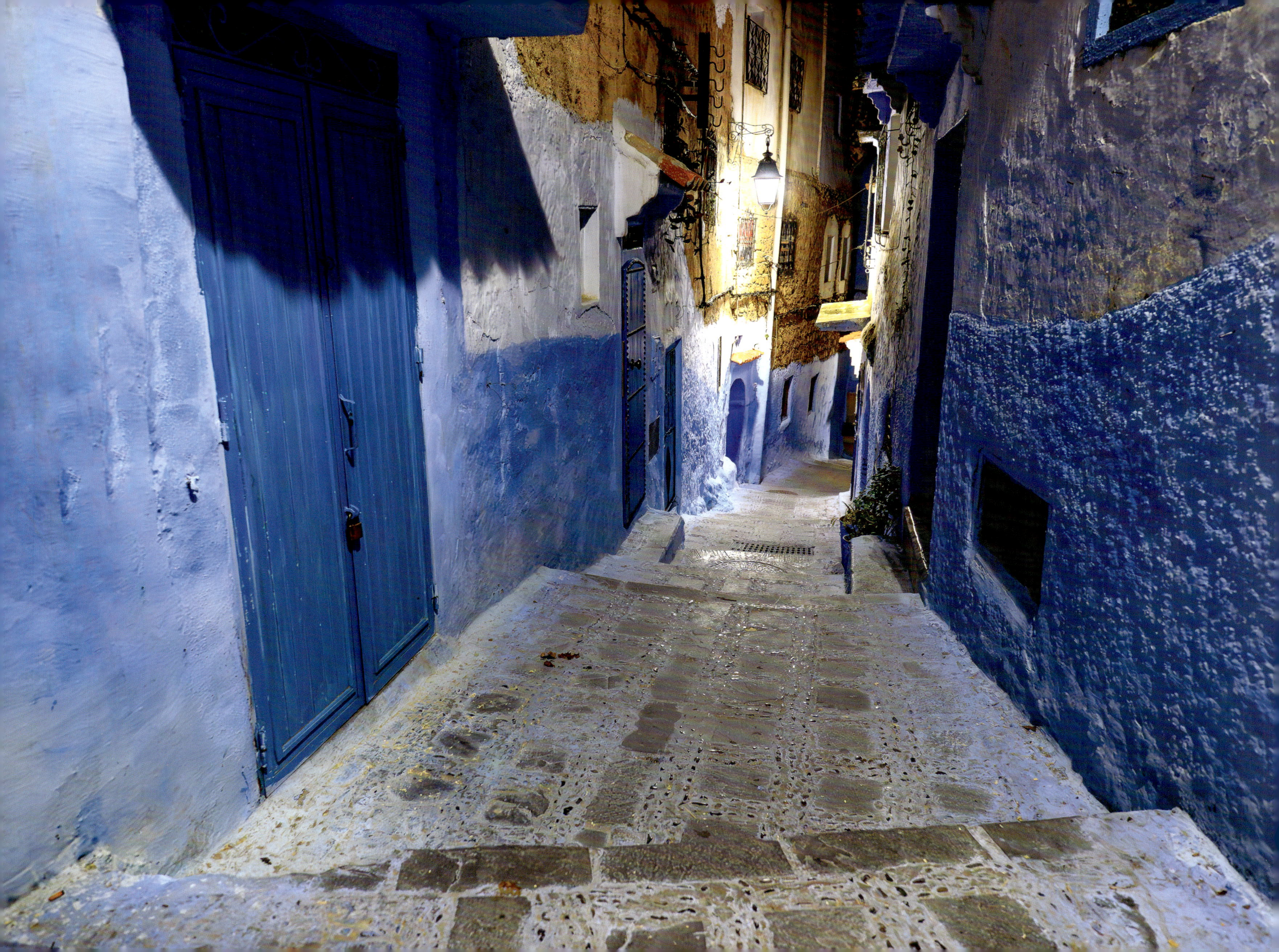

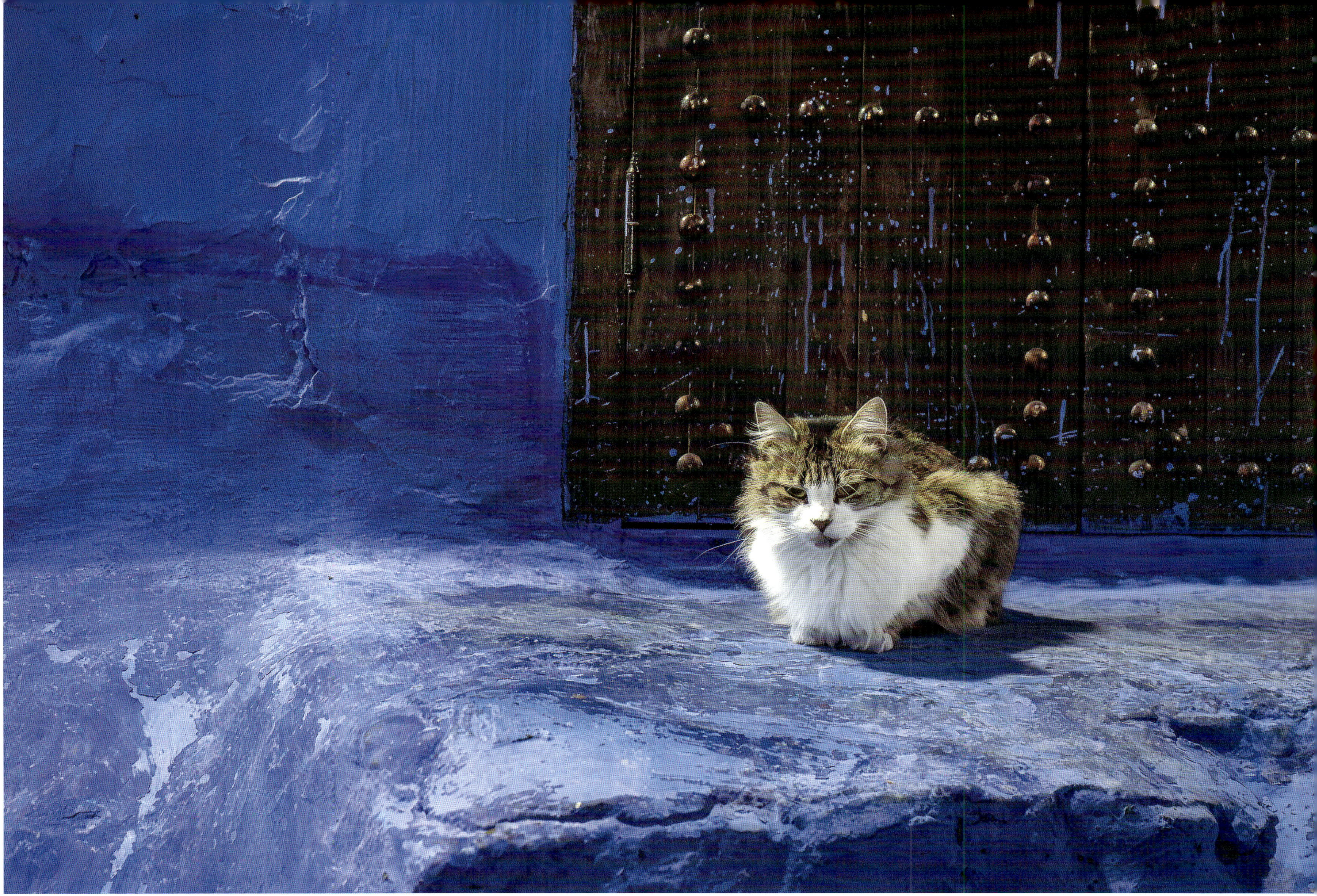

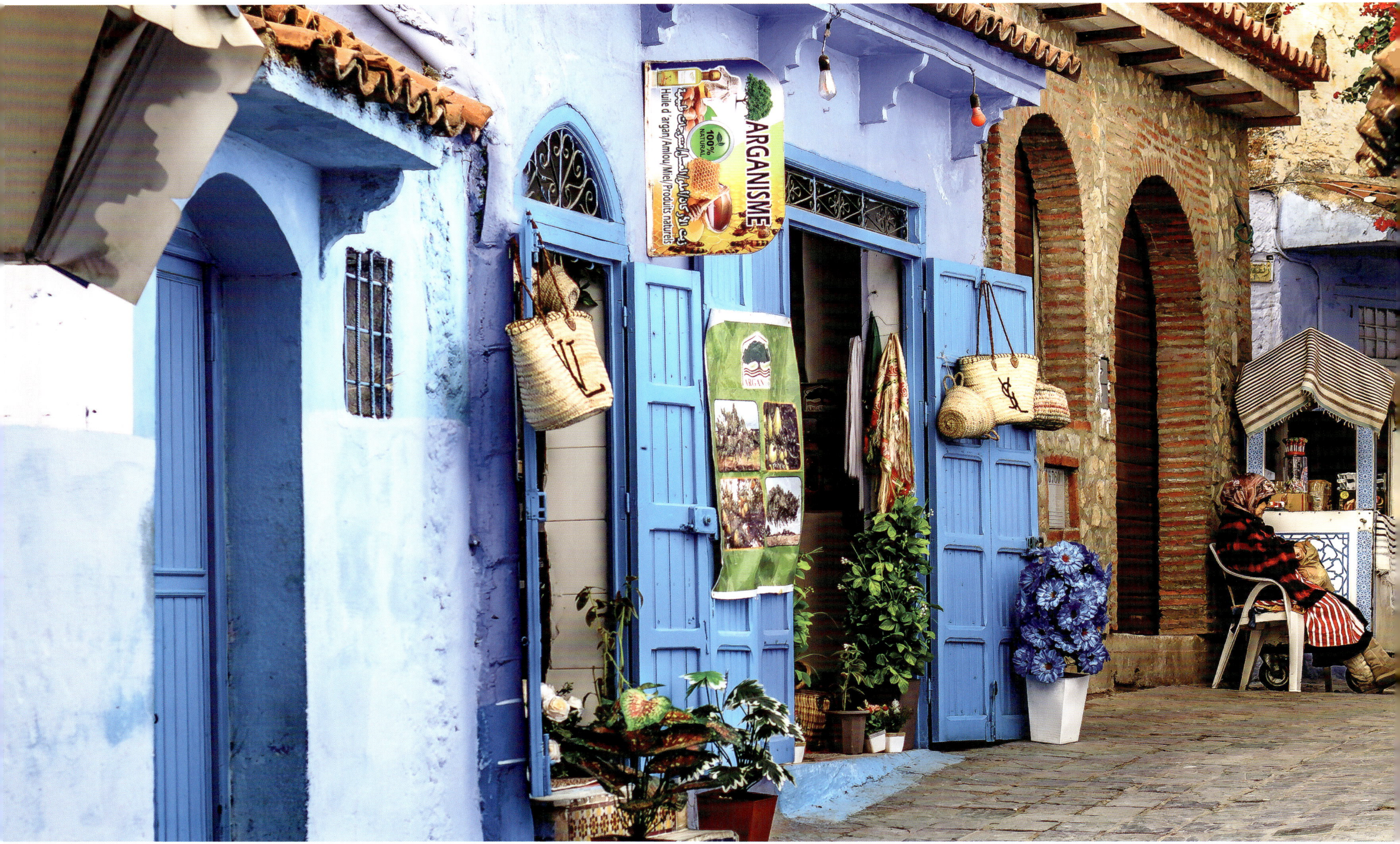
ARGANISME
100% NATURAL
Huile d argan/Amlou/Miel/Produits naturels

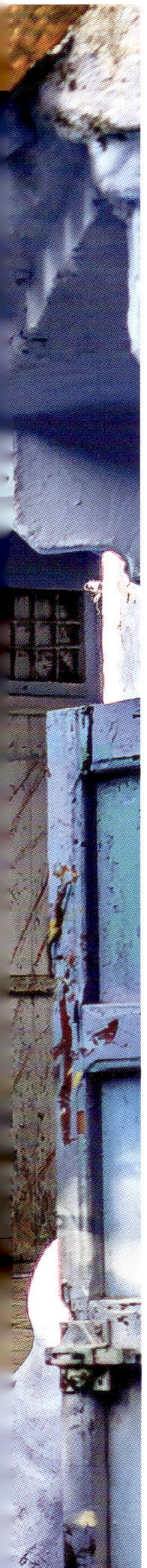

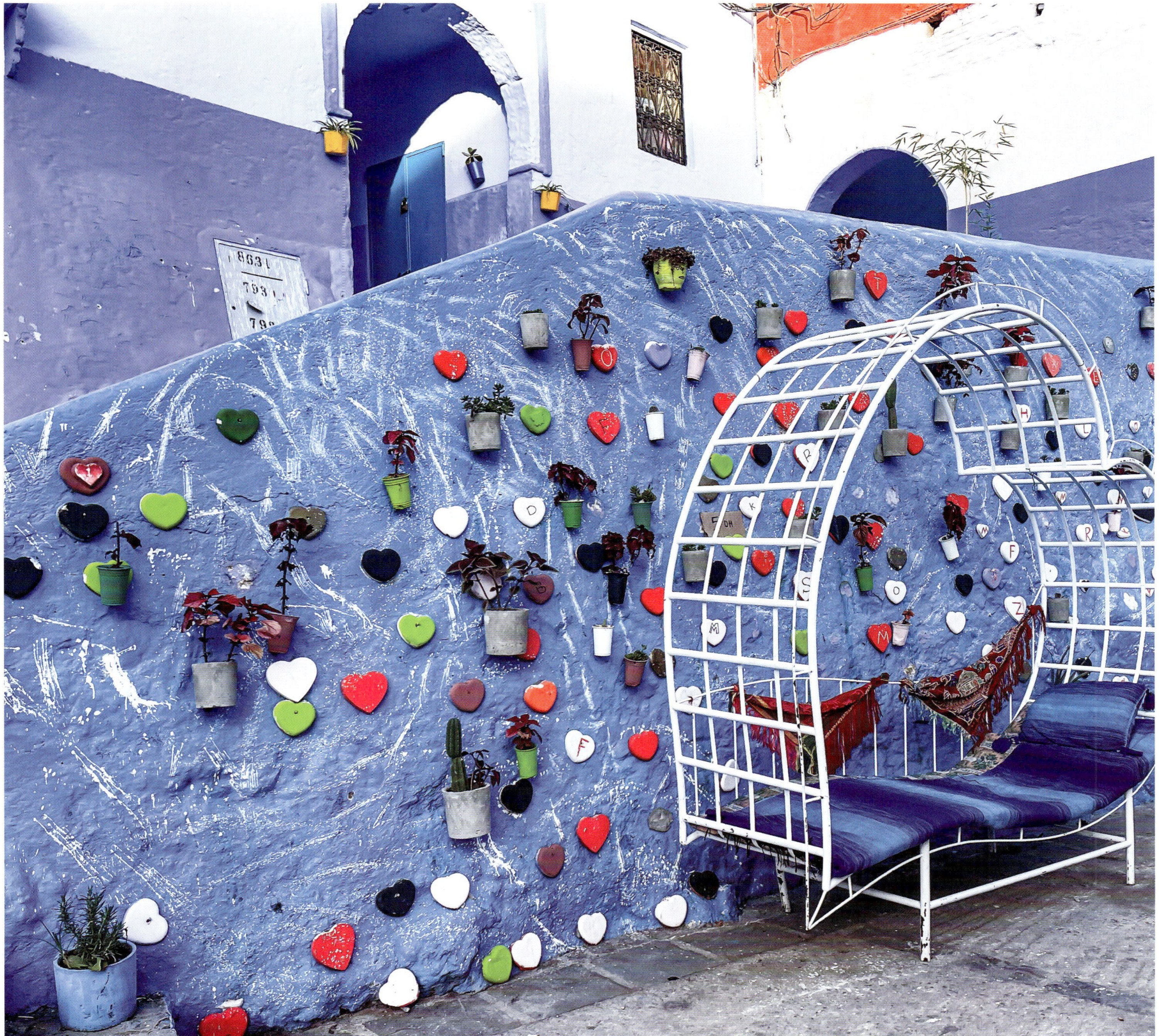

Previous page:
Blue walled homes line an alley at dawn.

It's been said that there are as many street cats in Morocco as there are people.

Woman merchant tending a souk.

Wall decorated with ceramic hearts.

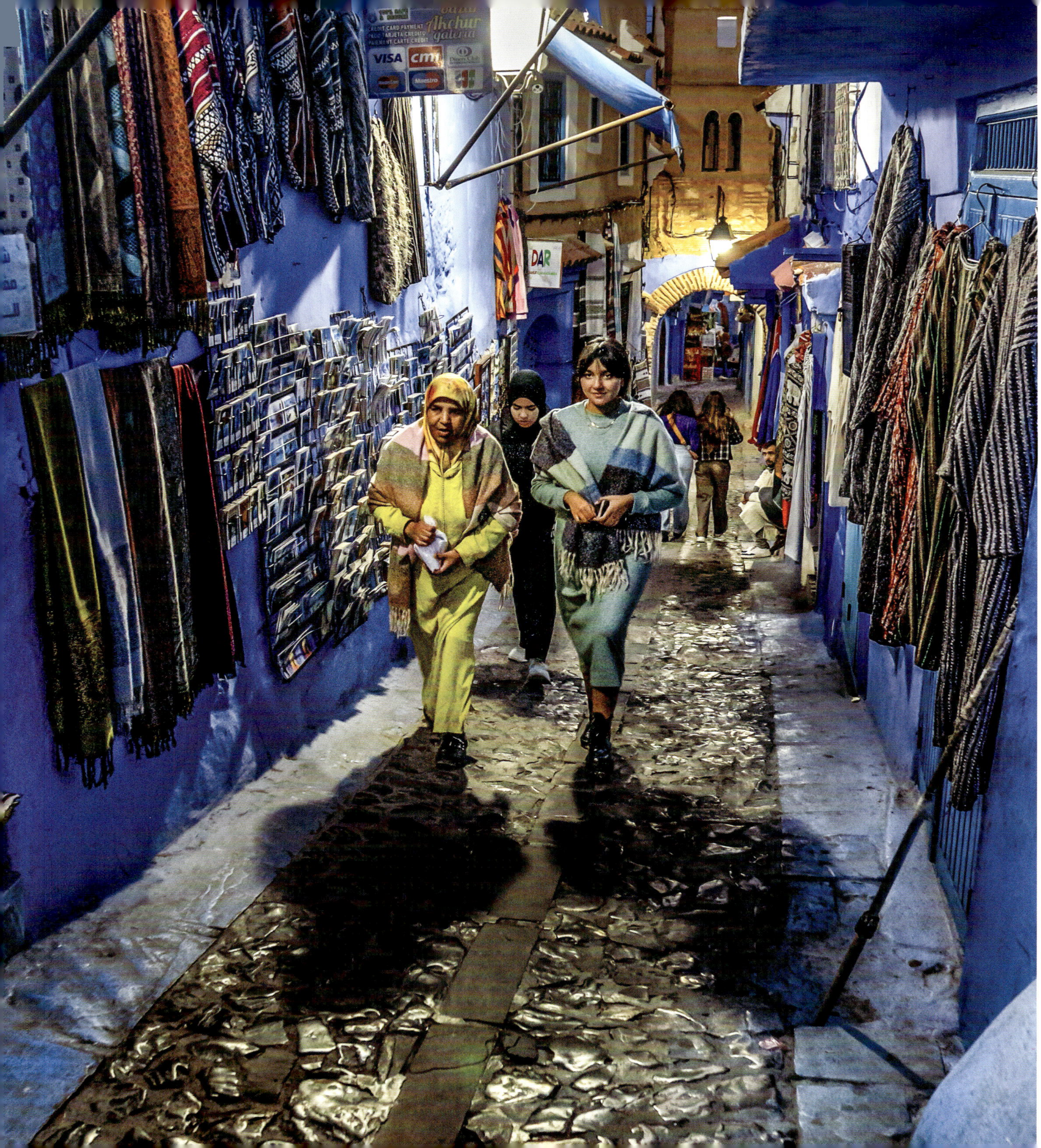
VISA
cmi
DAR

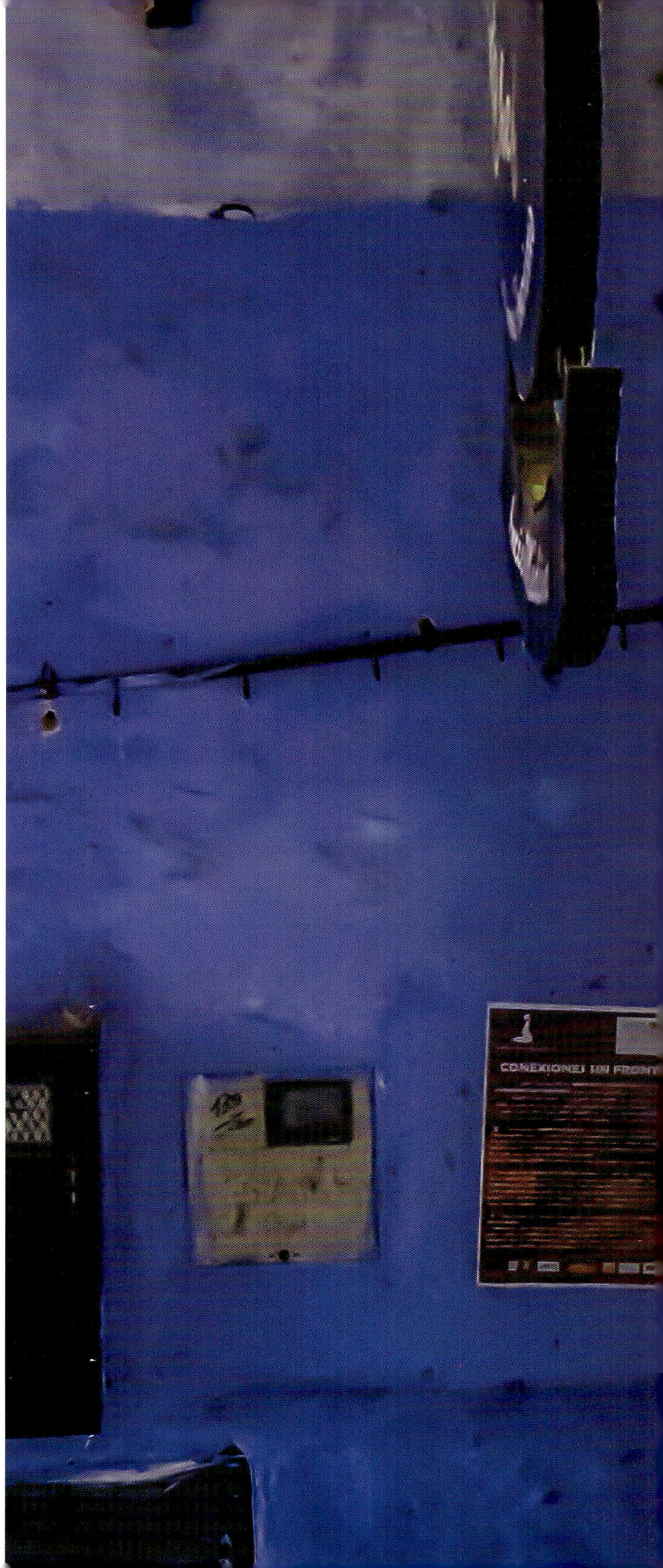

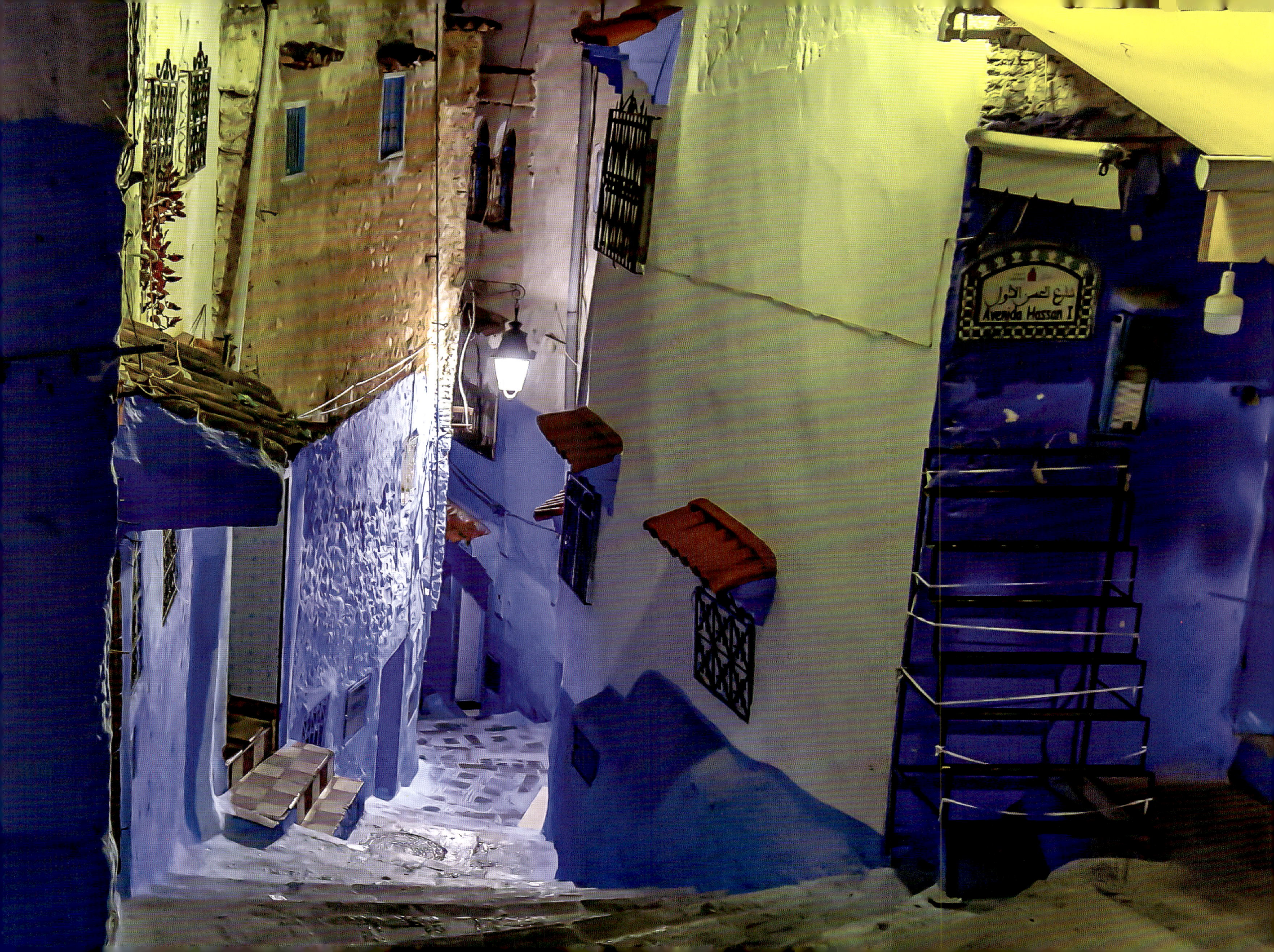
Avenida Hassan I

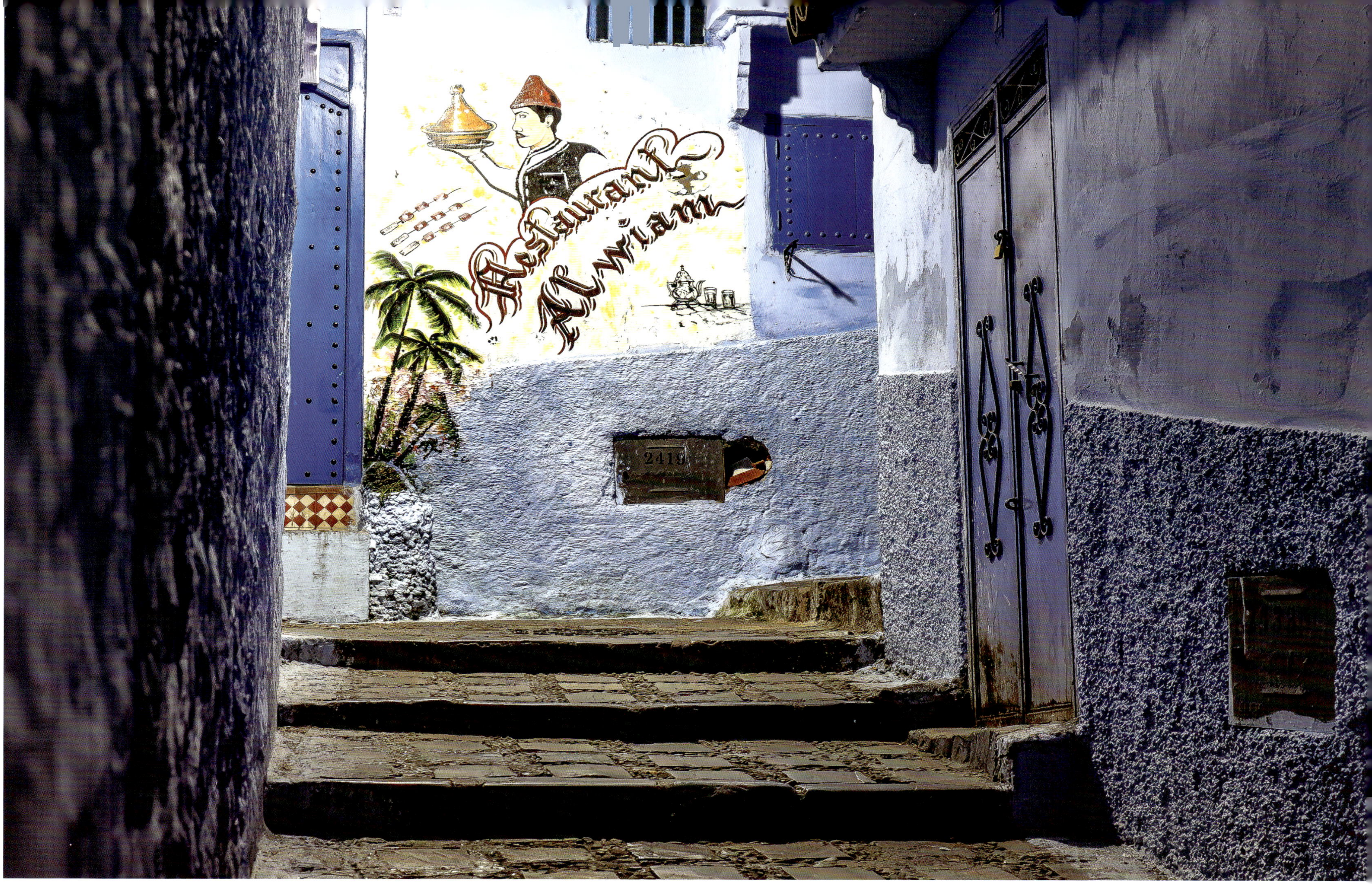


Previous and current pages:
Chefchaouen locals and the city
coming to life in the early morning.

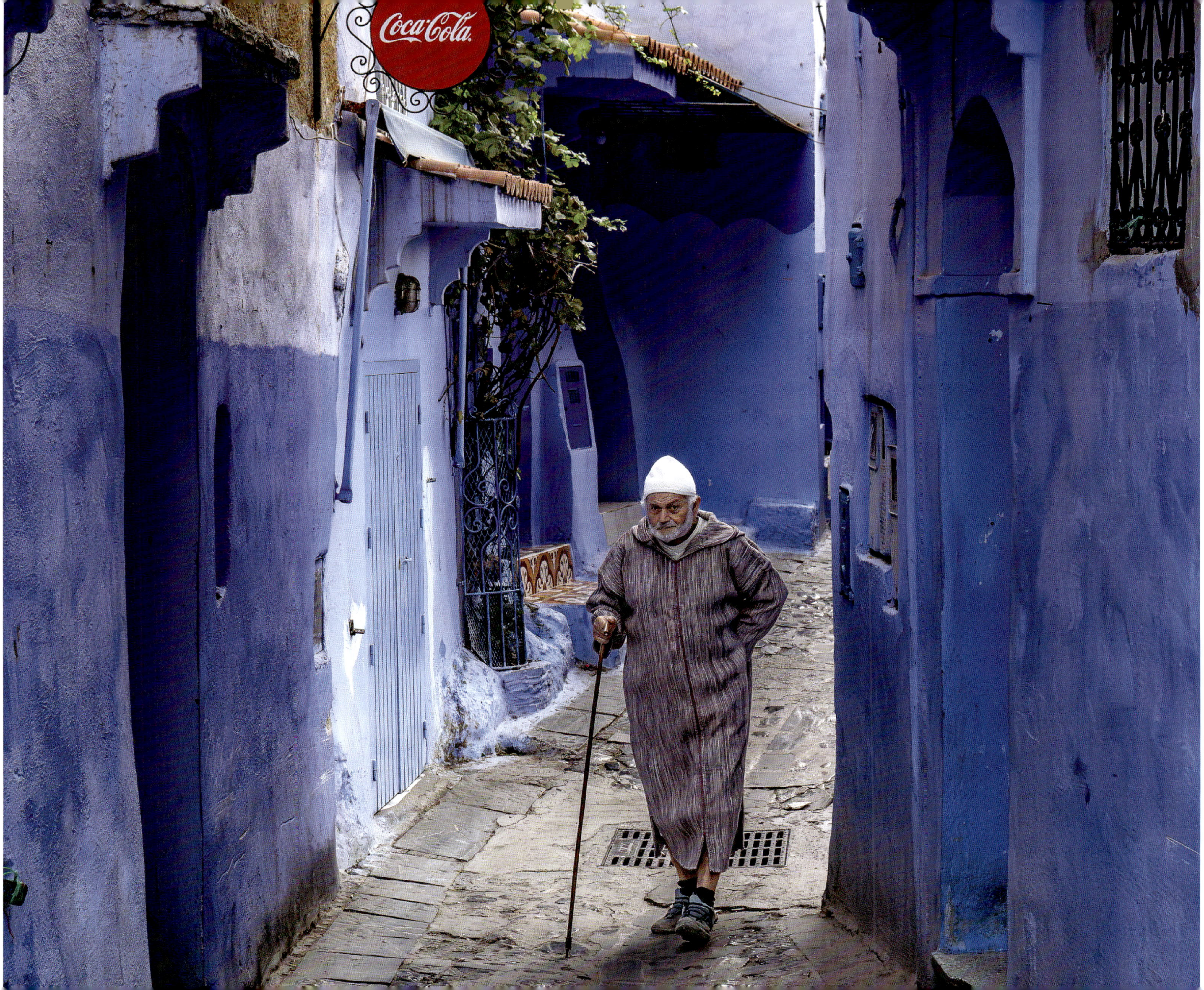
Coca-Cola

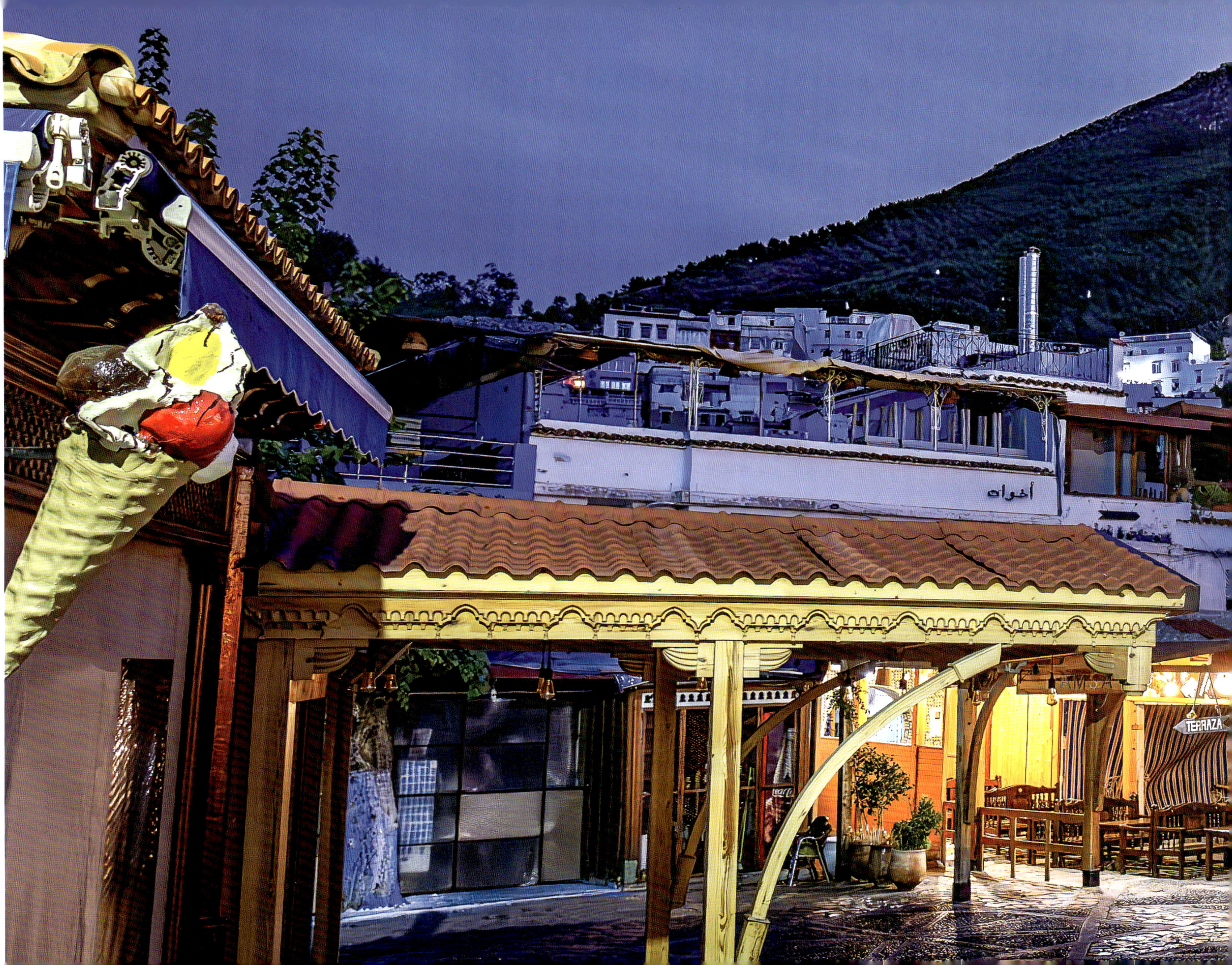
أخواه
TERRAZA

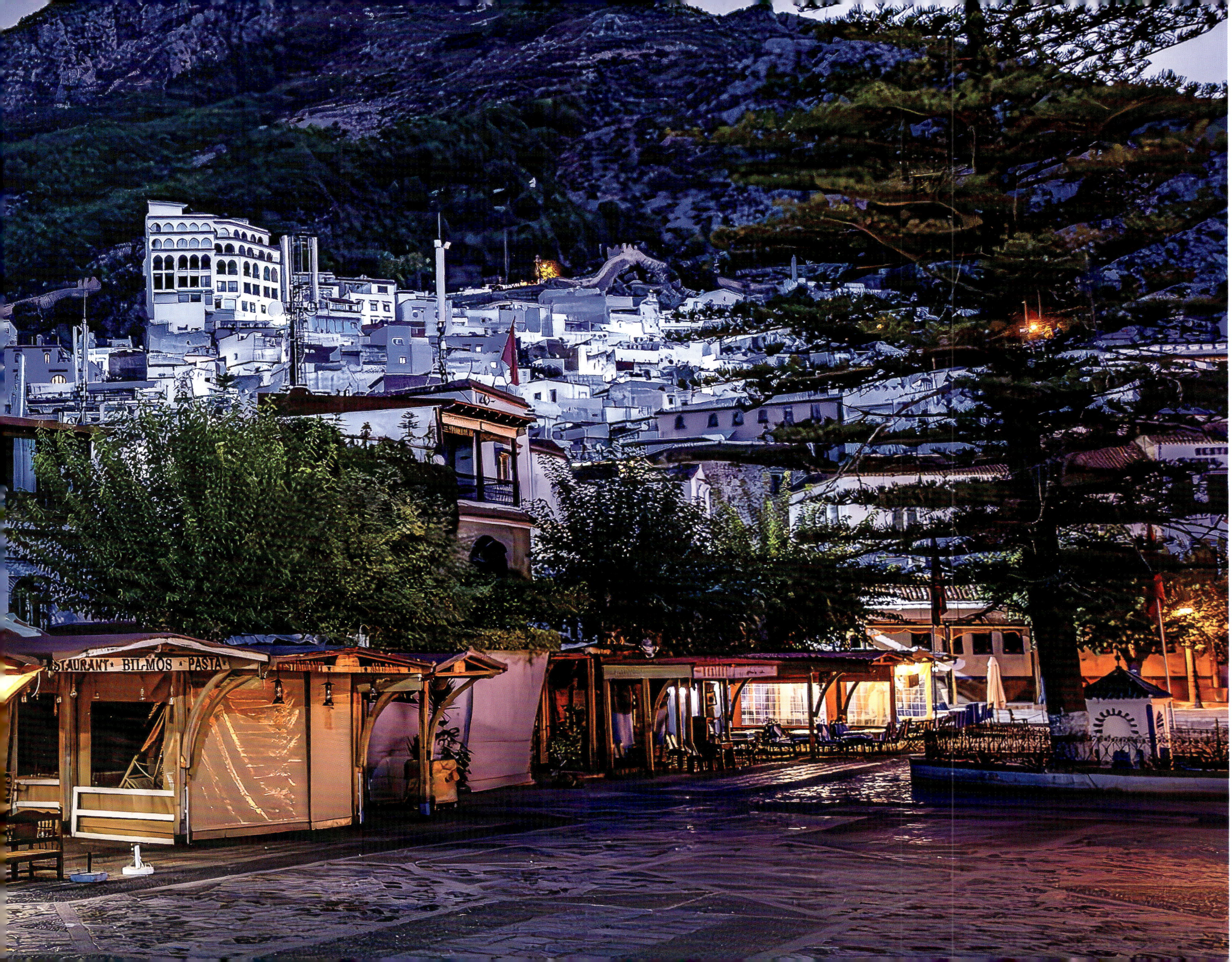
STAURANT · BILMOS · PASTA

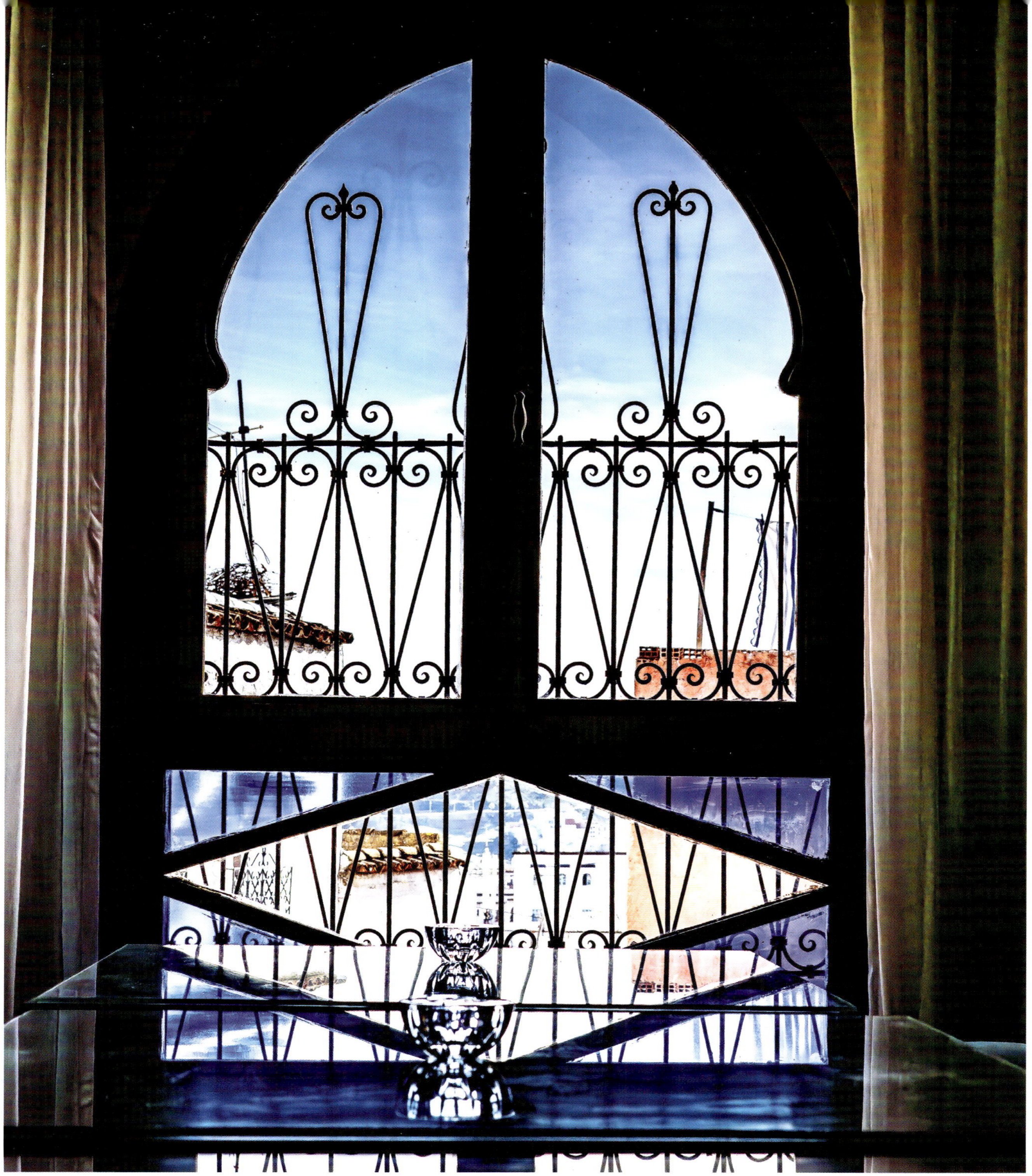

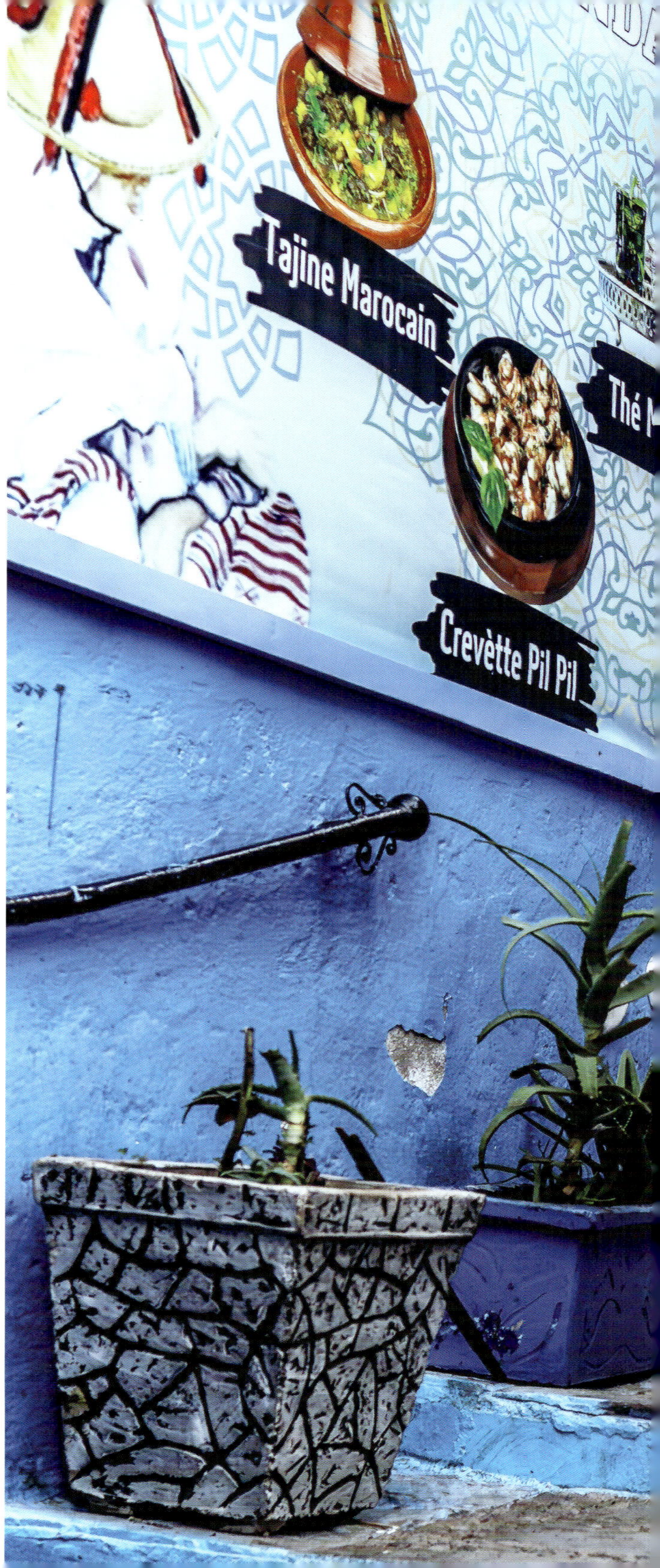
Tajine Marocain
Crevètte Pil Pil

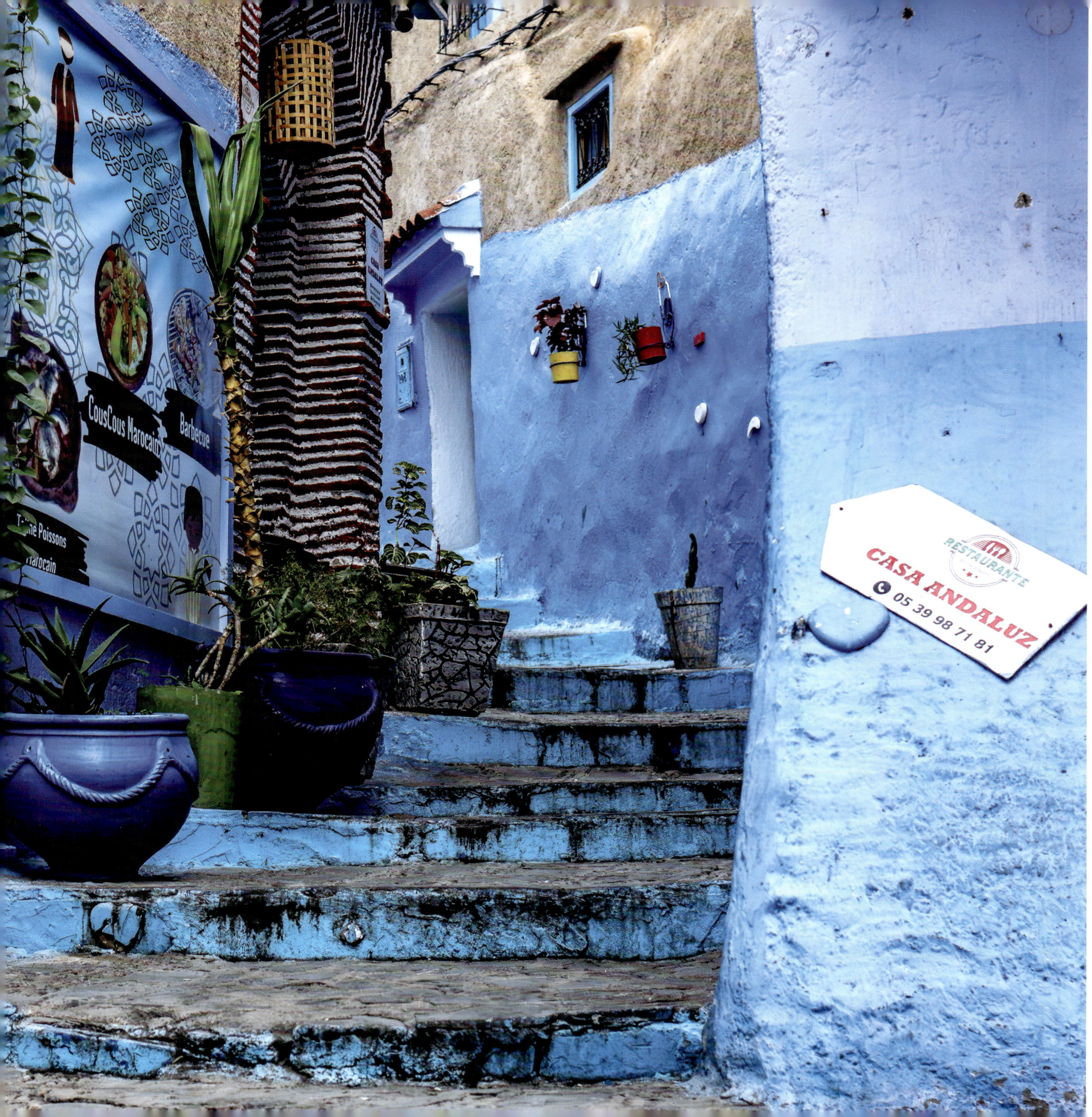


Previous page:
City center in the morning light.

Decorative riad window.

Staircase leading up to
Casa Andaluz.

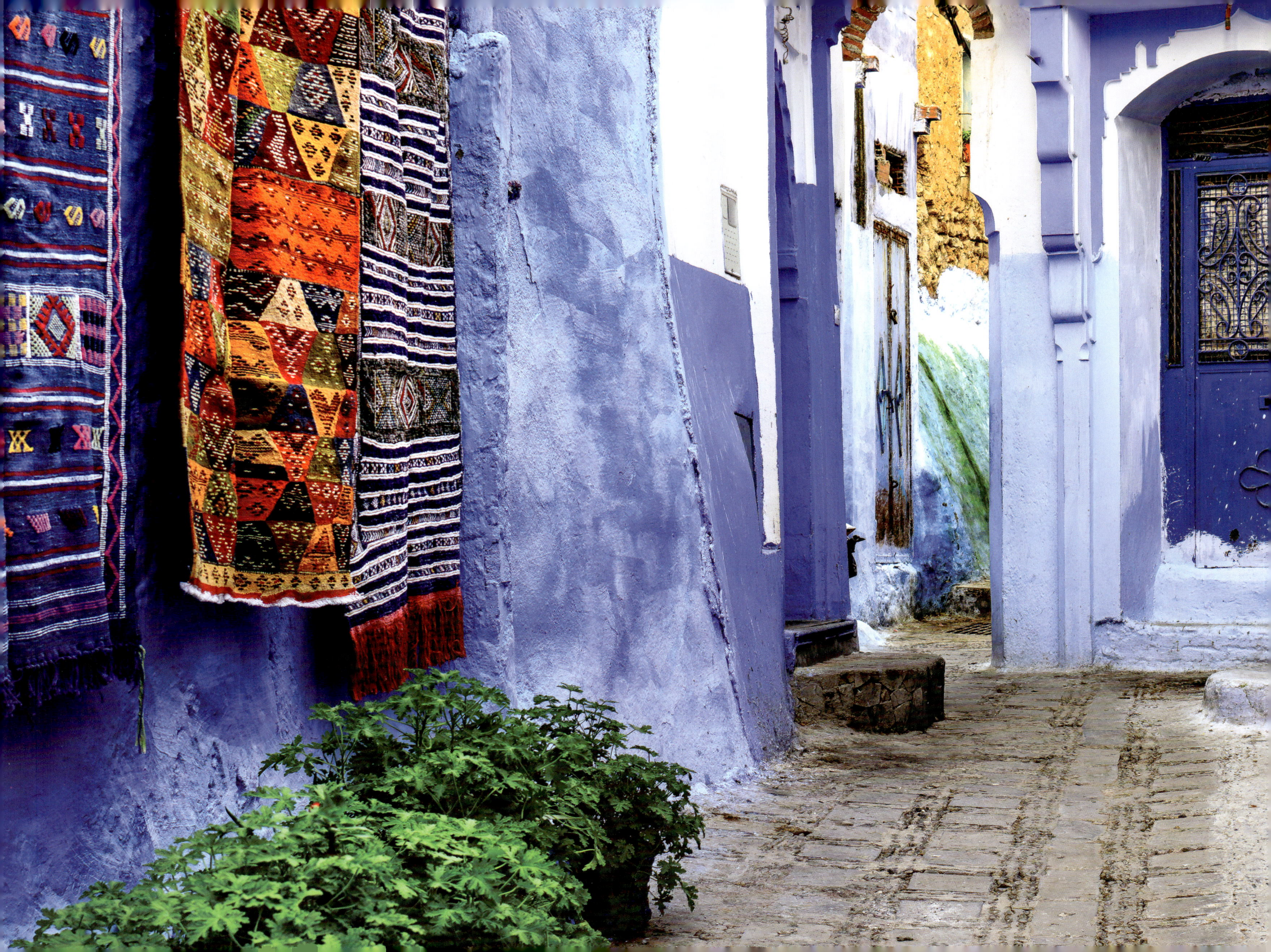

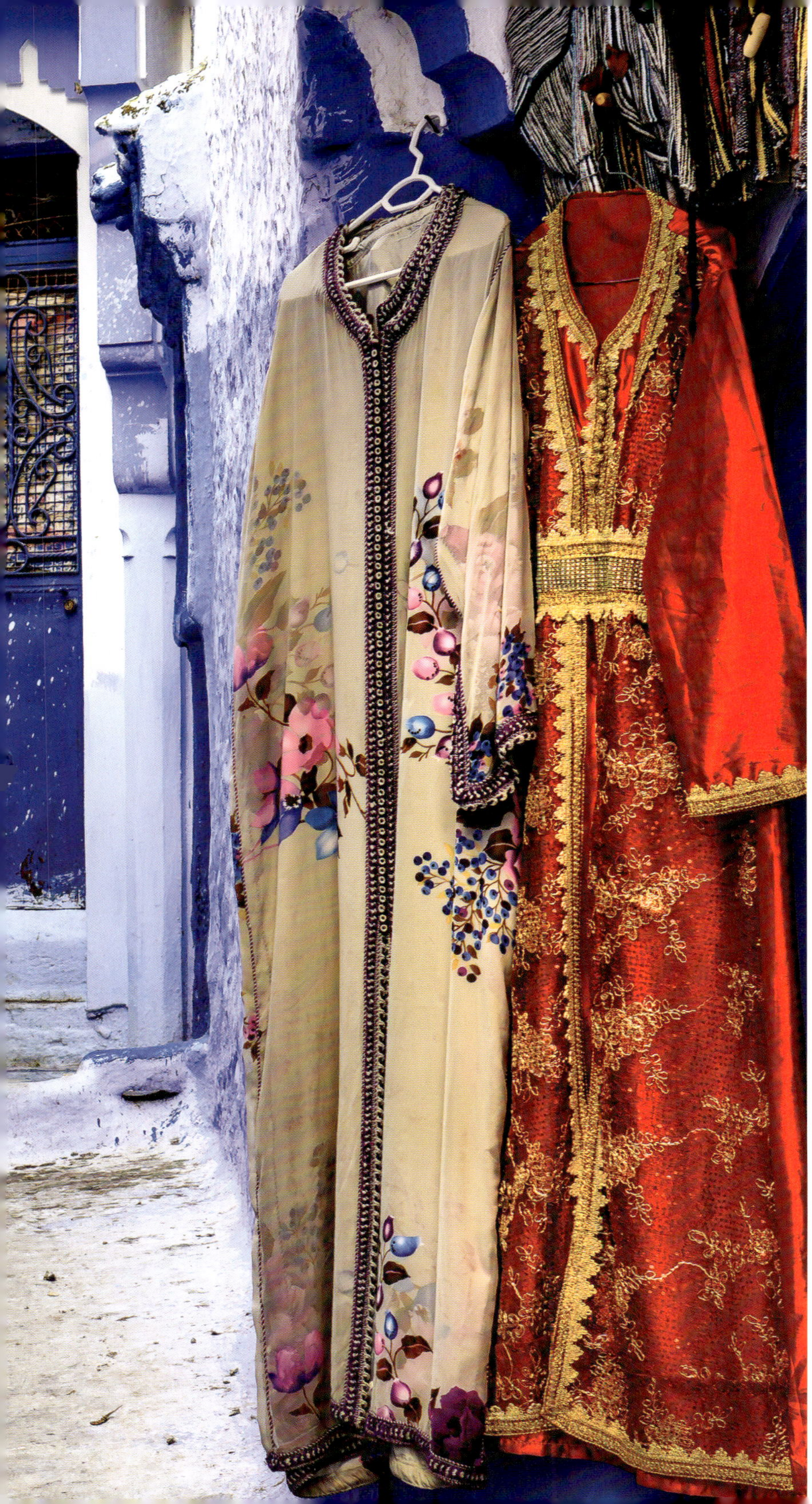
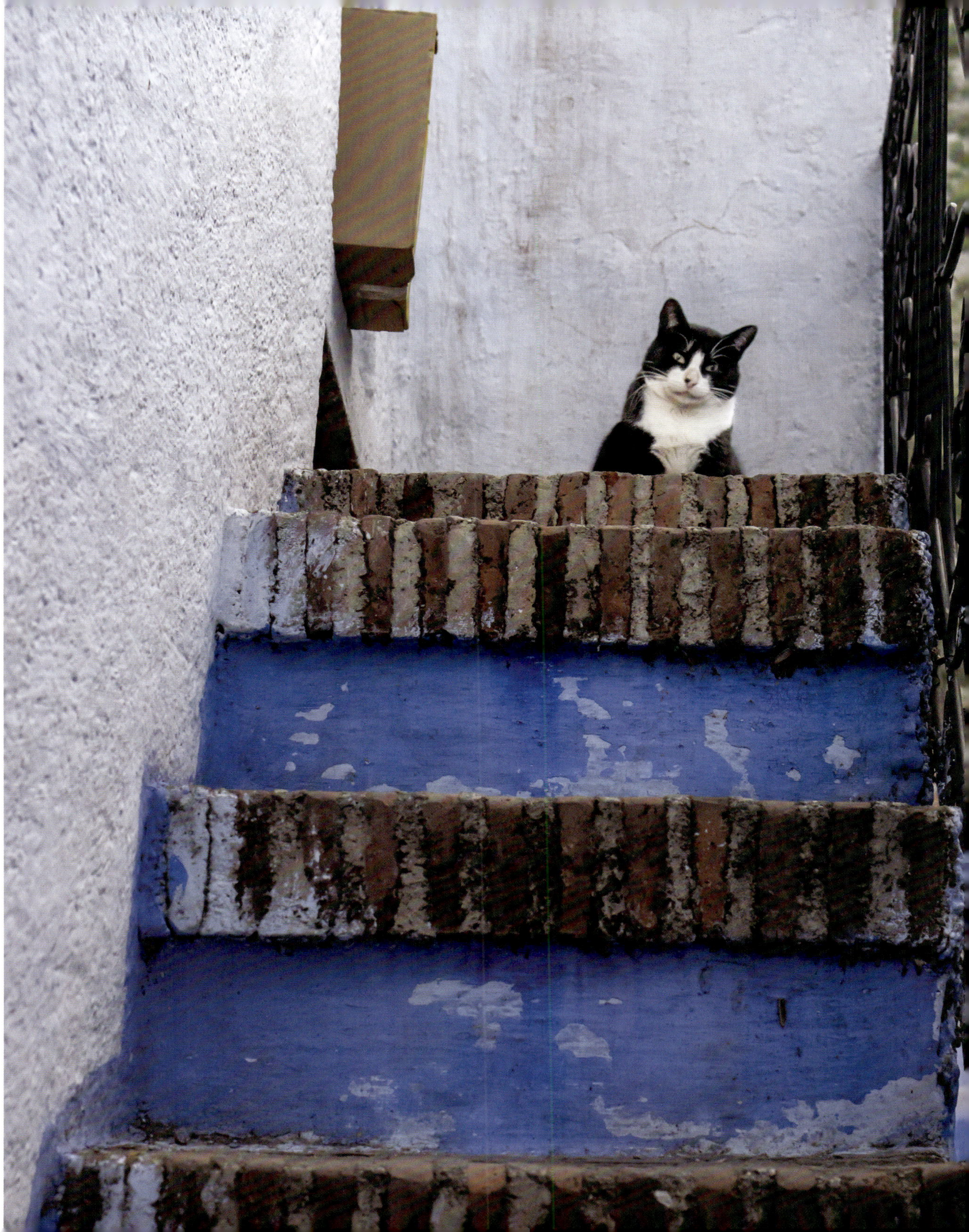

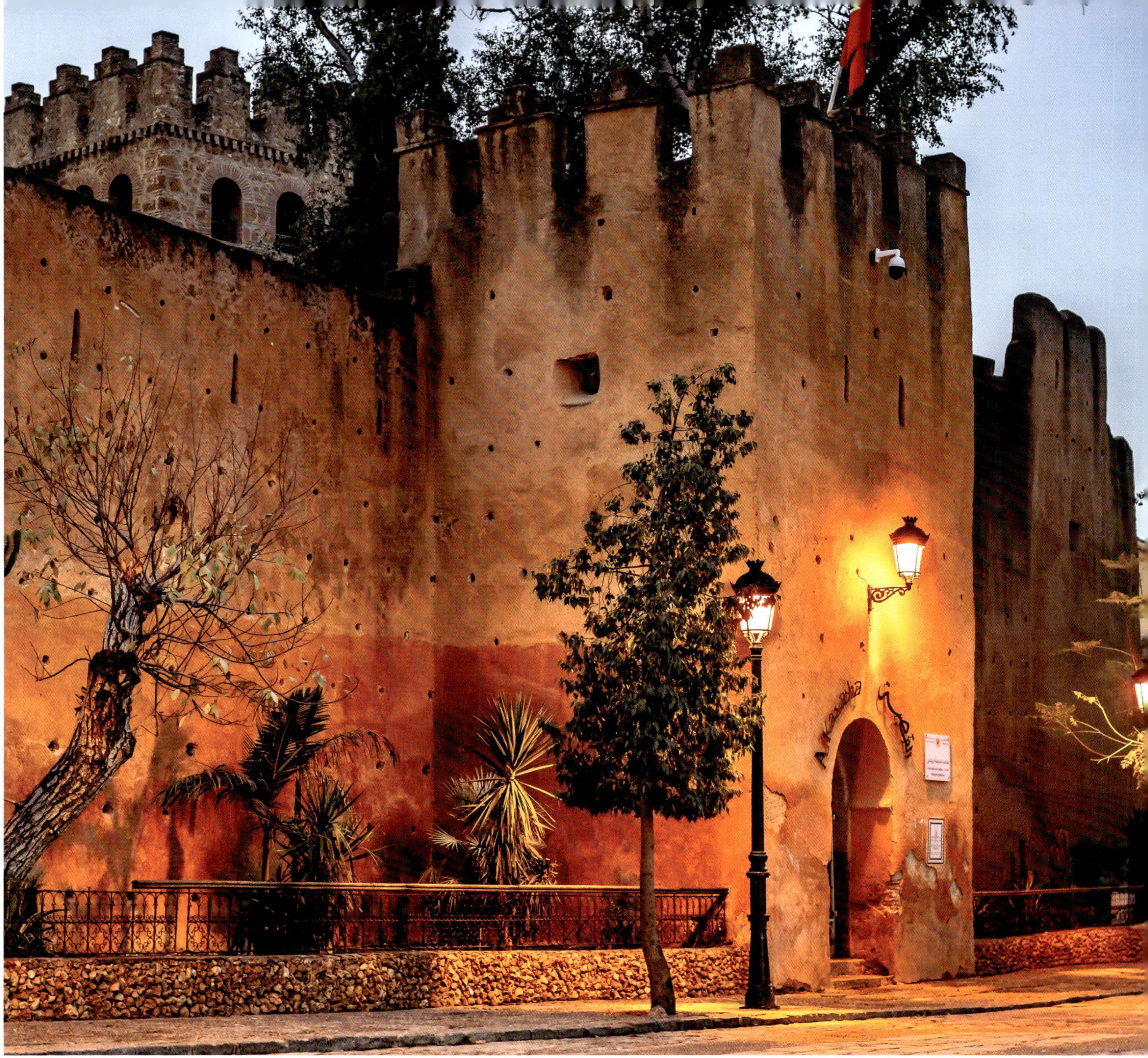

Previous page:
Colorful woven Moroccan rugs hang in an alley outside a souk.

There are always beautiful wandering street cats to see around every corner in Morocco.

This kasbah, a fortified quarter or citadel of a city, was built by Moualay Ali Ben Rachid, founder of Chefchaouen.

Blue walled stairways lead to many surprises and treasures to explore.

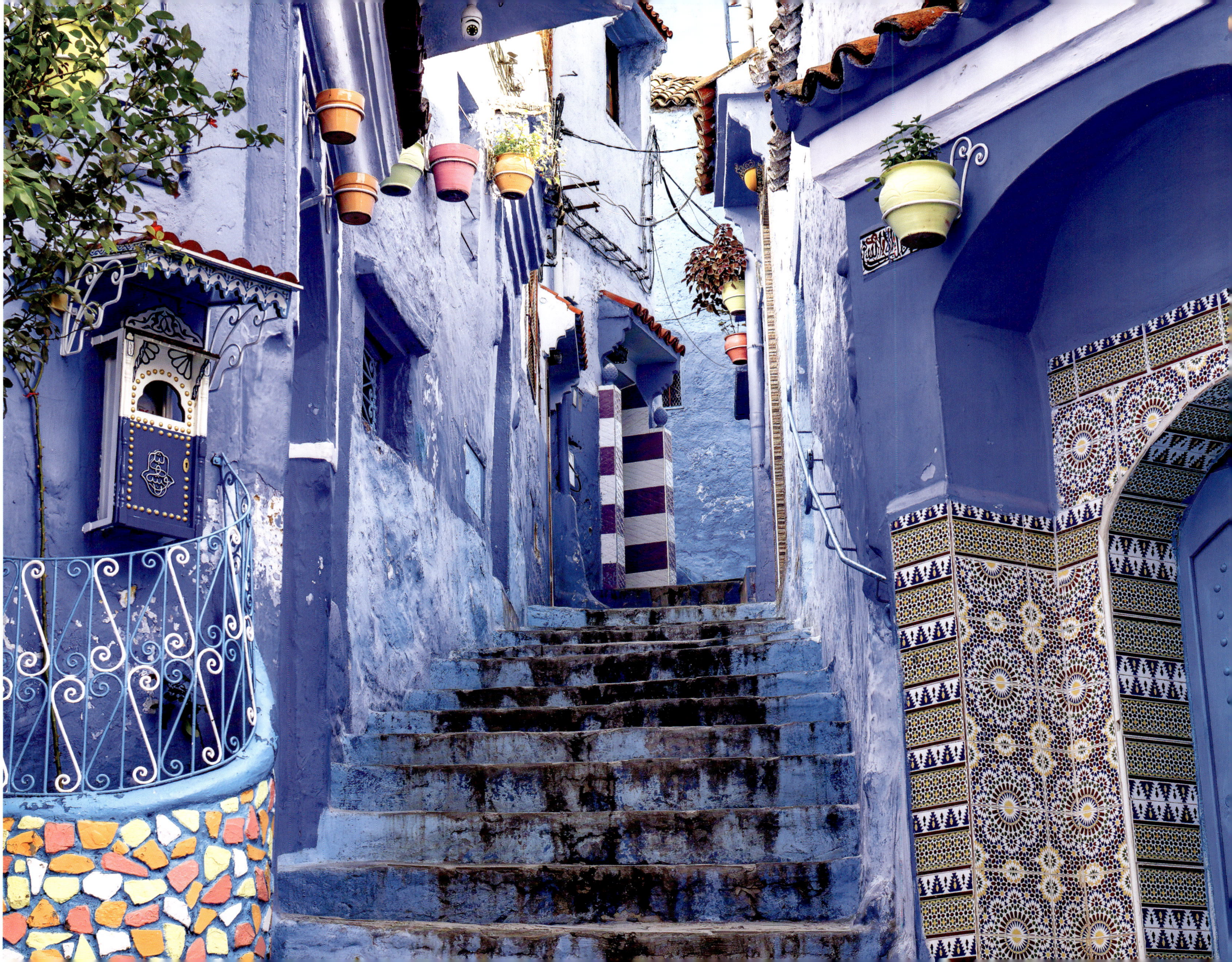

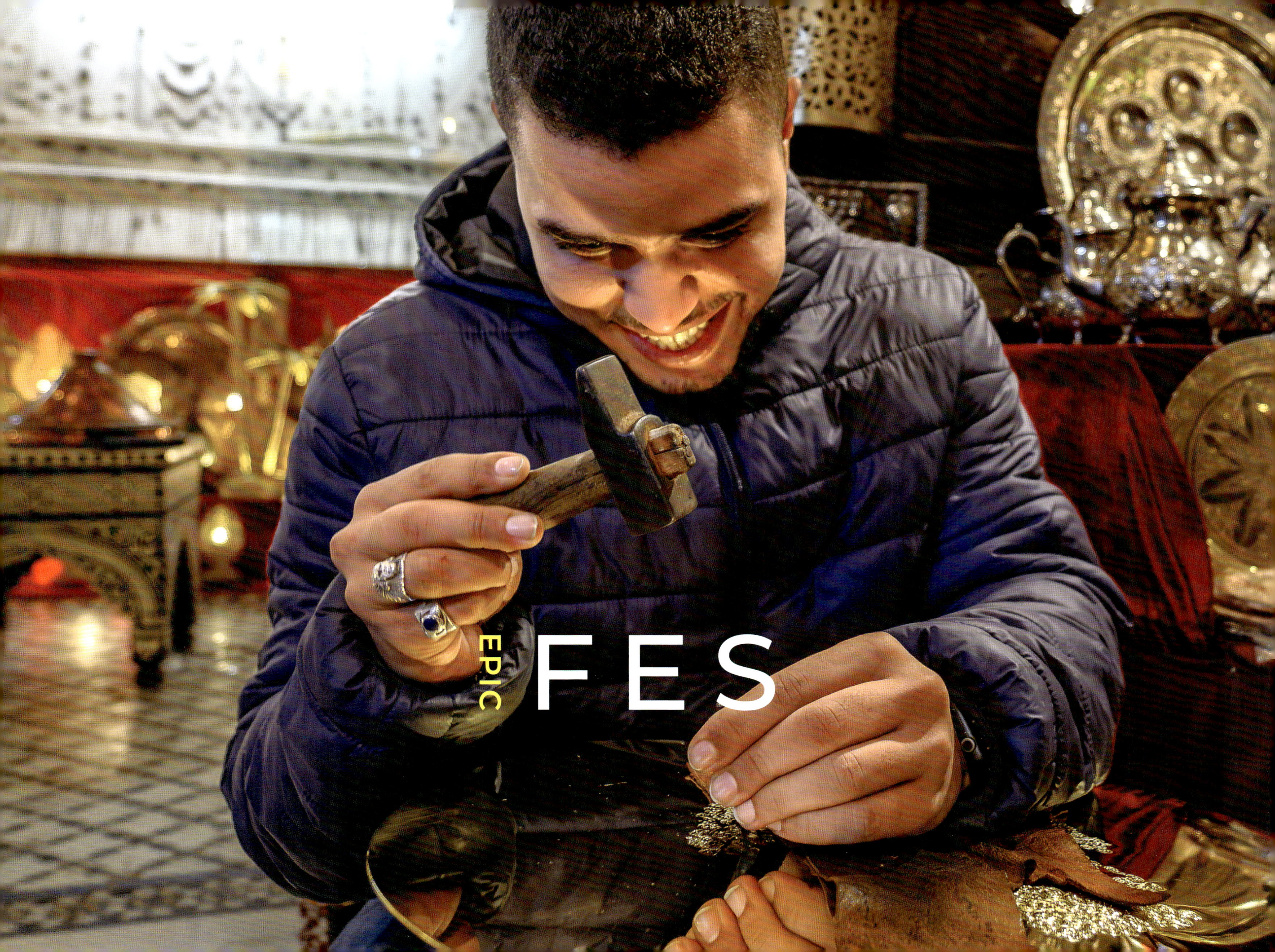
EPIC
FES

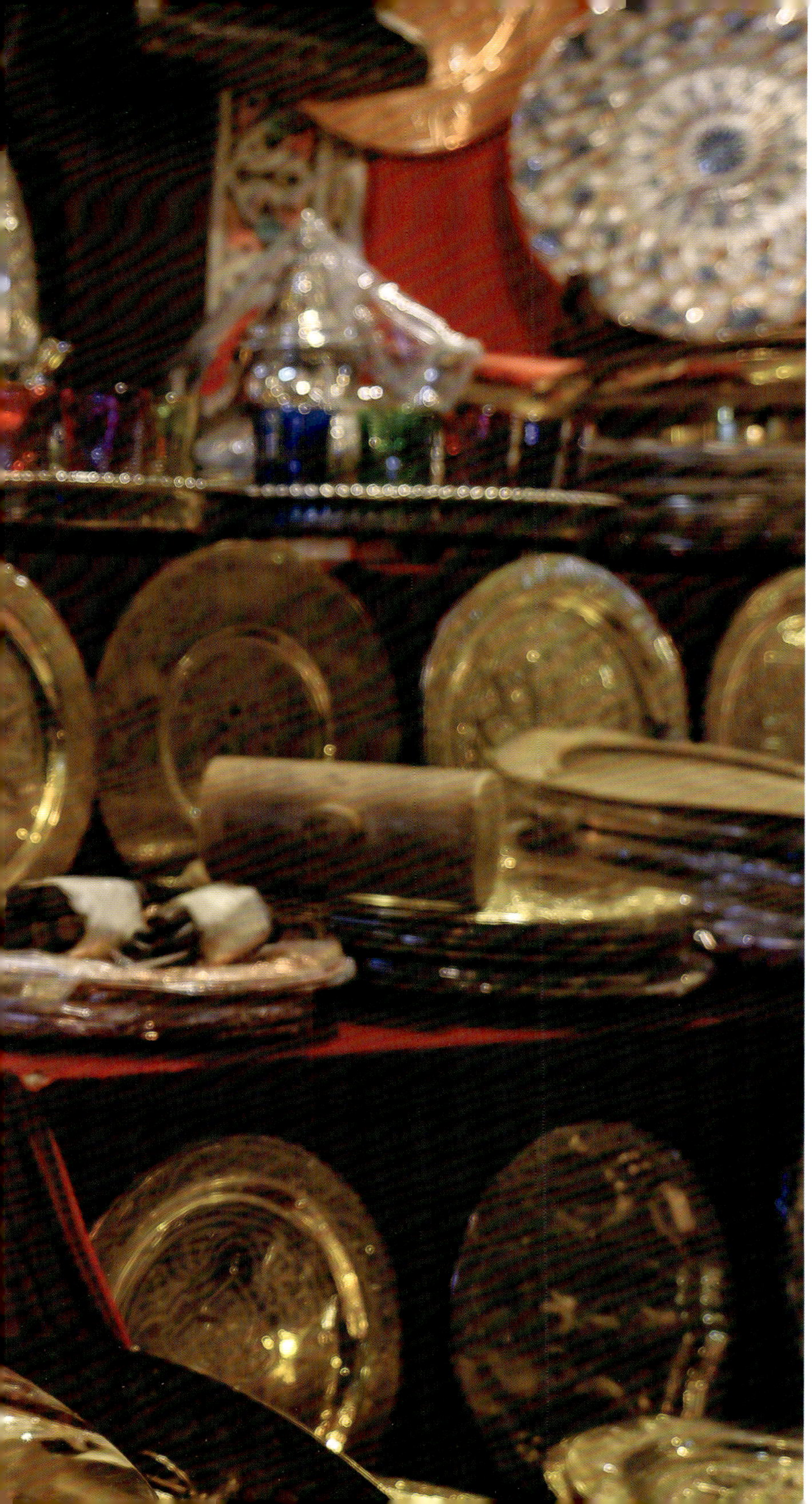

# A TIMELESS AND ENCHANTING IMPERIAL CITY

The oldest of Morocco's four imperial cities, Fes was founded in two sections in the 8th and 9th centuries by Idris I and Idris II. As the city developed it became a center of learning and Islamic education and home to the Sidi Mohamed Ben Abdellah University.

In the 13th century, the Royal Palace of Fes was built as one of the Royal residences for the King of Morocco. It is also the largest and oldest of the Royal residences. The city is mostly surrounded by low hills covered with olive groves and orchards. Ancient battlements flanked by stone towers partly enclose the old city, known as the Fès el-Bali. Inside the old city is a maze of some 9,000 alleys that wind through the world's oldest operating medina, another of Morocco's many UNESCO World Heritage Sites. The medina features a vast collection of souks and merchant stalls that offer a diverse selection of traditional Moroccan handcrafted goods including clothing, jewelry, carpets, pottery and leather goods.

The city is also known for a large section of tanneries that have been curing and coloring sheepskin, goatskin, and cow hides in almost the same way for over 800 years. The skins are cured and cleaned in a pungent mix of cow urine, salt, quicklime and water and then later dyed and made into clothing that is sold in the shops that surround the vats of curing mixture and can be viewed from surrounding terraces.

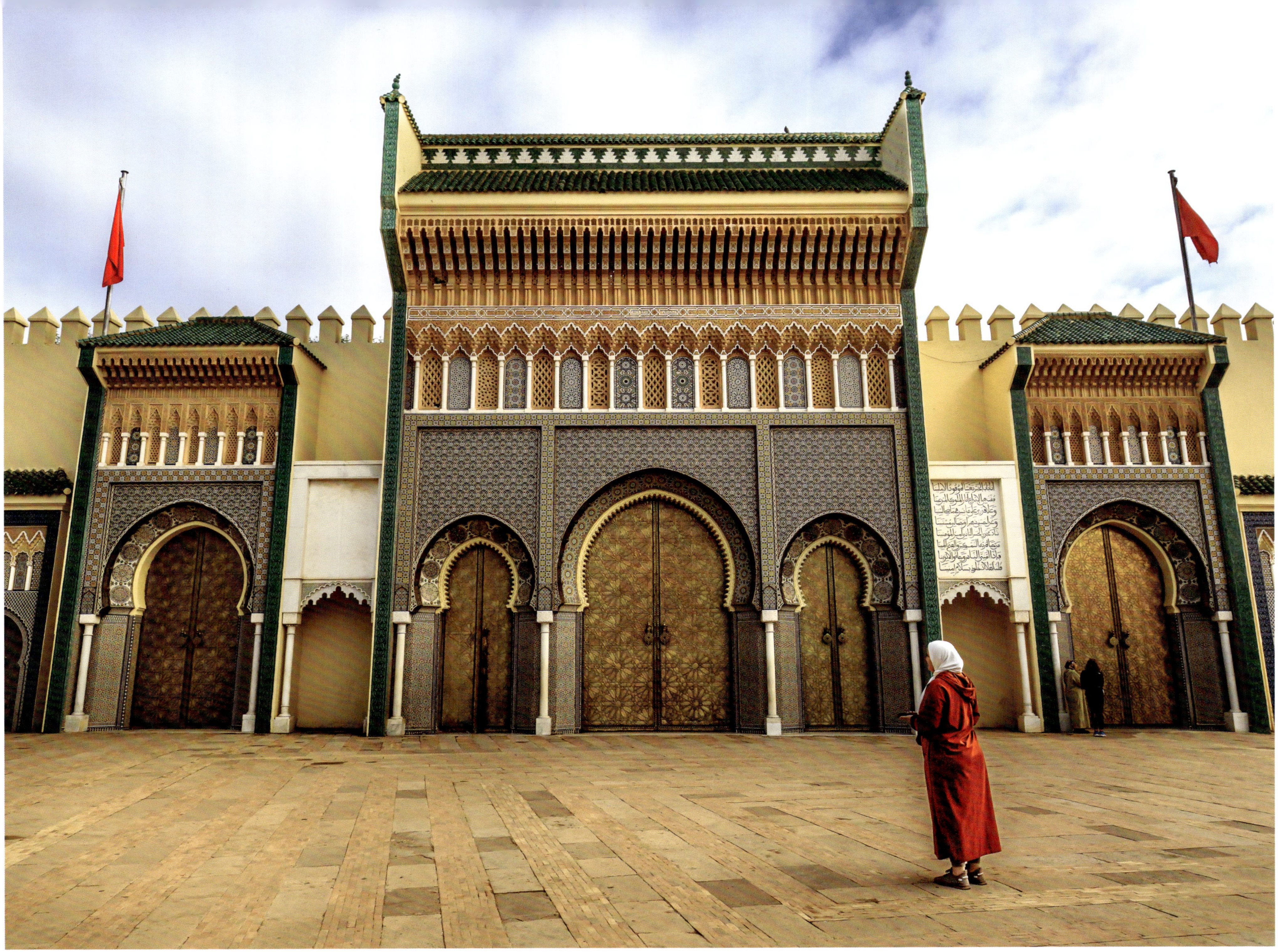

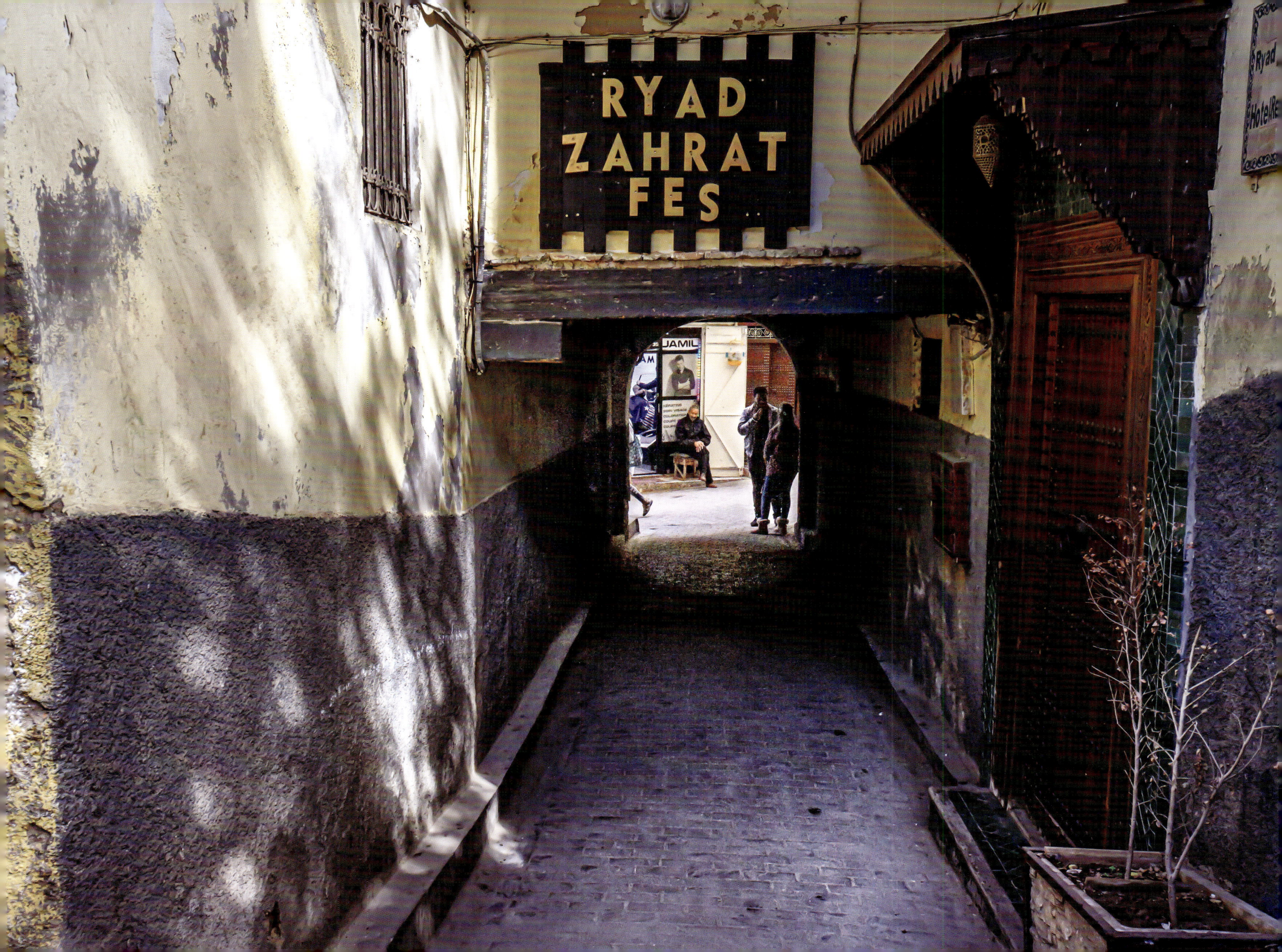
RYAD
ZAHRAT
FES
JAMIL

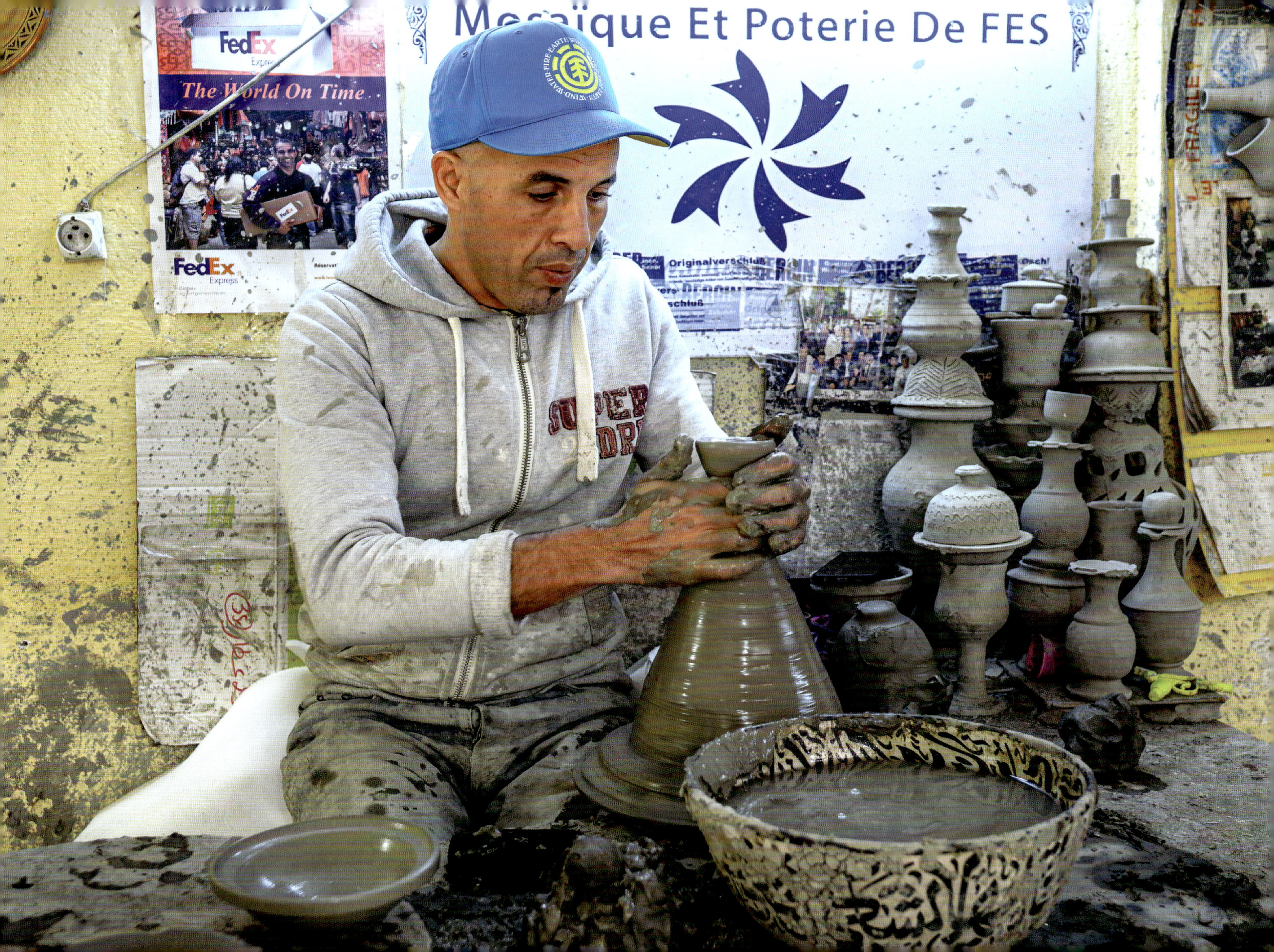
Mosaïque Et Poterie De FES
FedEx
The World On Time
FedEx
Express
Originalverschluß
FRAGILE

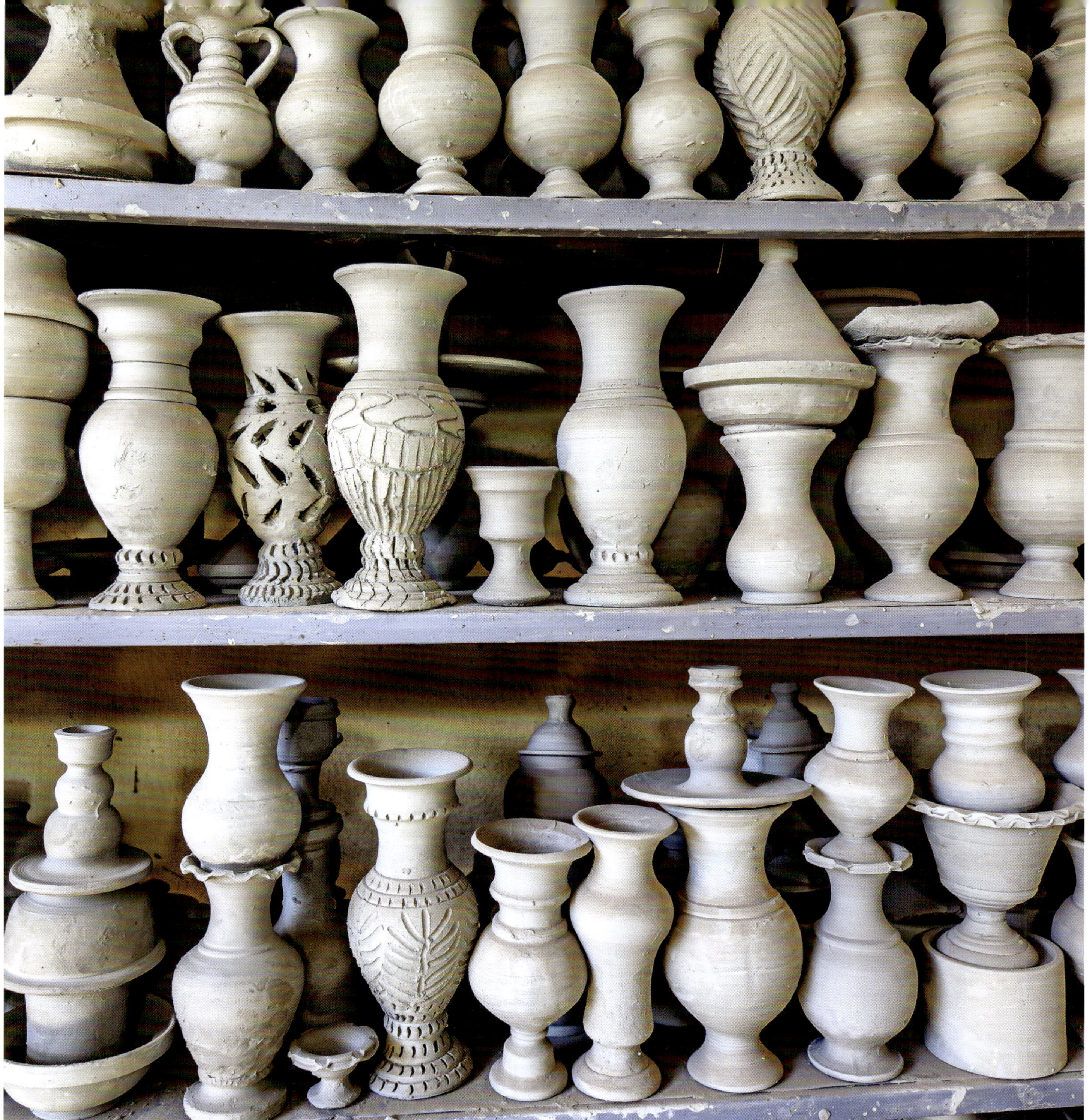

Previous page:
Gates to the Royal Palace.

Alley leading to Ryad Zahrat.

Next four pages:
Extremely skilled artisans and their creations in their Fes workshop.

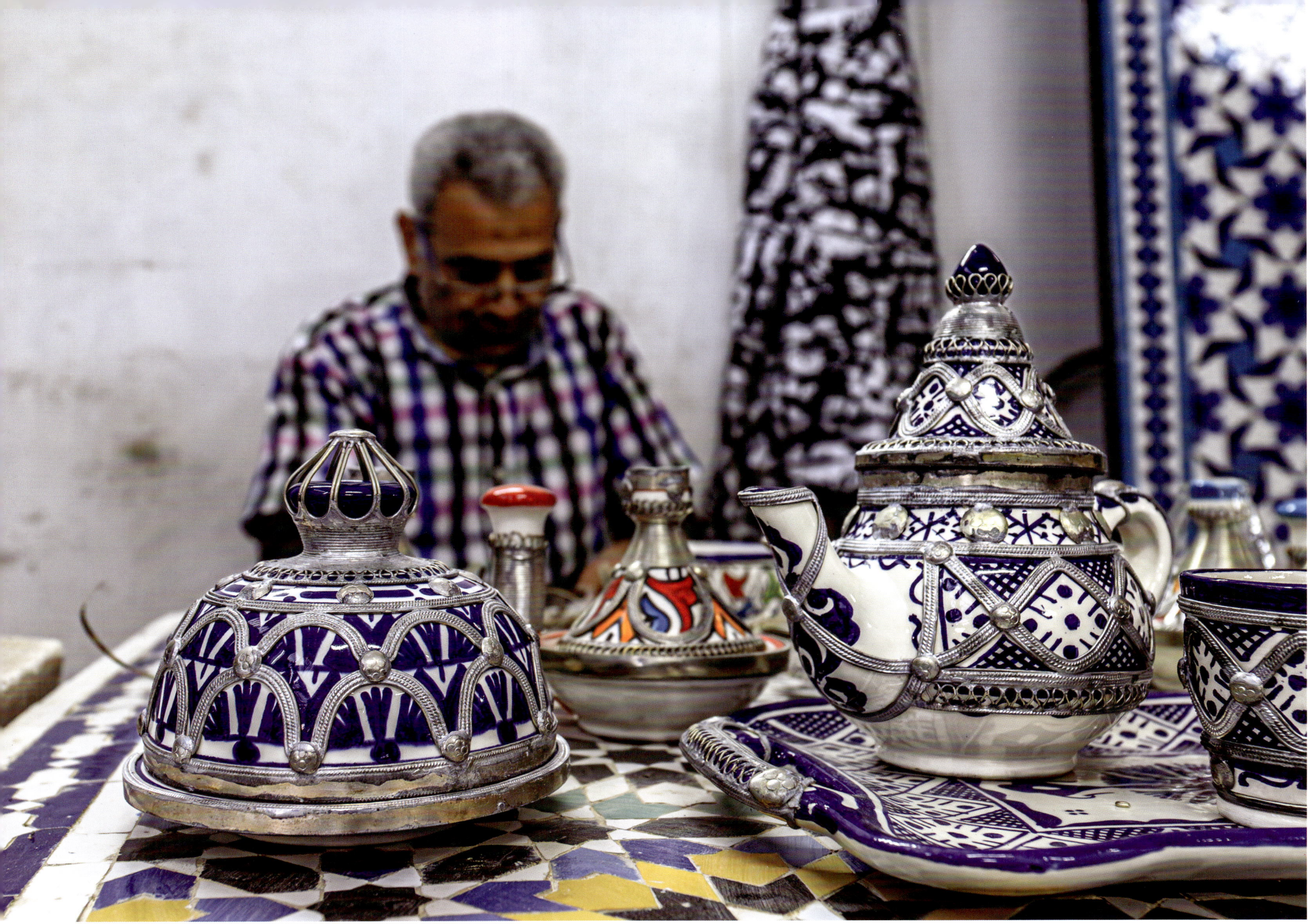

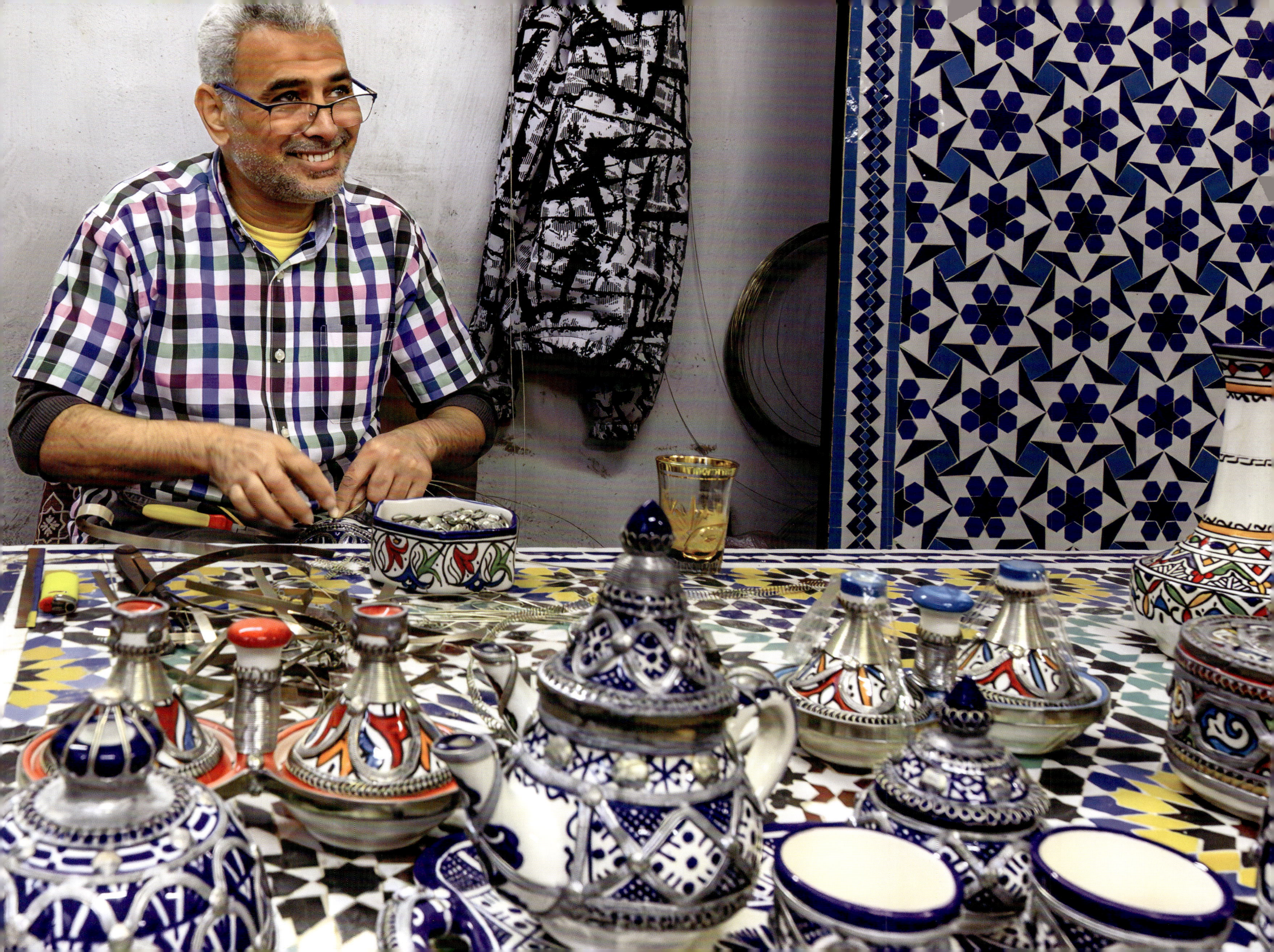

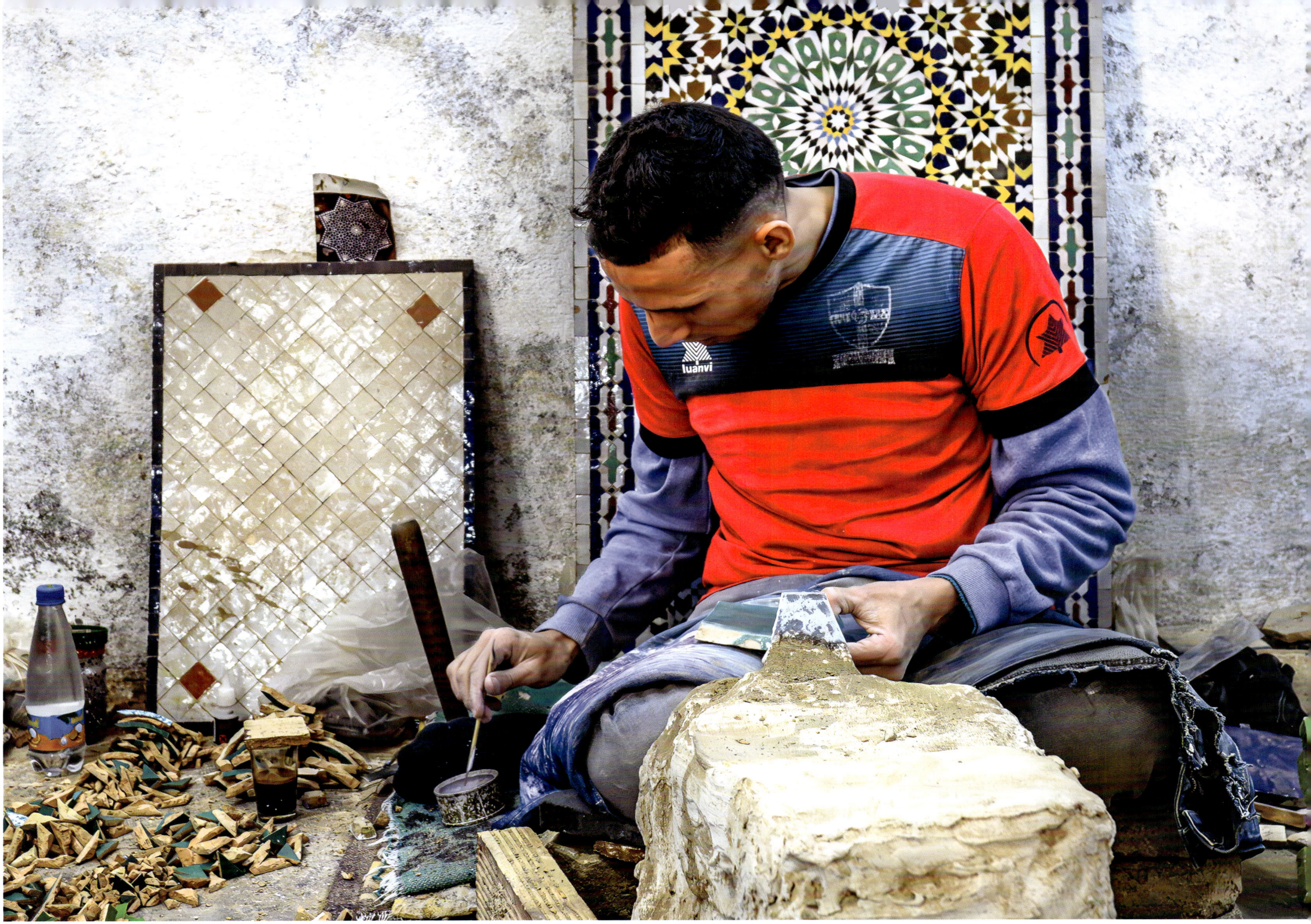
luanvi

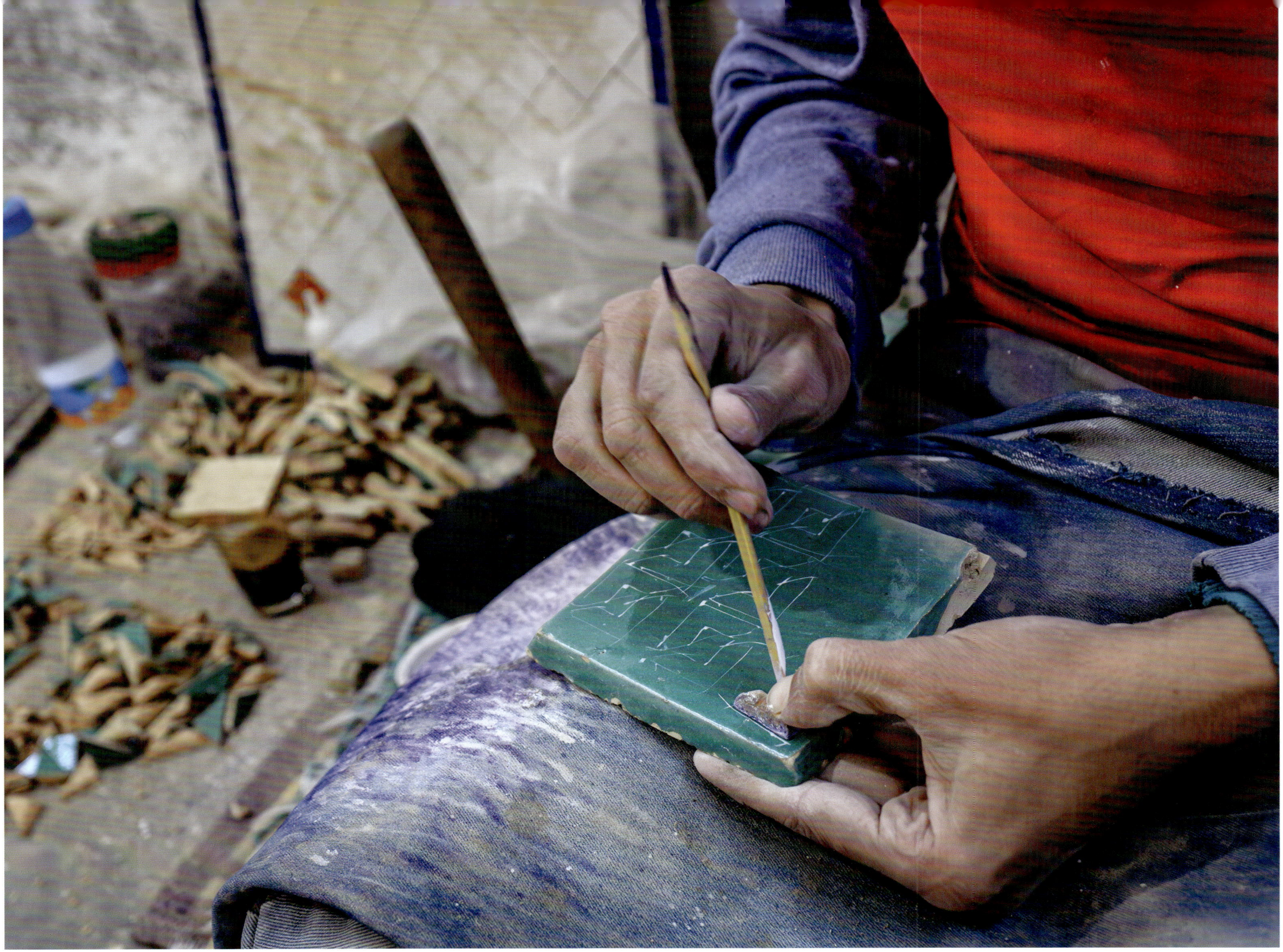

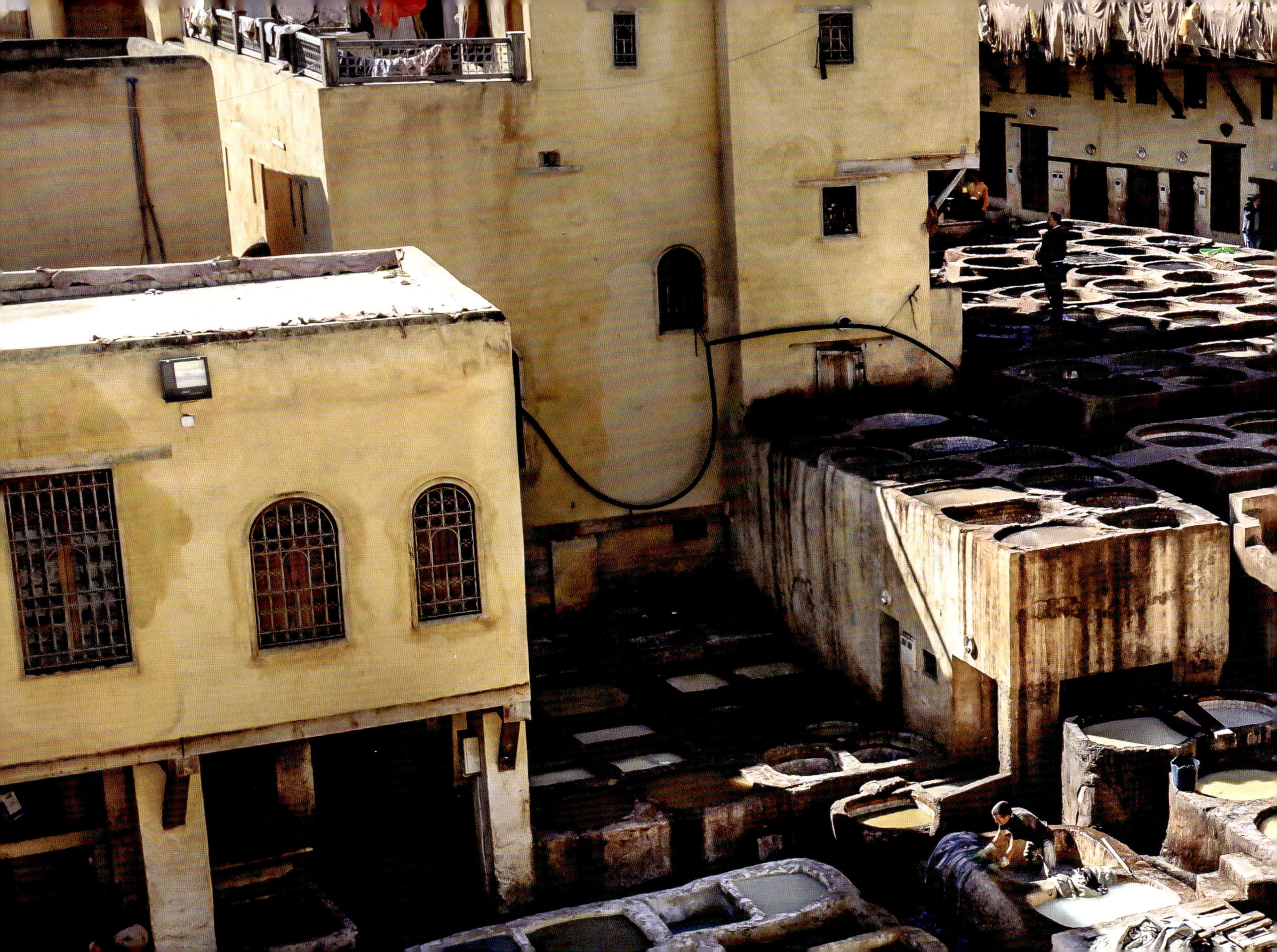

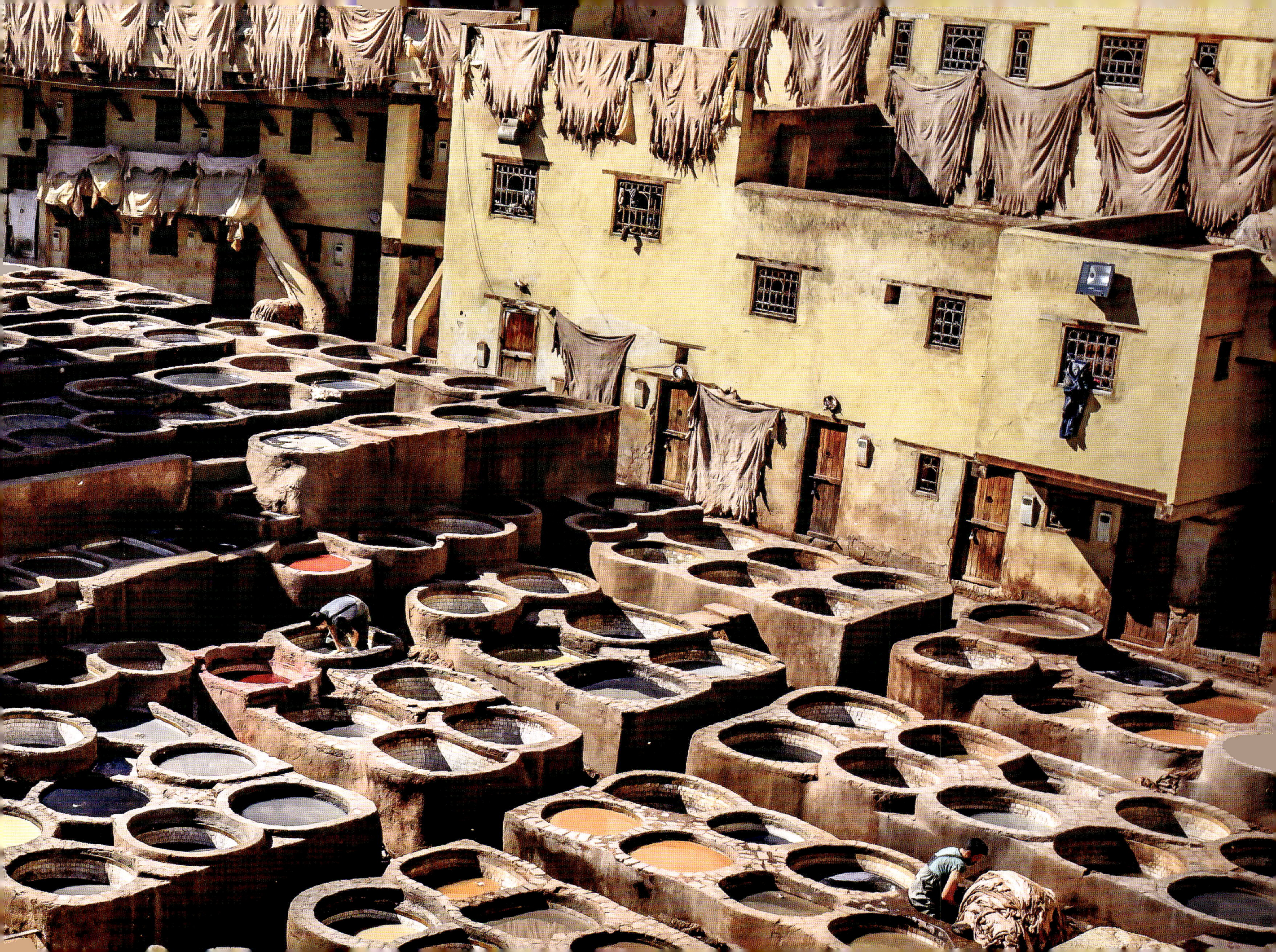

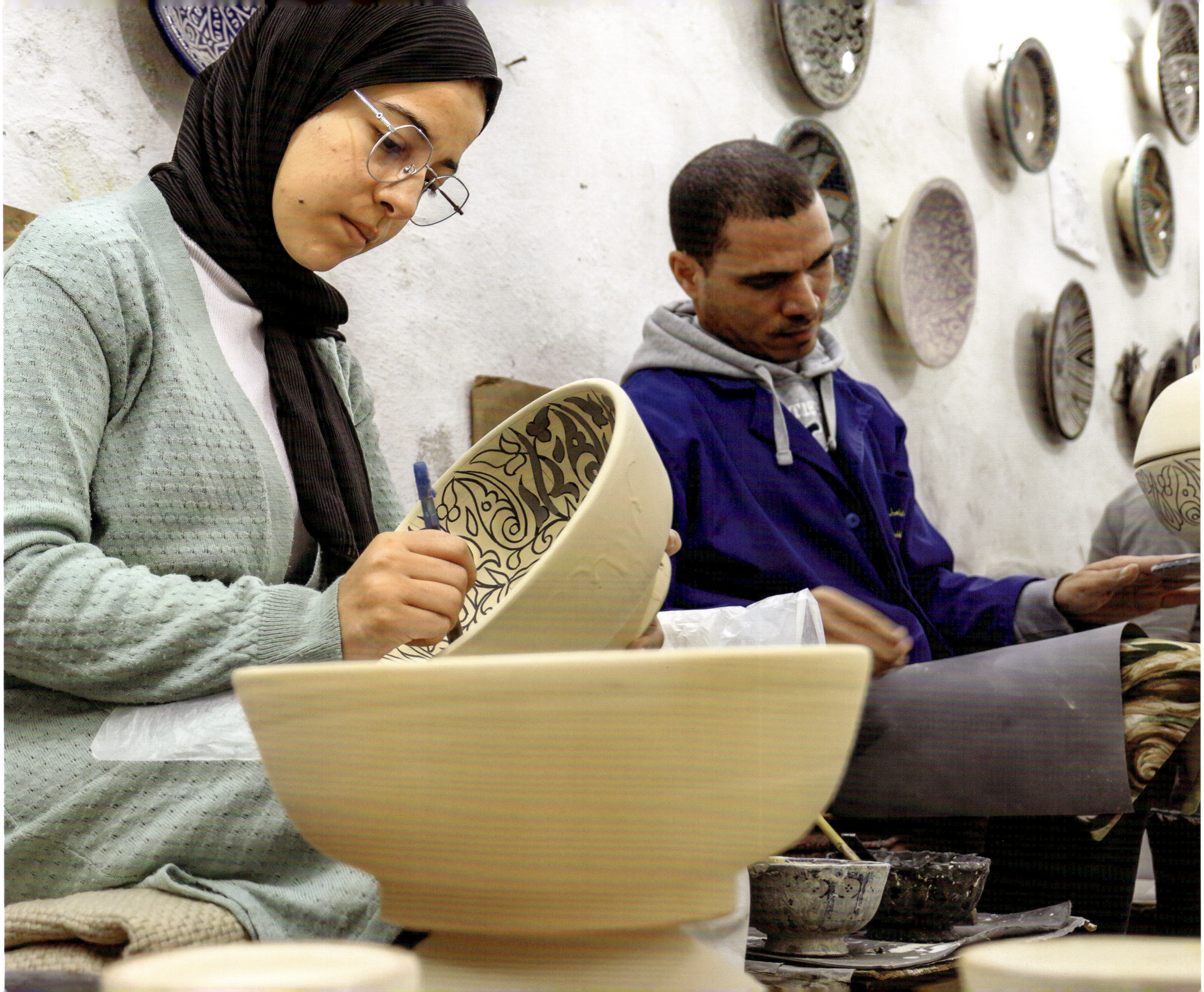

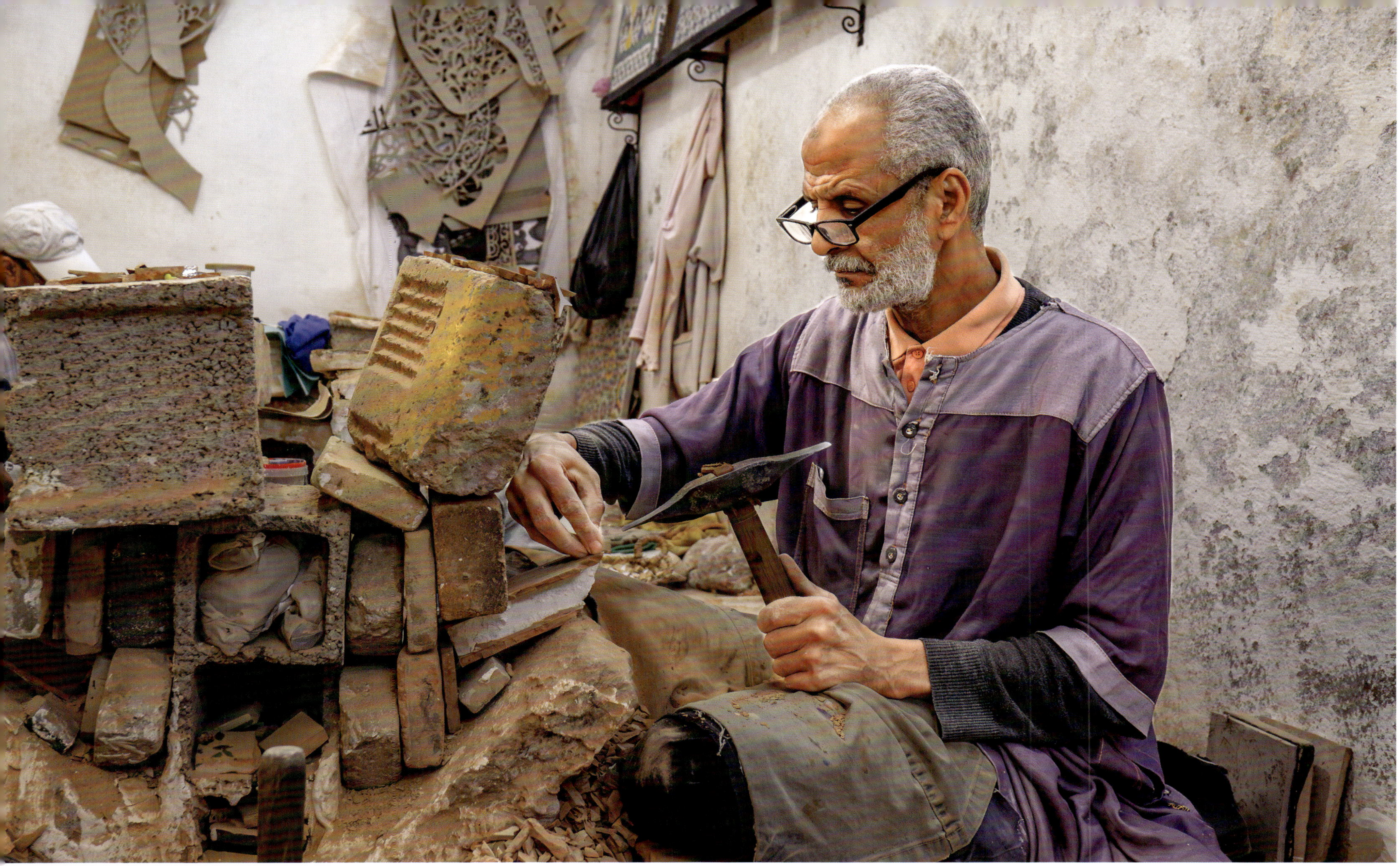

Previous page:
Tannery vats where hides are cured.

Fes artisans at work.

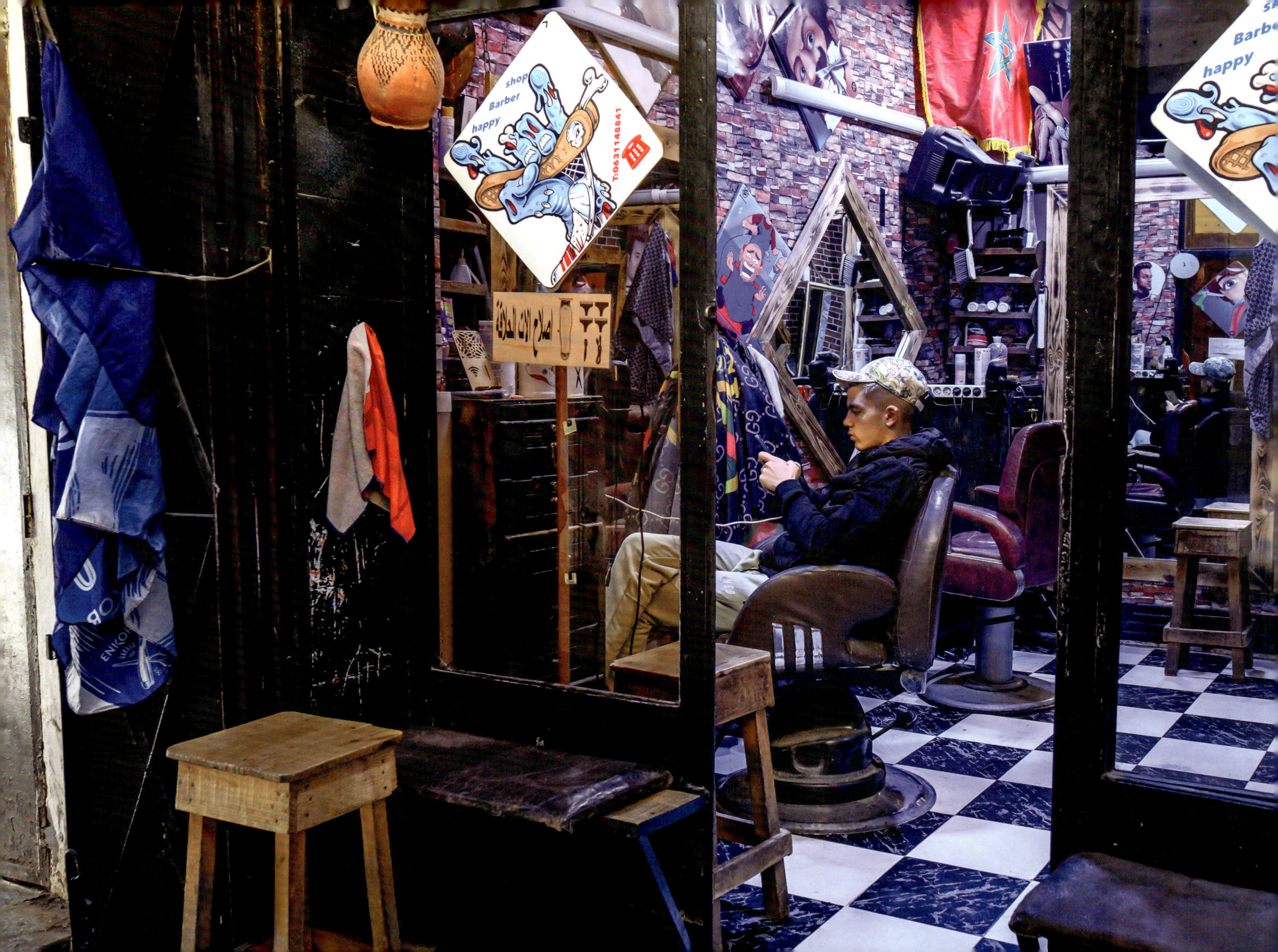
happy Barber shop
T:0631148841
اصلاح الآت الحلاقة

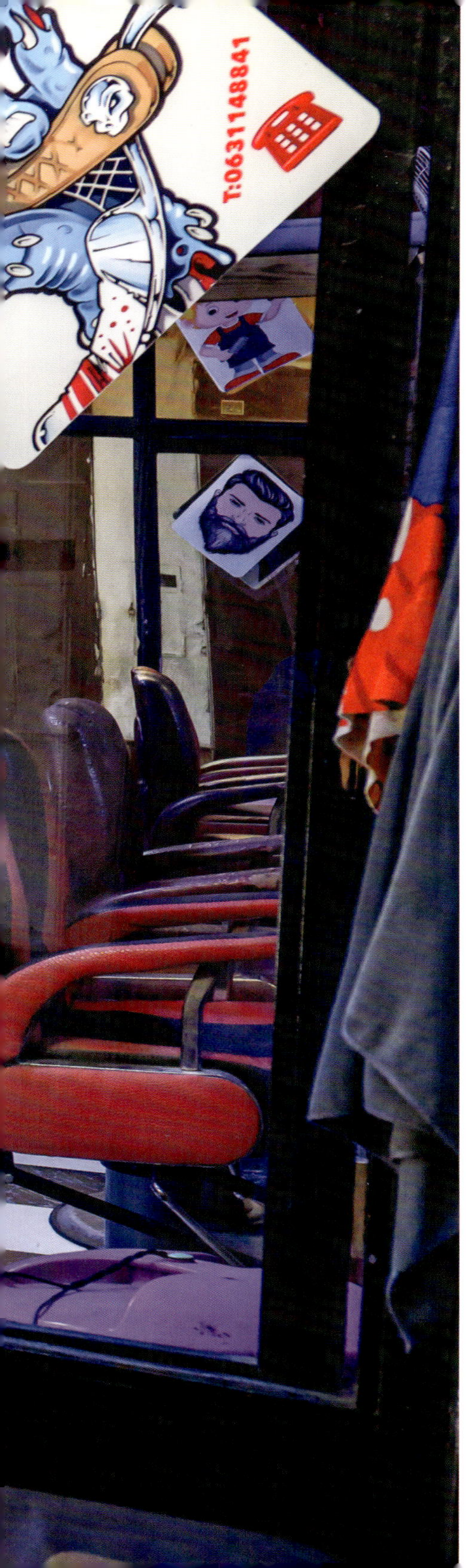
T:0631148841

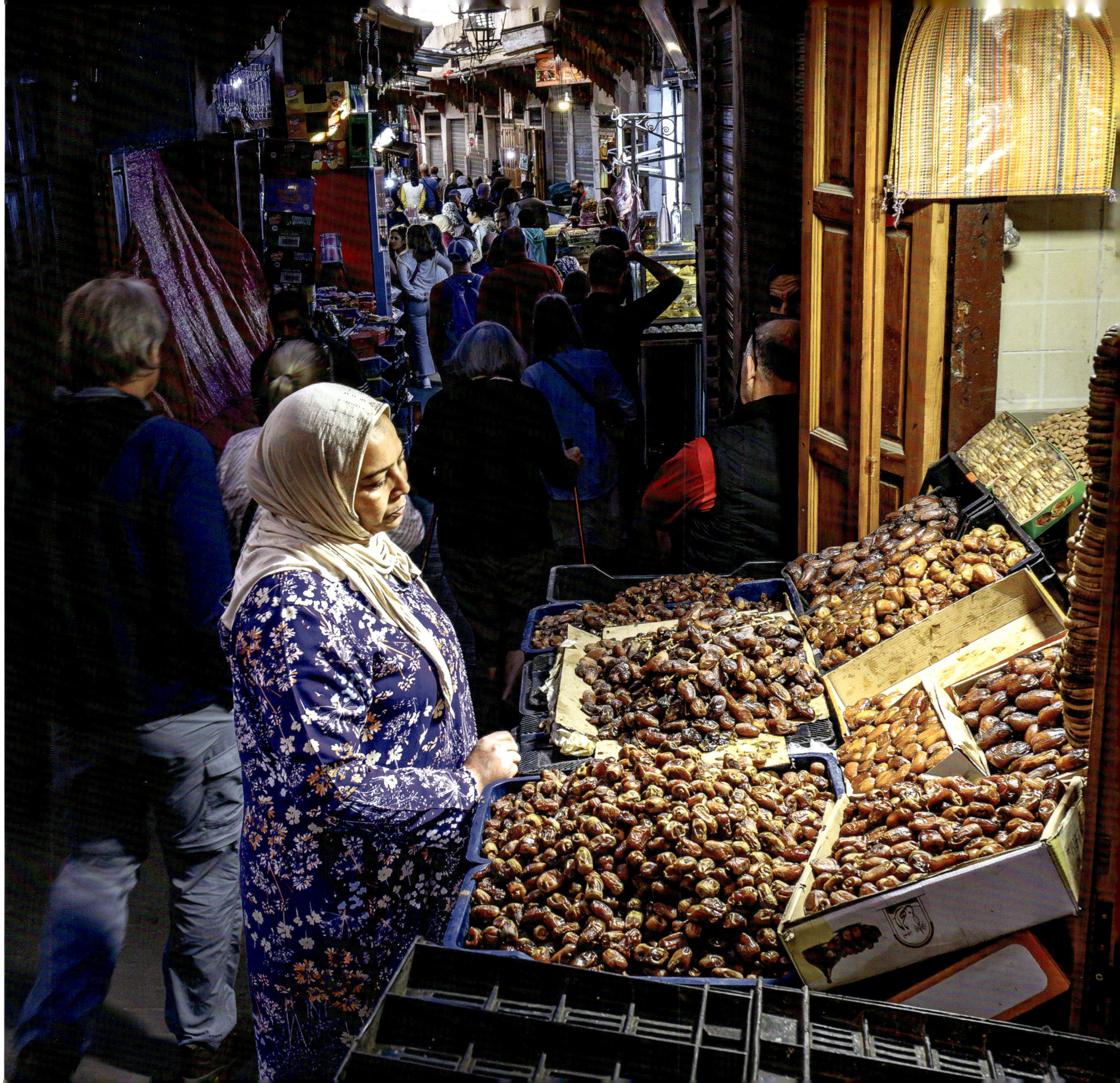

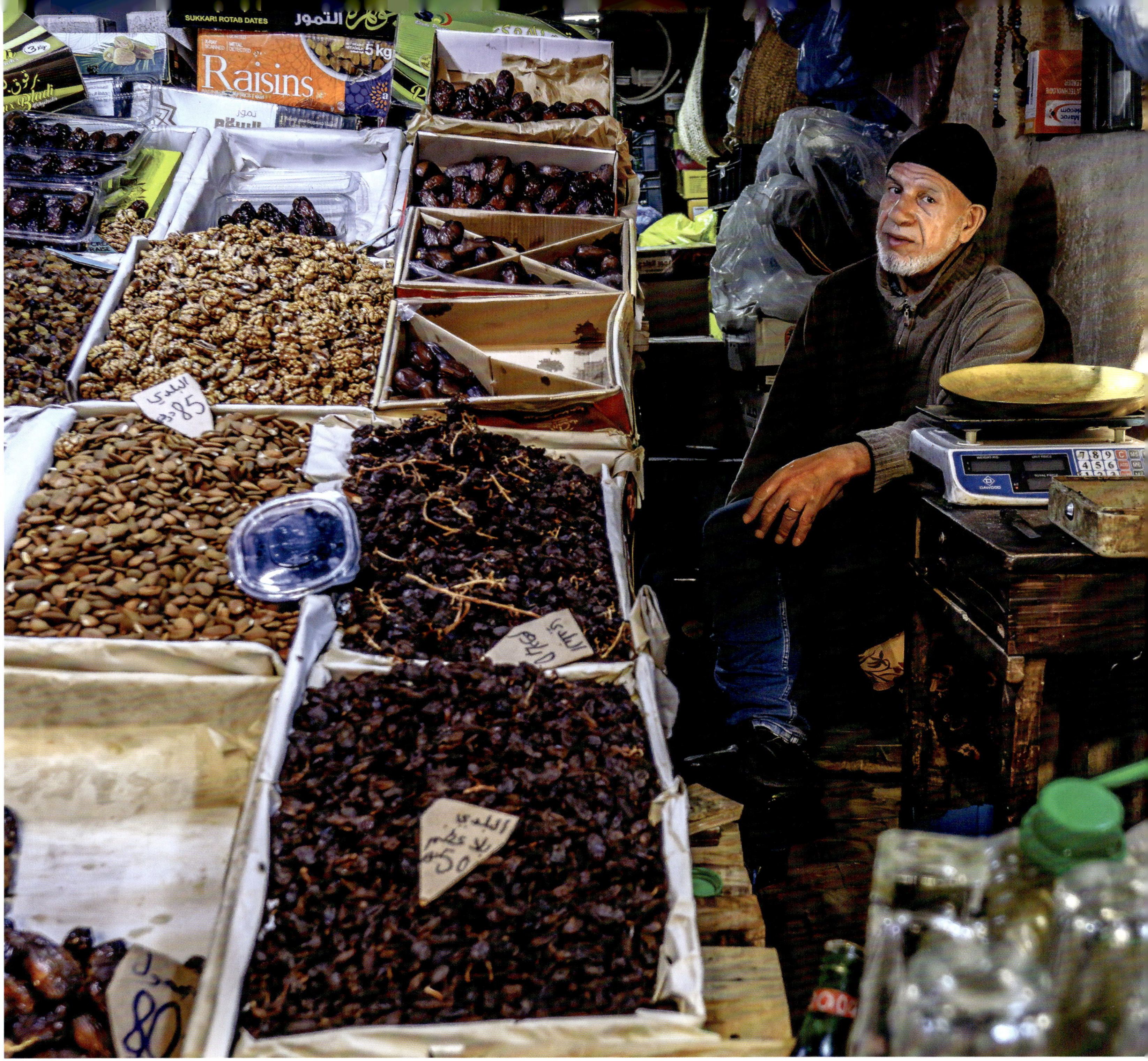


Previous page:
A barber waits for customers in his medina shop.

Woman shopping for dates in the sprawling souks of Fes.

Merchants and customers in the medina. Fes is called the cultural and religious heartland of the nation by many.

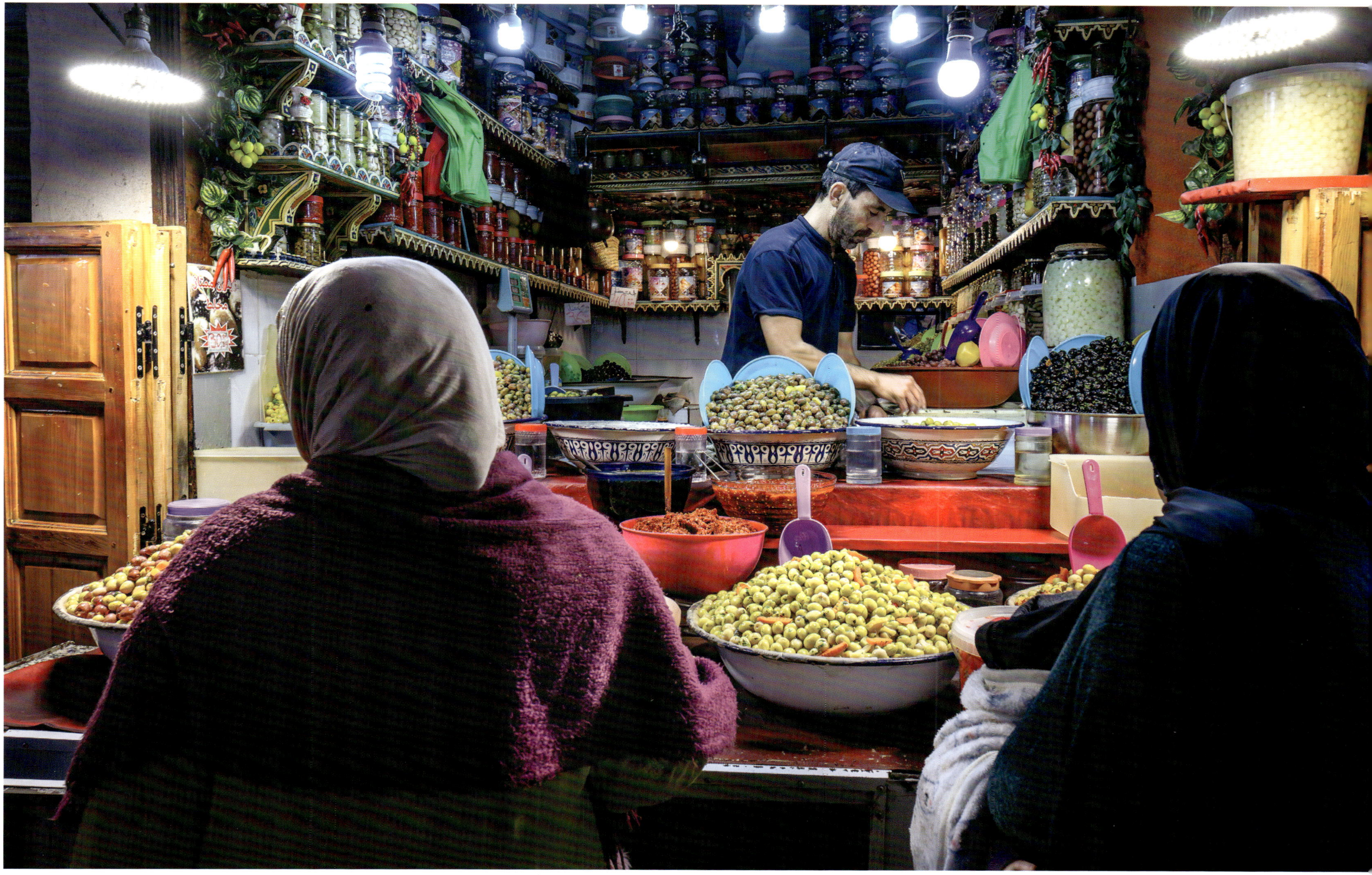

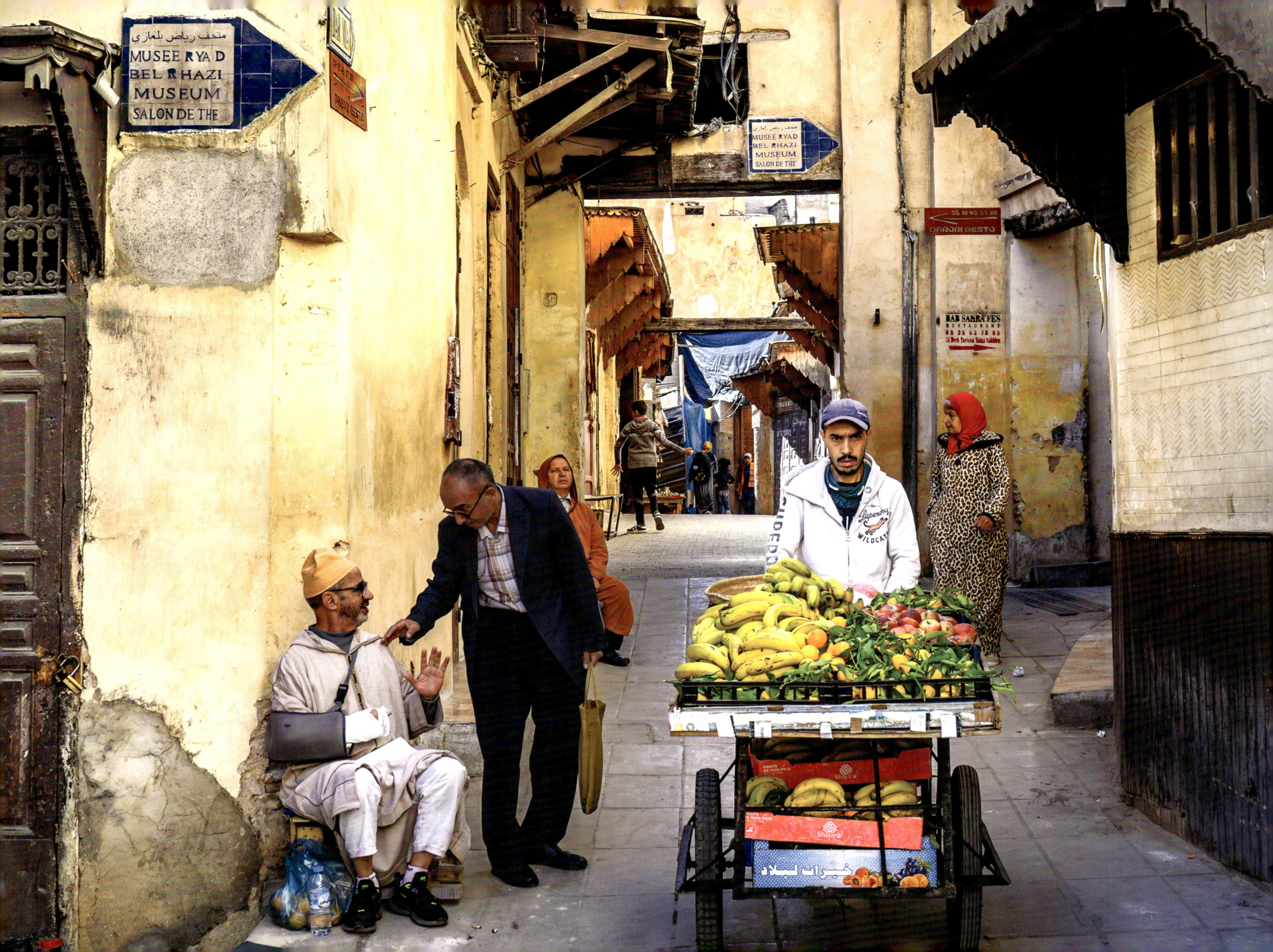
MUSEE RYAD
BEL RHAZI
MUSEUM
SALON DE THE
MUSEE RYAD
BEL RHAZI
MUSEUM
SALON DE THE
BAB SAHRA FES
RESTAURANT

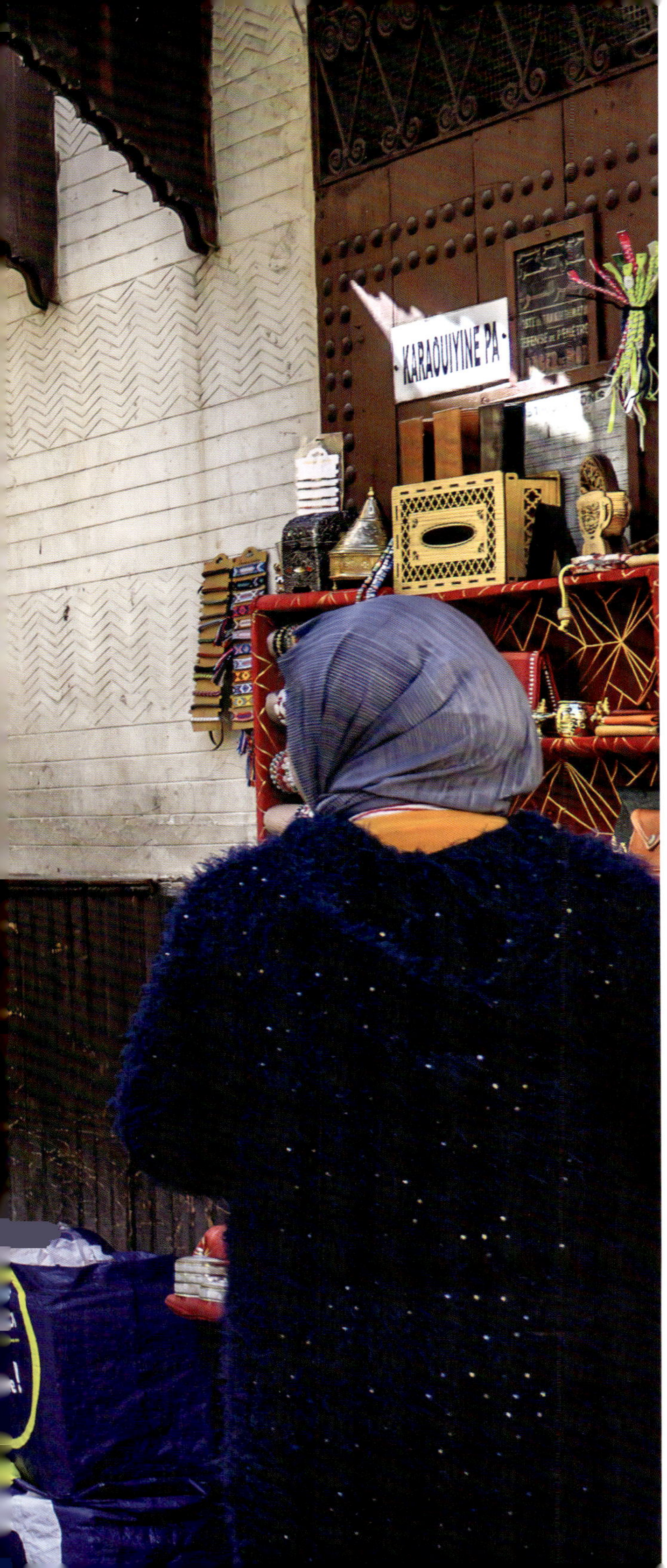
KARAOUIYINE PA

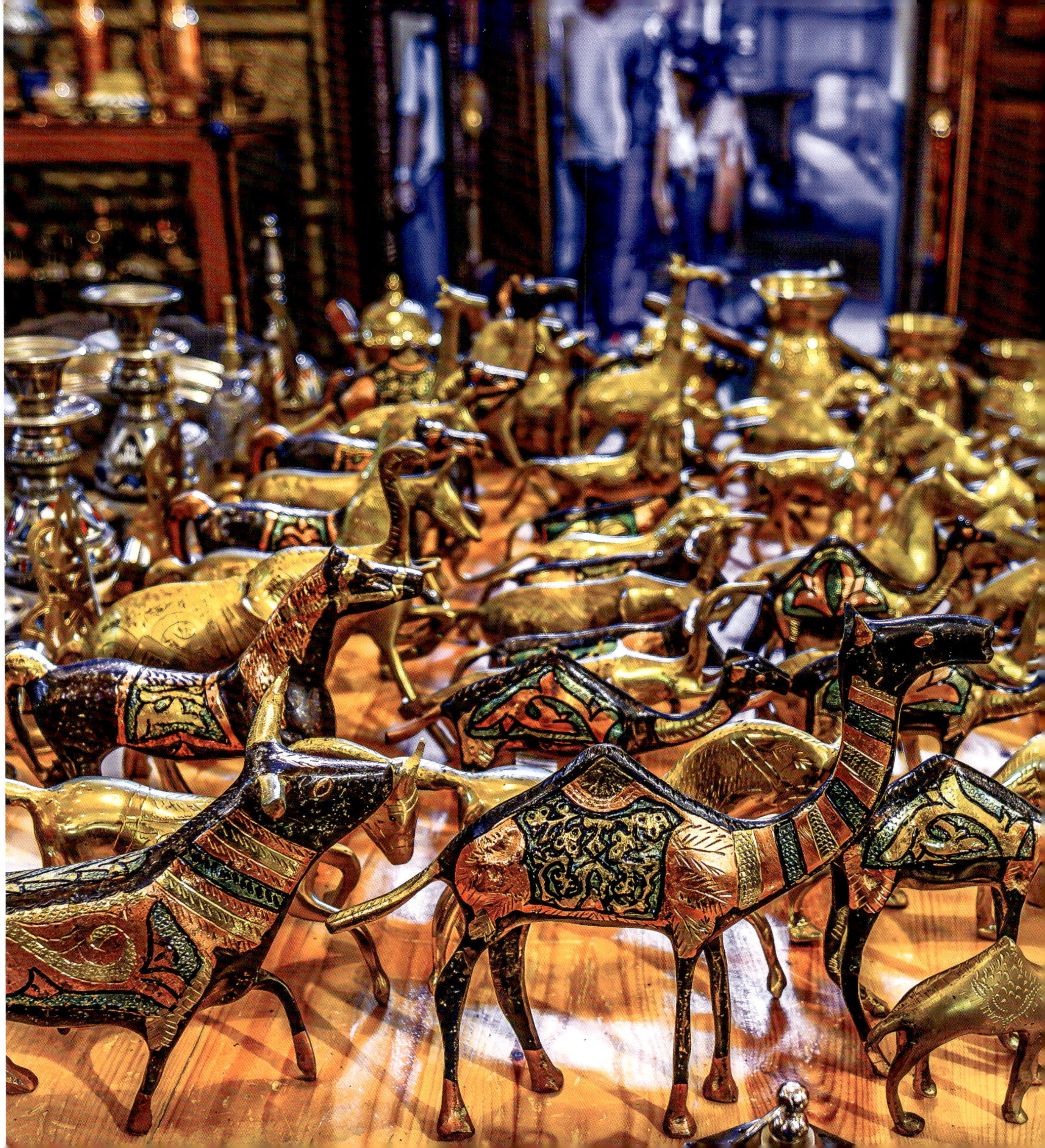

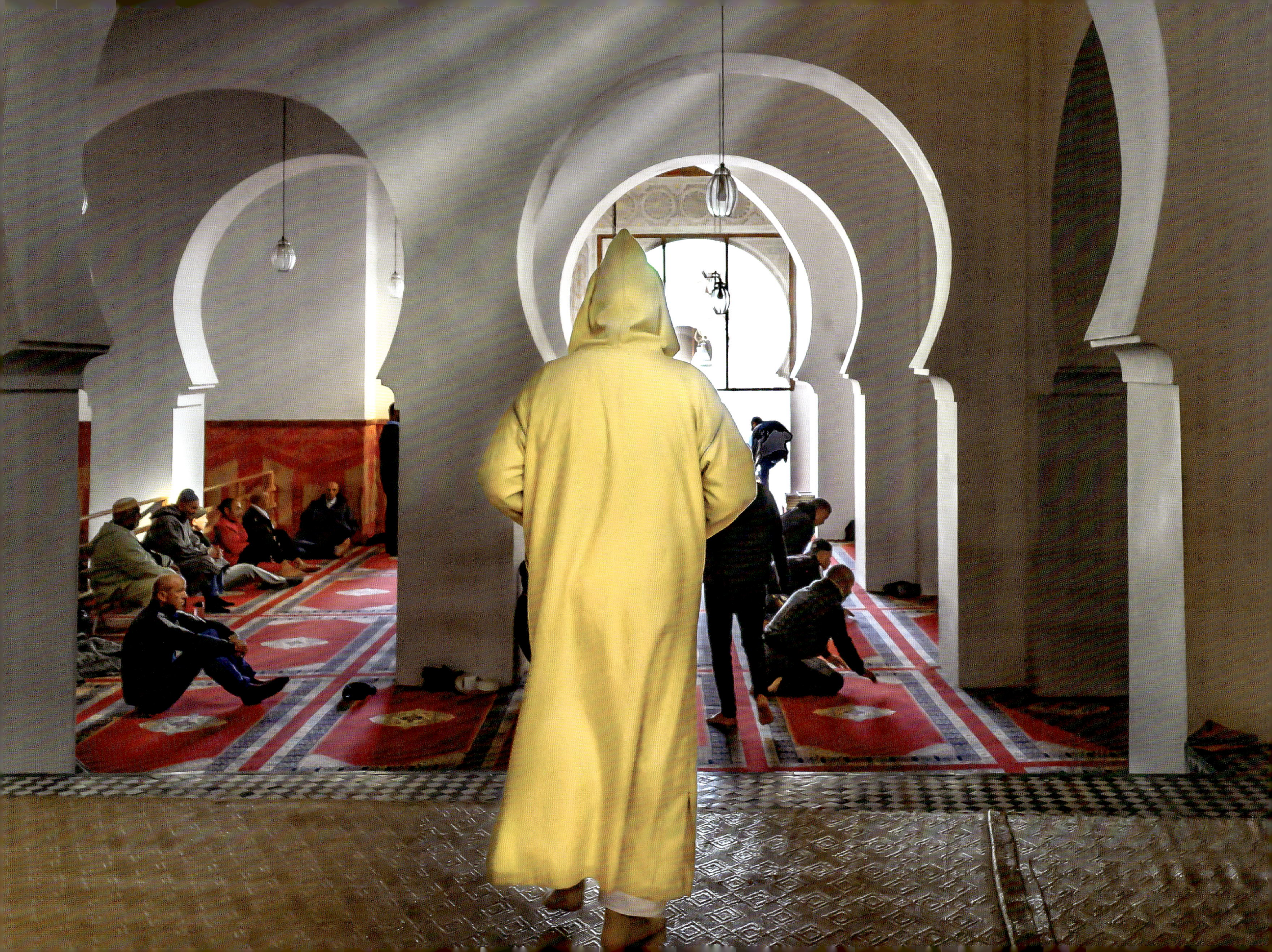

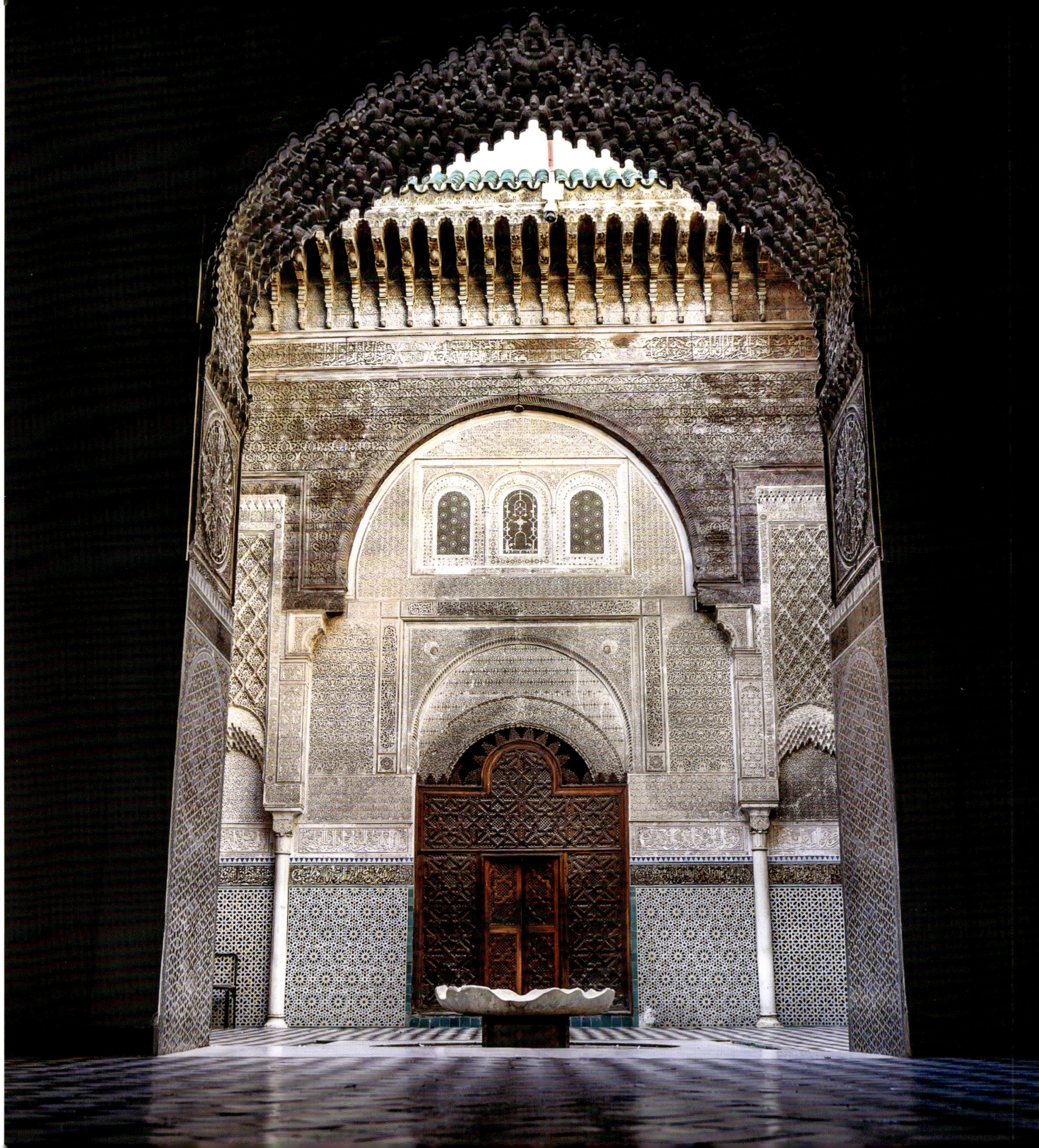

Previous page:
Fresh fruit being delivered in the medina.

Hand crafted figurines.

A man enters a mosque in the medina during prayer.

Inside view of the madrasa educational institution, Medersa Bou Inania, built by the Merinid sultan Bou Inan between 1351 and 1357.

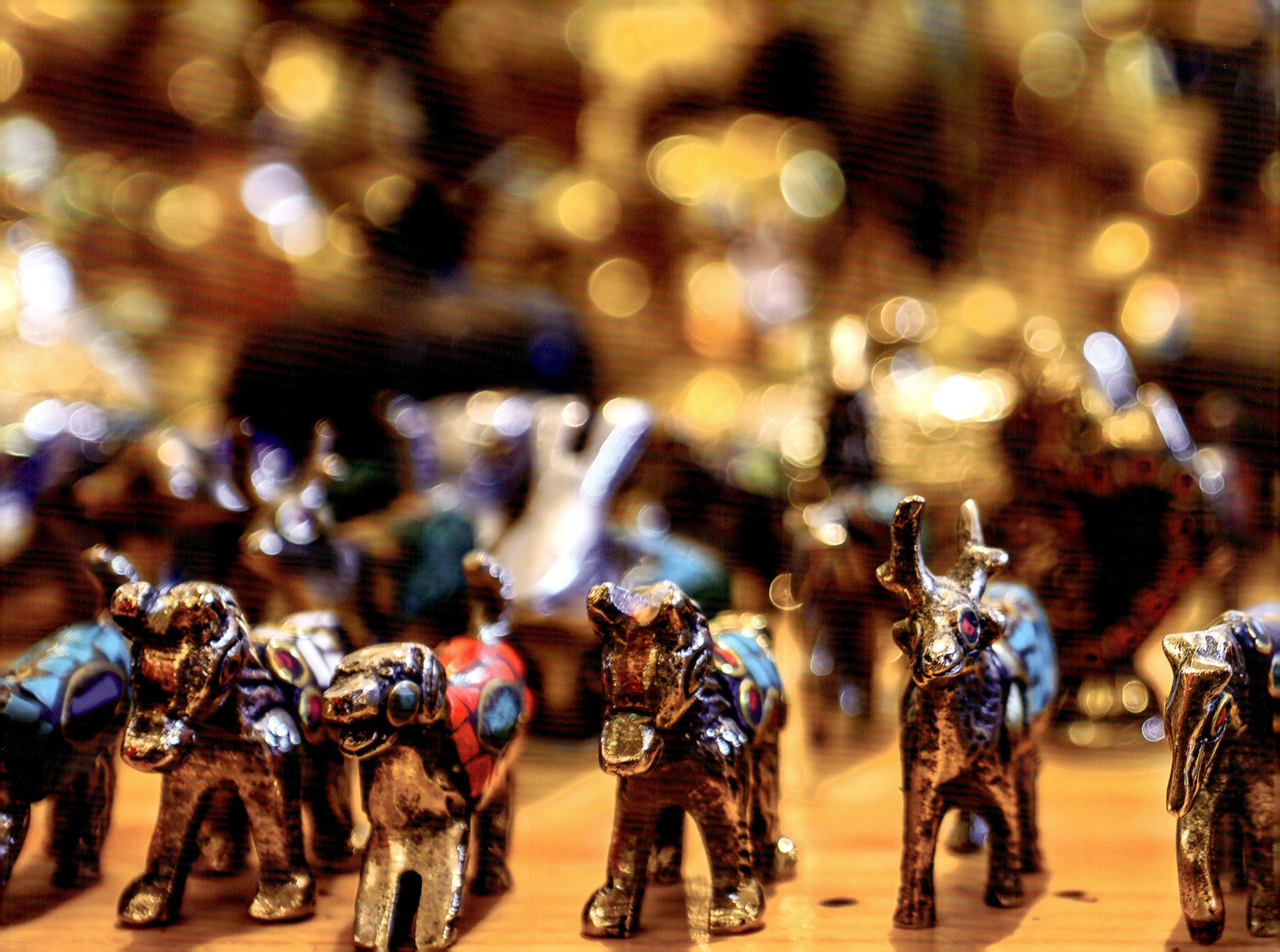

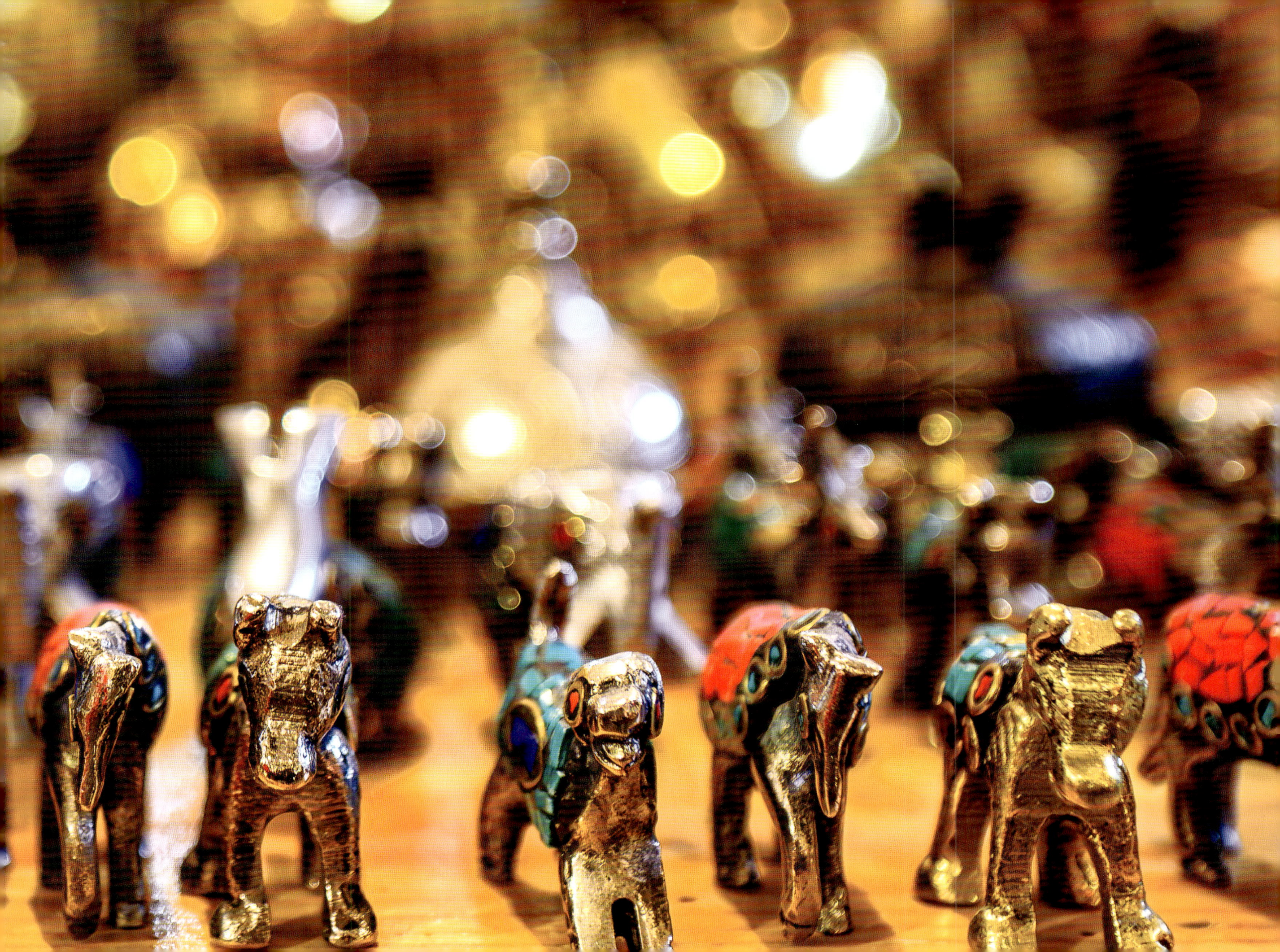

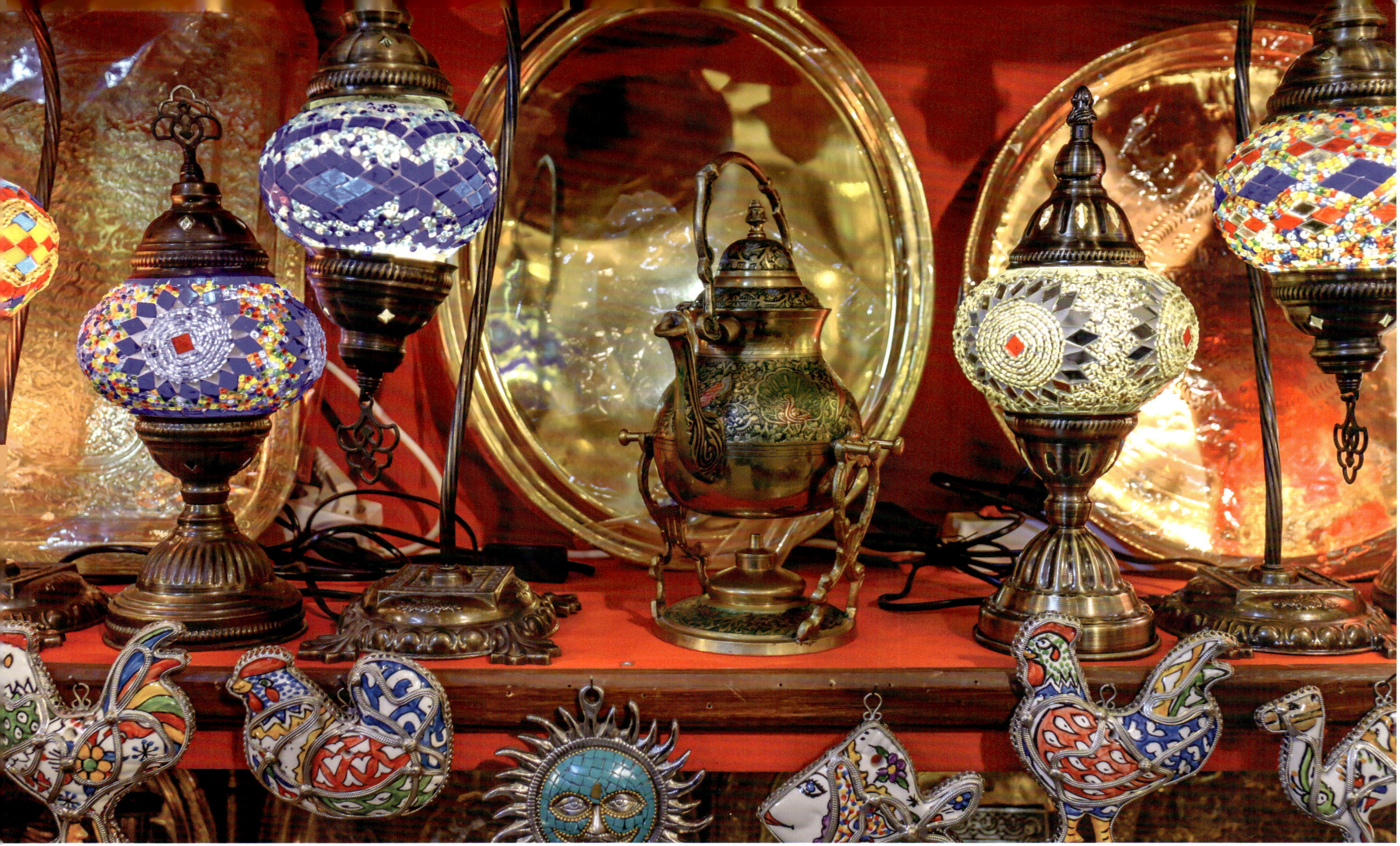

Previous page:
Figurines on display.

Shining lamps and shimmering teapots for sale.

A woman walking through a medina alley near the Riad Belghazi Museum.

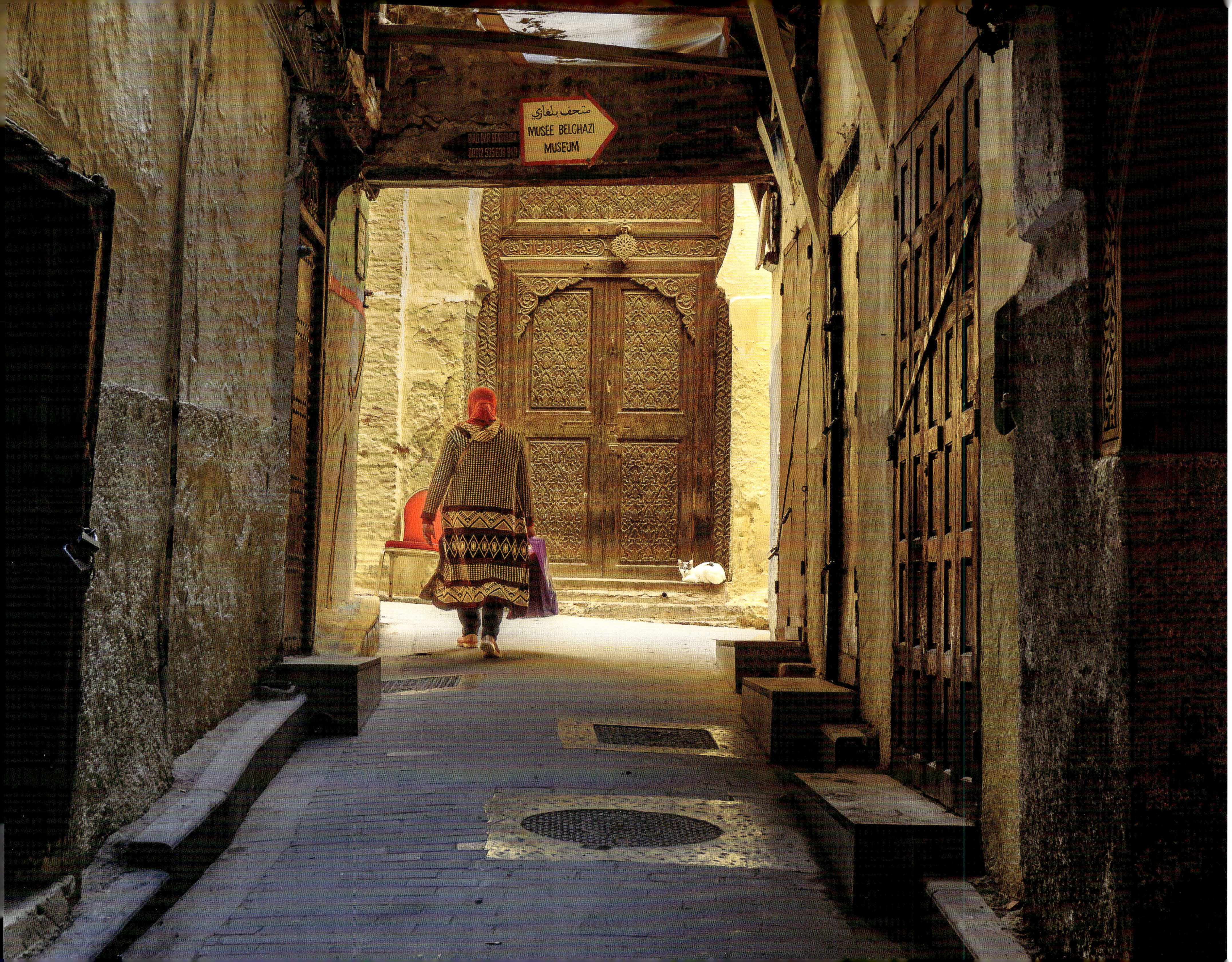
متحف بلغازي
MUSEE BELGHAZI
MUSEUM

# FORTIFIED KSAR AND MOVIE LOCATION

It may not take more than a few days to explore Ait Benhaddou, but it is sure to leave a lifelong impression. Consisting of buildings constructed from rammed earth, adobe straw, bricks and wood sometime in the 11th century, Ait Benhaddou was first developed as a critical stop on the trans-Saharan trade route between Sudan and the imperial cities of Marrakech, Fes and Meknes.

The site is surrounded by defensive walls and towers and was home to Amazigh families for centuries. The fortress is reinforced by angular towers that served as protection near its only two entry points. Inside is a maze of alleys, homes and old buildings. Once home to up to some 80 Amazigh families, there are only a handful of inhabitants who still live and work in artist workshops and small tourist shops.

Walking through the Ksar is like a journey into the past. Long winding stairs and alleys lead to the top of the hill where visitors gather to watch the sun set in the shadow of an old and crumbling grain silo. Because the materials used to build the site break down over time, there is little left of the original structures that were replaced and restored over time. Its preservation is helped by funds generated by being a UNESCO World Heritage Site—and from its value as a unique movie location.

The list of films shot at Ait Benhaddou is long and includes, *The Mummy, Jesus of Nazareth, Gladiator, Lawrence of Arabia*, and the television series *Game of Thrones*.

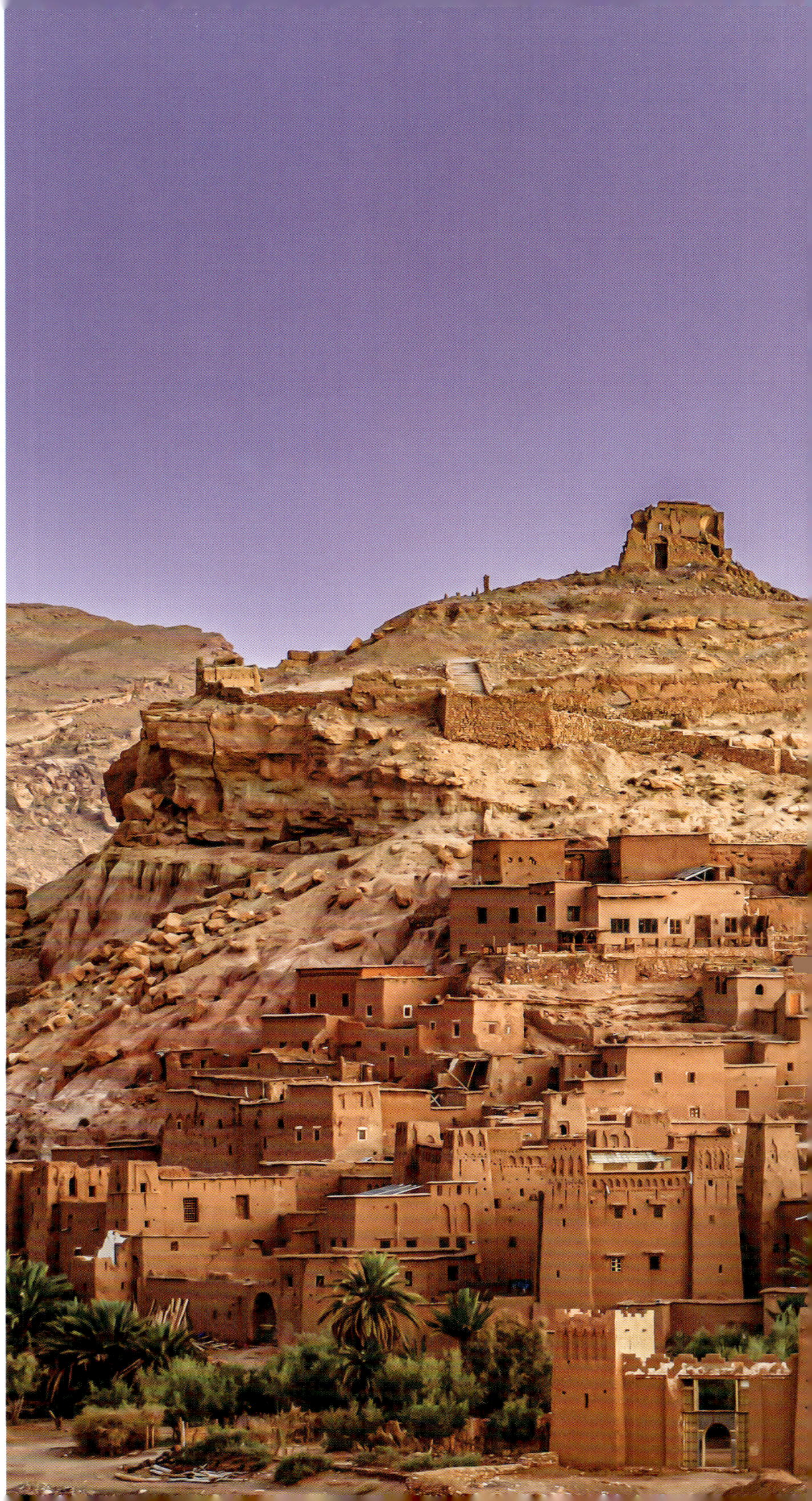

# EPIC AIT BENHADDOU

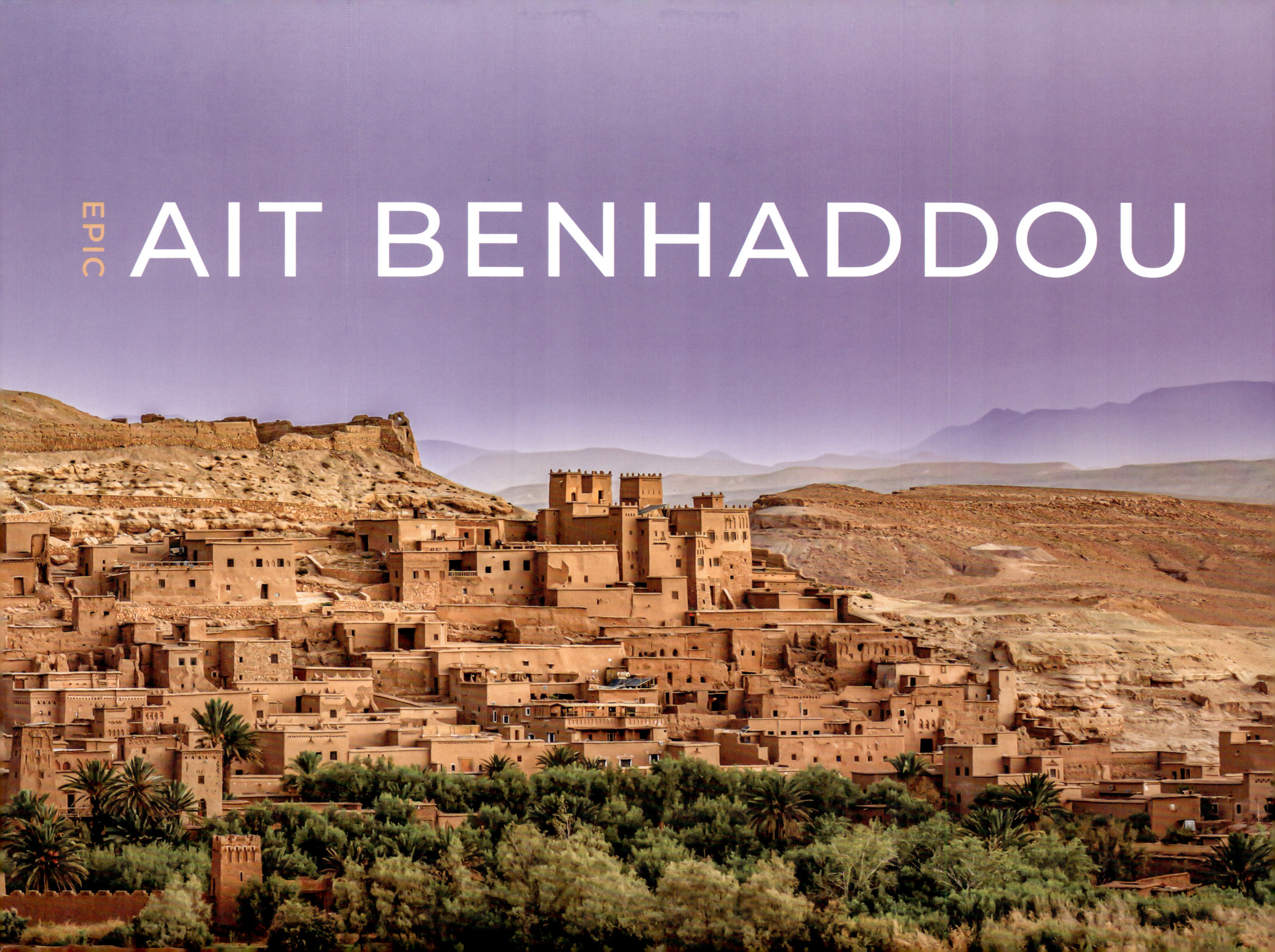

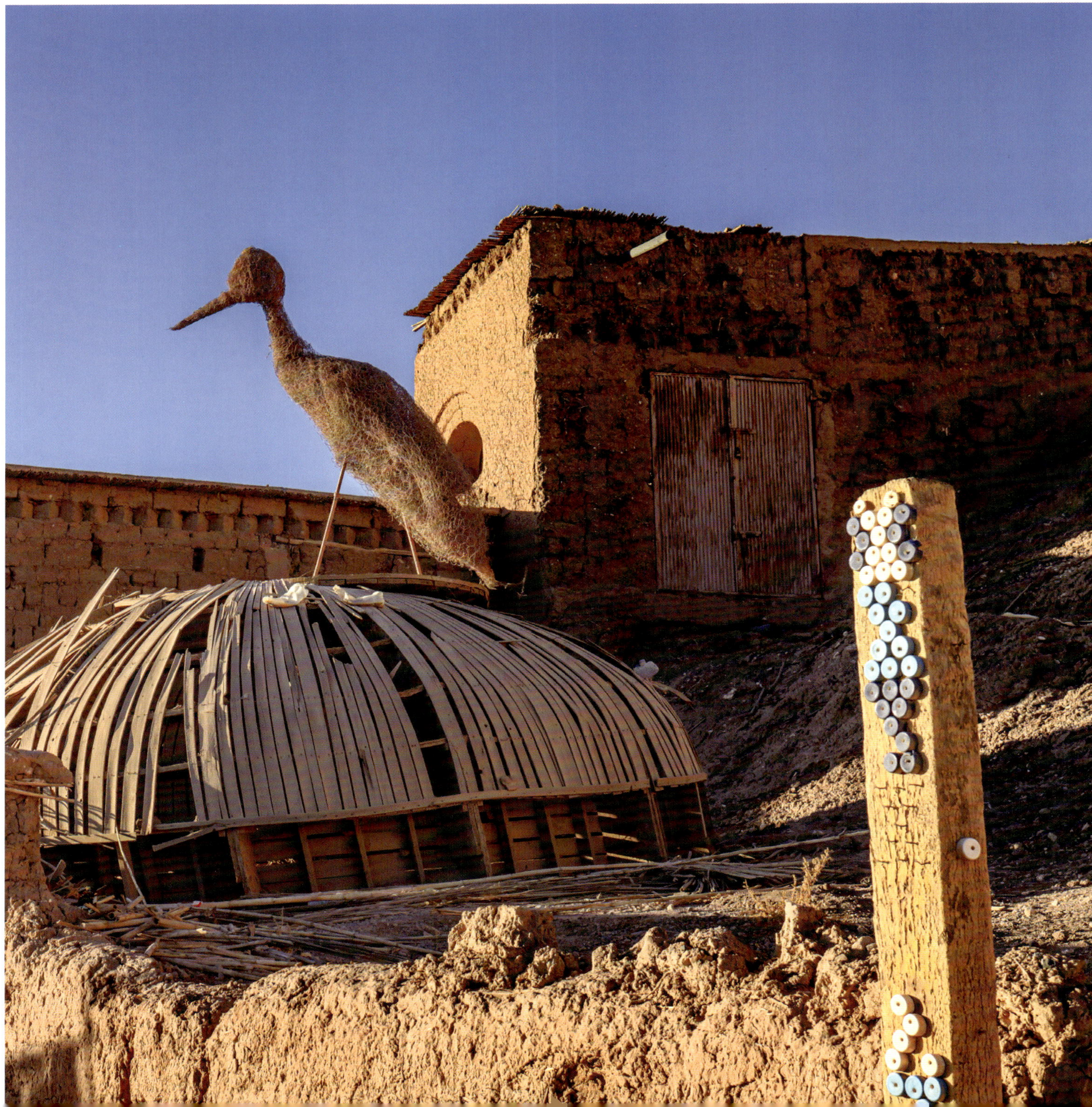

Wire pelican on the roof of a shop.

Man riding a horse through the village.

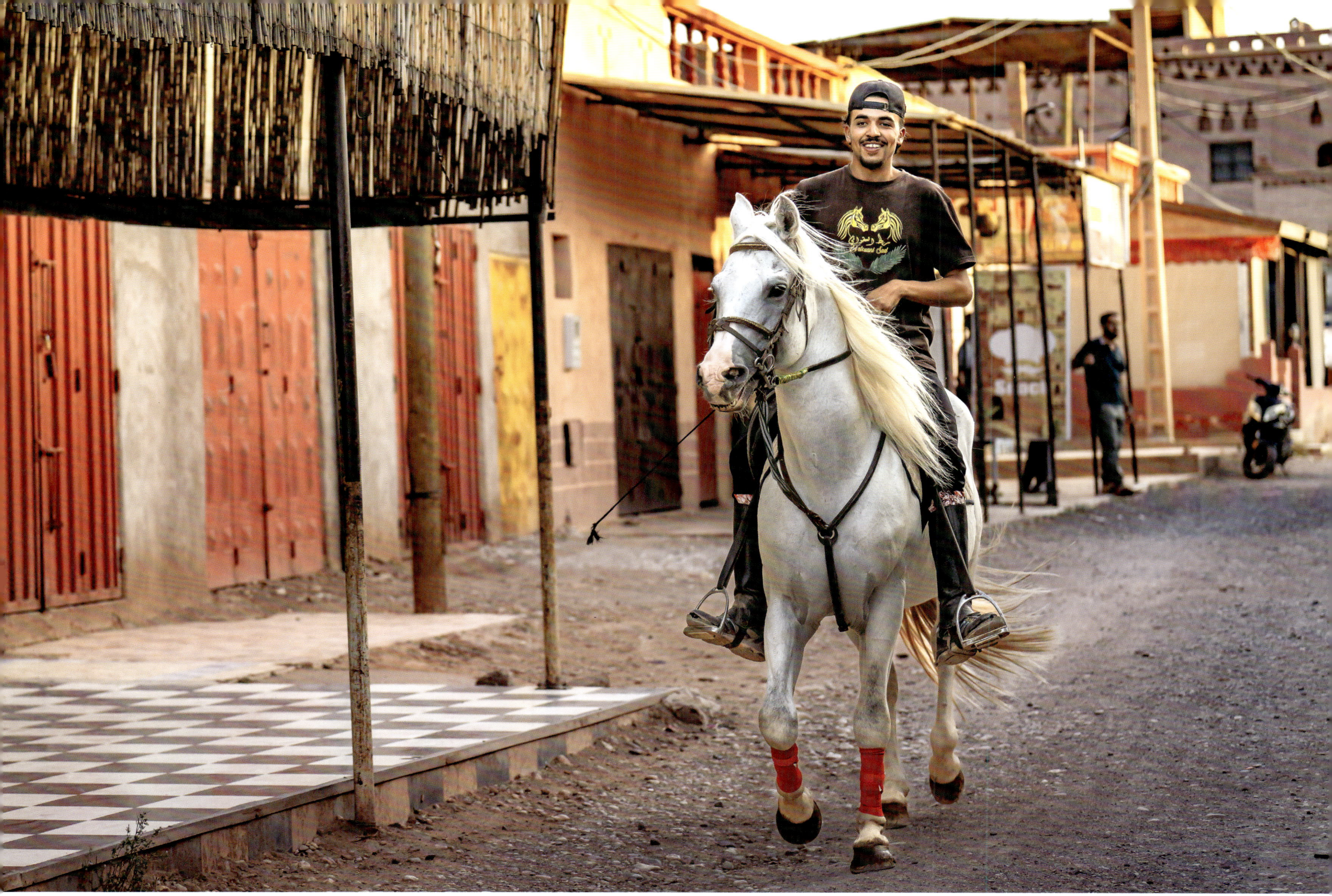

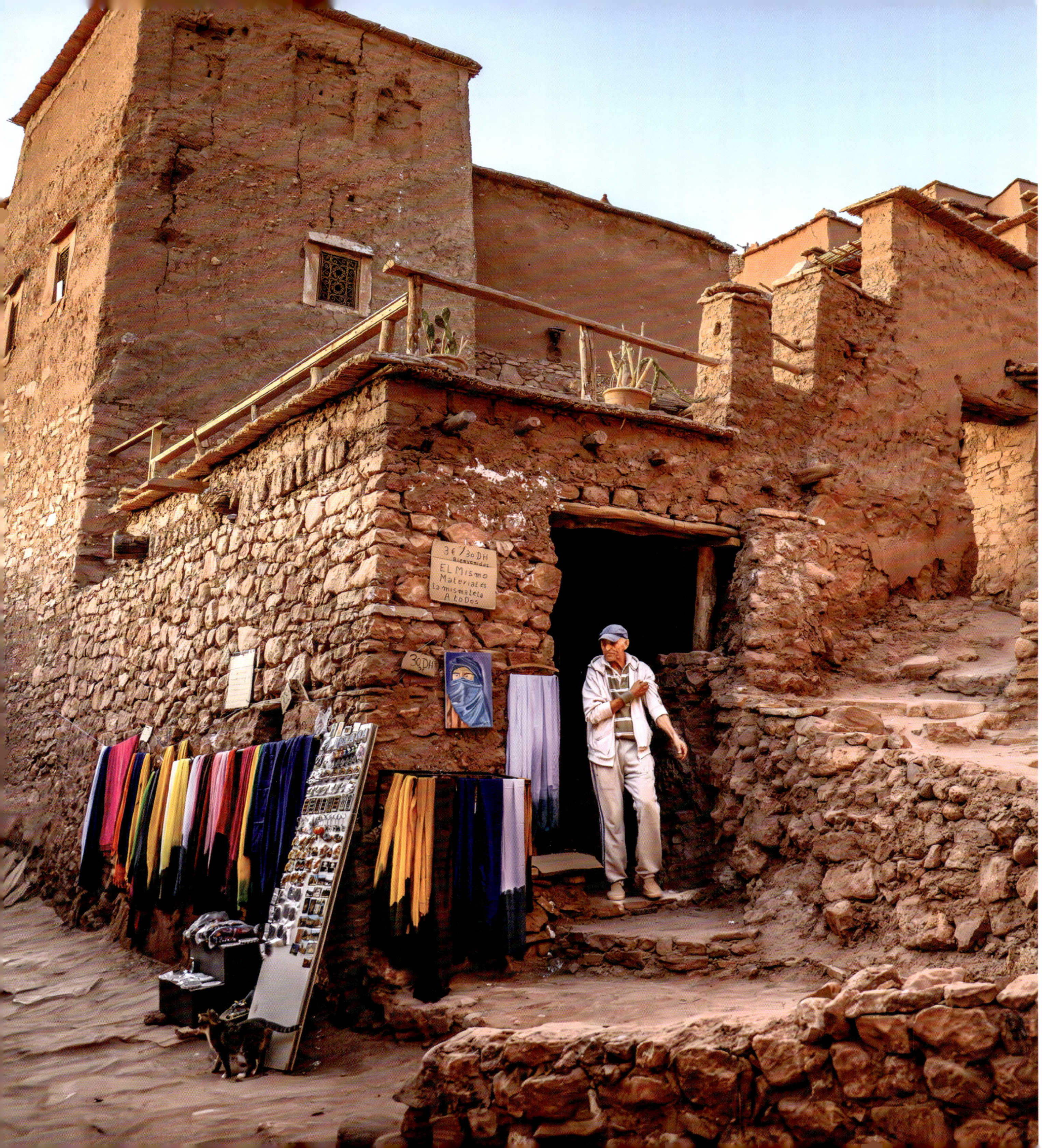
3€/30DH
EL Mismo
Materiales
la mismatela
A toDos
30DH

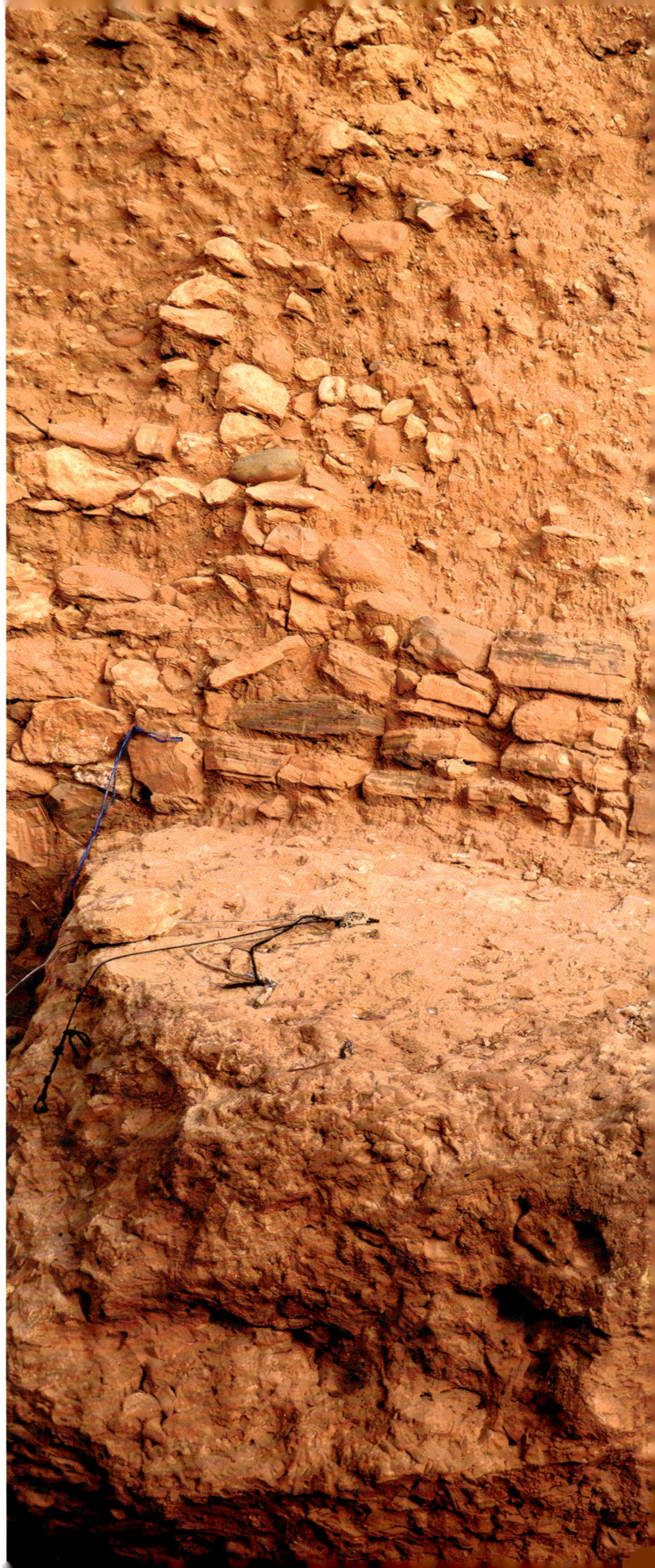

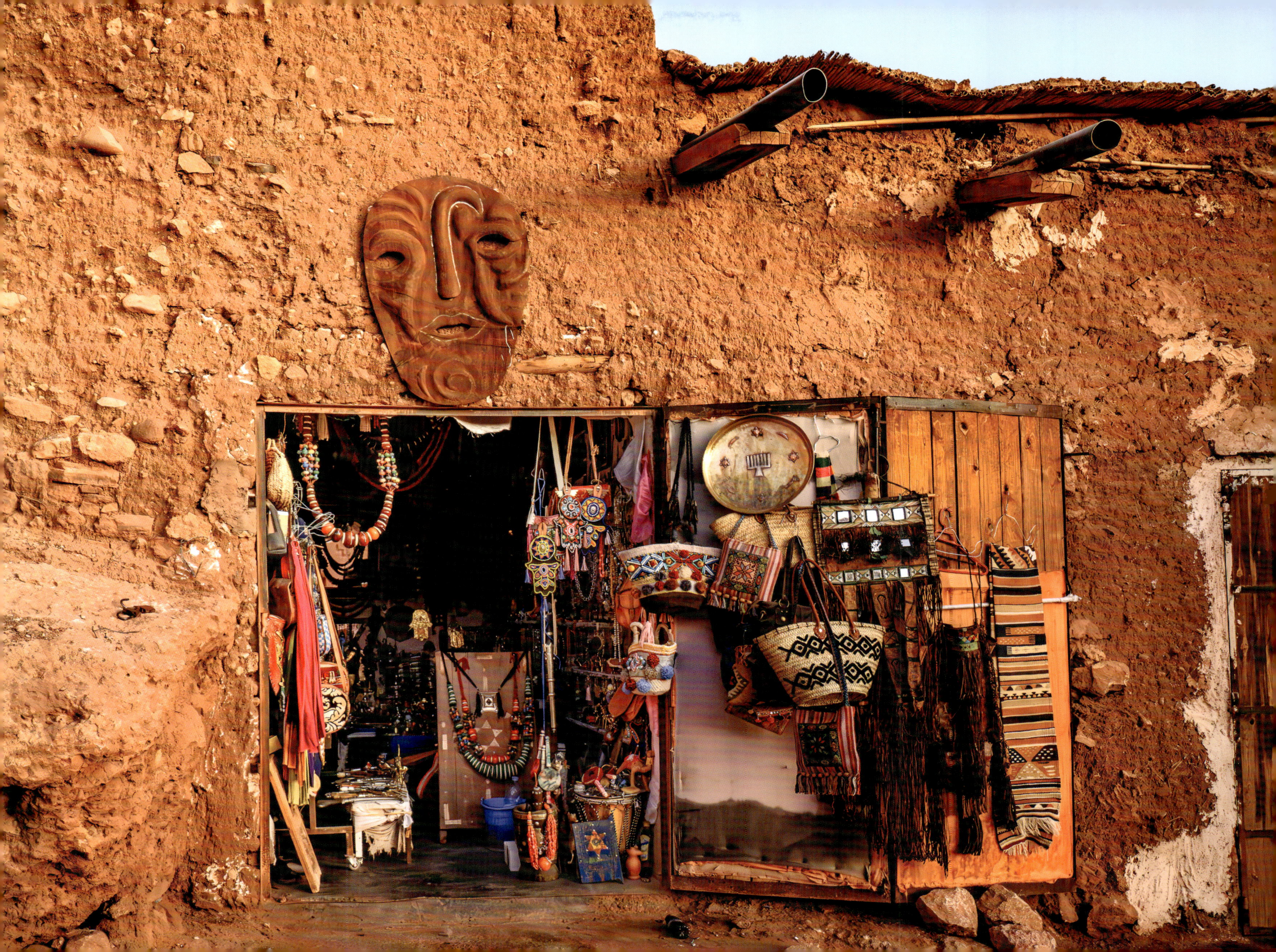

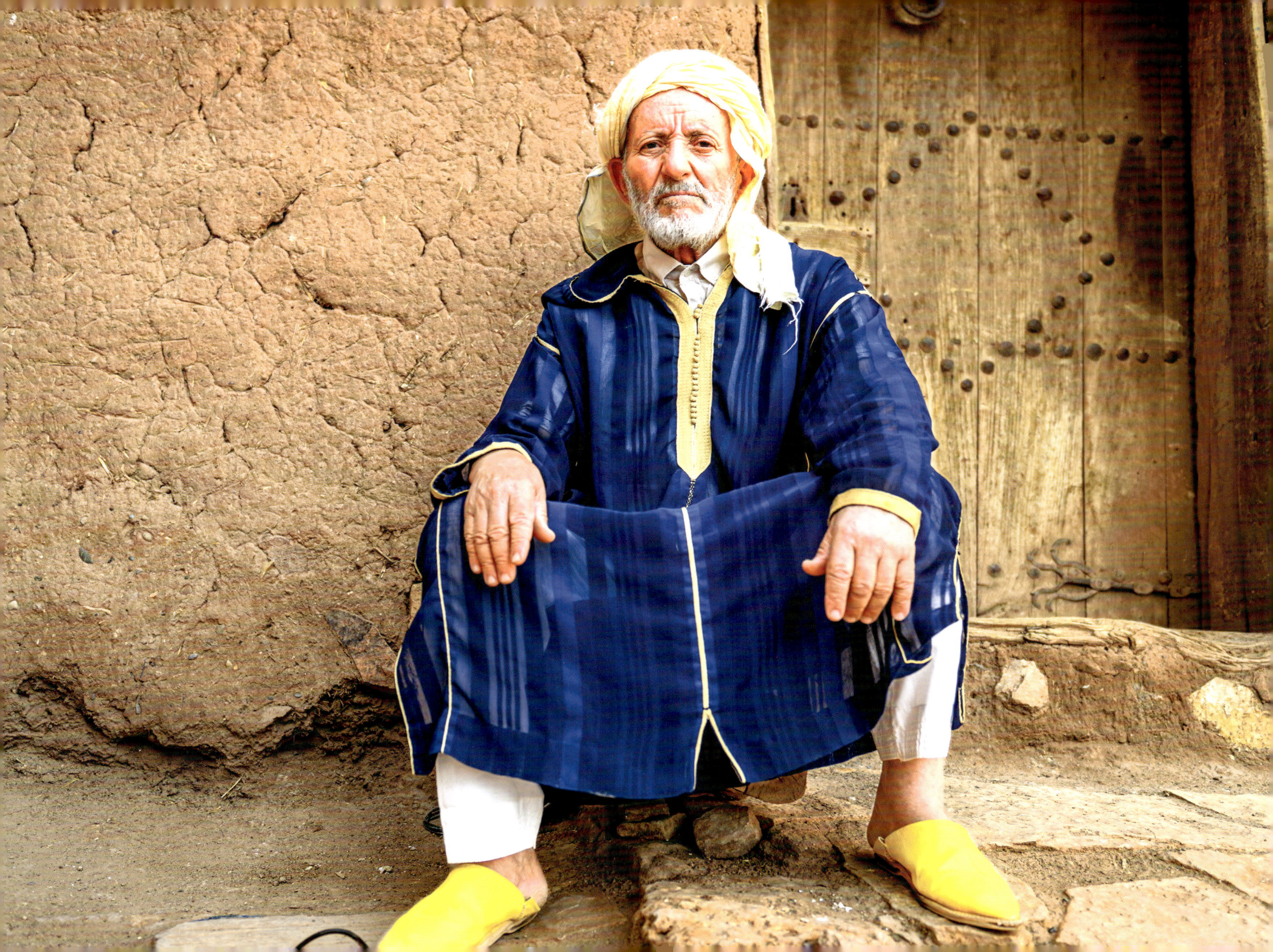

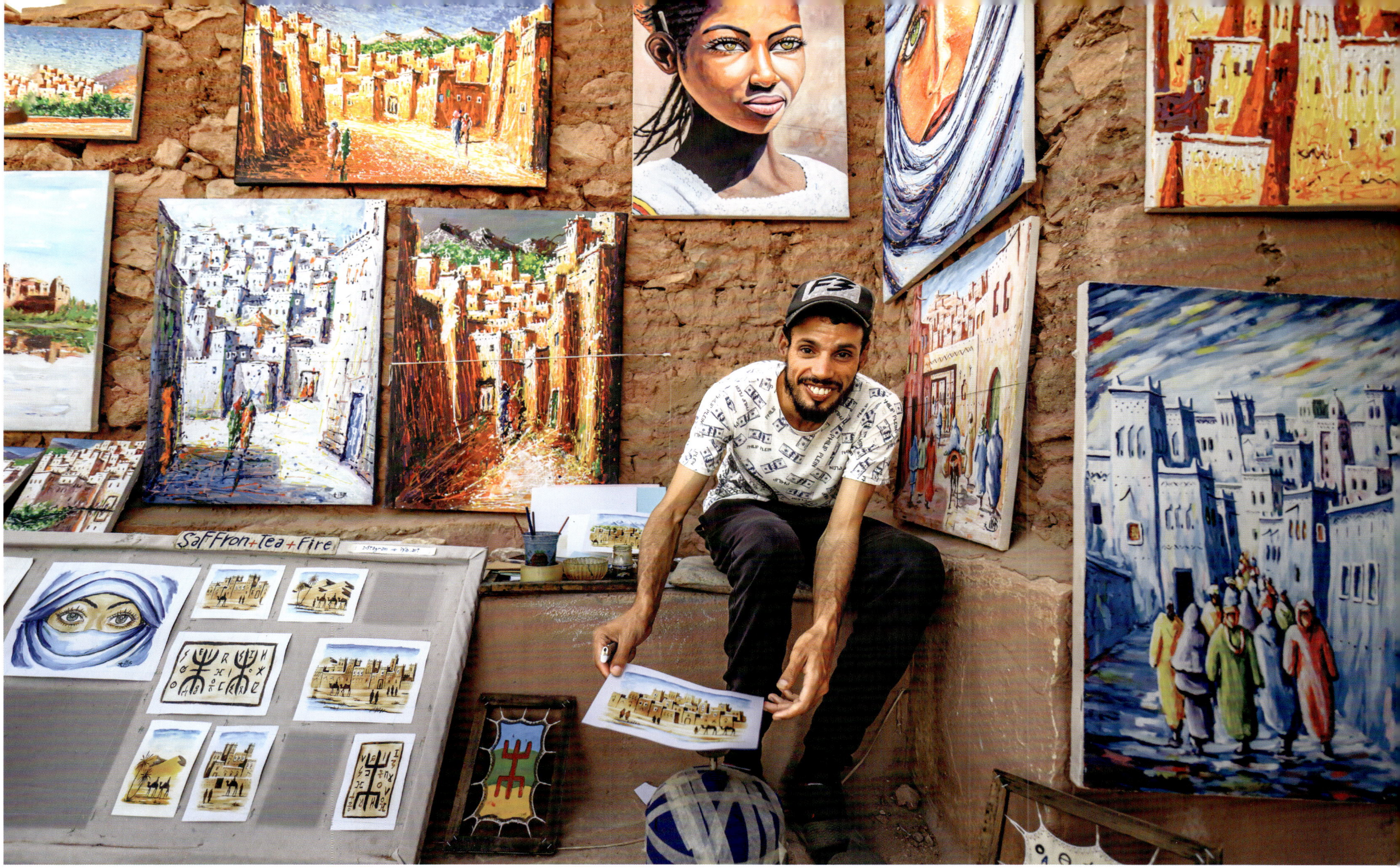


Previous page:
An artist who lives in the Ksar outside of his shop.

Kasbah owner Mohamed Jamal Edi sits in front of the Kasbah entrance.

Artist selling work at his shop inside the Ksar.

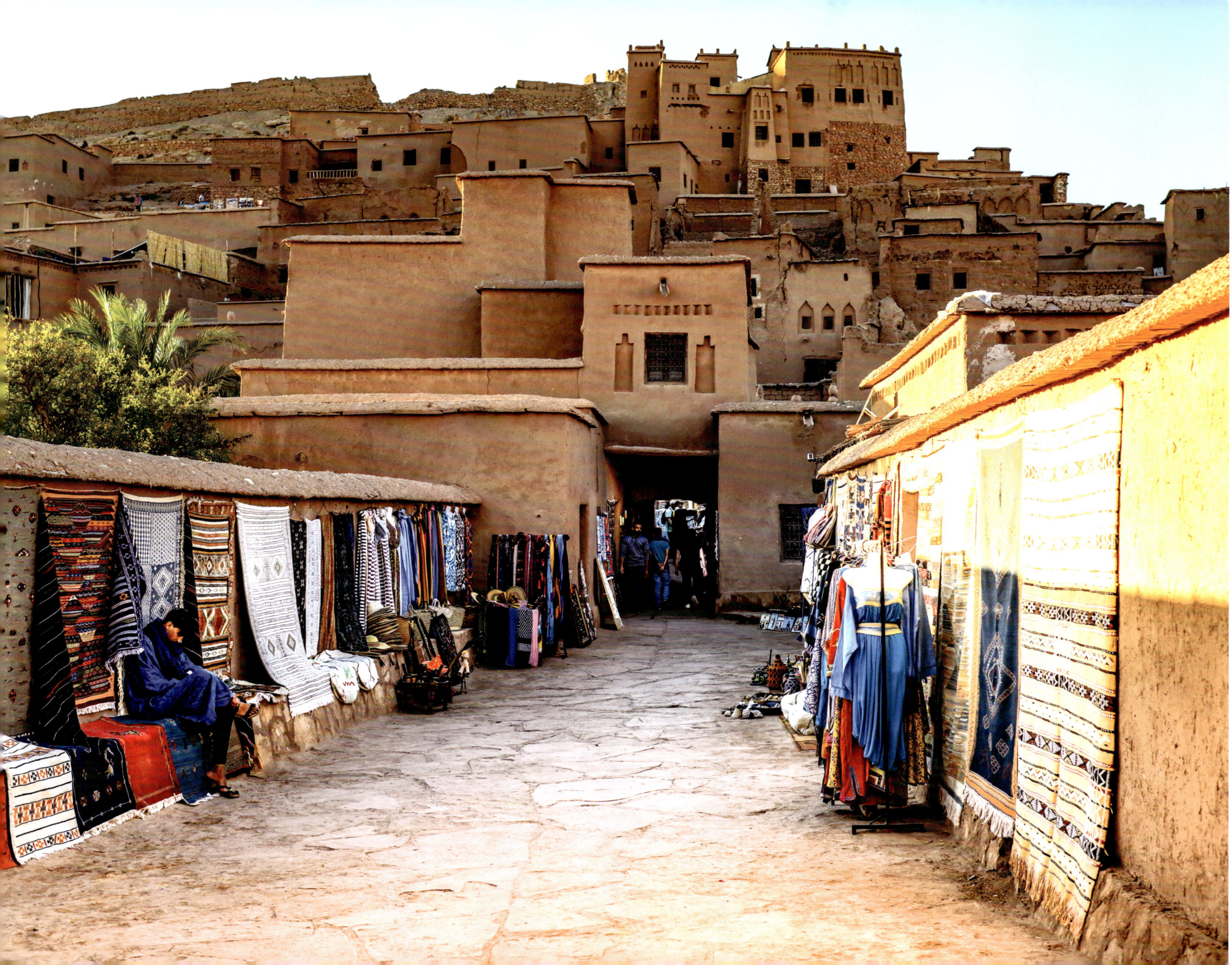

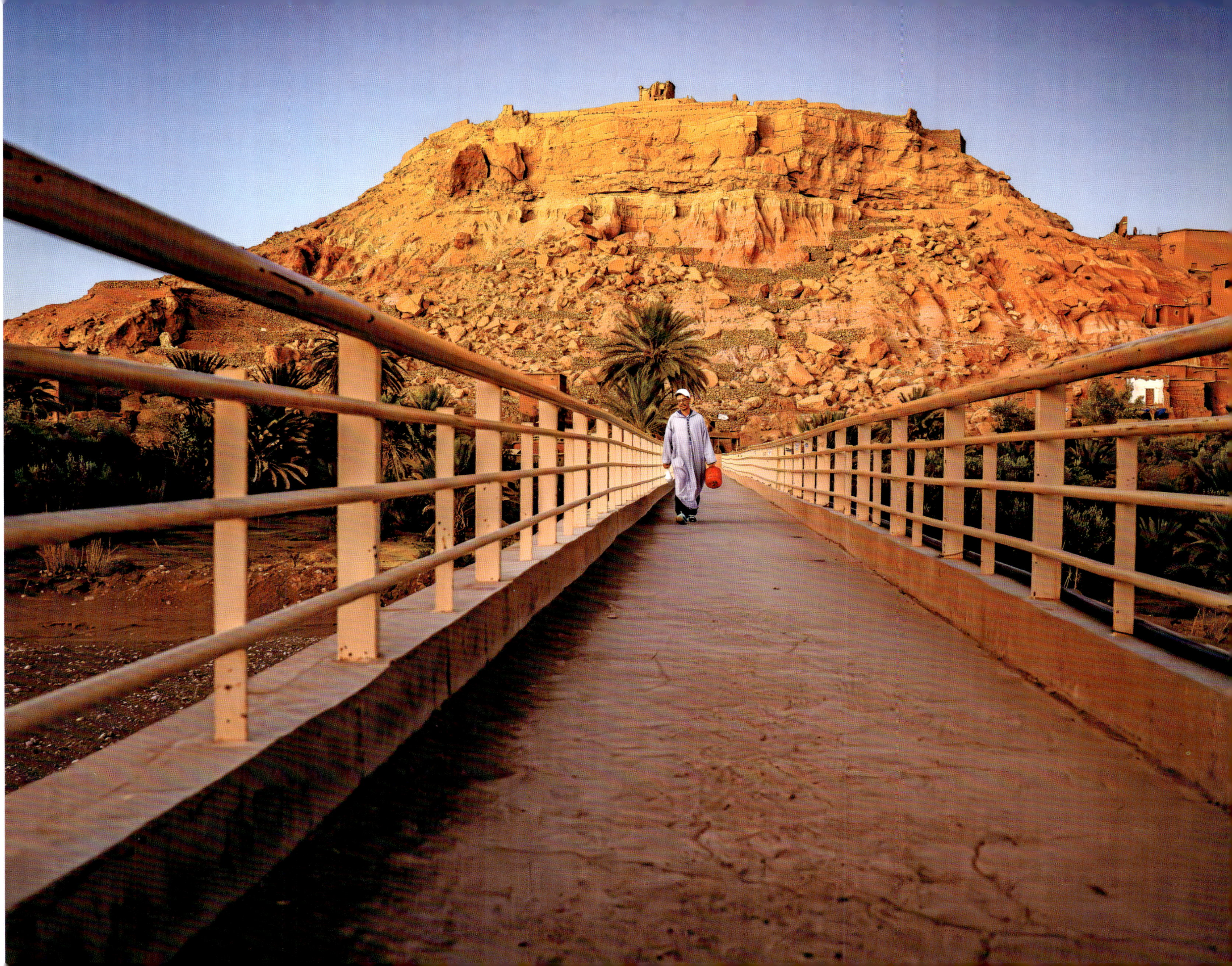

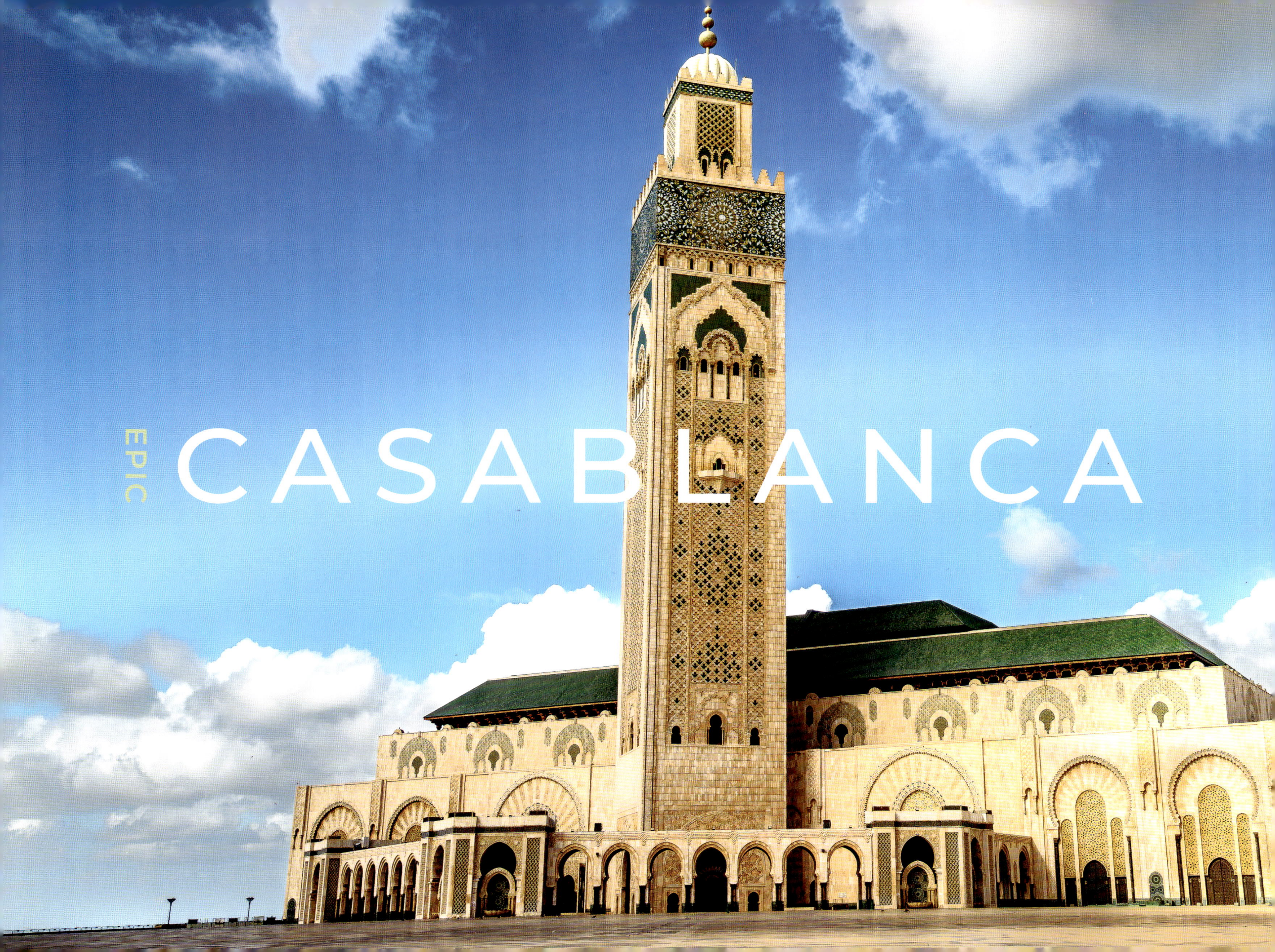
EPIC
CASABLANCA

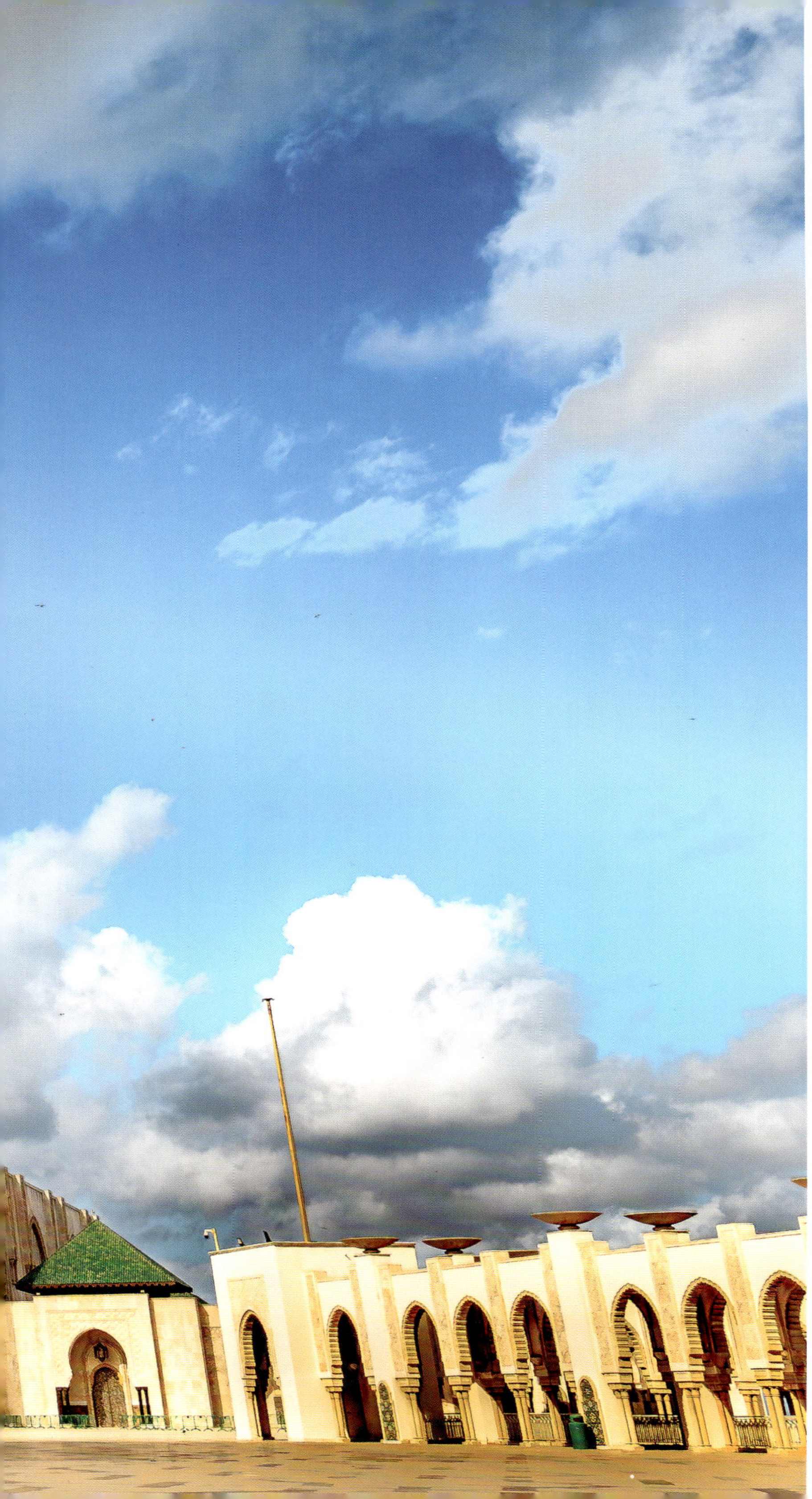

# CENTER OF COMMERCE AND HOME TO THE HASSAN II MOSQUE

The largest city in Morocco, Casablanca, is the country's economic and business center. It is located on the Atlantic Coast, in central-western Morocco. It has a population of nearly four million and is the eighth largest Arab city in the world. While the city's airport, Mohammed V International, receives most of the international flights into Morocco, it is not seen as a typical tourist destination. But it does include the breathtaking Hassan II Mosque, the second largest functioning mosque in Africa. The mosque was completed in 1993, and was designed by French architect, Michel Pinseau. Its construction was commissioned by King Hassan II and built by Moroccan artisans.

King Hassan II commissioned the project to honor King Mohammed V, who died in 1961. When summoning artisans from across the Kingdom, King Hassan II announced that he wished the mosque to be a building all of Morocco would be proud of. Work on the mosque began in July 1986, and over the seven years it took for construction, thousands of workers labored day and night, and some 10,000 artisans and craftsman participated in building the stunning masterpiece.

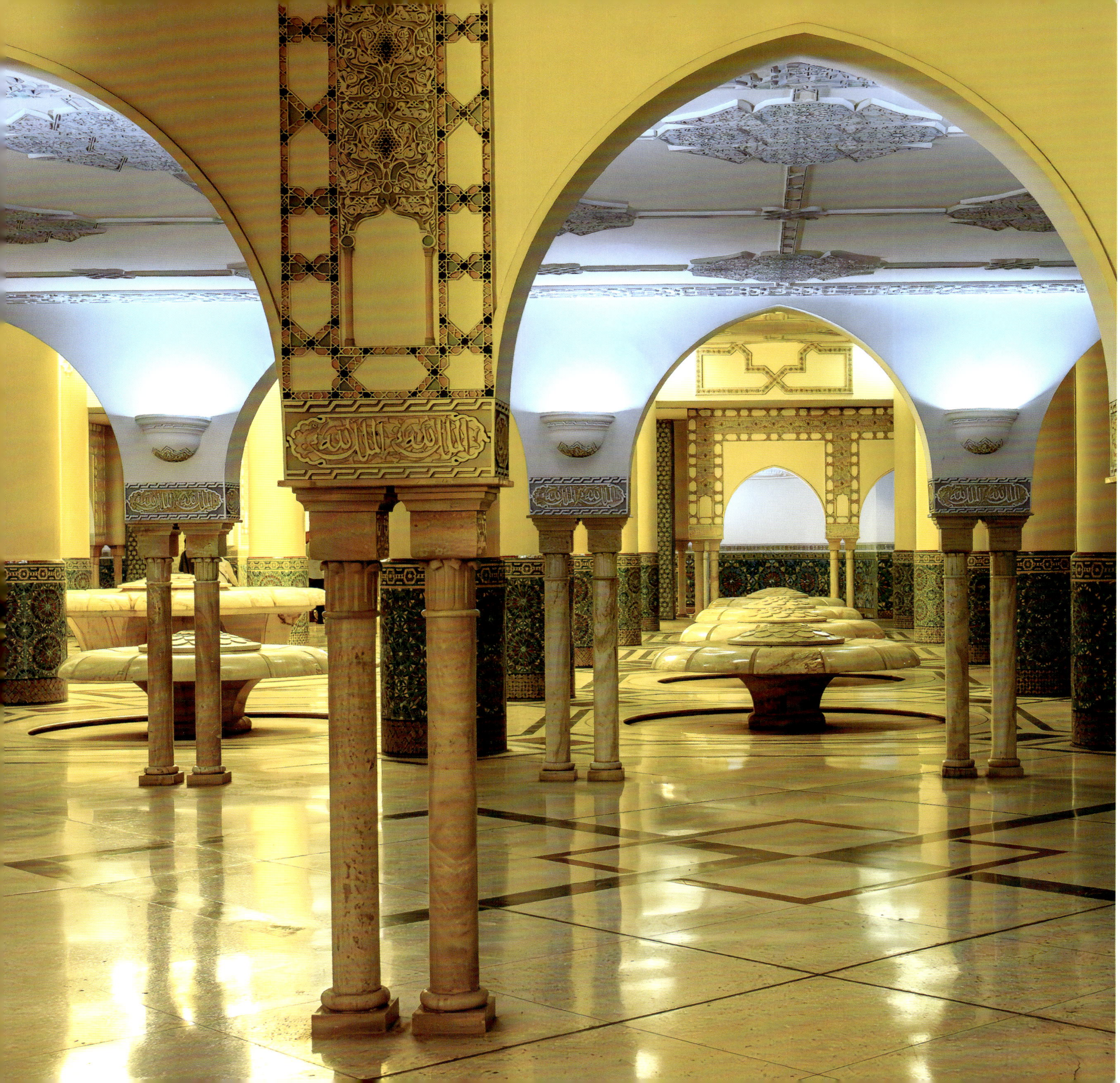

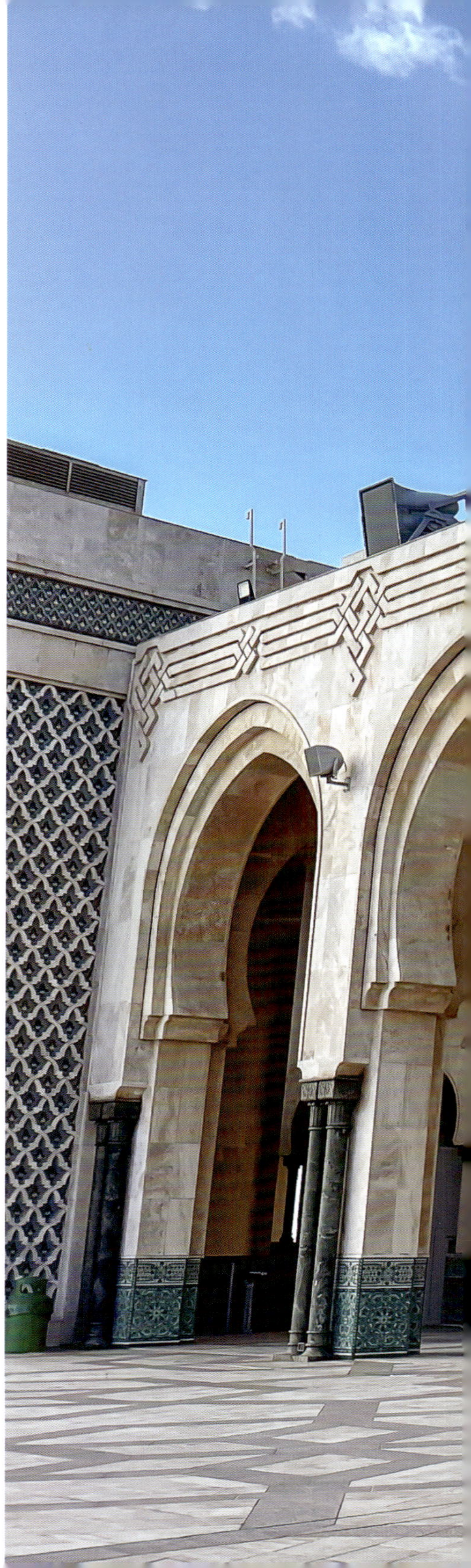

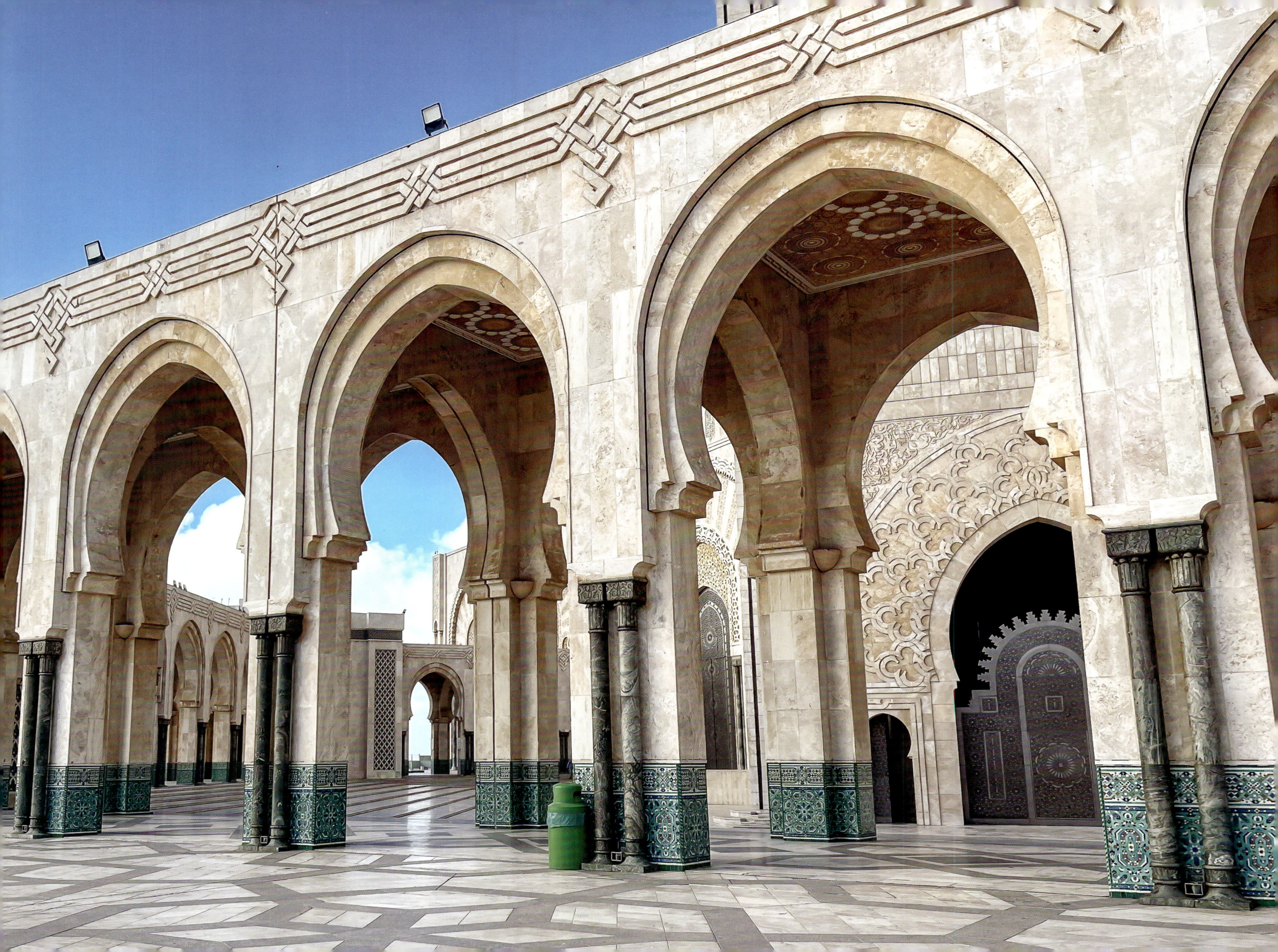

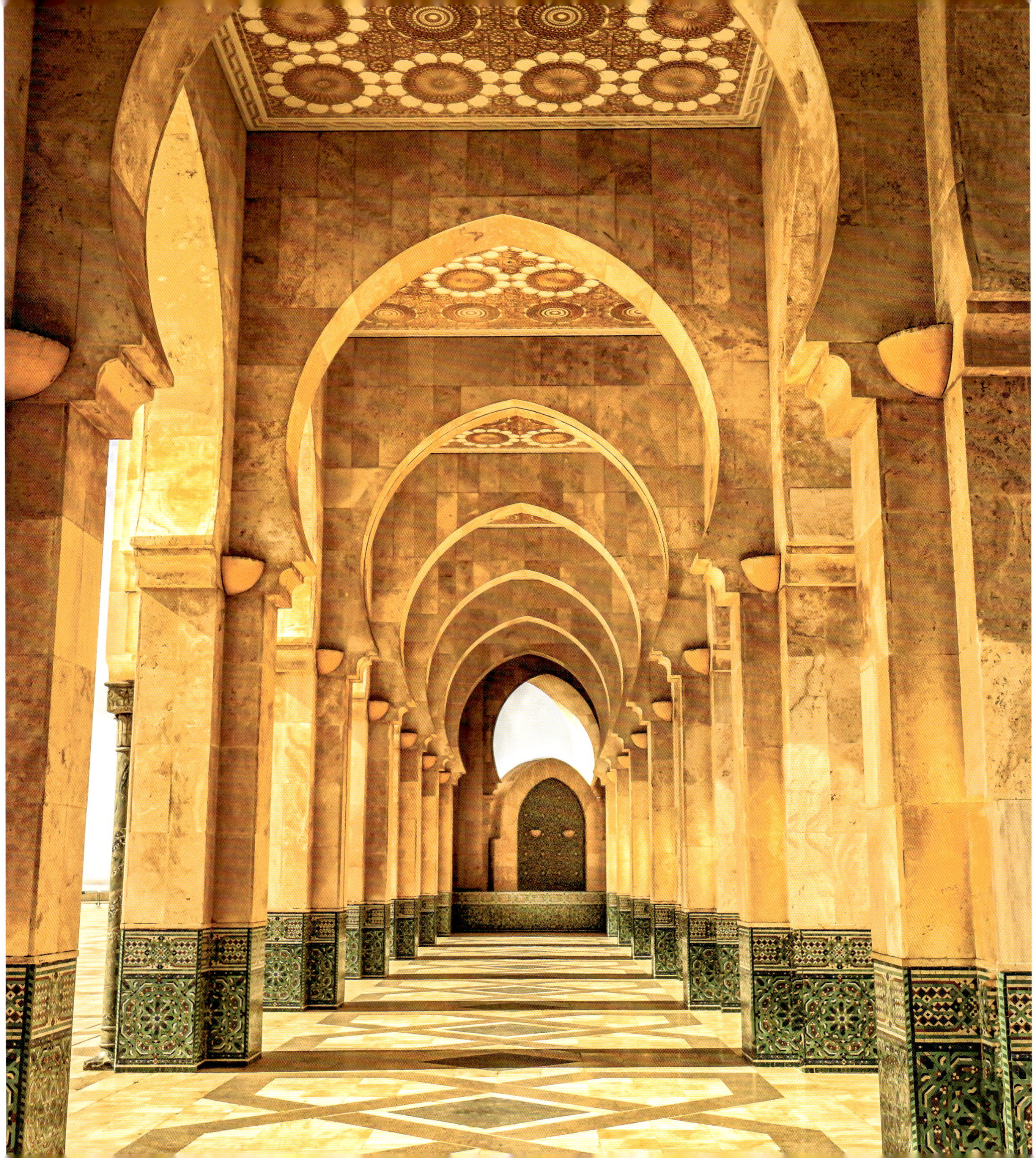

Previous page:
Lower-level Ablution Hall. The ablution hall houses marble fountains that represent lotus flowers and there are separate areas for men and women.

Outside columns. Columns form an archway of stone.

Interior of Hassan II Mosque.

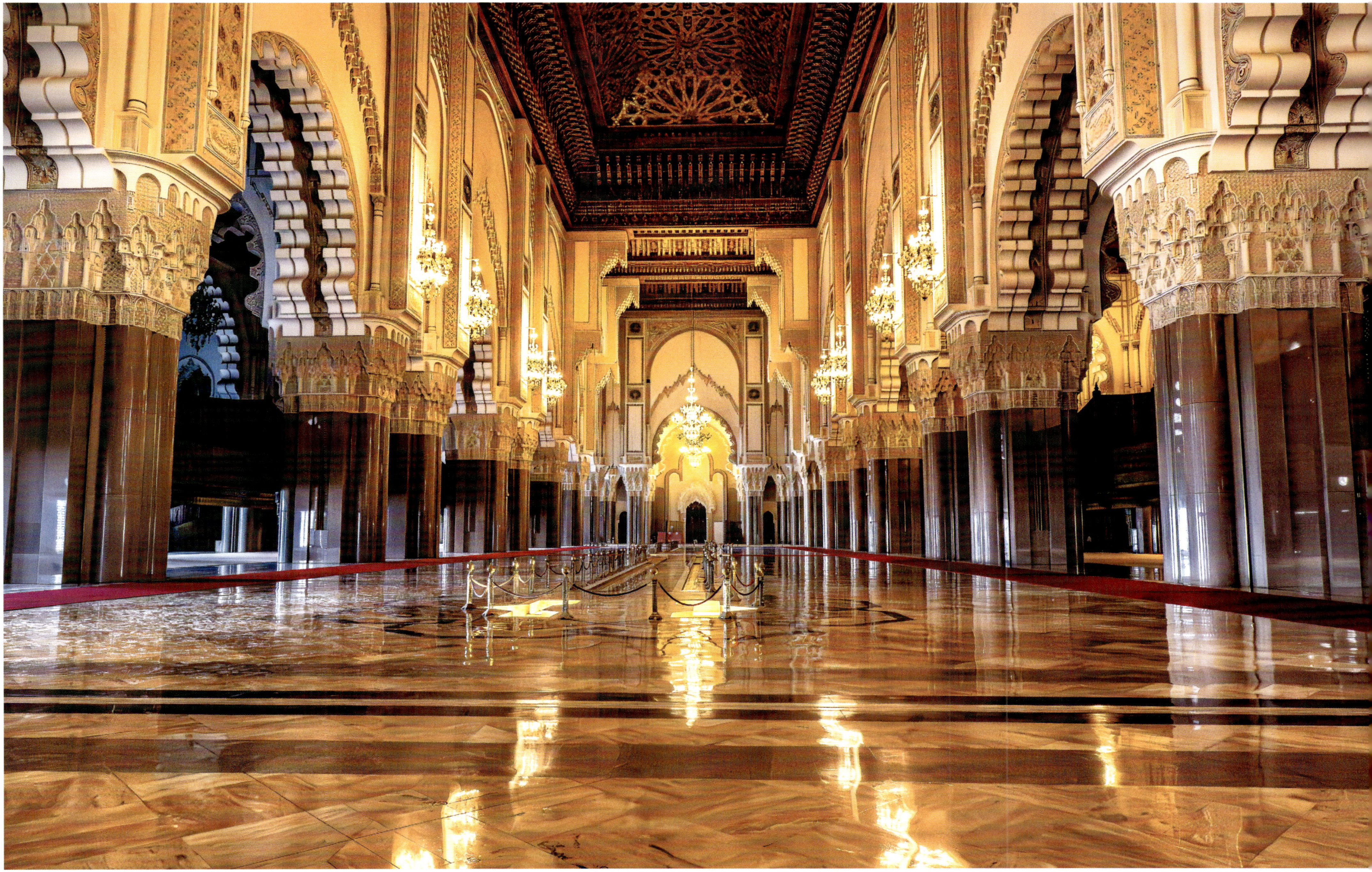

# IMPERIAL CITY AND MOROCCO'S CAPITAL

Just 50 miles north of Casablanca are the neighboring cities of Rabat and Sale. Rabat was founded in the 12th century as a fortified monastery and has been the Moroccan capital since 1912. It is one of the four Imperial Cities, along with Fes, Marrakech and Meknes.

The city is built behind a fortified wall and includes an old medina surrounded by ramparts located near the coast. It features the 17th-century fortress, the Kasbah des Oudayas, and an Andalusian Garden with an adjoining religious college that houses a museum of Moroccan Art.

Also located within the city is the "unfinished mosque" and the Tower of Hassan. Across from the Hassan Tower is the mausoleum of Muhammad V. The Tower grounds and mausoleum is guarded around the clock by members of the elaborately dressed Royal Guard who stand watch on foot or mounted on horses at entrances to the mausoleum and around the gates outside Hassan Tower.

In addition to its ancient sites, Rabat is also home to the large performing arts Grand Theatre de Rabat. Across the river Wadi Bou Regreg, and in view of the red sandstone walls of the medieval fortified Muslim necropolis Chellah, is the city of Sale, and one of Morocco's most modern structures, the still unfinished 250 meter tall Mohammed VI high rise. Rabat and Sale are two different cities that are historically and geographically linked and often thought of as one.

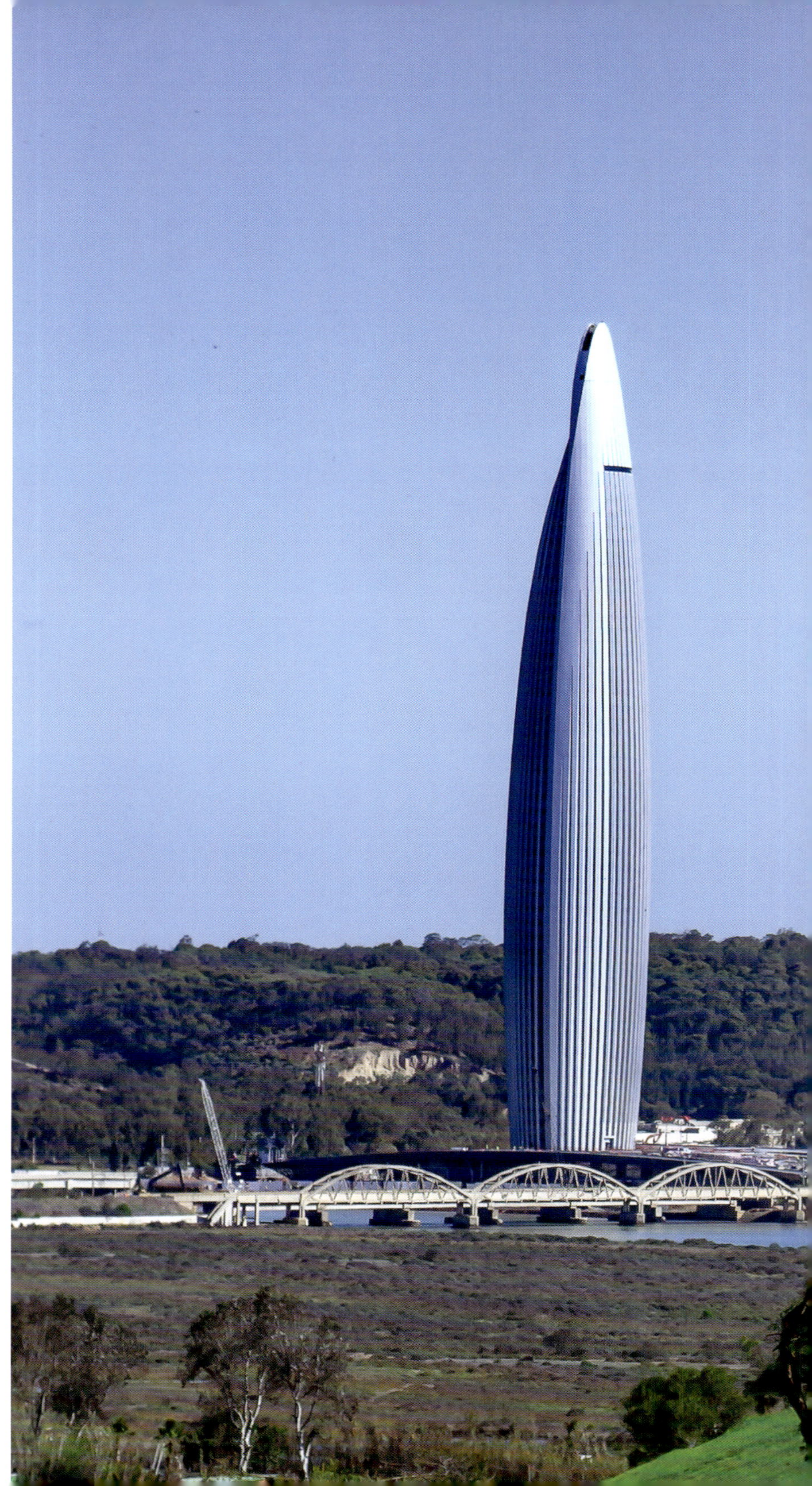

# EPIC RABAT

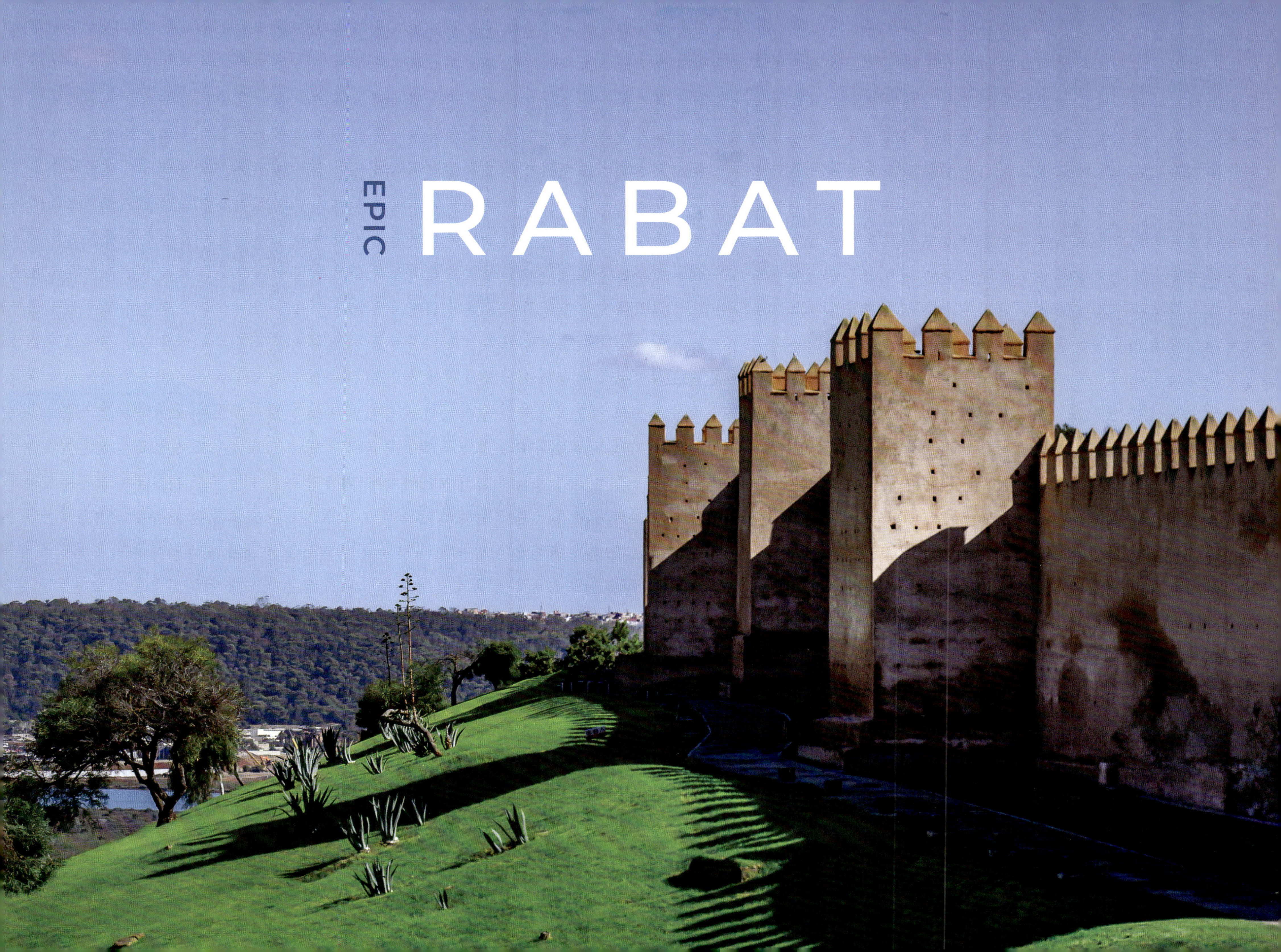

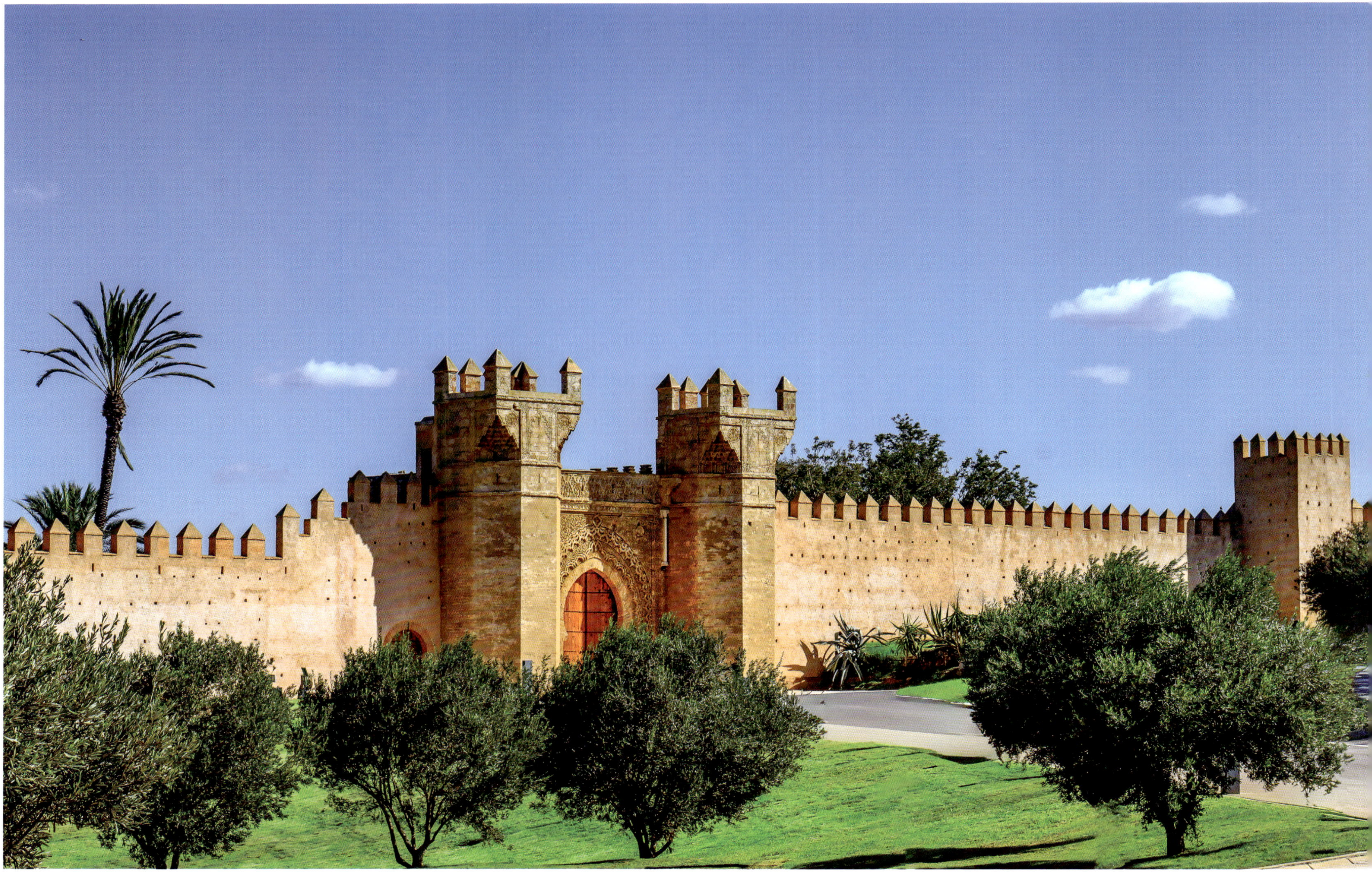

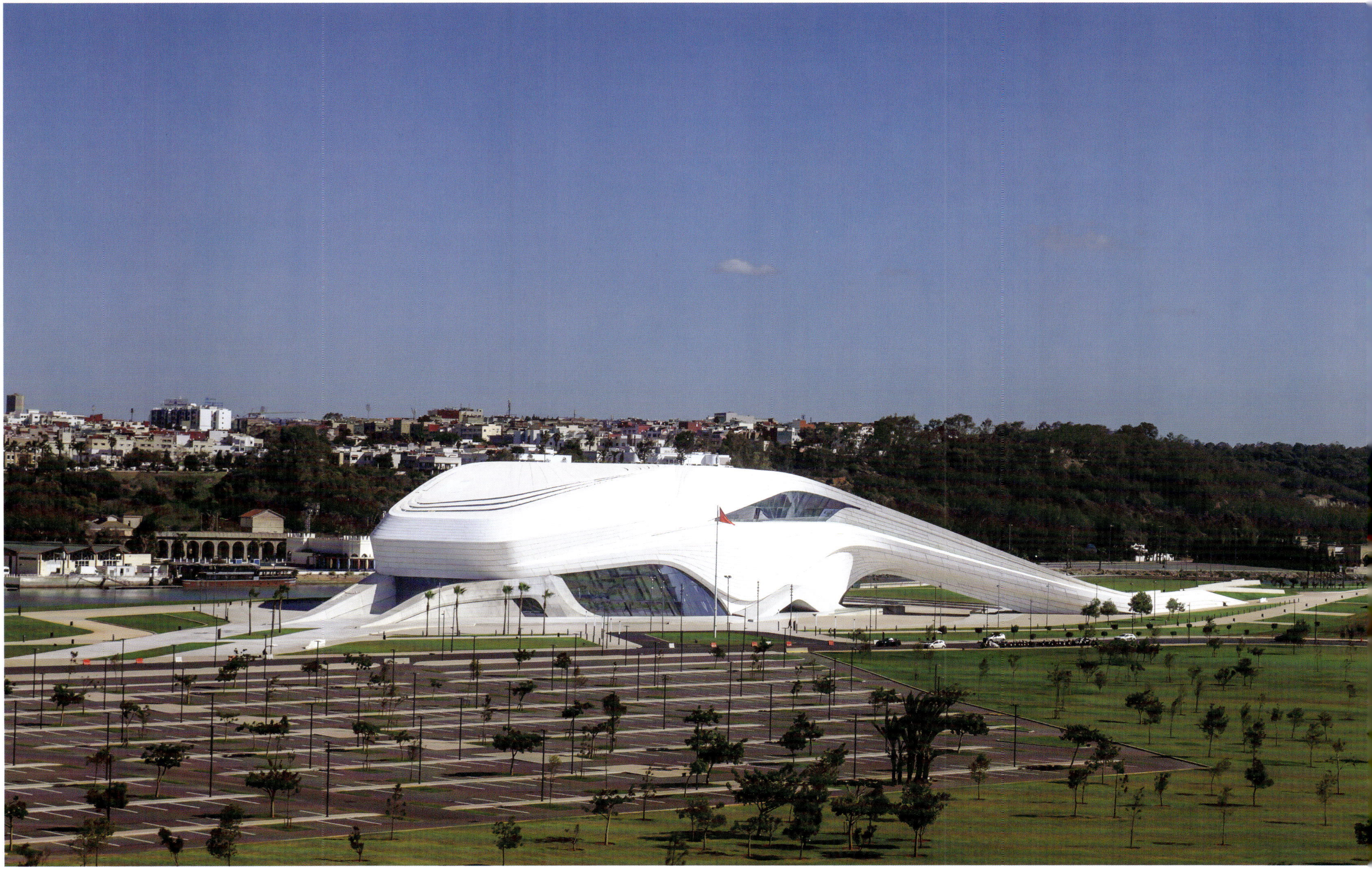

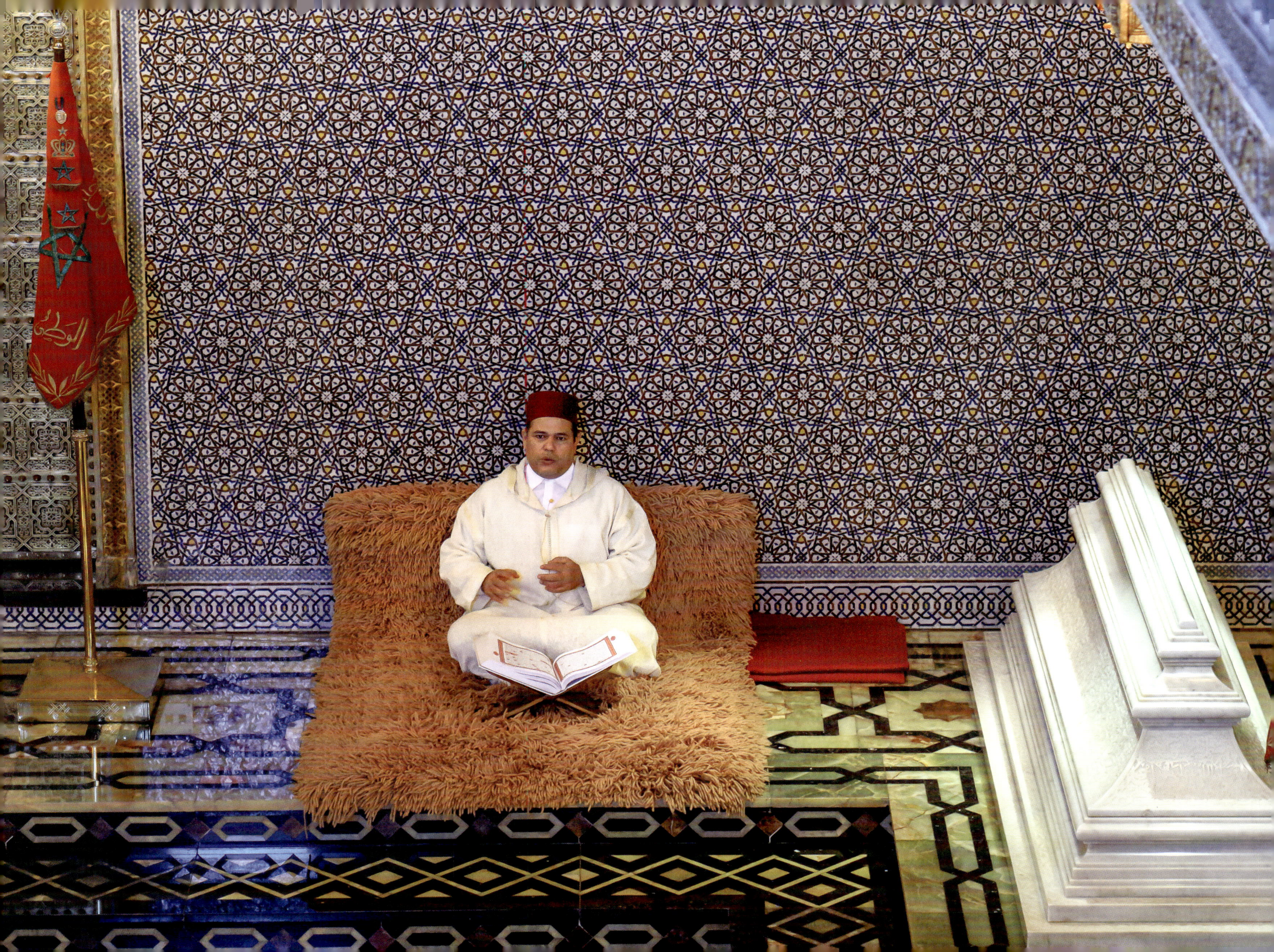

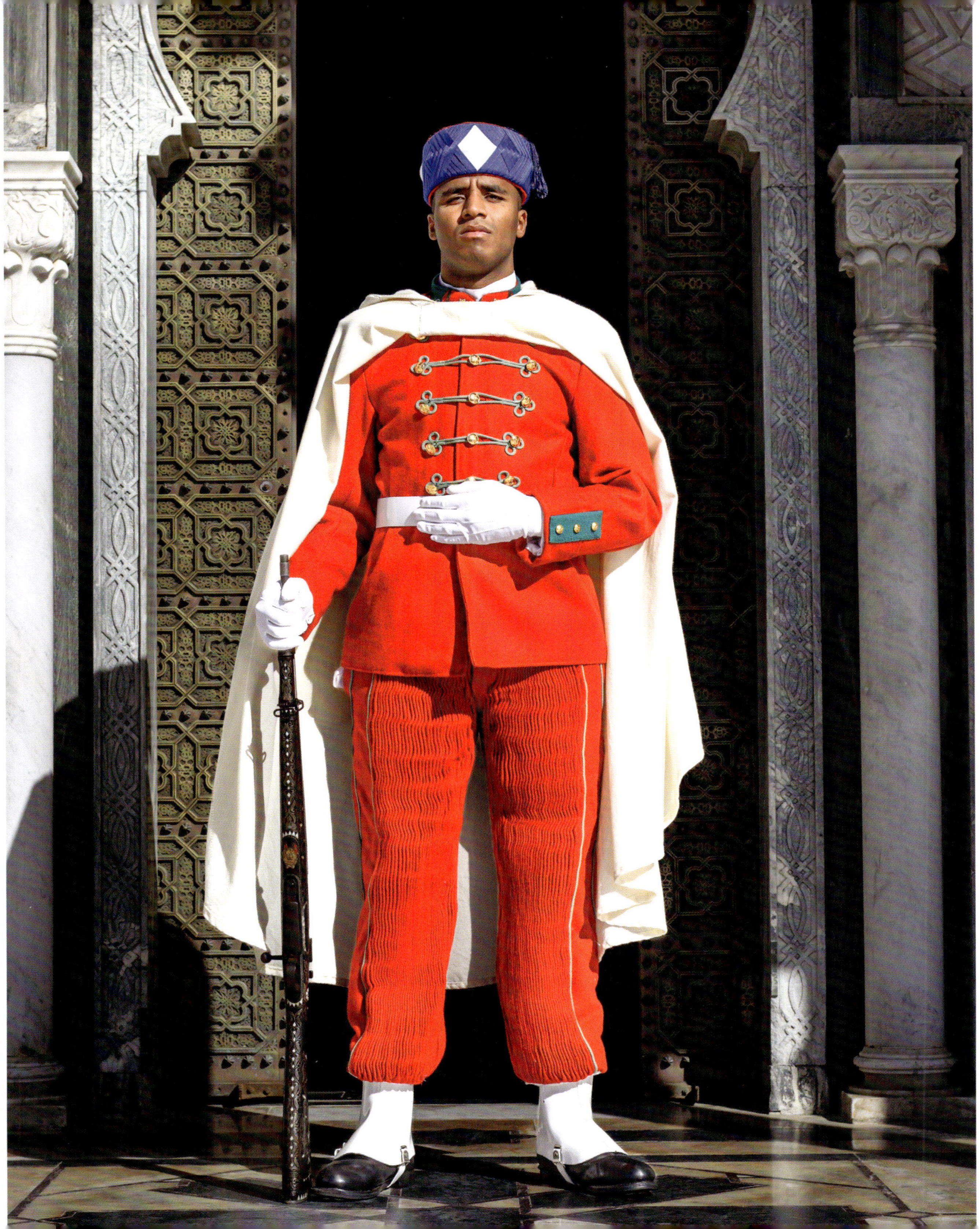

Previous page:
Exterior of the Kasbah
des Oudayas.

Grand Theatre. Imam (prayer leader of a mosque) reading from the Quran inside the Muhammad V mausoleum.

Left and next page:
Royal Guards outside the mausoleum and mounted outside the tower and unfinished mosque.

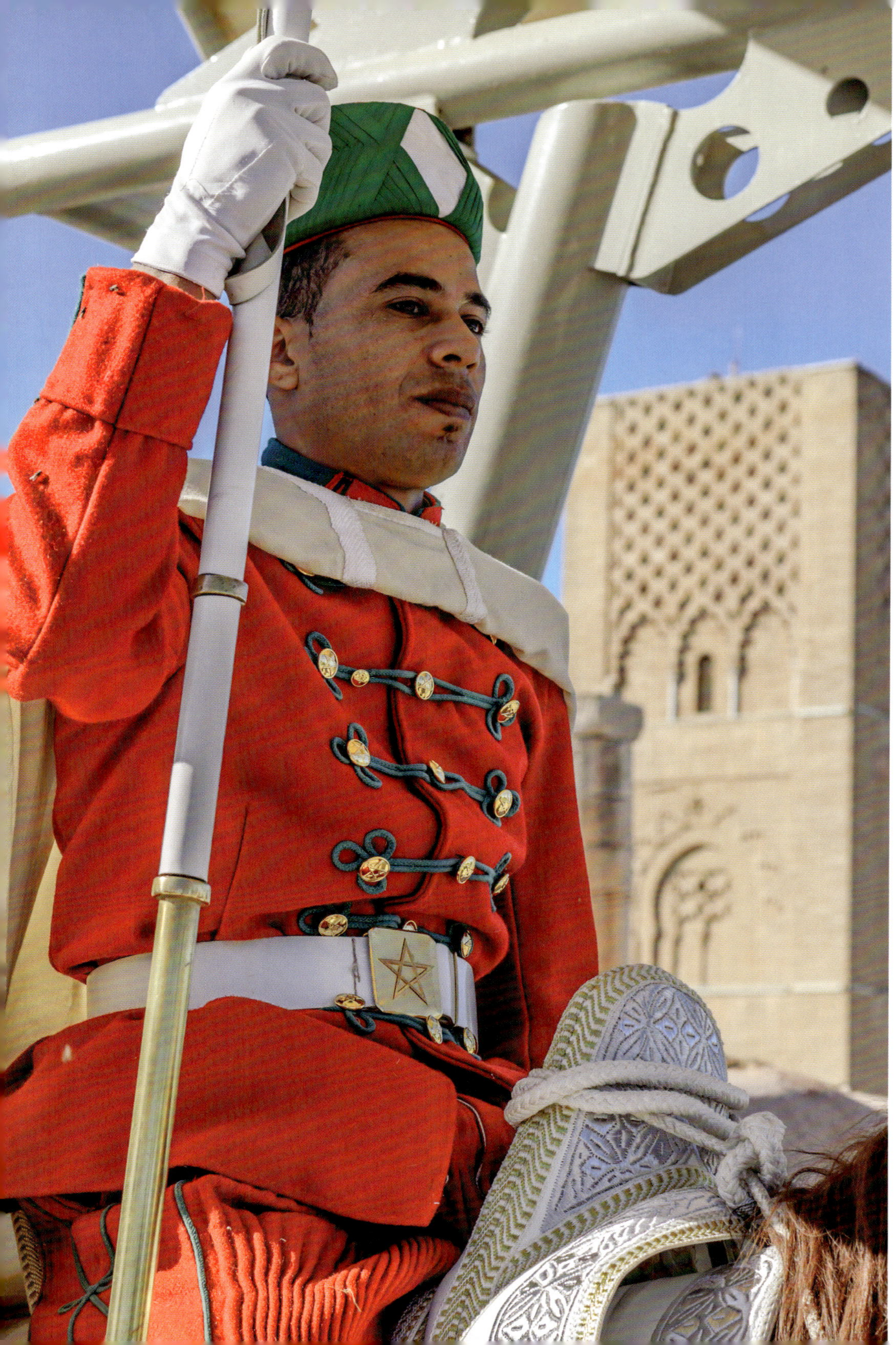

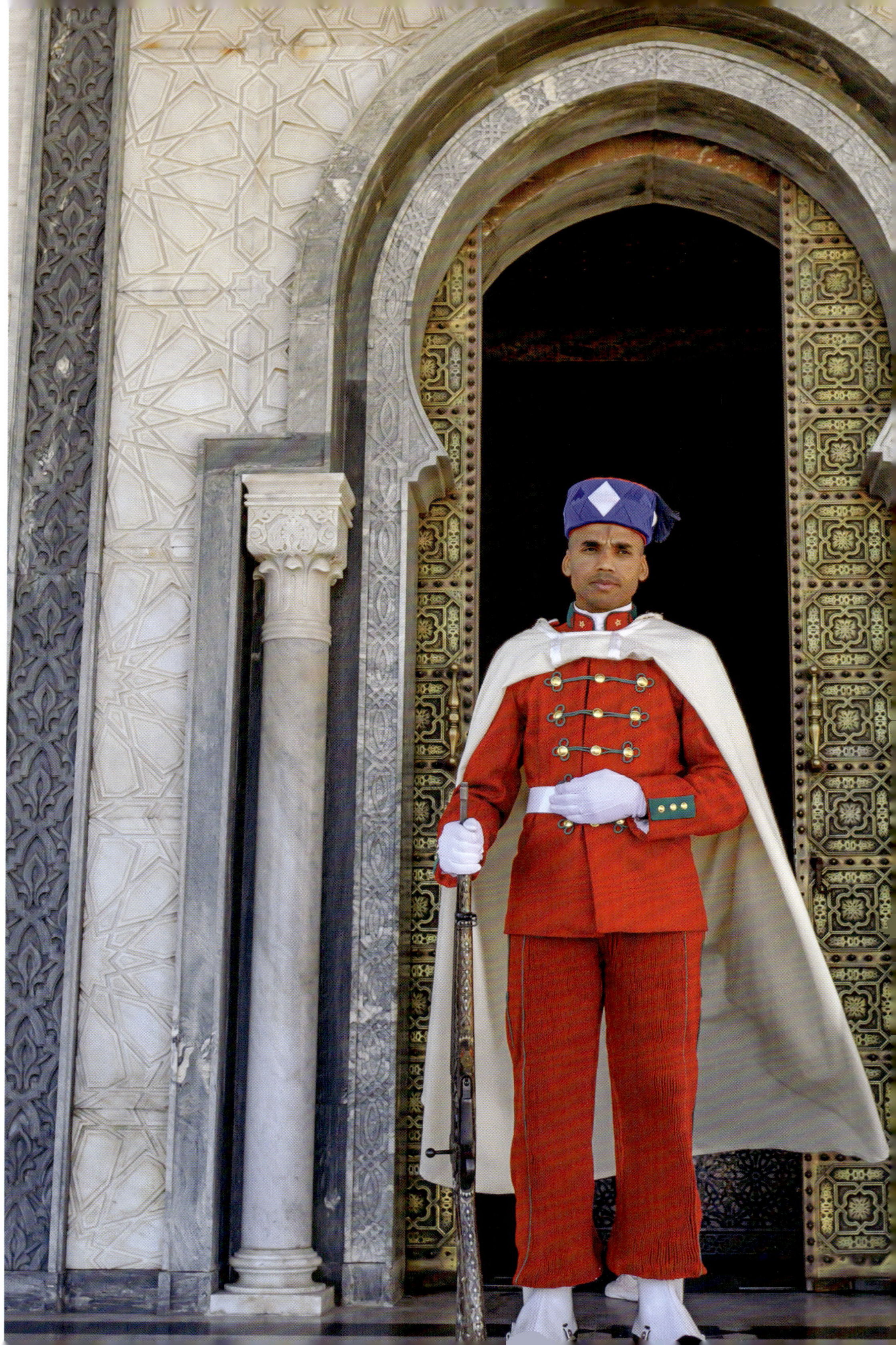

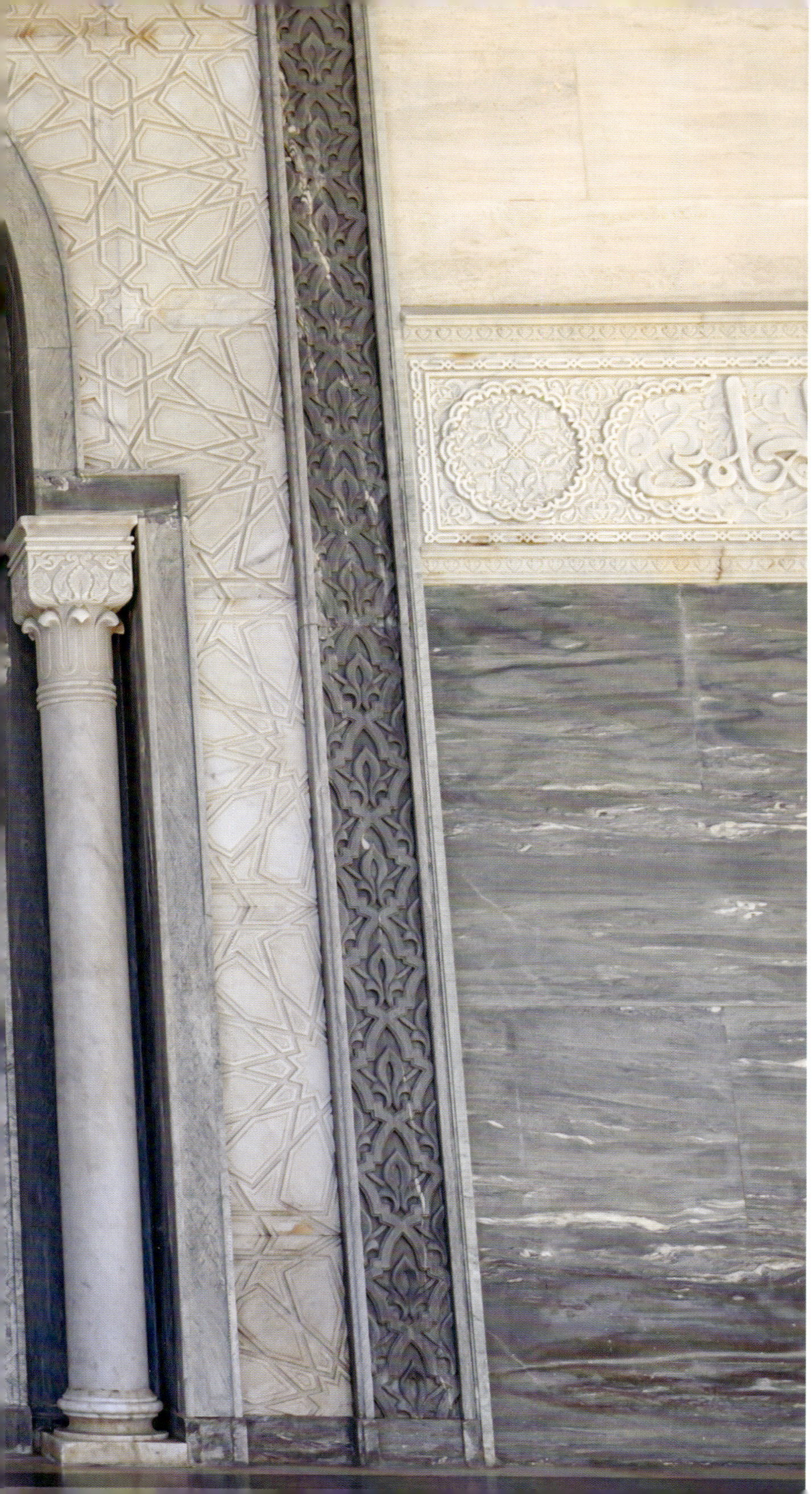

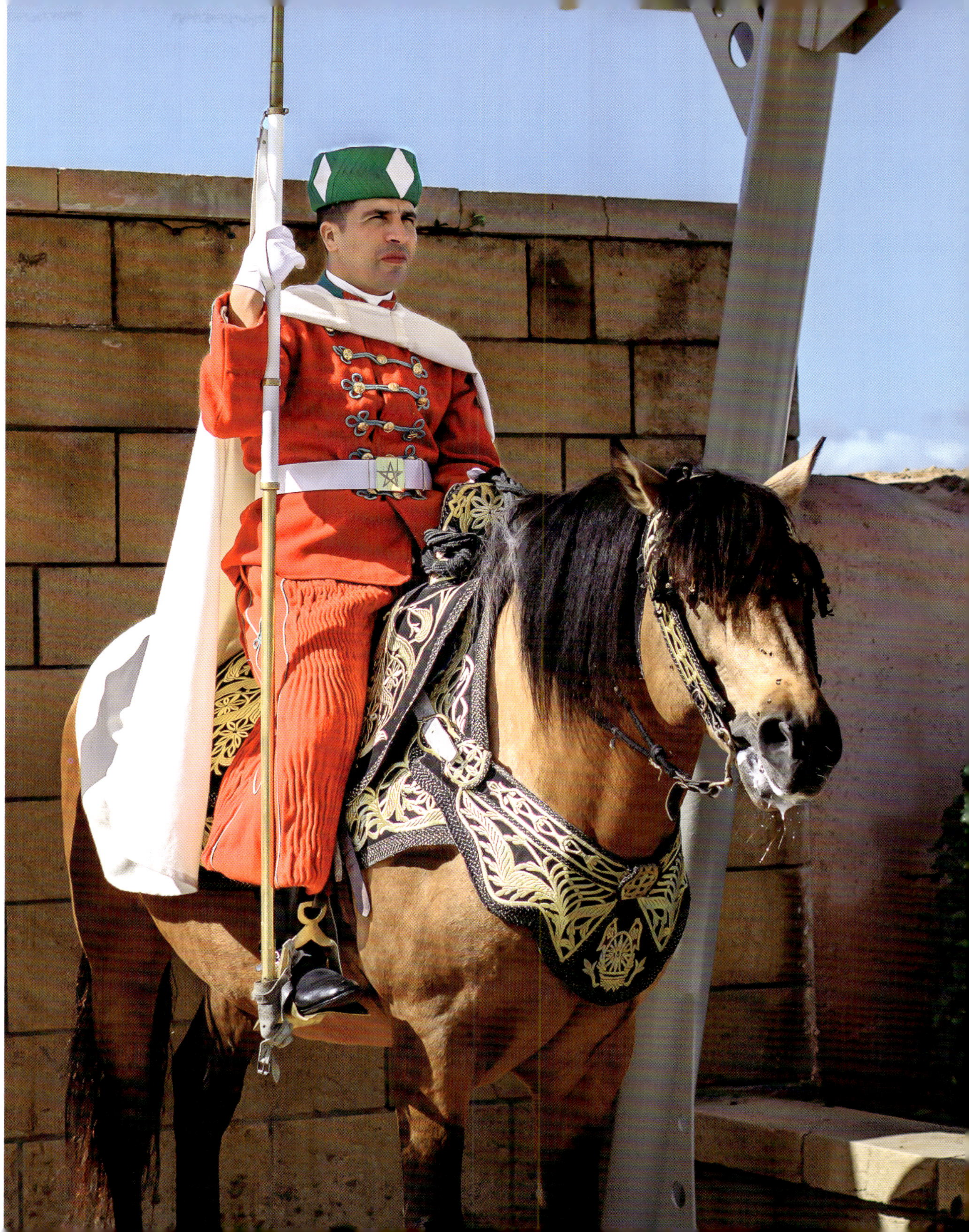

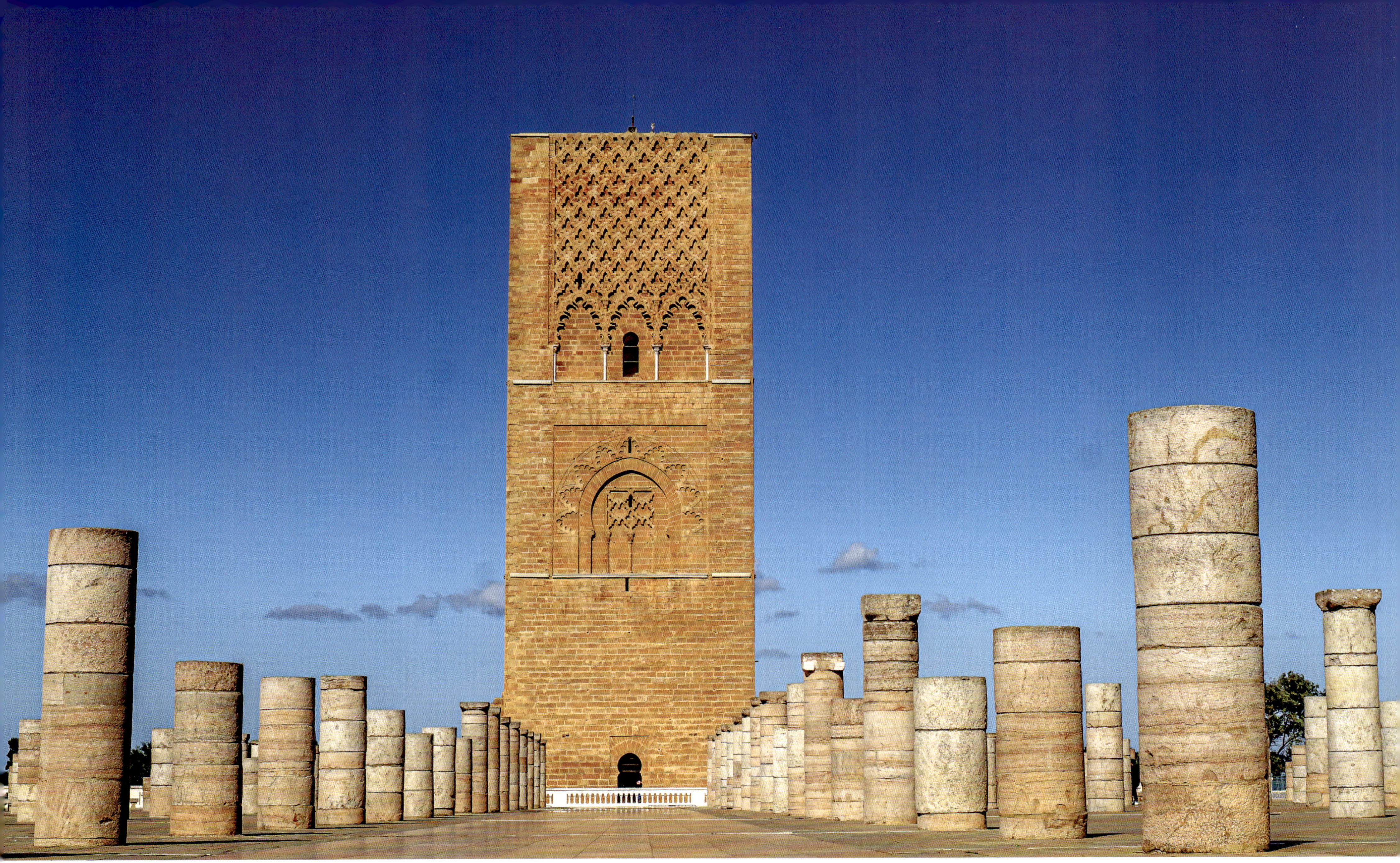

Grounds of the unfinished mosque and the Tower of Hassan.

Beautifully ornate doors to the mosque.

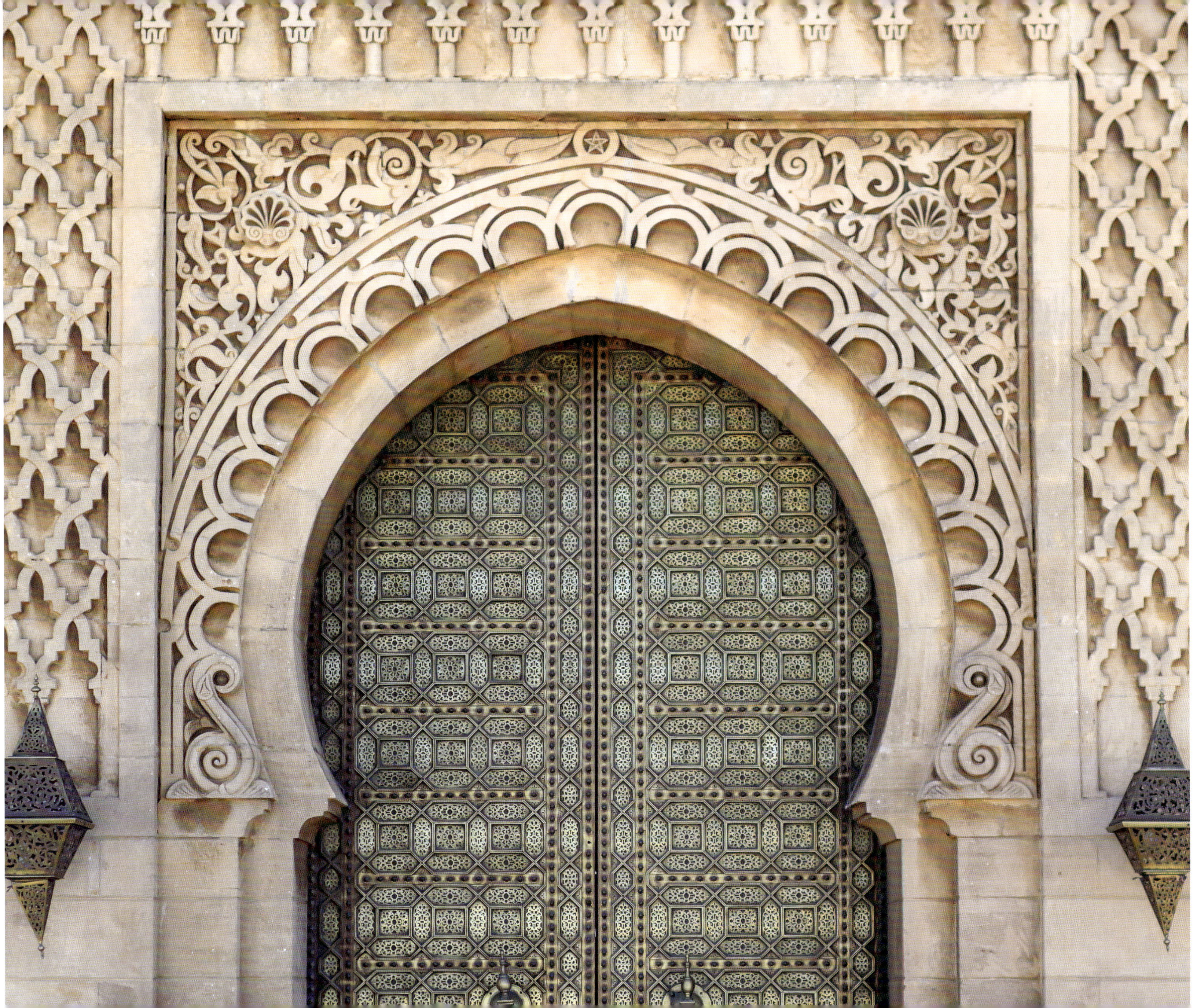

EPIC

# TODRA GORGE

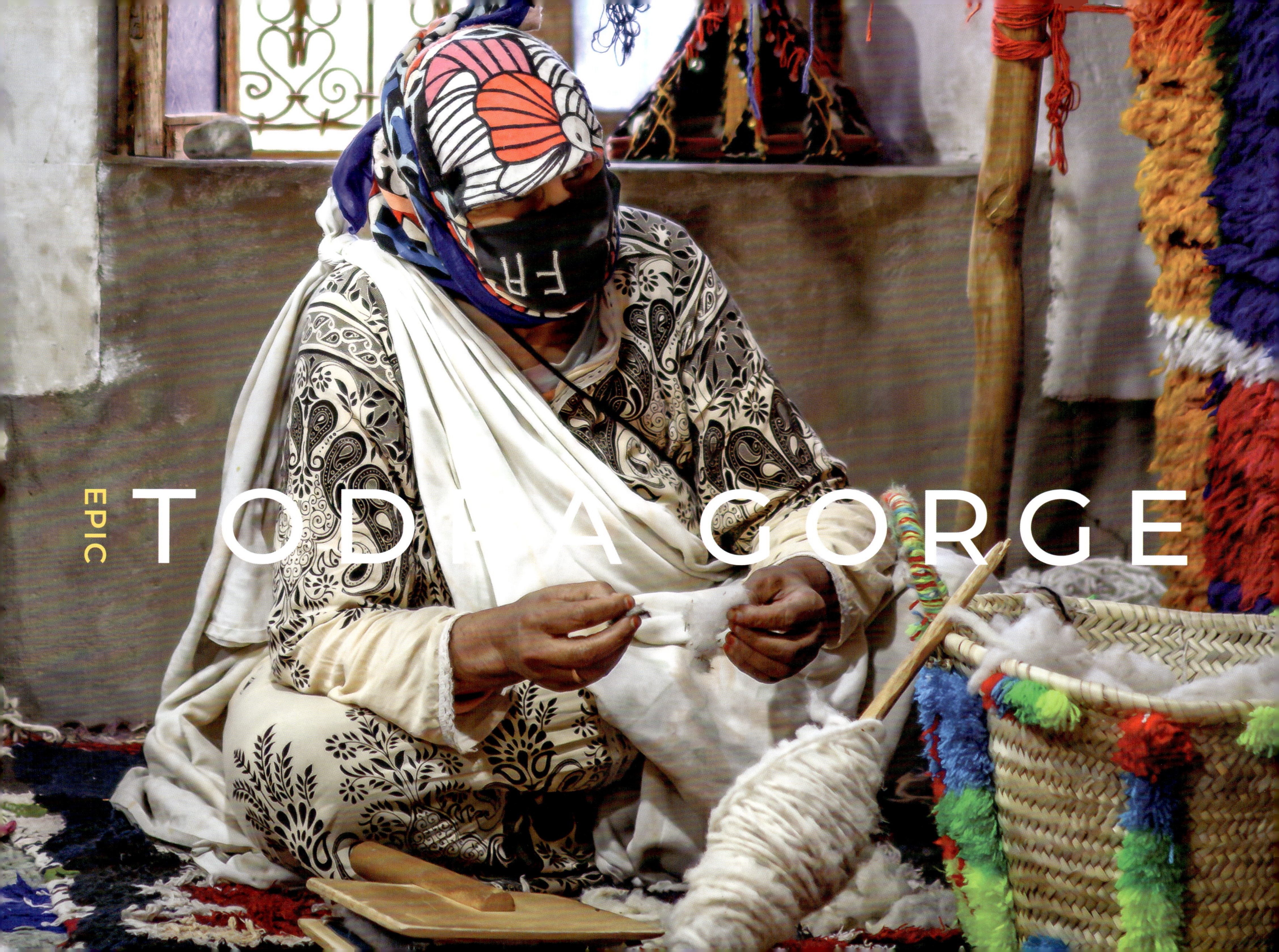

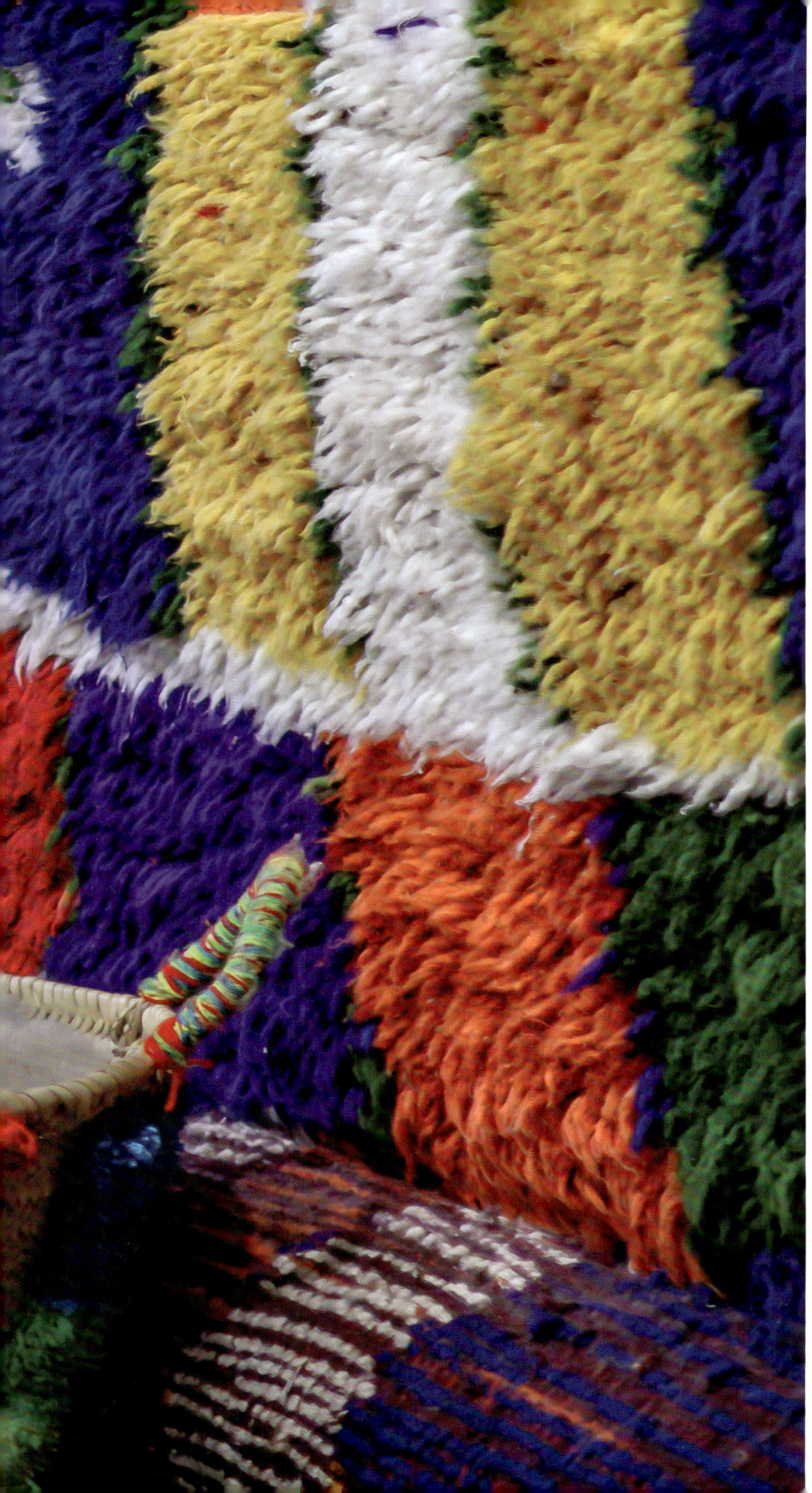

# MOROCCO'S LIMESTONE MOUNTAIN PASS PLAYGROUND

Set in the rocky Atlas Mountains, Todra Gorge is a natural oasis carved through limestone rock by the River Todra and has narrow canyon walls that can reach 400 meters in places. The center attraction of the gorge is a narrow, two-lane road that runs between the steep rock walls and alongside the River Todra.

Todra Gorge is a top destination for rock climbing enthusiasts. It is also an ideal spot for hiking and camping. Depending on the time of year, Todra Gorge can be either empty—during the fall and winter months—or packed during the hot months with Moroccan families on vacation who come to camp in the shadow of the rock walls and play in the cool flowing river.

While the gorge itself is an attraction that can fill a day of adventure, there are plenty of things to see and visit in the surrounding area, including a small village with several local cooperatives that offer handcraft rugs in their shops.

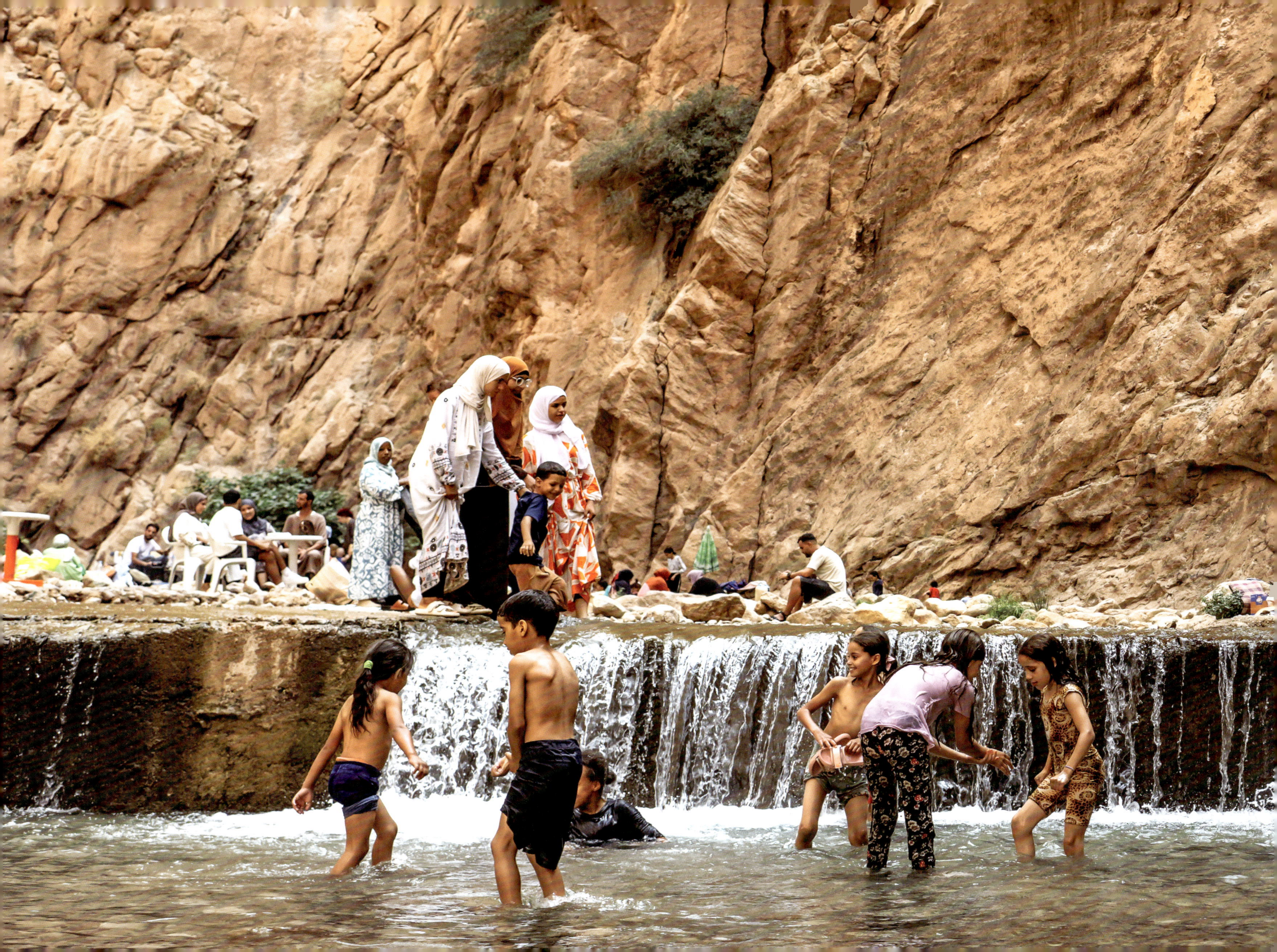

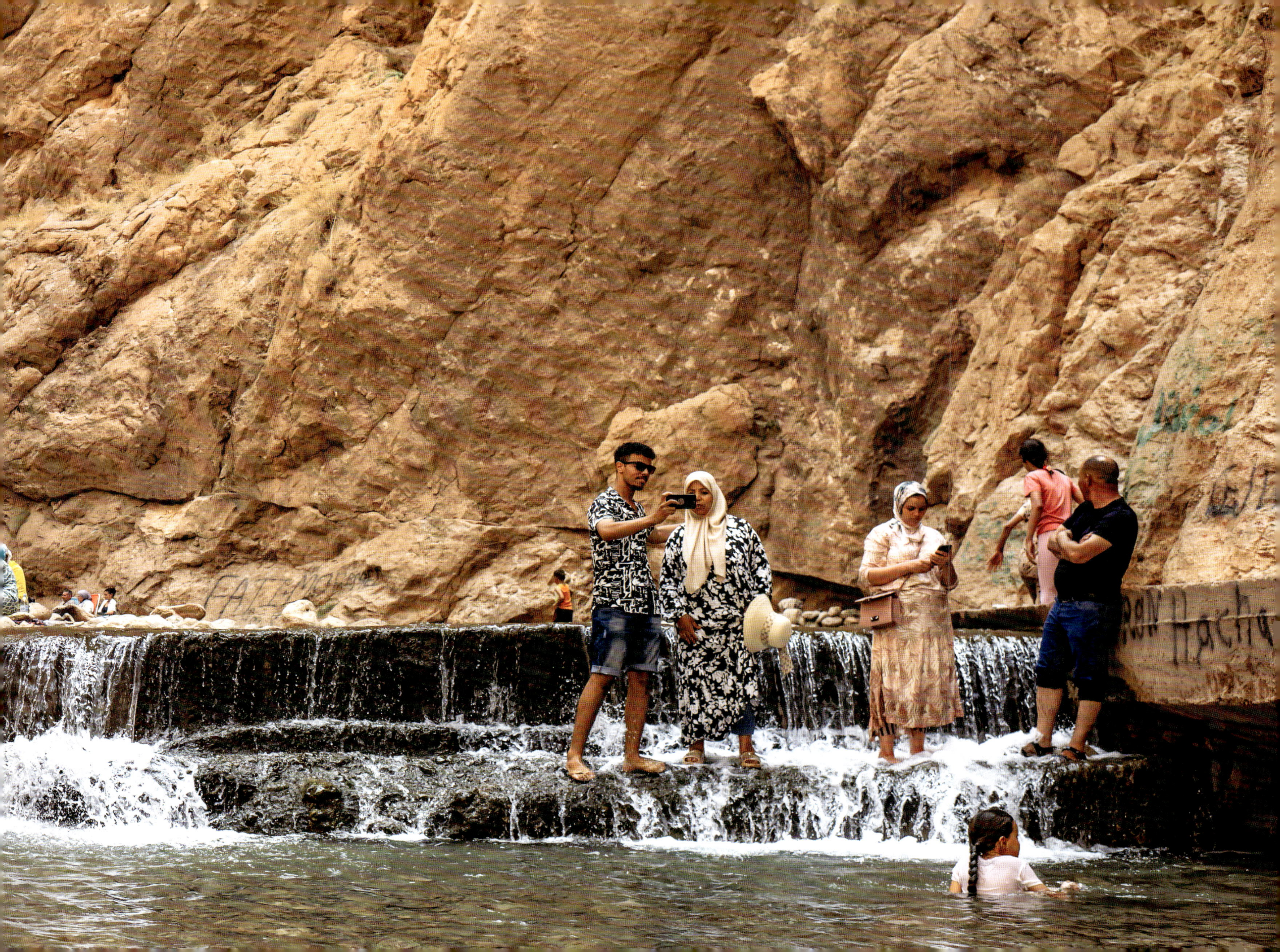

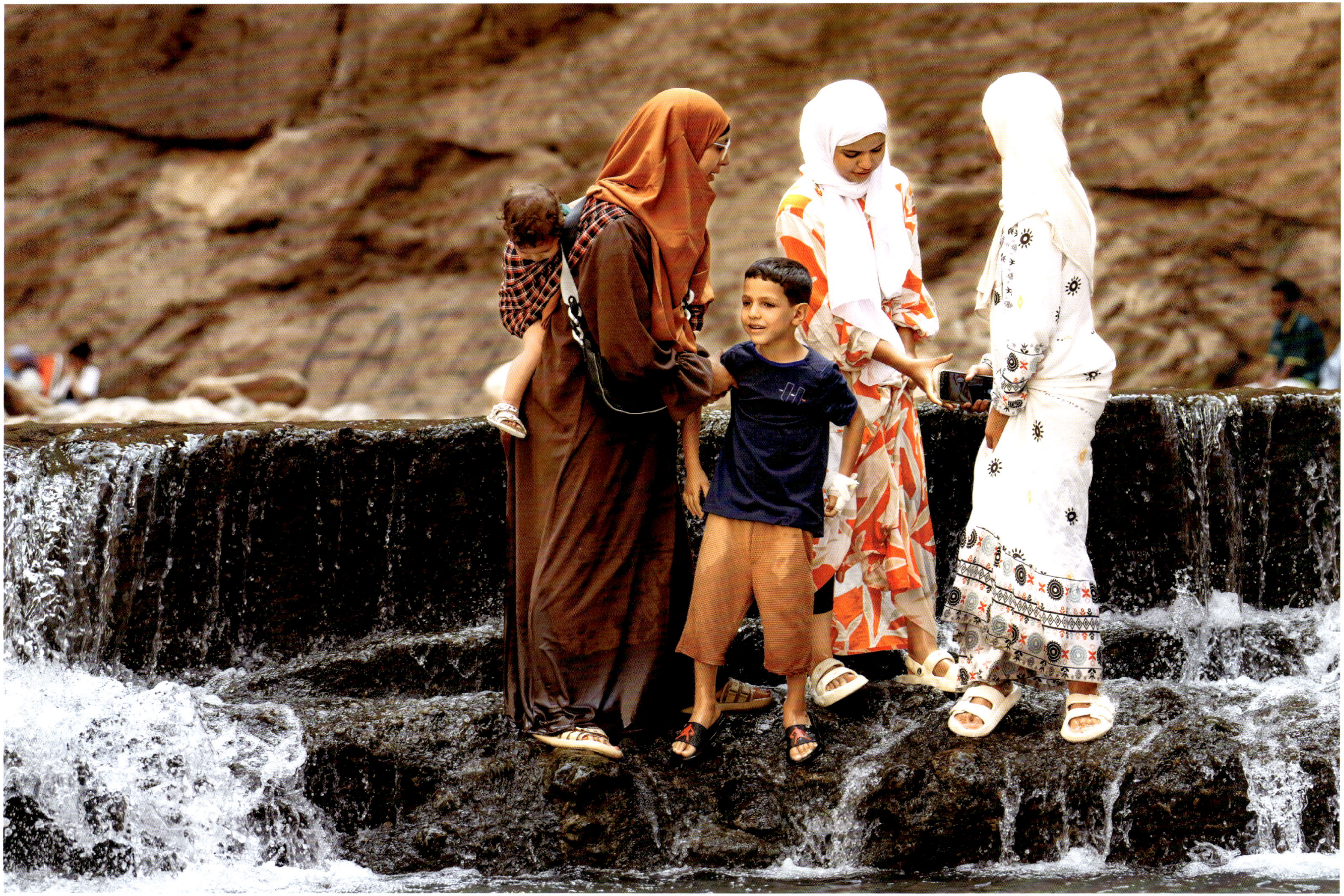

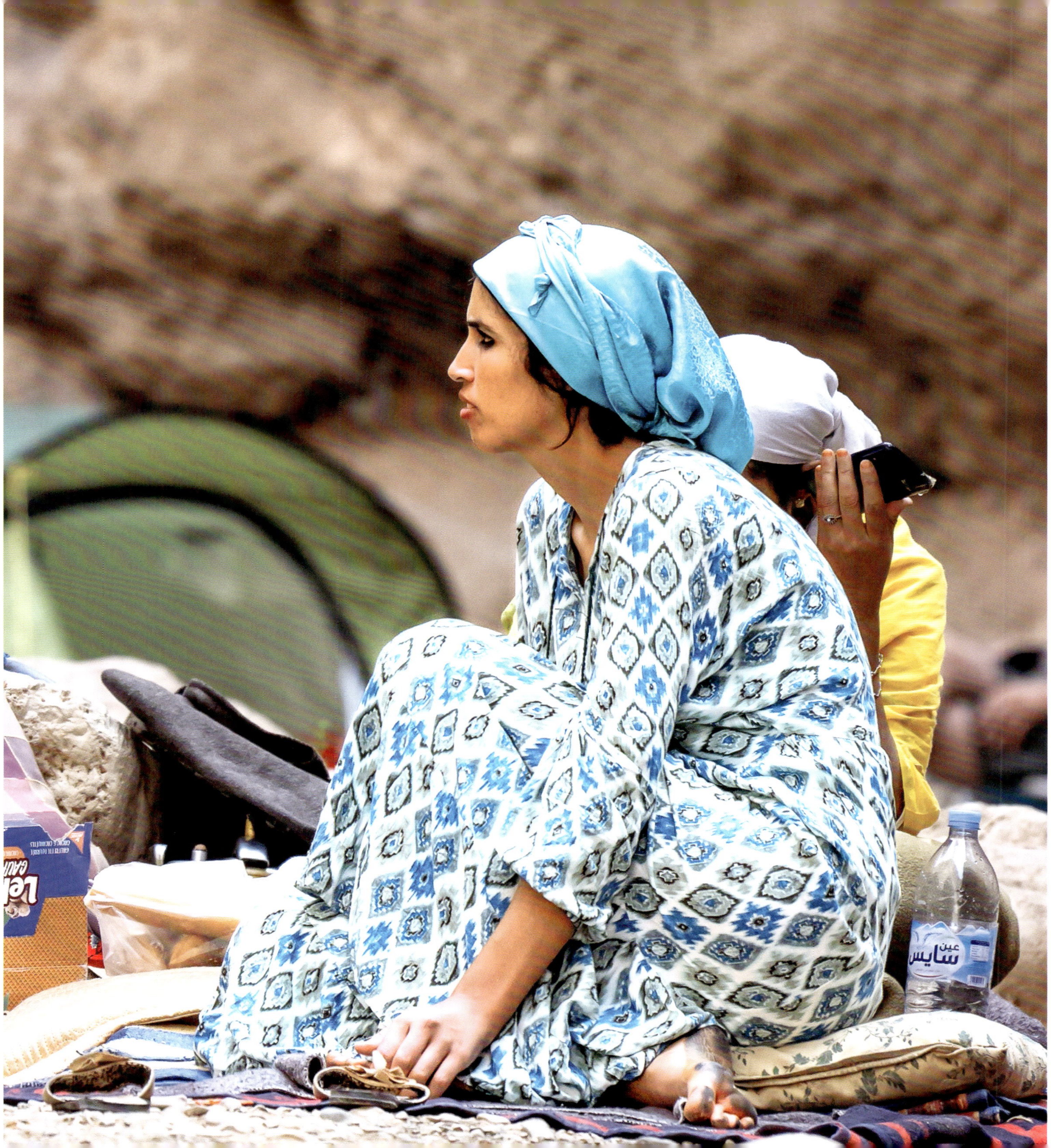


Moroccans enjoy vacationing and camping in the Todra Gorge.

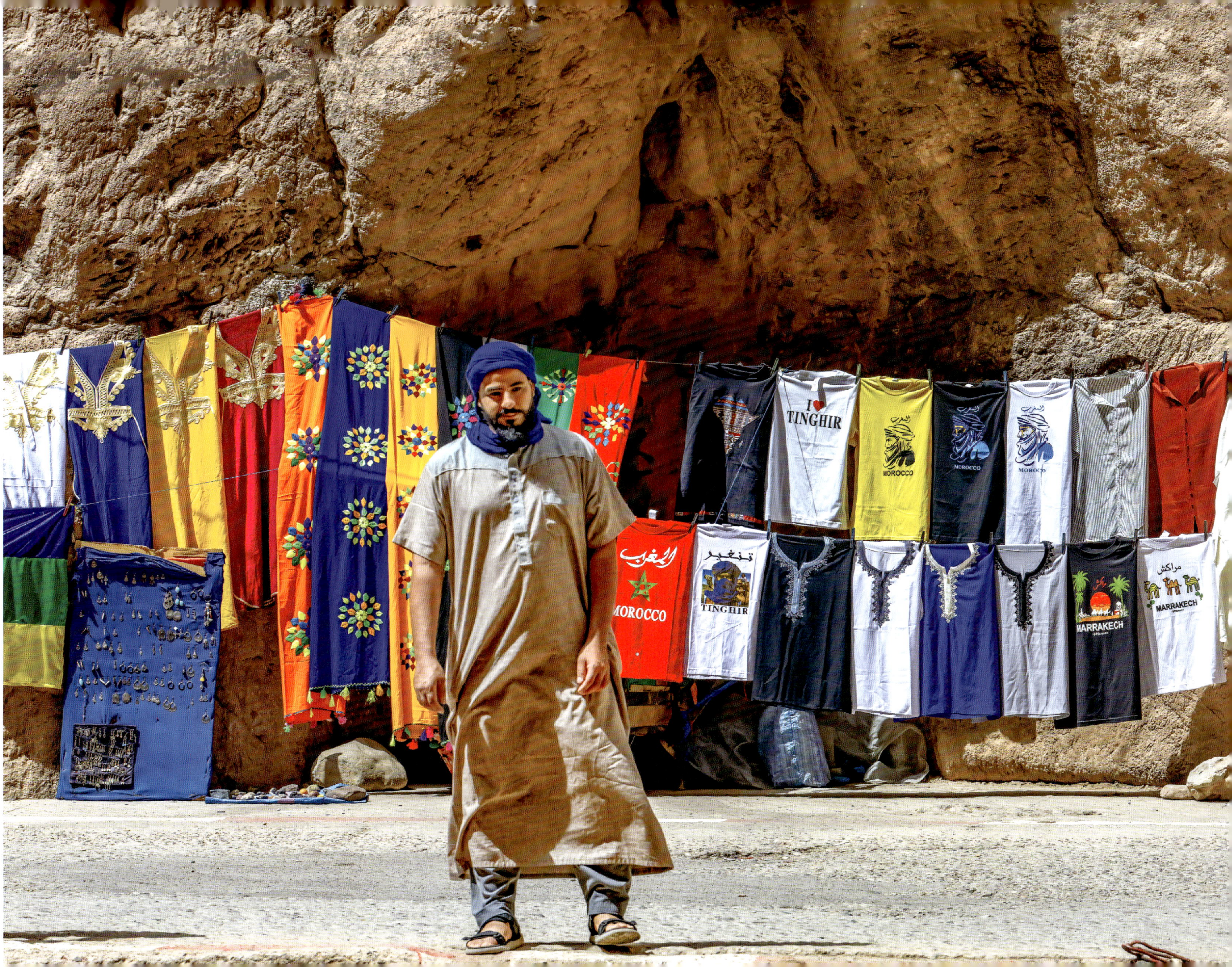

I ♥ TINGHIR
MOROCCO
المغرب
MOROCCO
تنغير
TINGHIR
MARRAKECH
مراكش
MARRAKECH

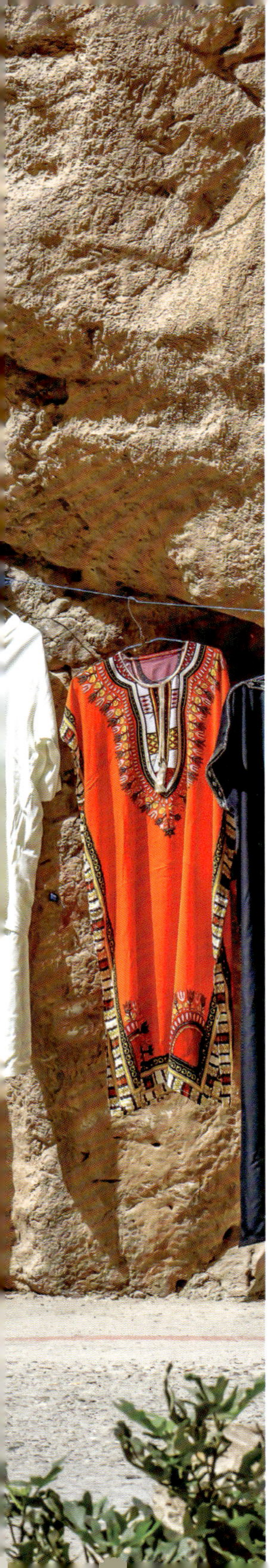

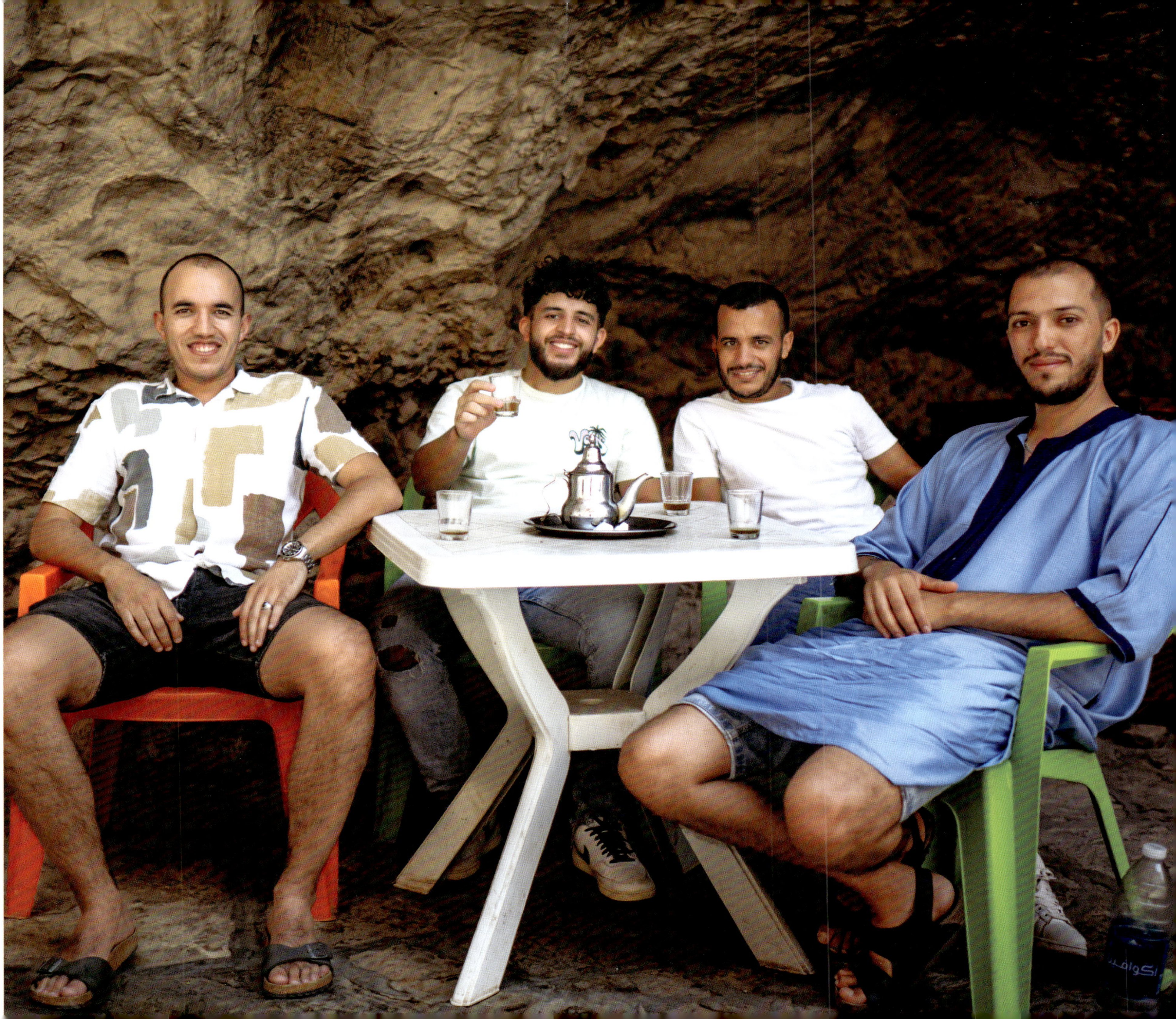

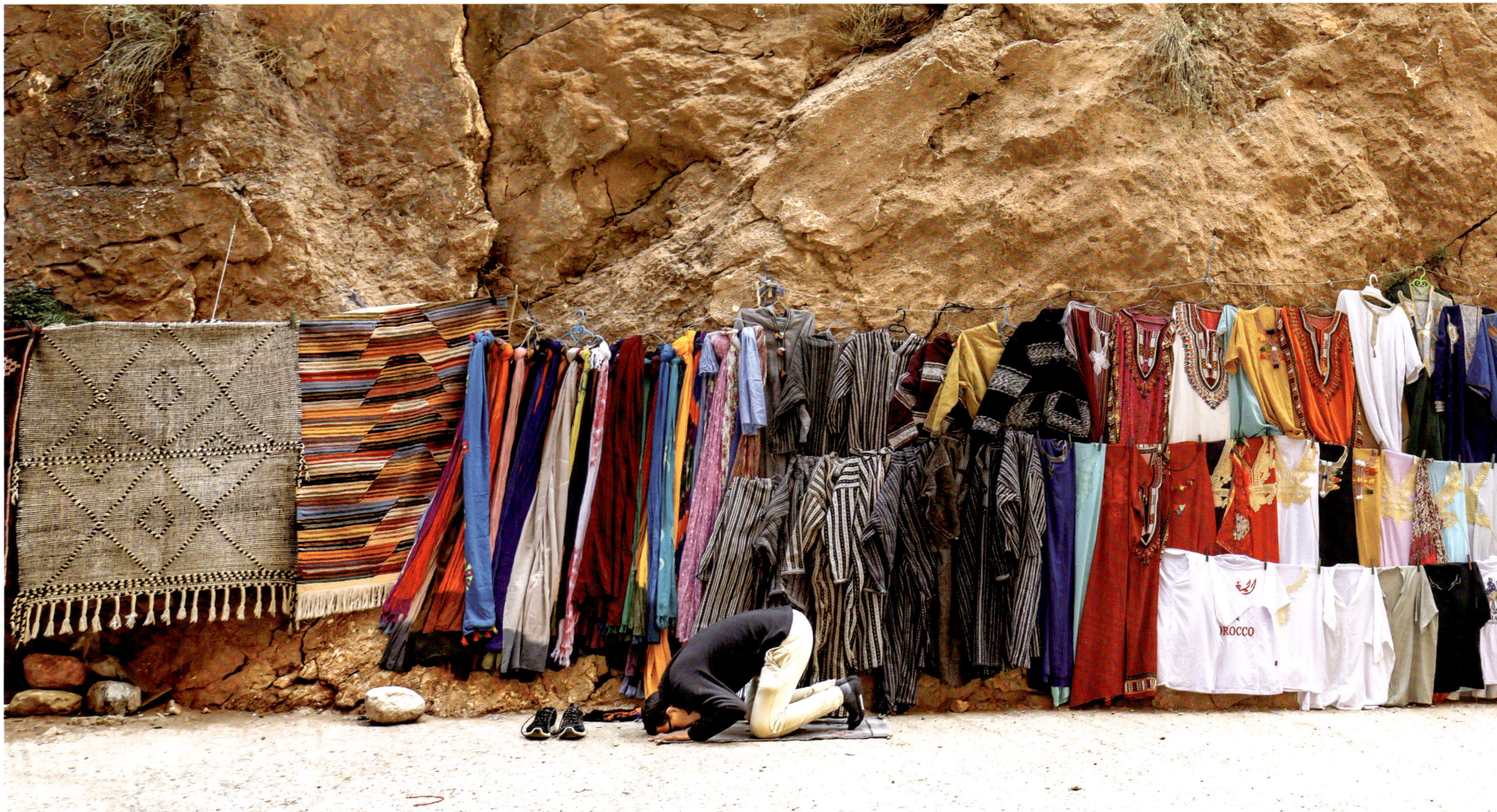


Previous page:
Merchant selling shirts and scarves.

Men enjoying traditional Moroccan mint tea.

Man taking time for prayer.

Rock climbing is a popular pastime in the Todra Gorge, attracting climbers from around the world.

Merchants relaxing in the shade.

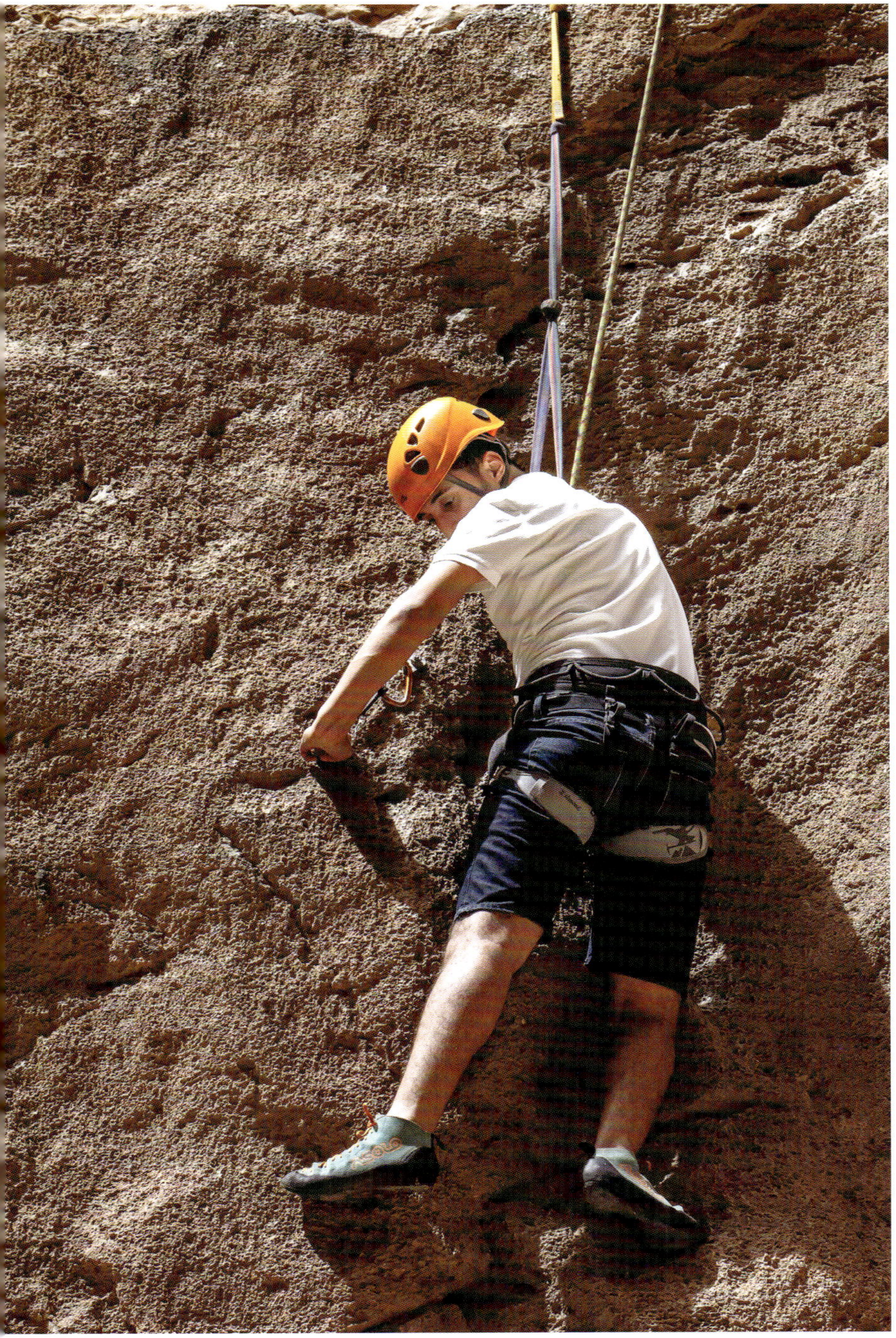

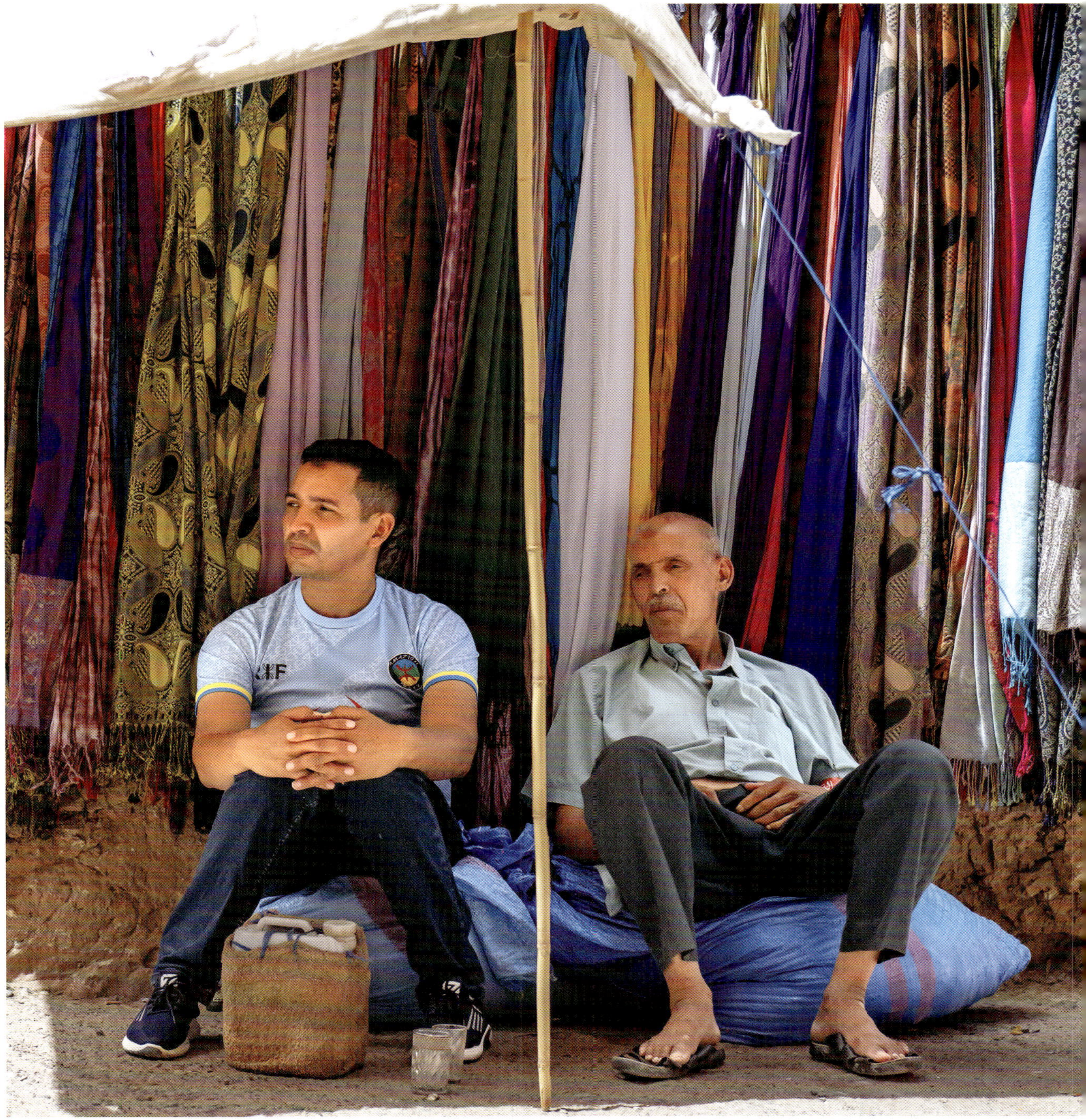

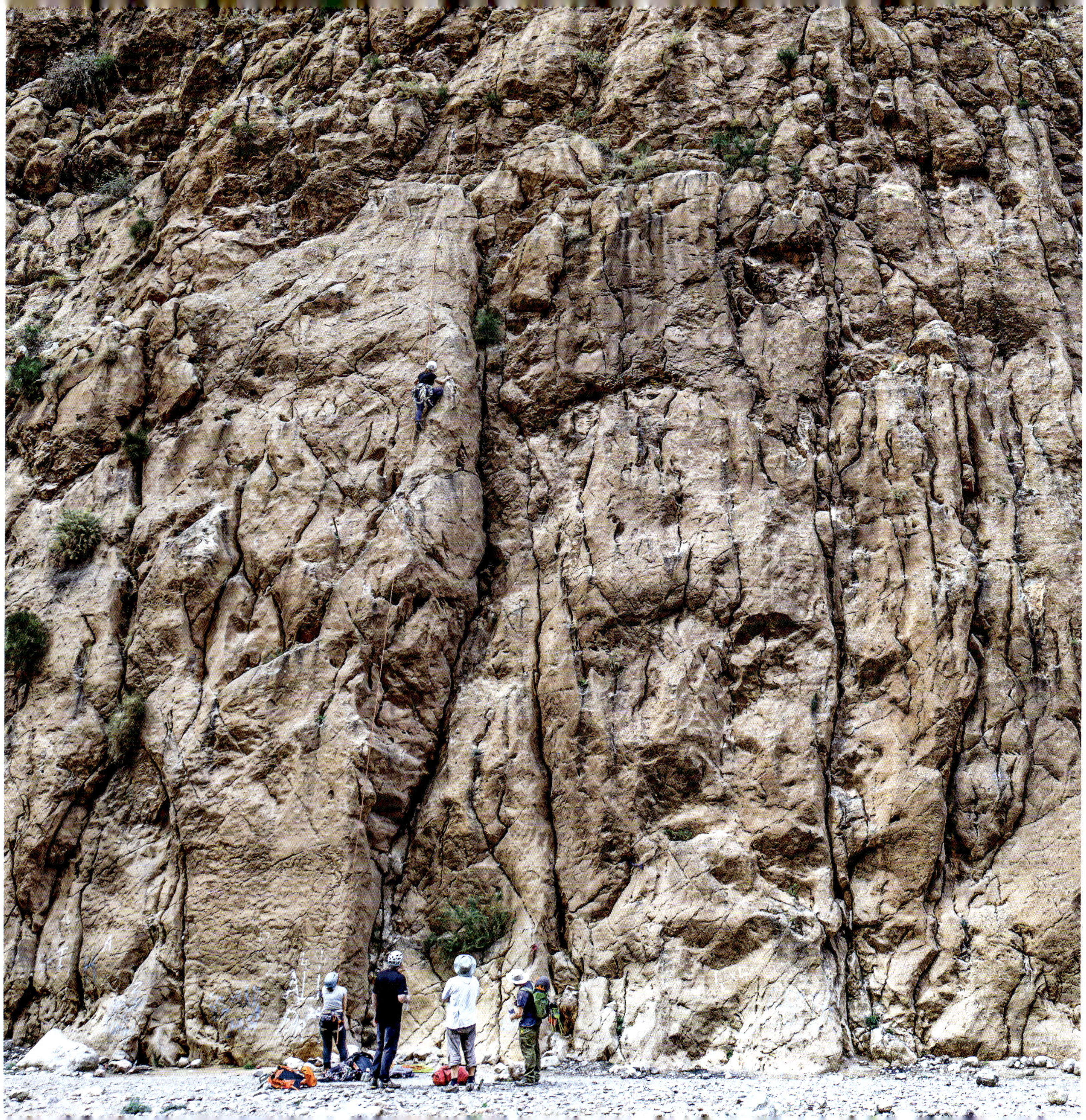

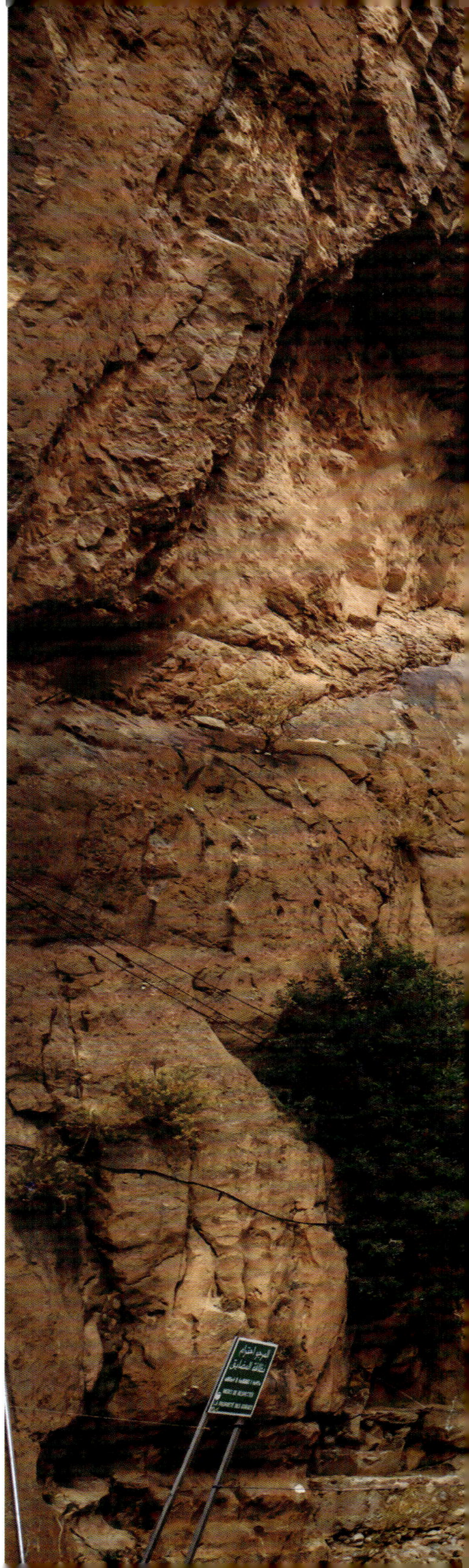

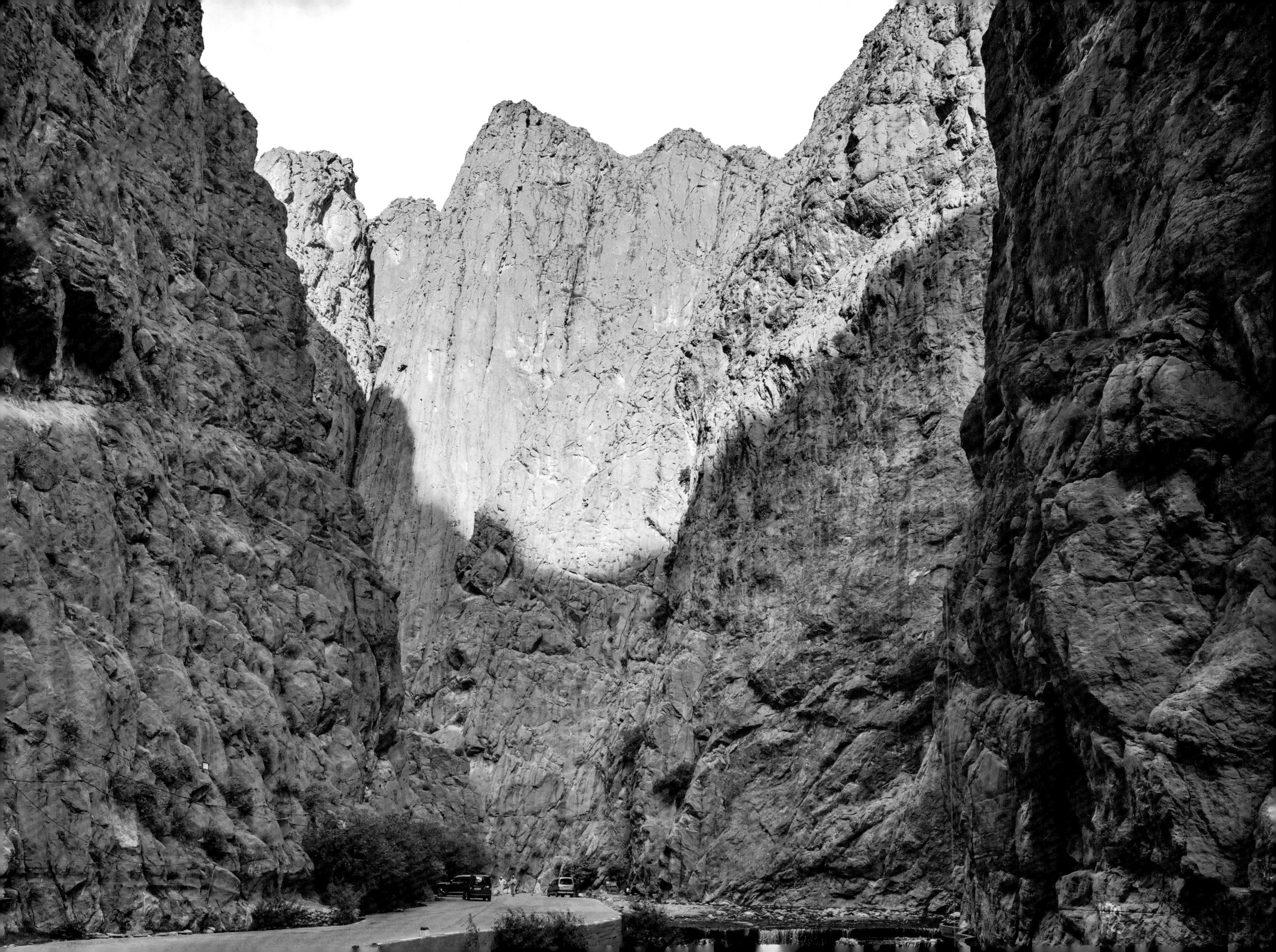

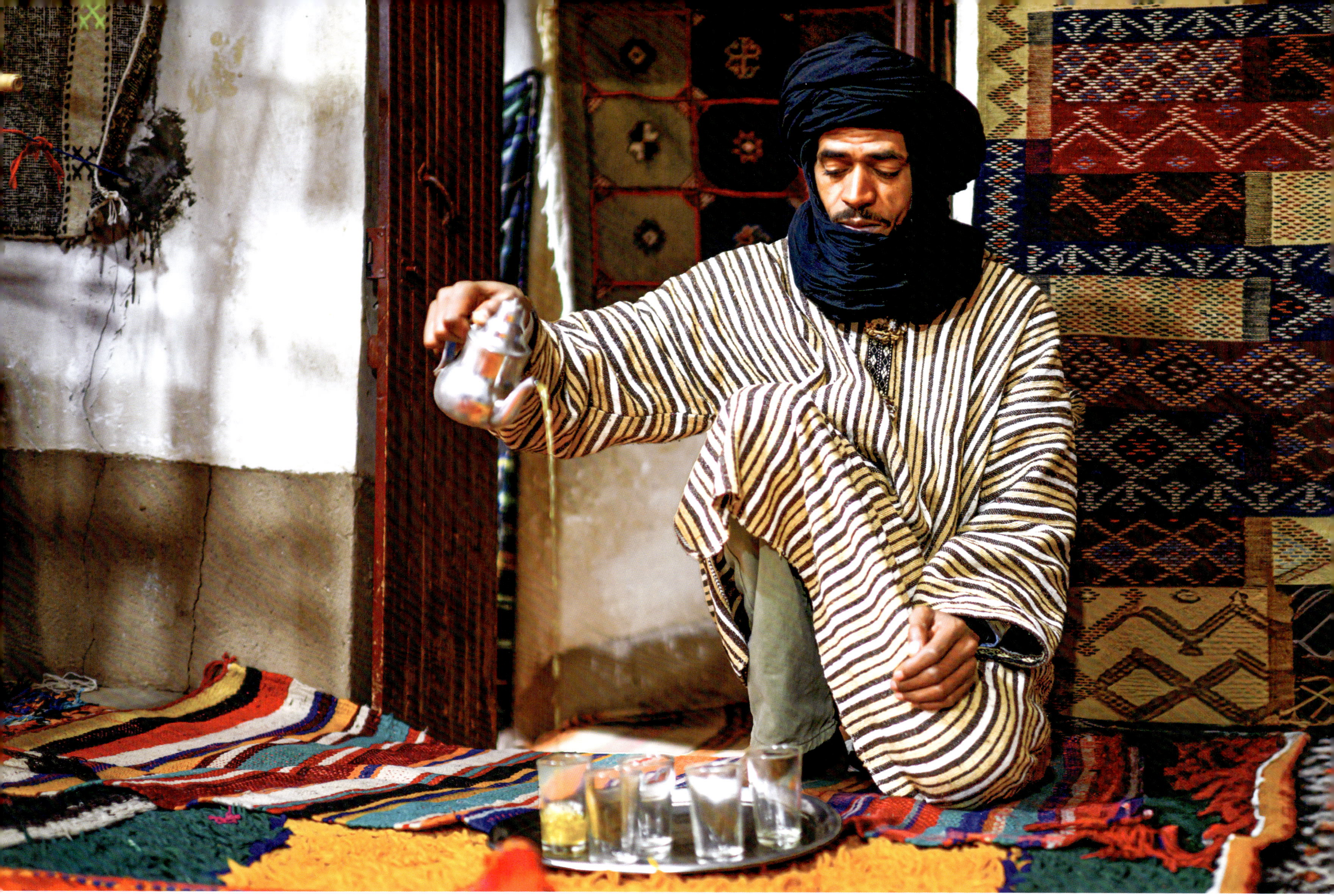

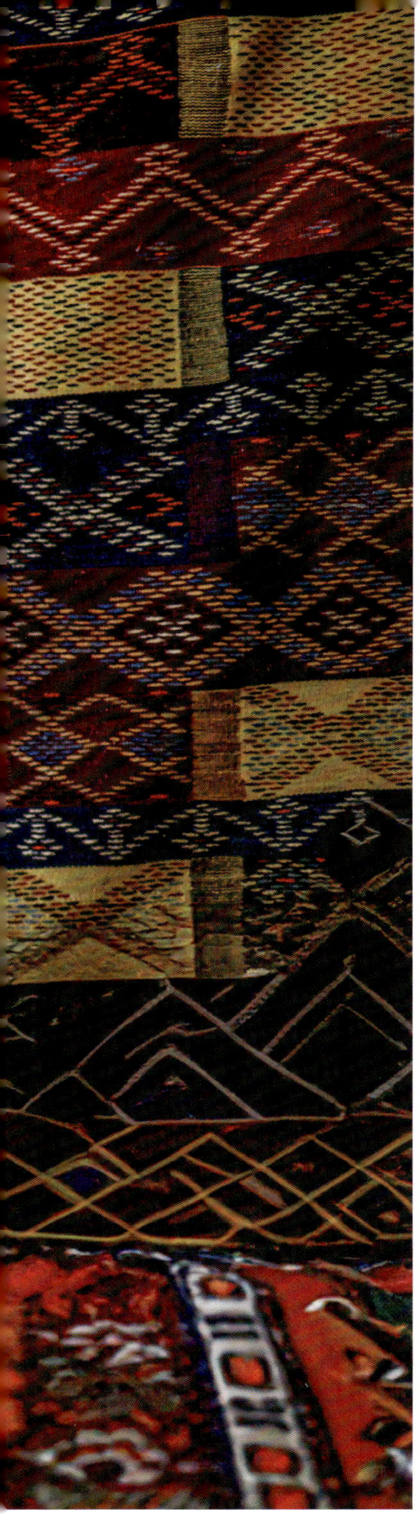

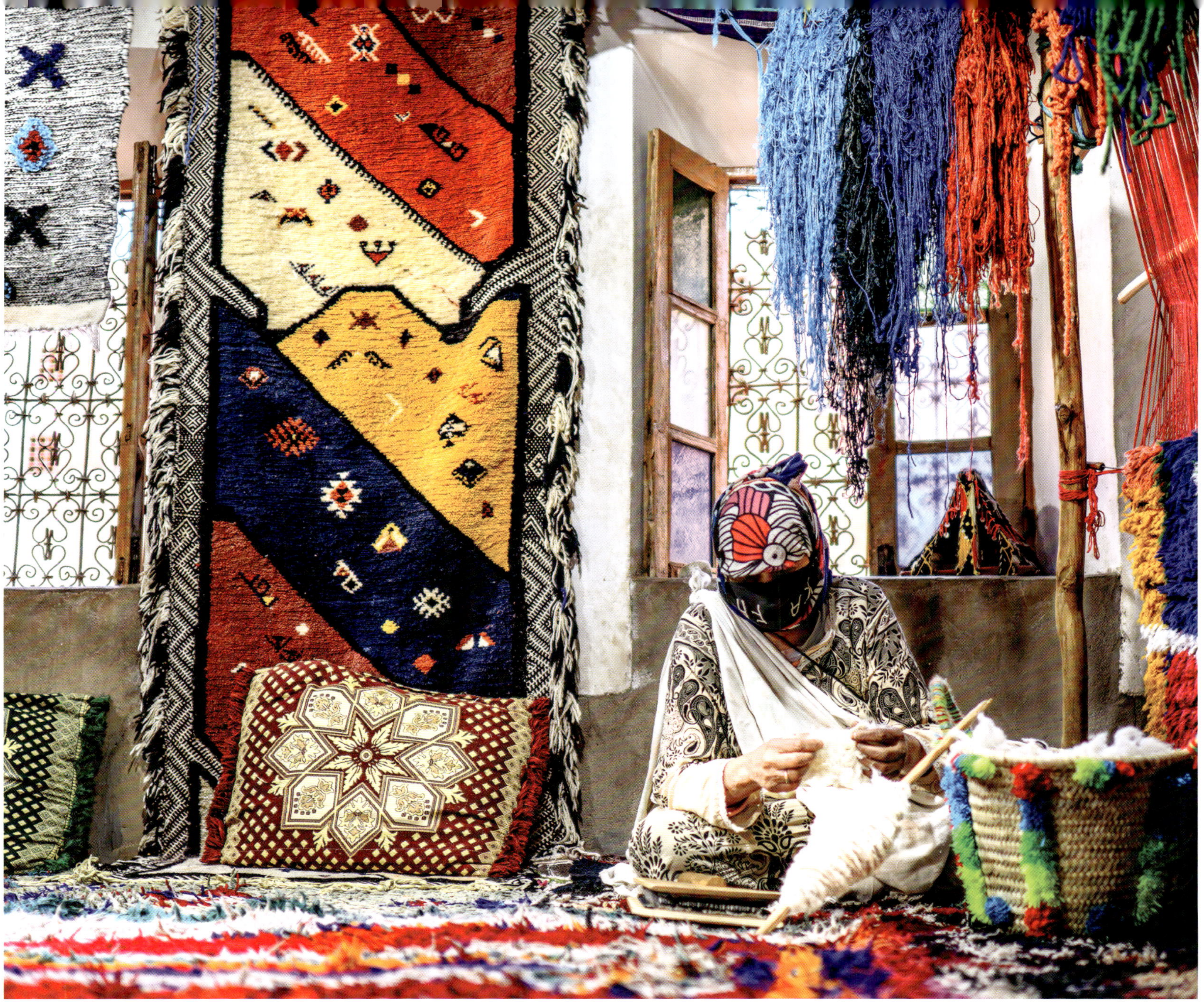

Previous page:
The rock walls of the Todra gorge, sometimes called "The Grand Canyon of Morocco."

Rug merchant pouring tea for shoppers.

Woman weaving traditional rug.

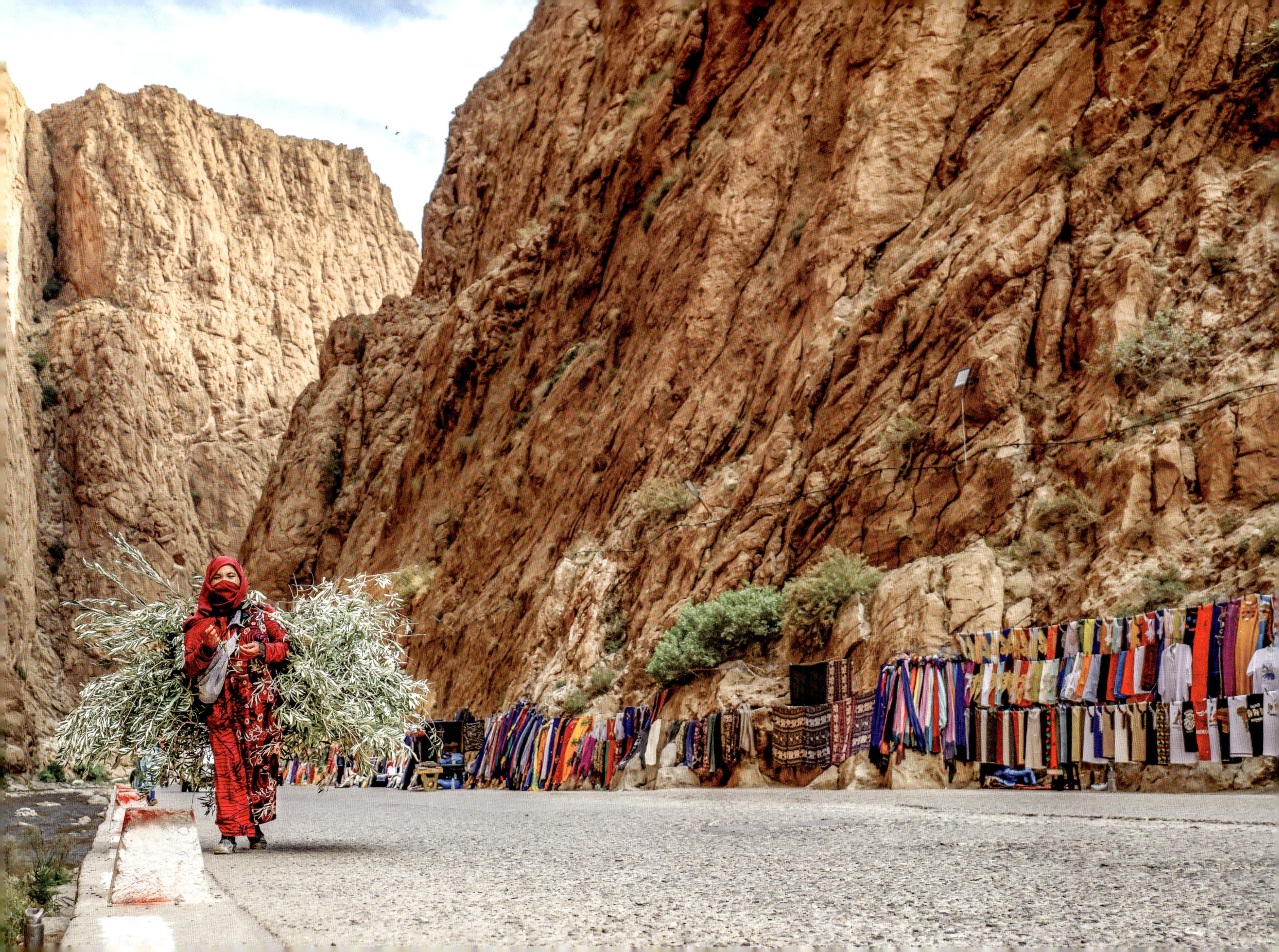

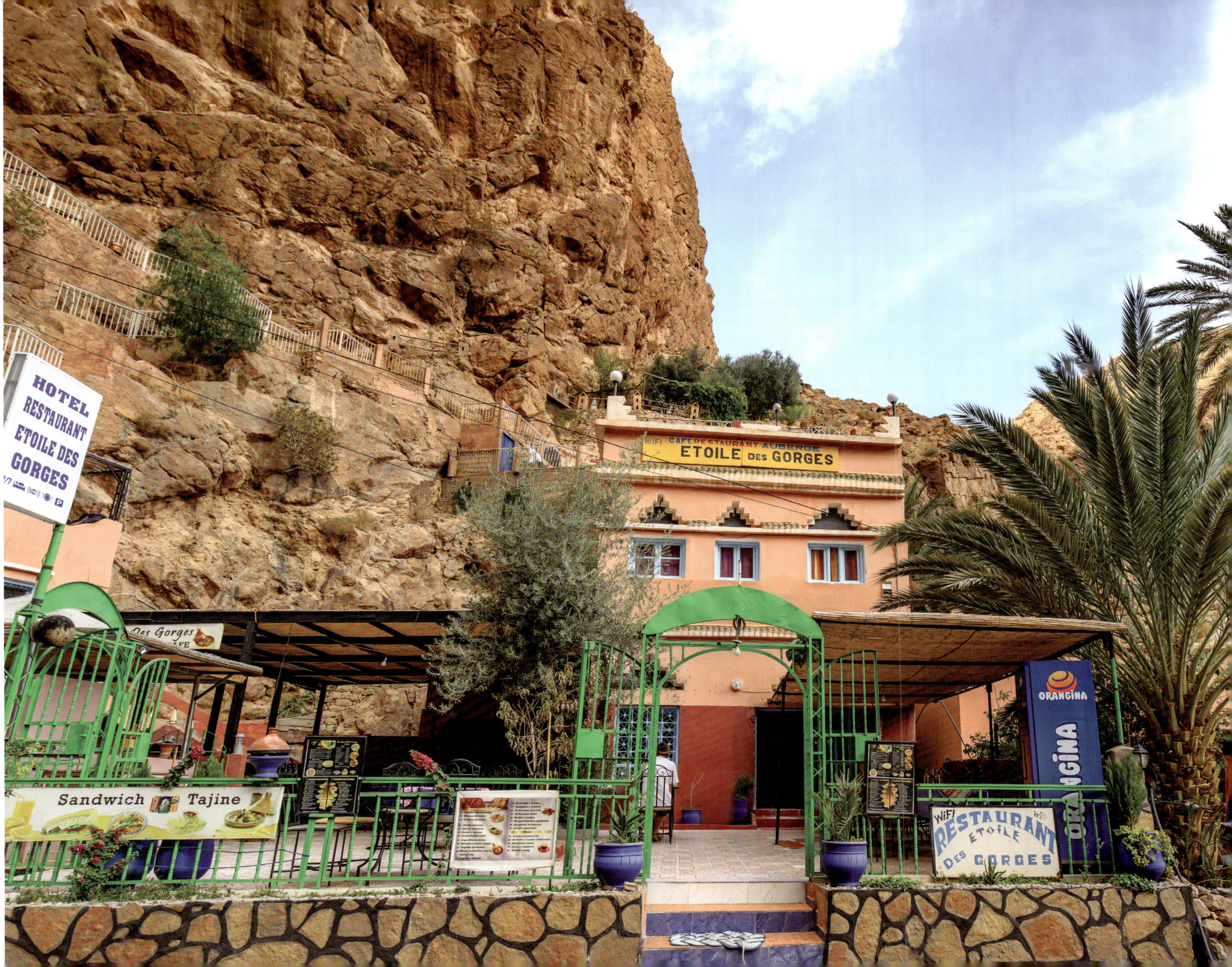
HOTEL
RESTAURANT
ETOILE DES
GORGES
WIFI
CAFE RESTAURANT AUBERGE
ETOILE DES GORGES
Des Gorges
Sandwich
Tajine
ORANGINA
ORANGINA
WiFi
RESTAURANT
ETOILE
DES GORGES

# WHERE HOLLYWOOD GOES TO FILM

Sometimes called "the Door of the Desert," Ouarzazate was once a stop for merchants and traders on their way from Northern Morocco and Europe. The small city is close to Todra Gorge, Ait Benhaddou, and the Sahara Desert, and is a stopping point for tourists visiting those locations.

Two of the main sites in Ouarzazate are the Kasbah Taourirt and the Atlas Corporation Film Studio, where many of the movies and television shows staged in Morocco are filmed. This location was first used as a movie set when Lawrence of Arabia was shot there in 1962. In all, the Atlas Studios has been used as a shooting location for some 200 films. Some of the most notable movies include *Cleopatra, Ben Hur, Gladiator, The Mummy, The Passion of the Christ, Kundun, Alexander the Great, Black Hawk Down,* and *Star Wars*.

Some scenes of the television hit series, *Game of Thrones*, were filmed at a studio set built for the episodes shot there. The studio is open for public tours of the various sets that were created and then left behind, including a massive Egyptian set used in *The Mummy, Asterix, Tutankhamen, Cleopatra,* and *Game of Thrones*.

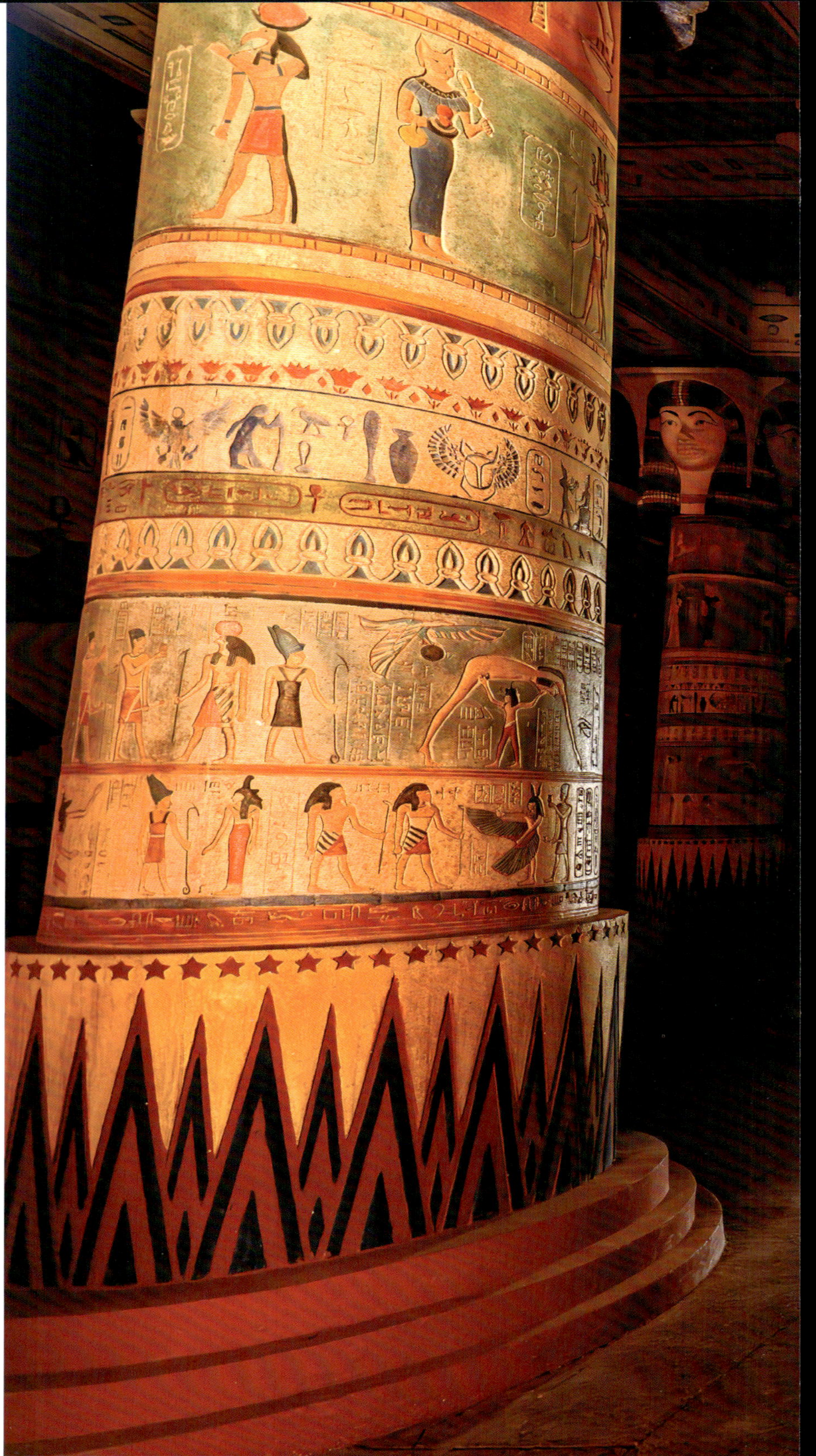

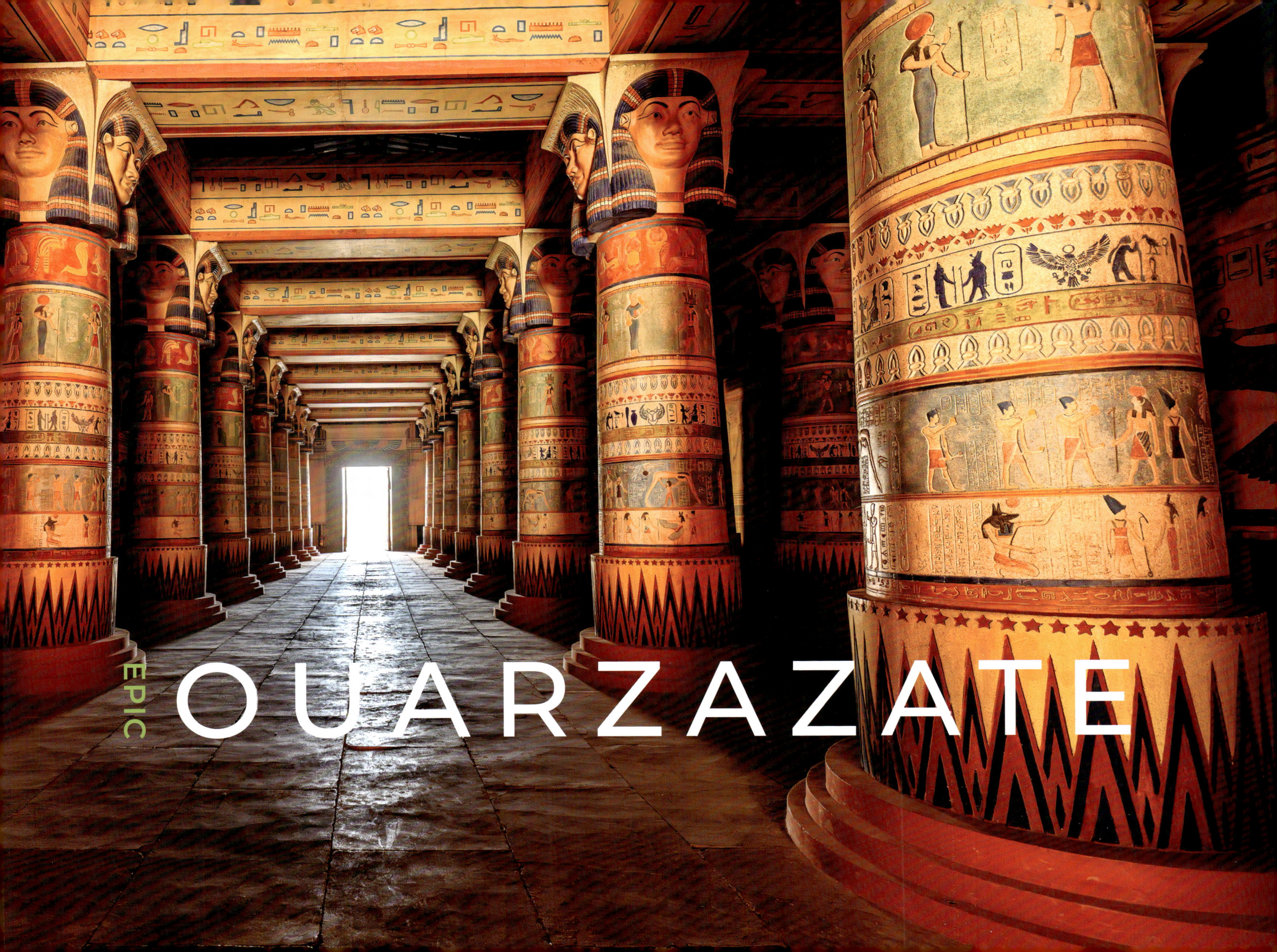

EPIC

# OUARZAZATE

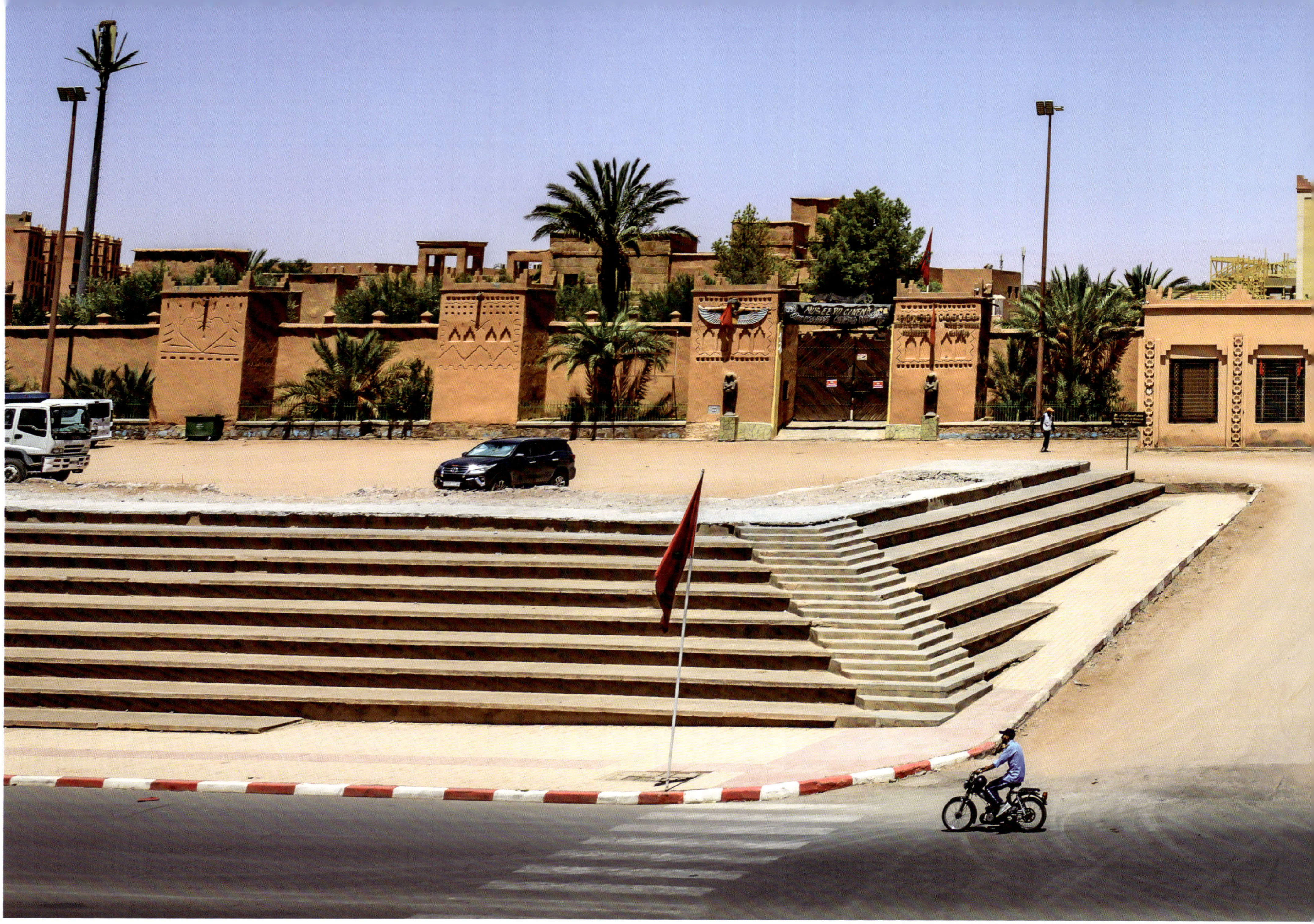

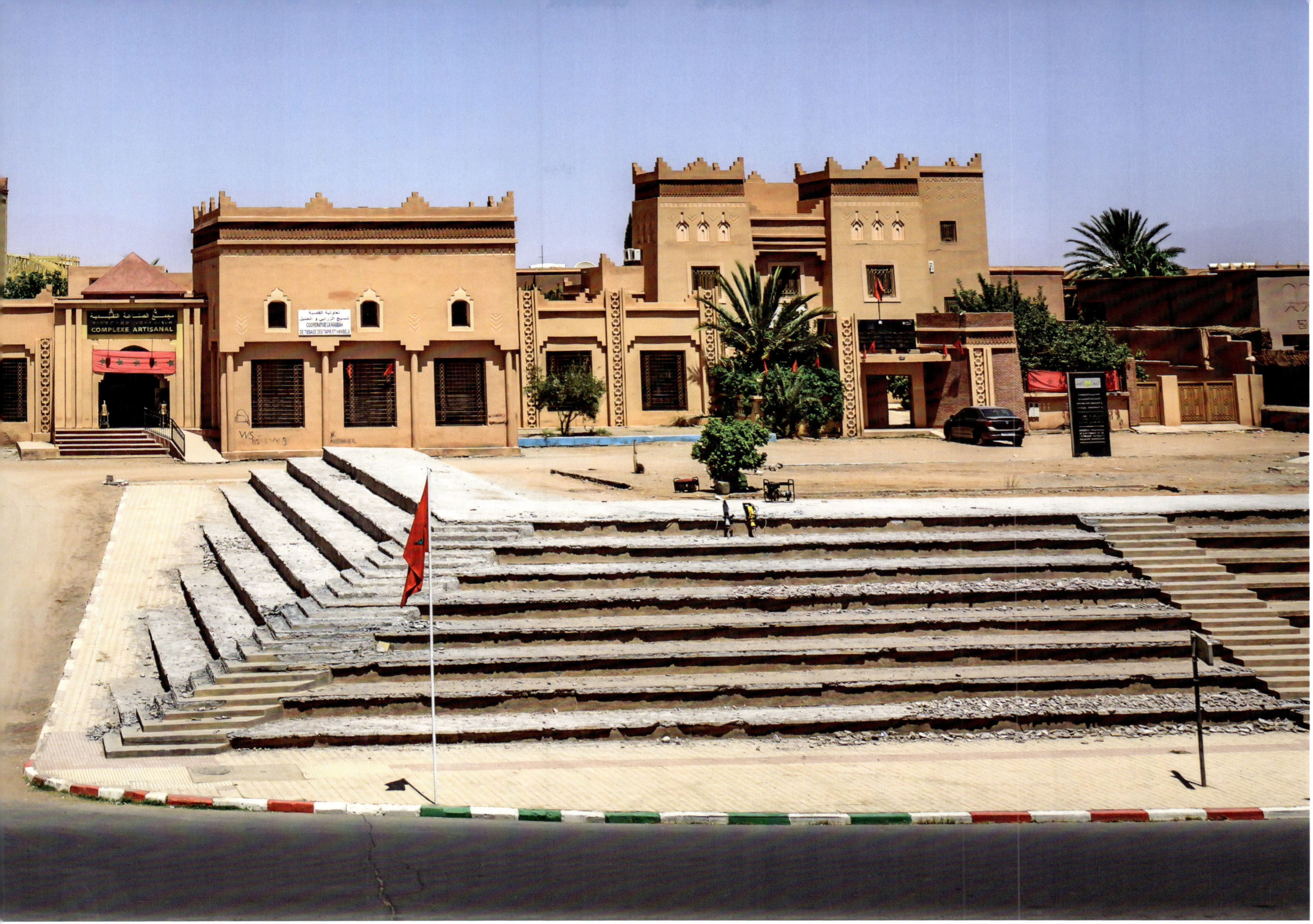
مجمع الصناعة التقليدية
COMPLEXE ARTISANAL
تعاونية القصبة
لنسيج الزرابي و الحنبل
COOPERATIVE LA KASBAH
DE TISSAGE DES TAPIS ET HANBELS

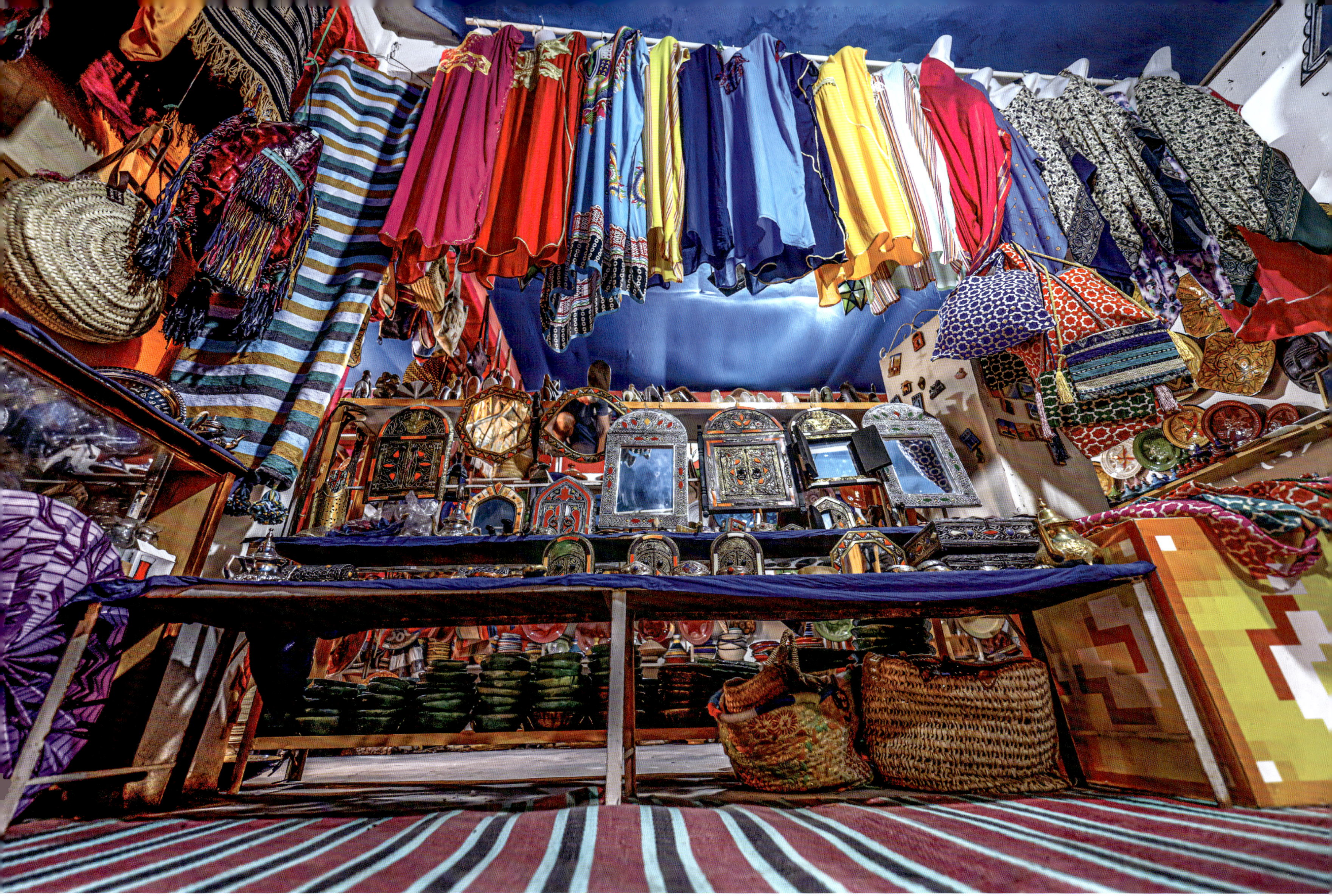

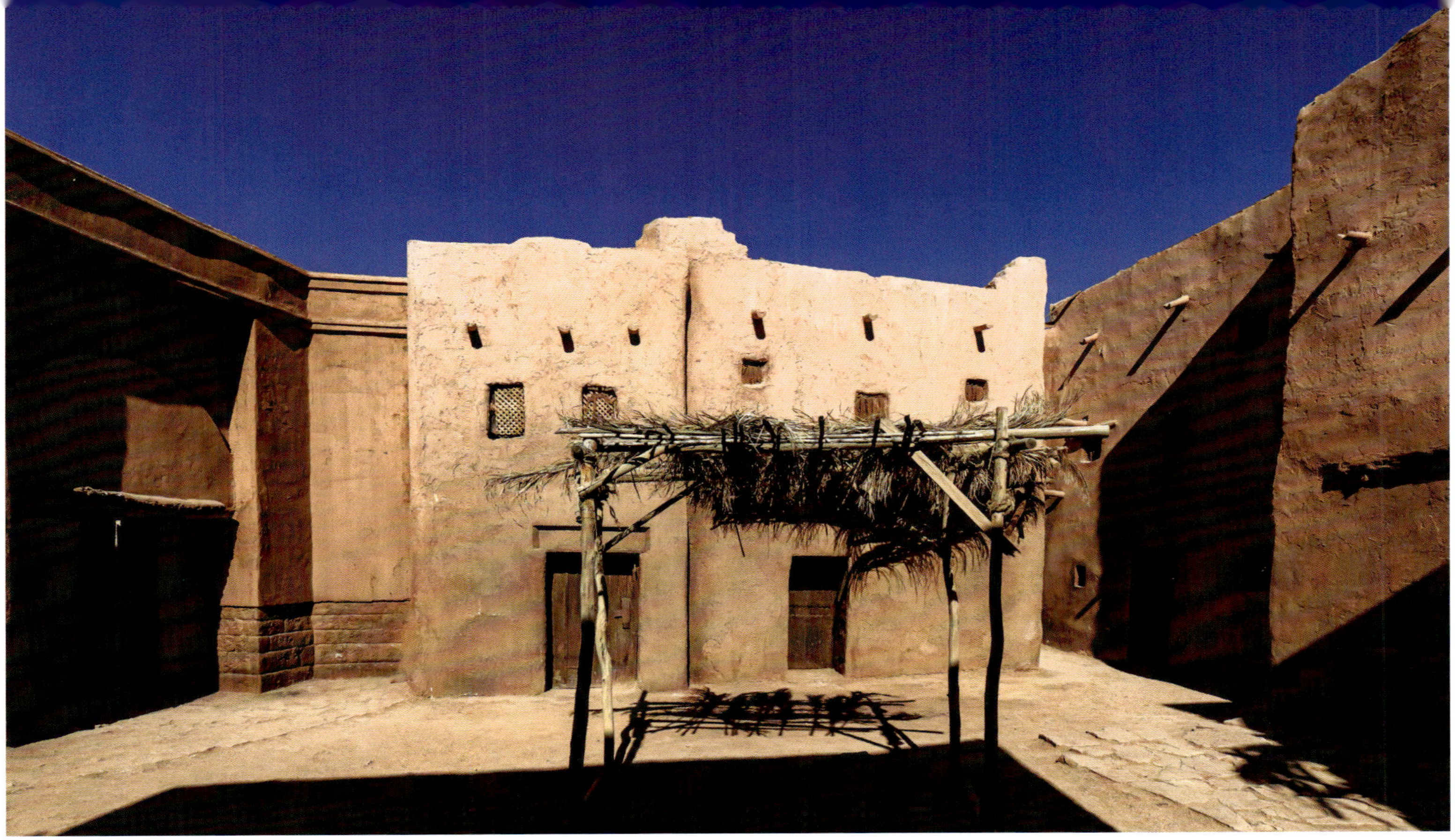

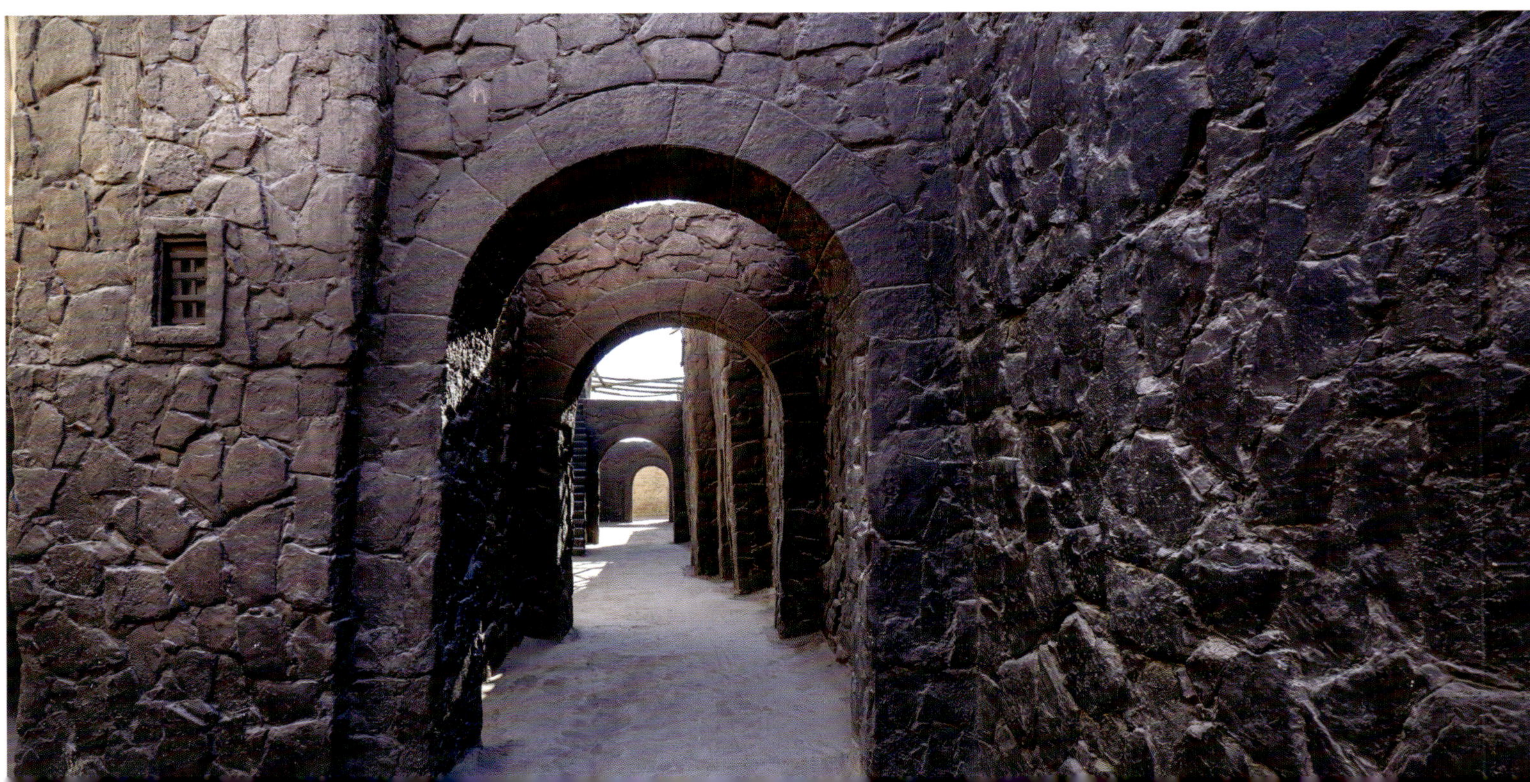

Previous page:
View of the front of the Atlas movie studio.

Photos of scarves and baskets inside a shop.

Section of the movie set used in the film, *Gladiator*.

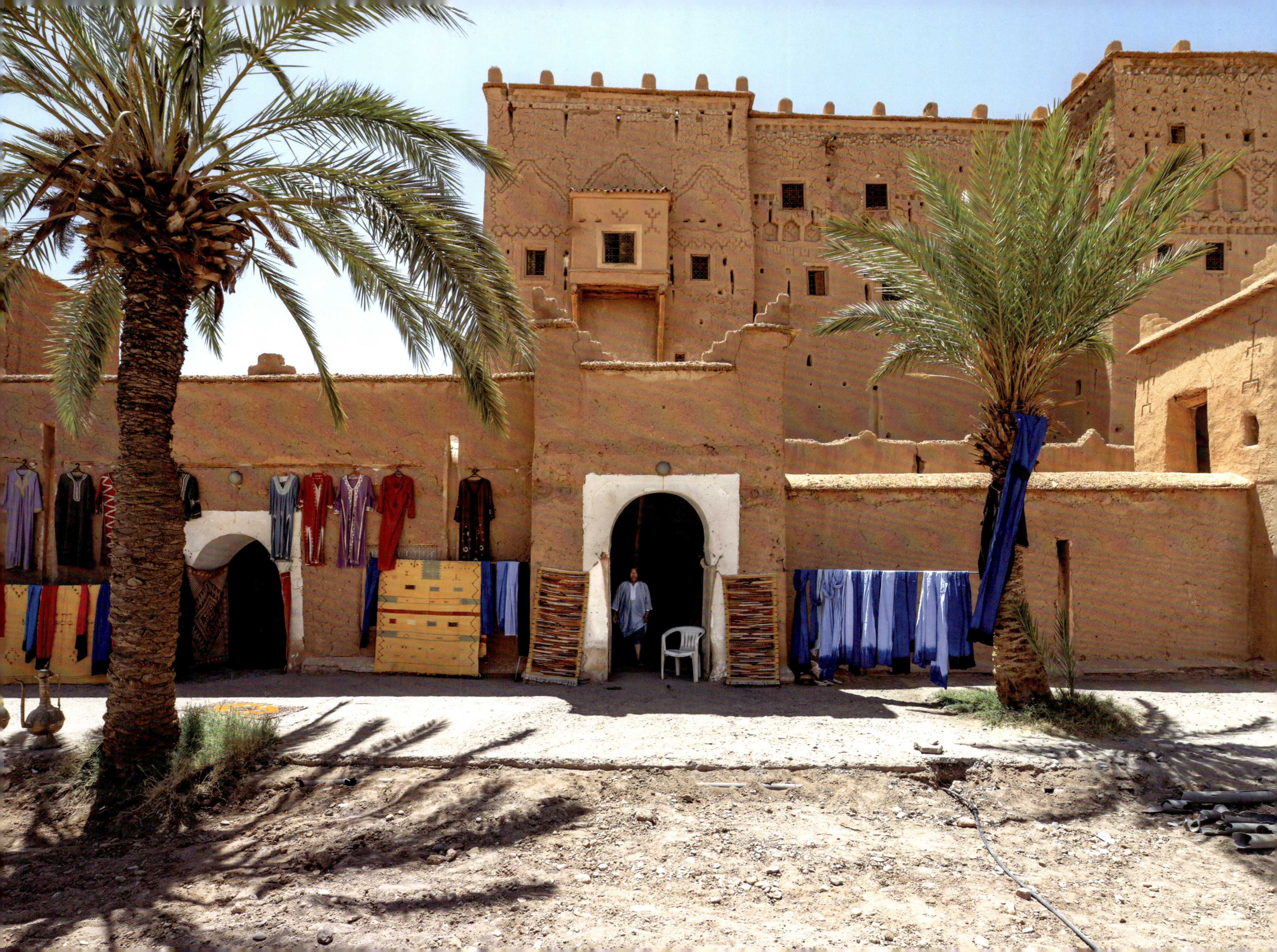

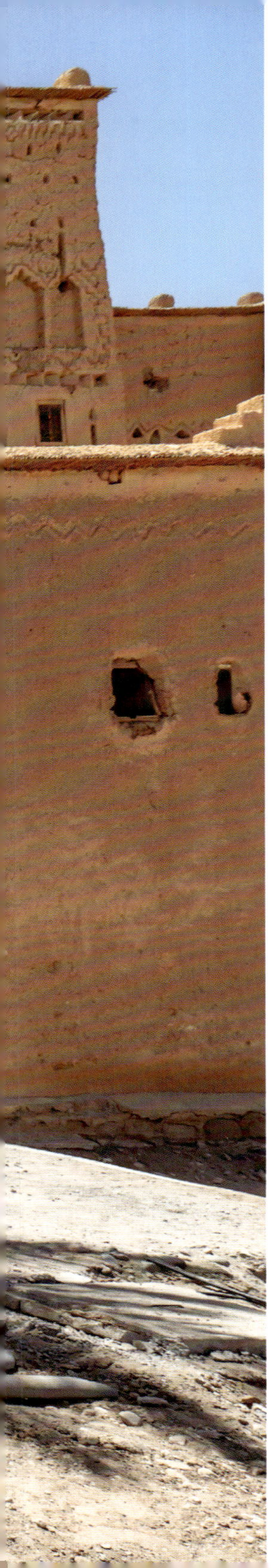

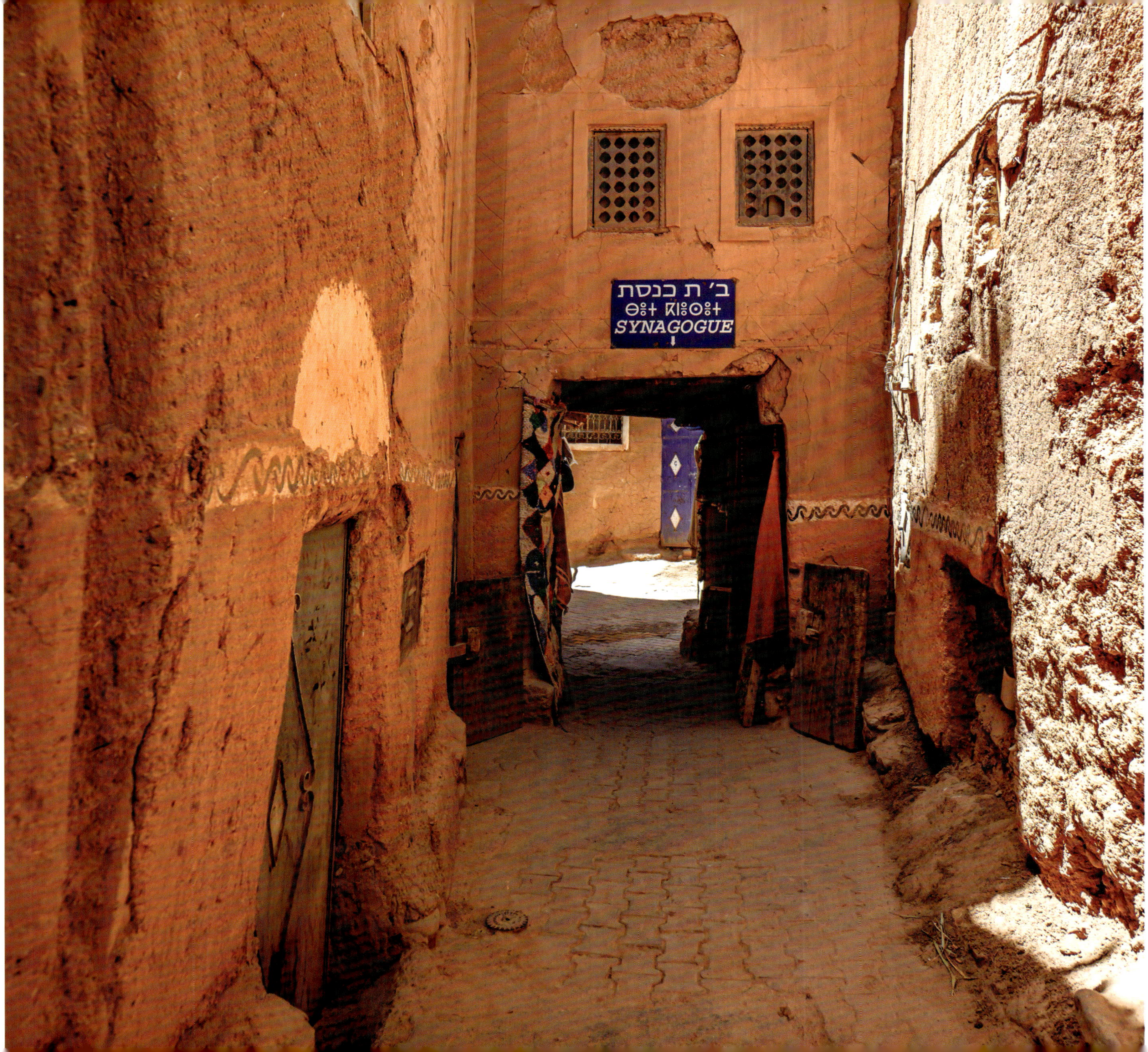
בית כנסת
SYNAGOGUE

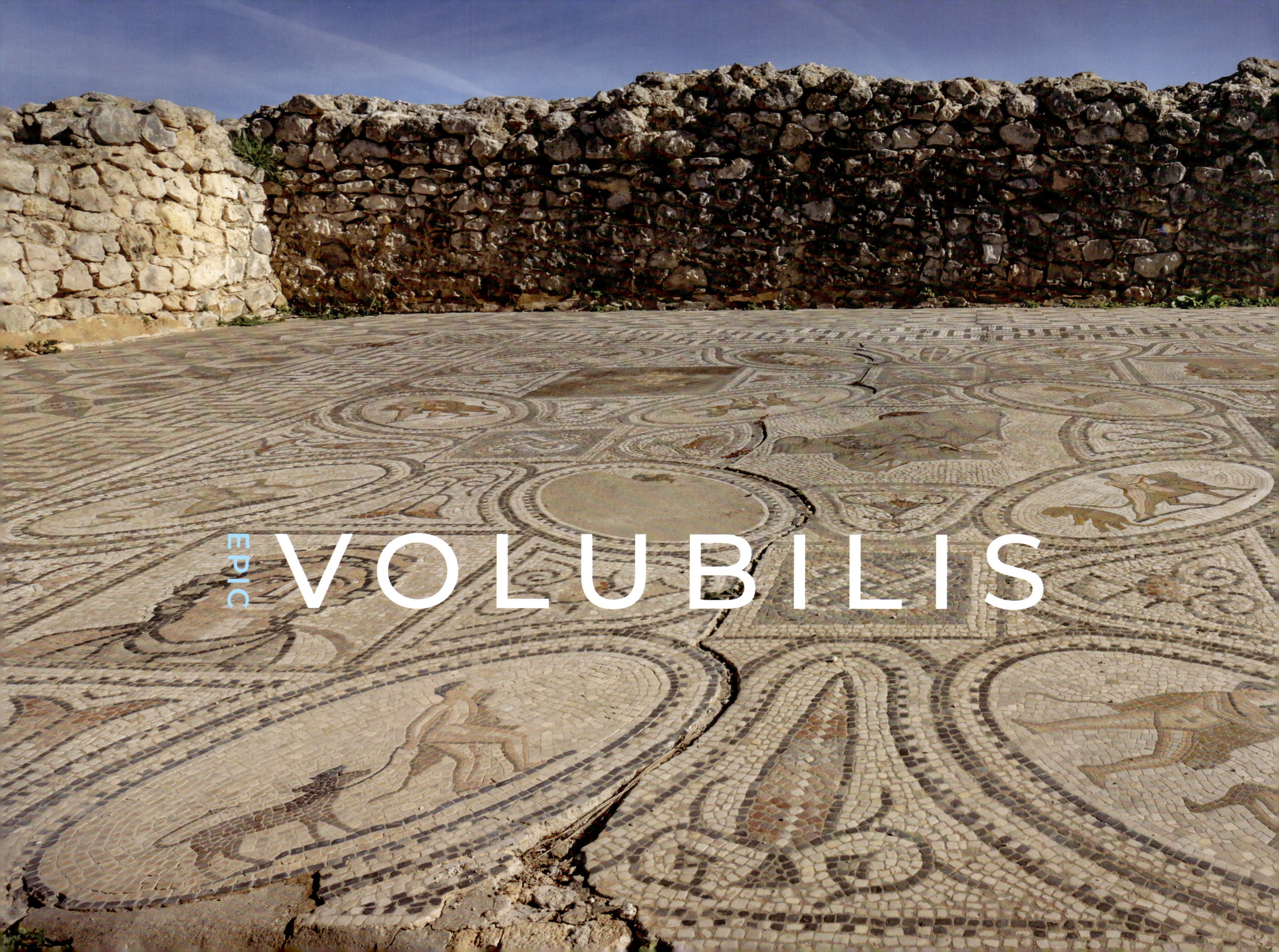
EPIC
VOLUBILIS

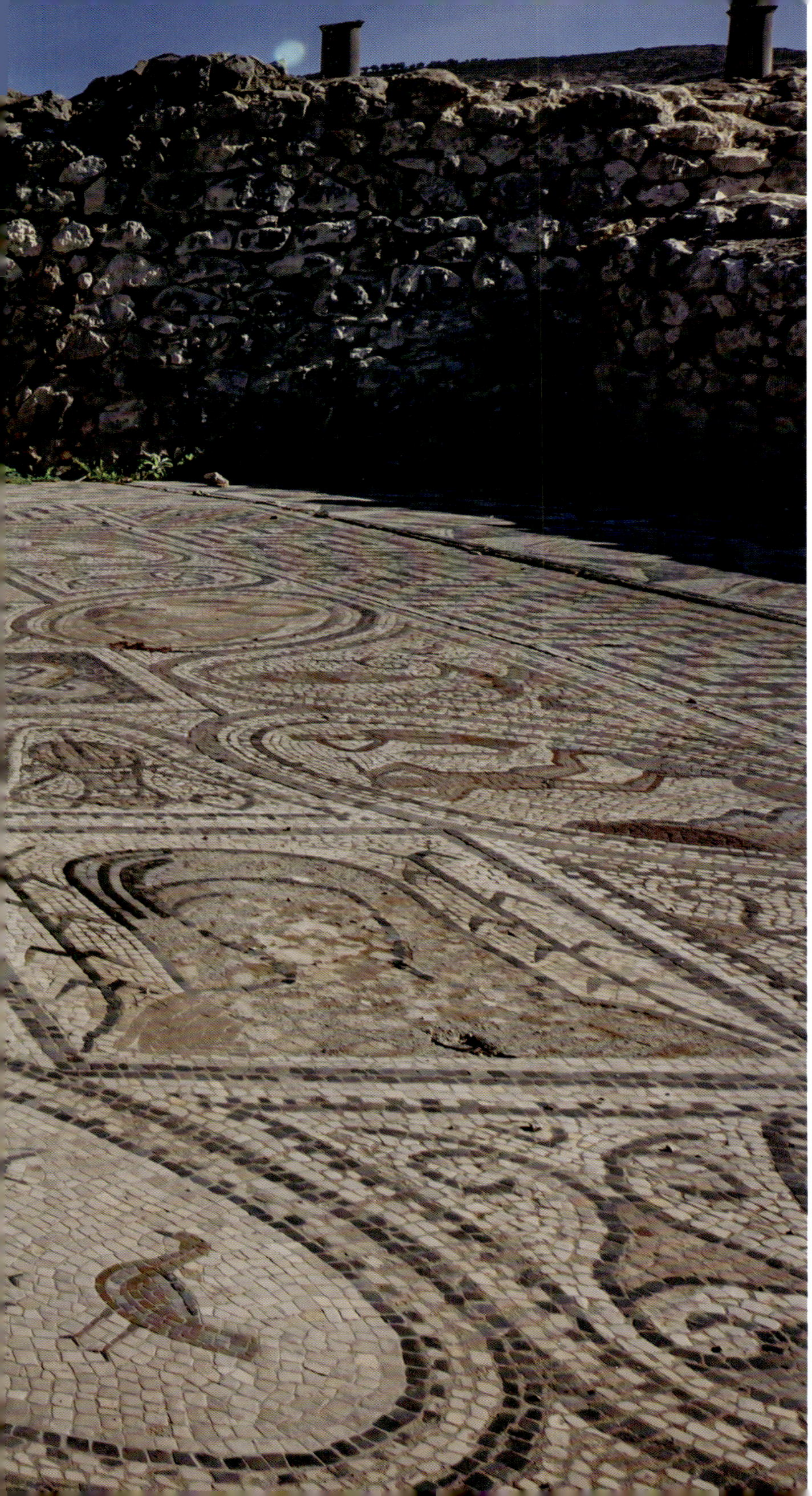

# AN ANCIENT ROMAN CITY

Not far from the city of Meknes is Volubilis, a once thriving Roman outpost that was established by Amazigh tribes in the 1st century and later annexed to Rome. The city was a thriving community that was deserted by Romans in 285 after it fell to local Amazigh armies.

Today, Volubilis is a UNESCO World Heritage Site and an existing example of what Roman culture and life were like. Among the ruins available for touring are several private homes, some decorated with mosaic floors that remain intact, a basilica, a thermal bath, and Pa ace of Gordian, believed to once be the home of the imperial procurator.

All the ruins sit before the great Triumphal Arch, which spans the city's main streets. Much of the arch was once decorated with Roman figures, a chariot and horses, portions of which remain. In addition to the arch, the partial remains of The Capitoline Temple rises behind the site of the basilica and a courtyard. It features the remains of an altar at the top of 13 steps leading to the Corinthian columned temple.

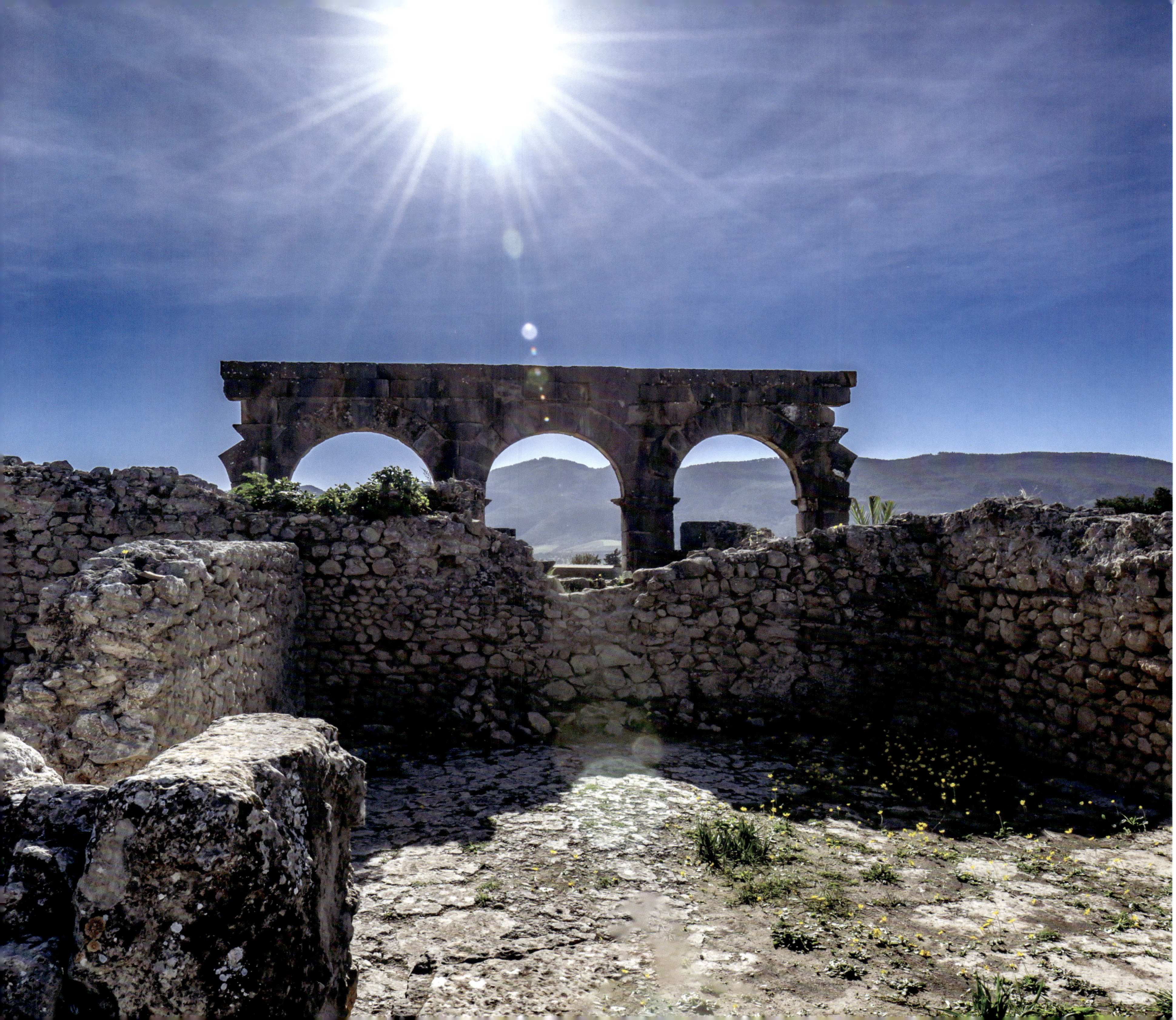
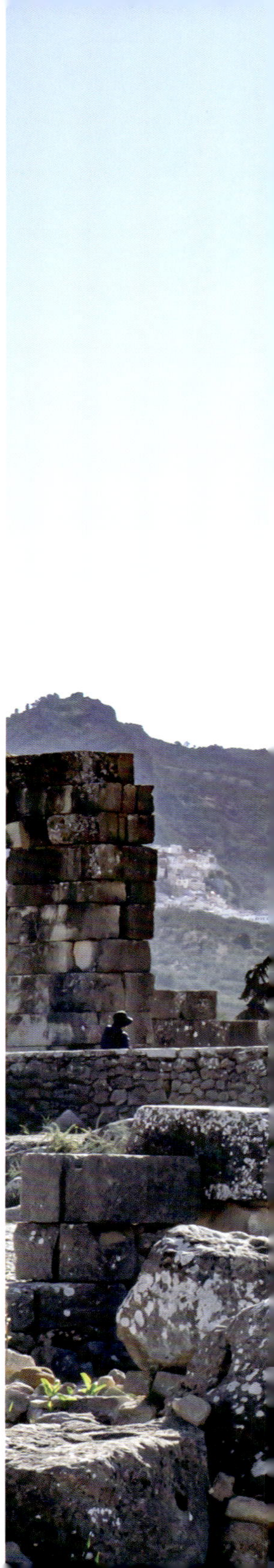

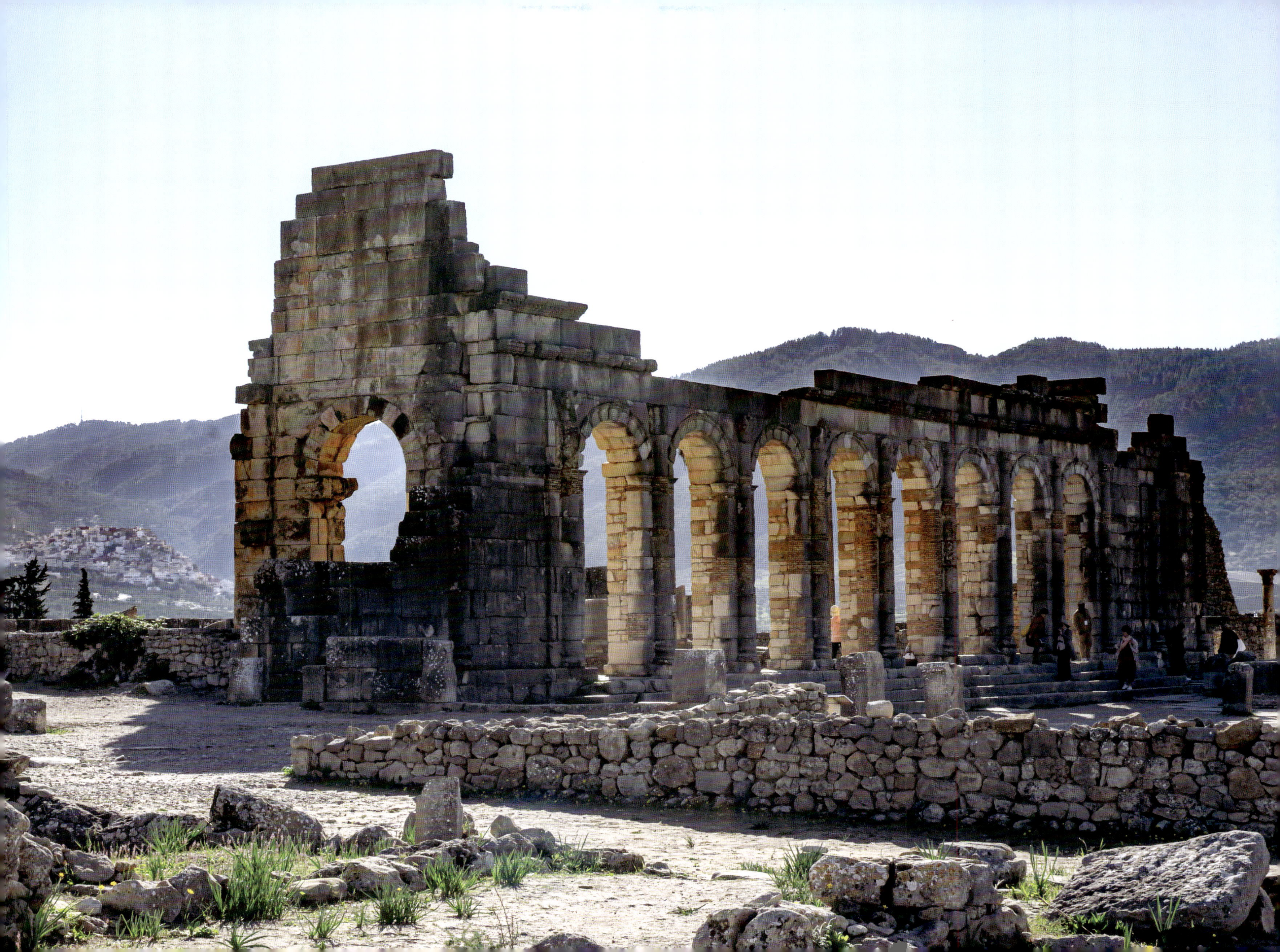

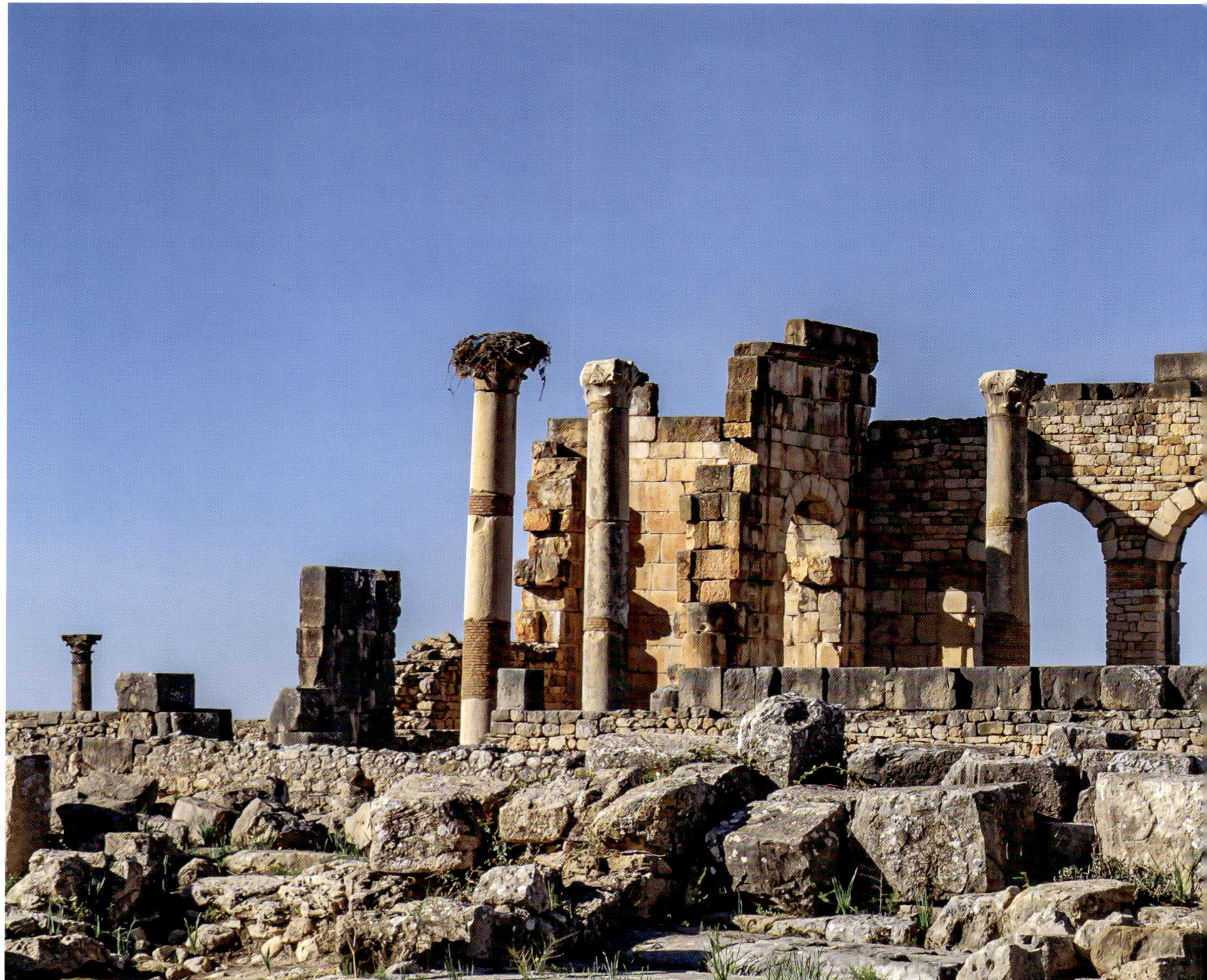

Previous page and right: Various views of the Triumphal Arch inside the ruins of the Roman city of Volubilis.

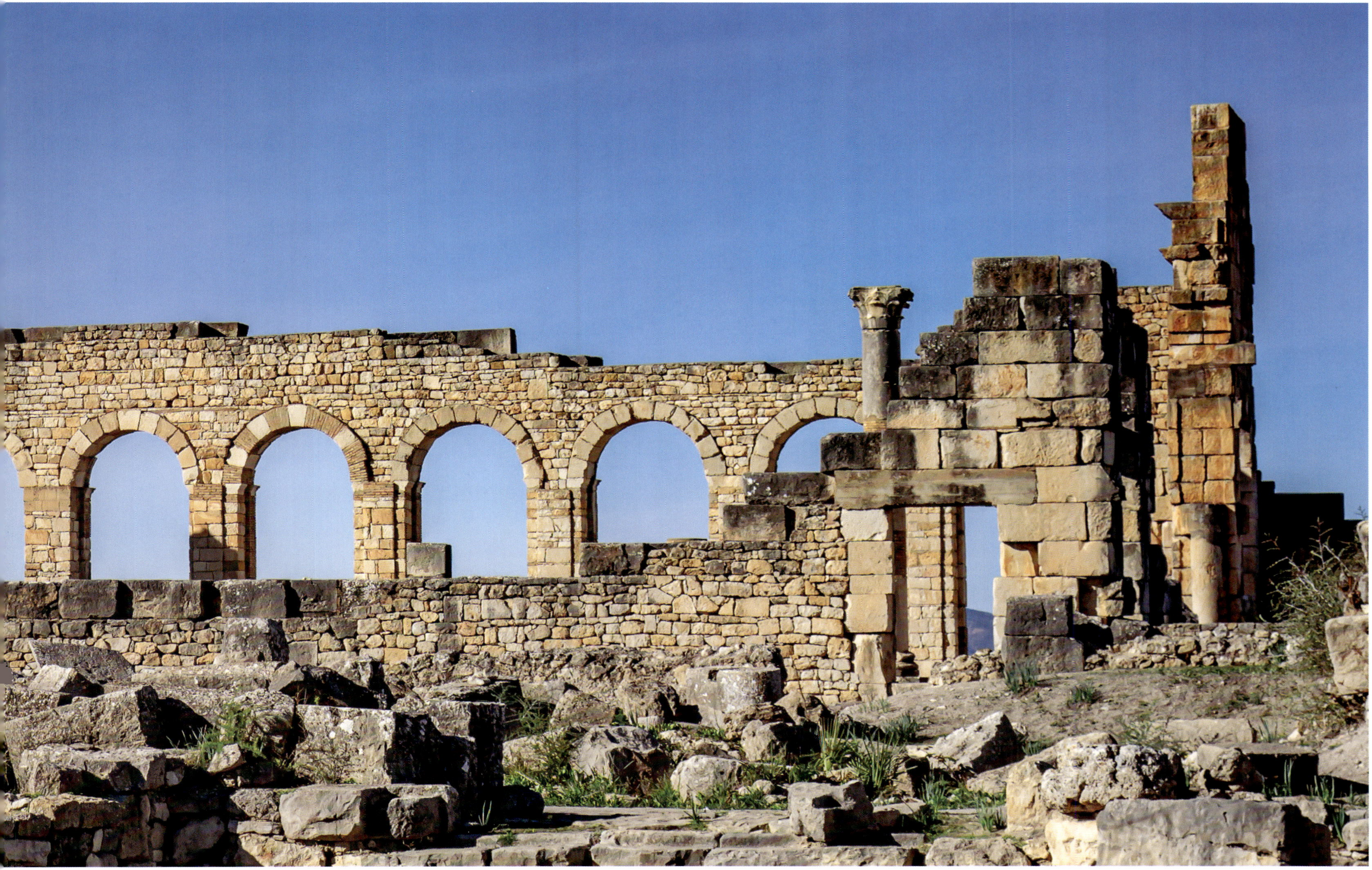

# EPIC FACES OF MOROCCO

Any tour of the Kingdom of Morocco is going to involve a lot of driving and moving from city to city can take hours. Along the way there is plenty to view and varies from geographic location to location.

But the one constant anywhere in the Kingdom are the always engaging Moroccan people. Some are not thrilled to be photographed—many will just not allow it, and politely ask that they not be, but they are always friendly and happy to help. Still, others do not mind the attention, and a big part of this project was about documenting the many faces and people along the way.

People watching, according to Nomadic Tour guide Khalid El-Ouafy, is "the official pastime," in Morocco. And why wouldn't it be? The Moroccans encountered were always interesting, kind and inviting. They offered mint tea, were always generous and warm in every way. They were genuinely kind, and while they say they don't like to be photographed, their easy smiles said otherwise.



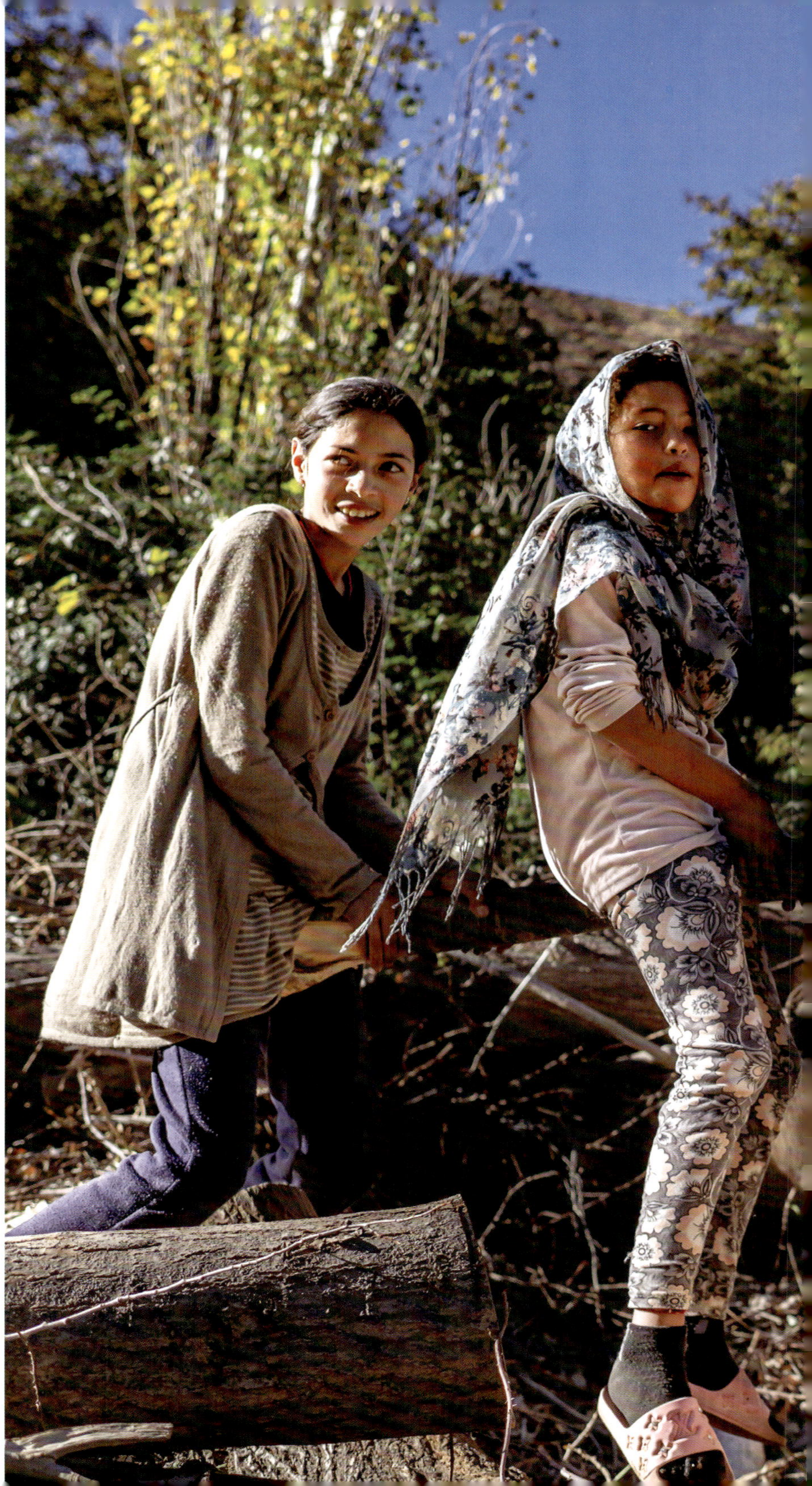

# EPIC FACES

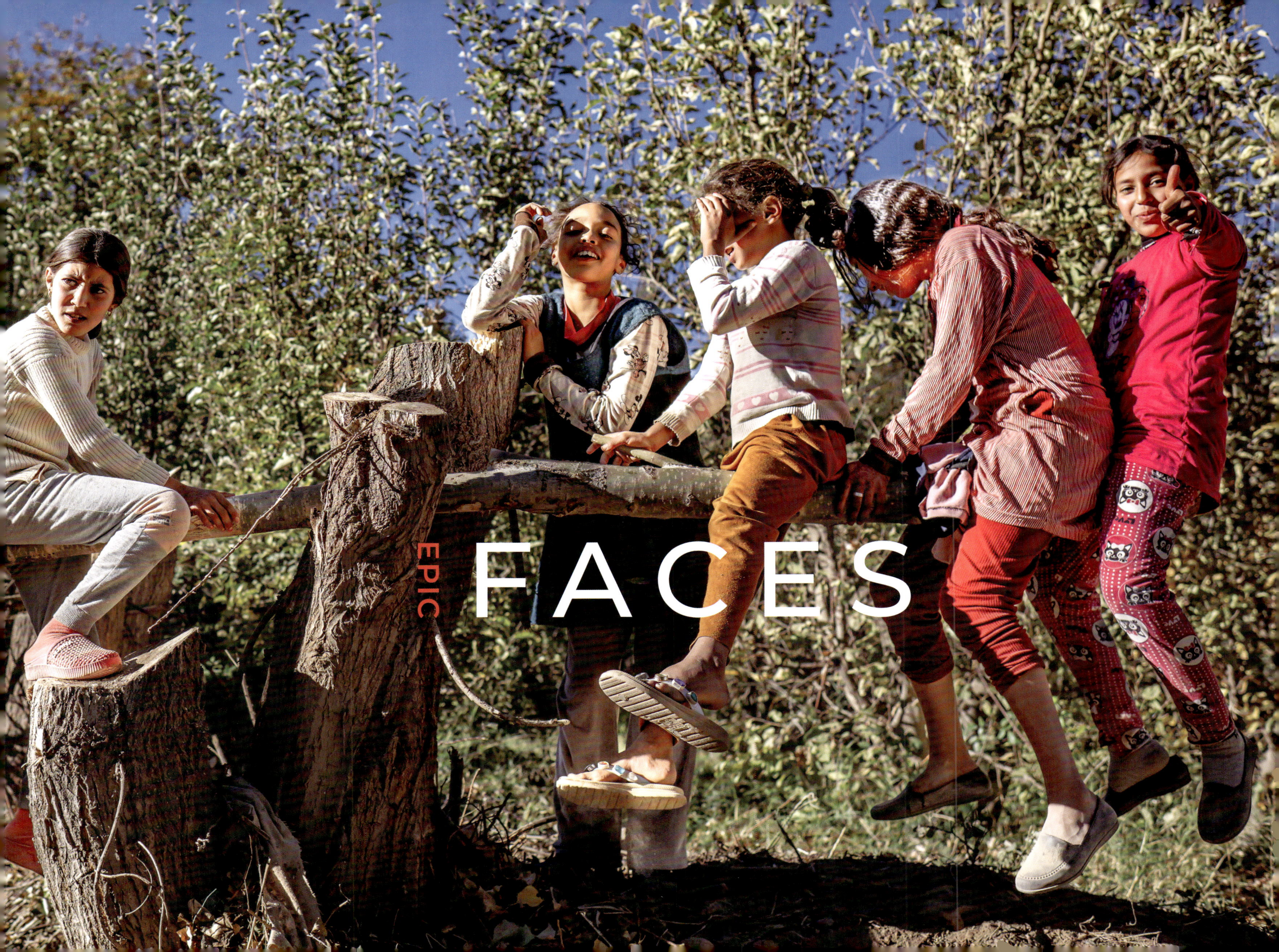

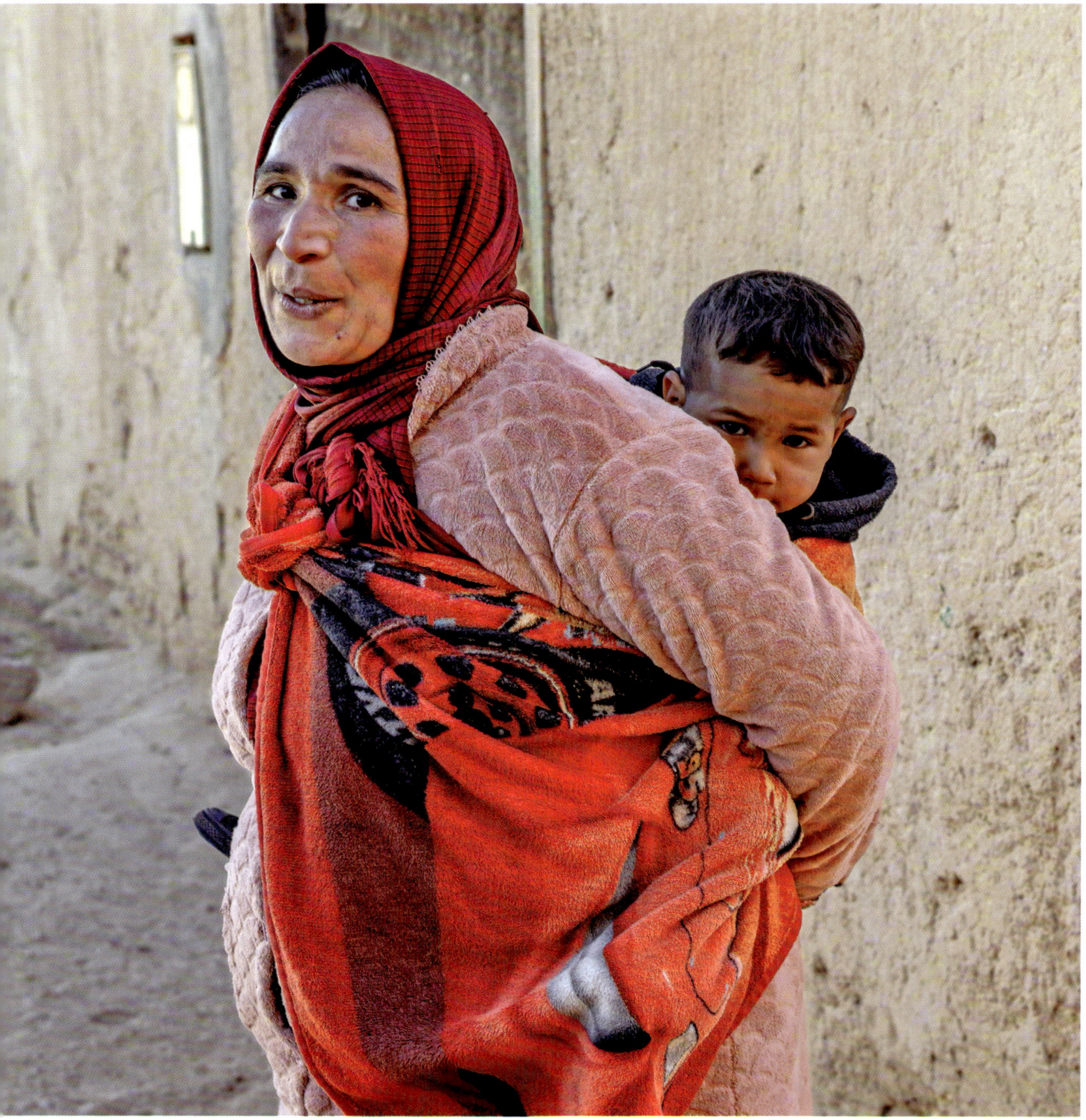

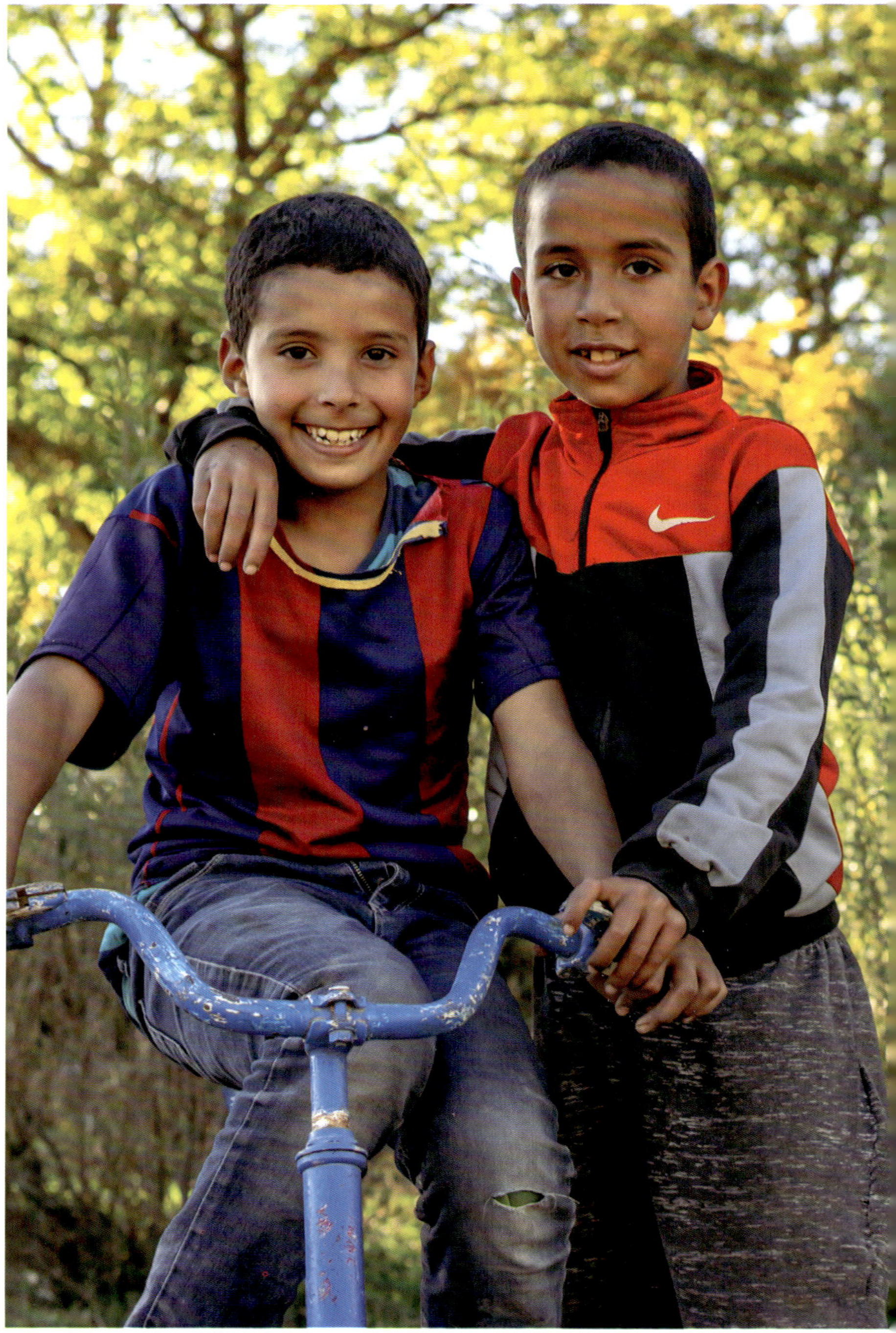

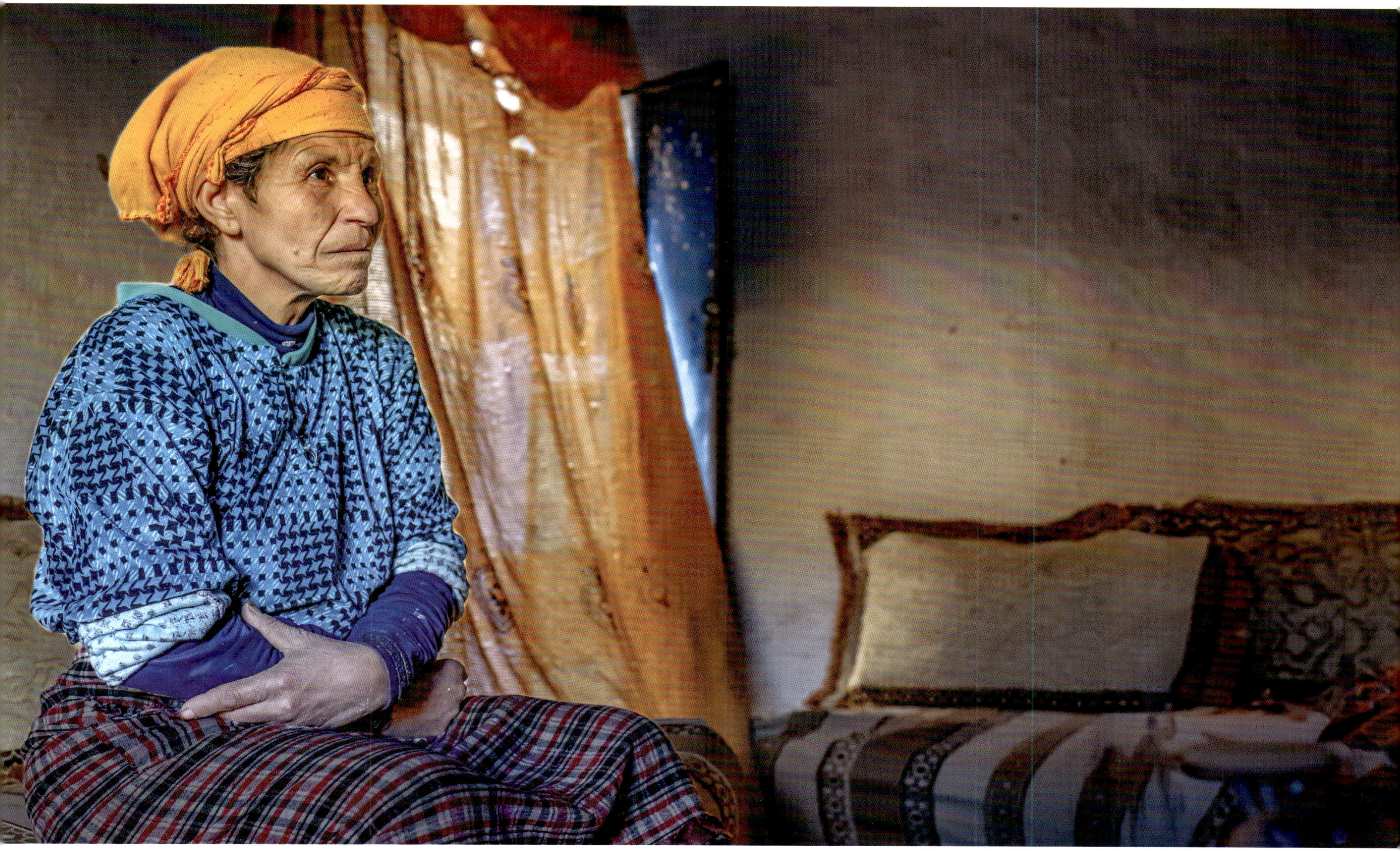

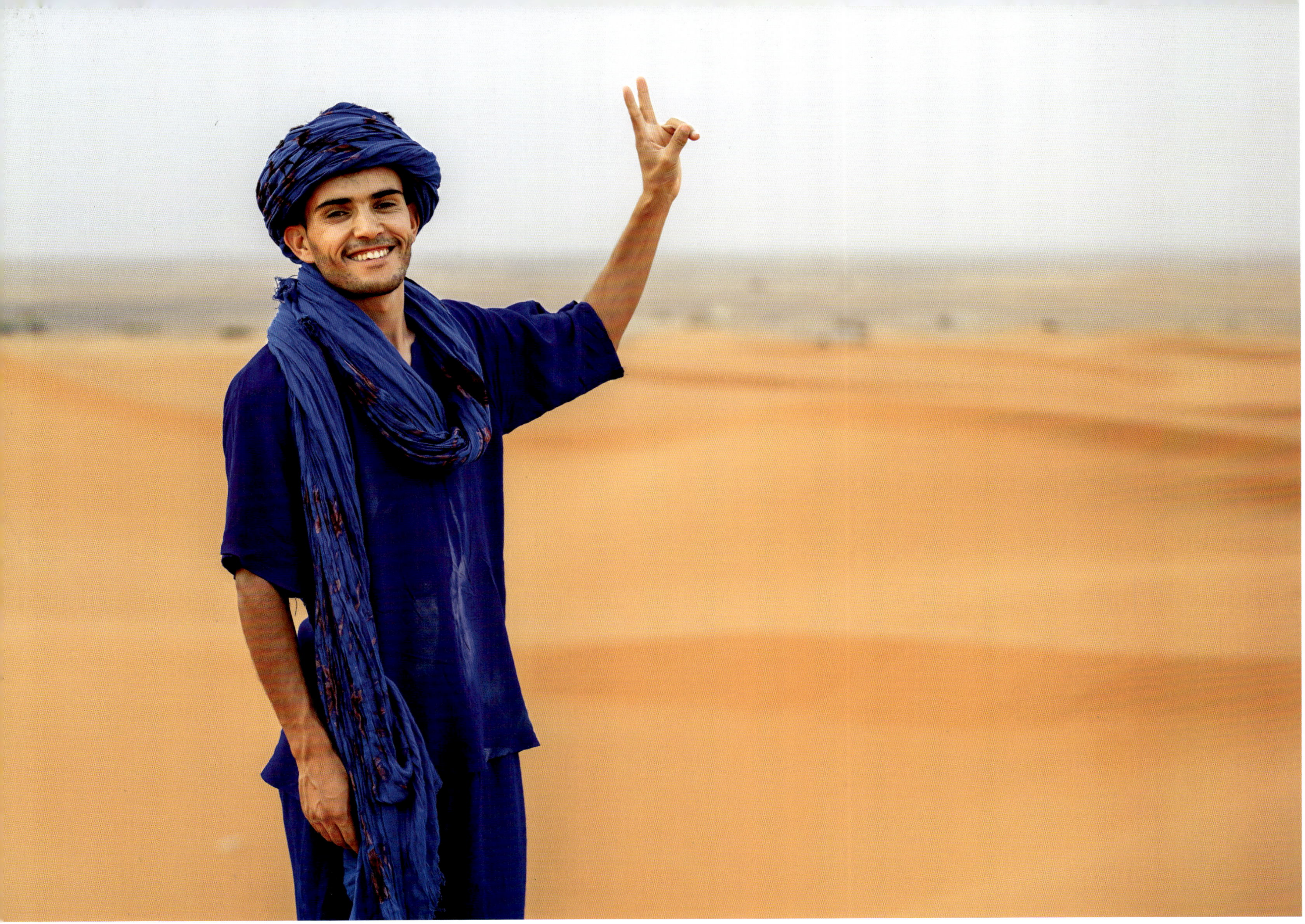

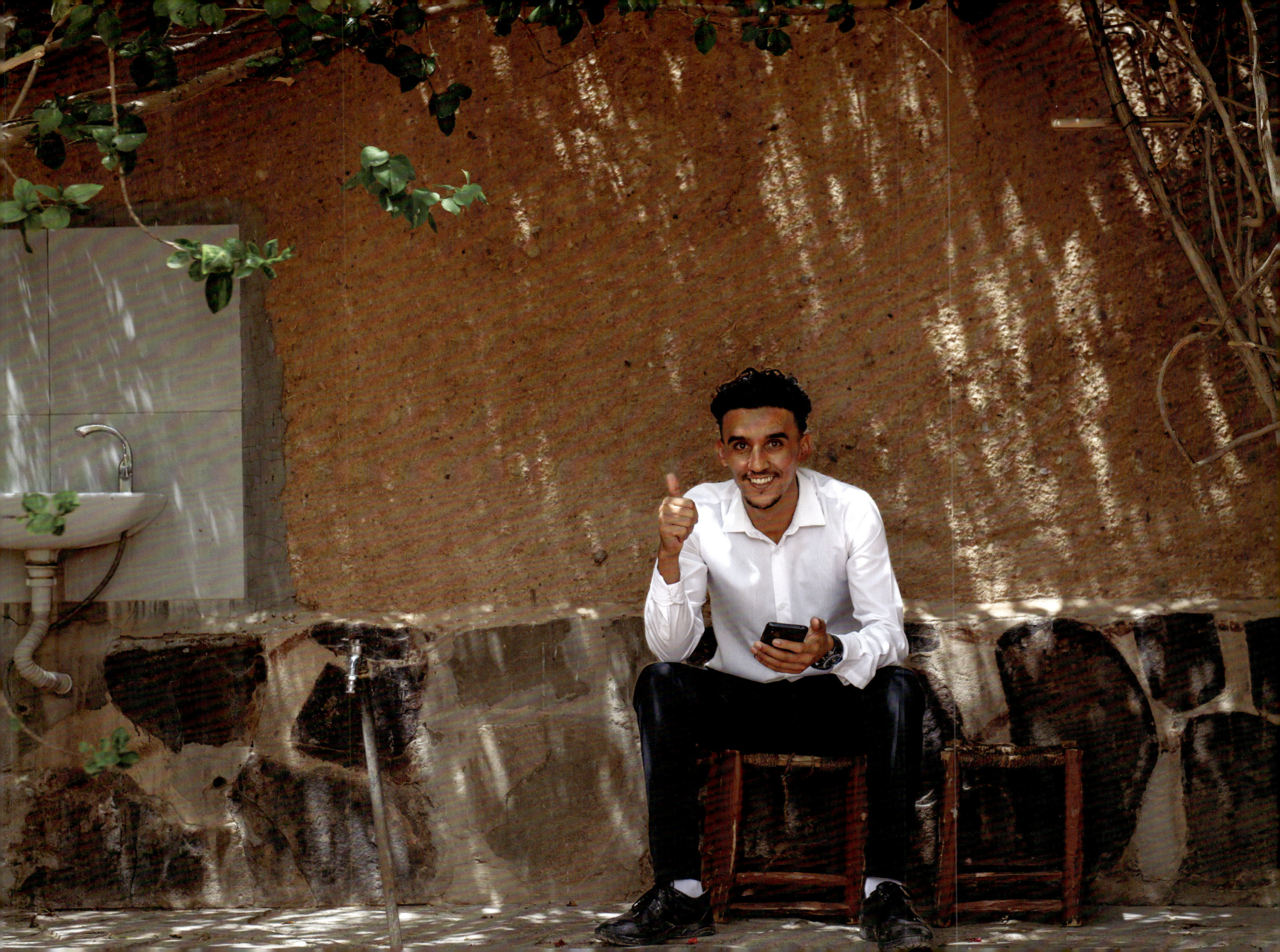

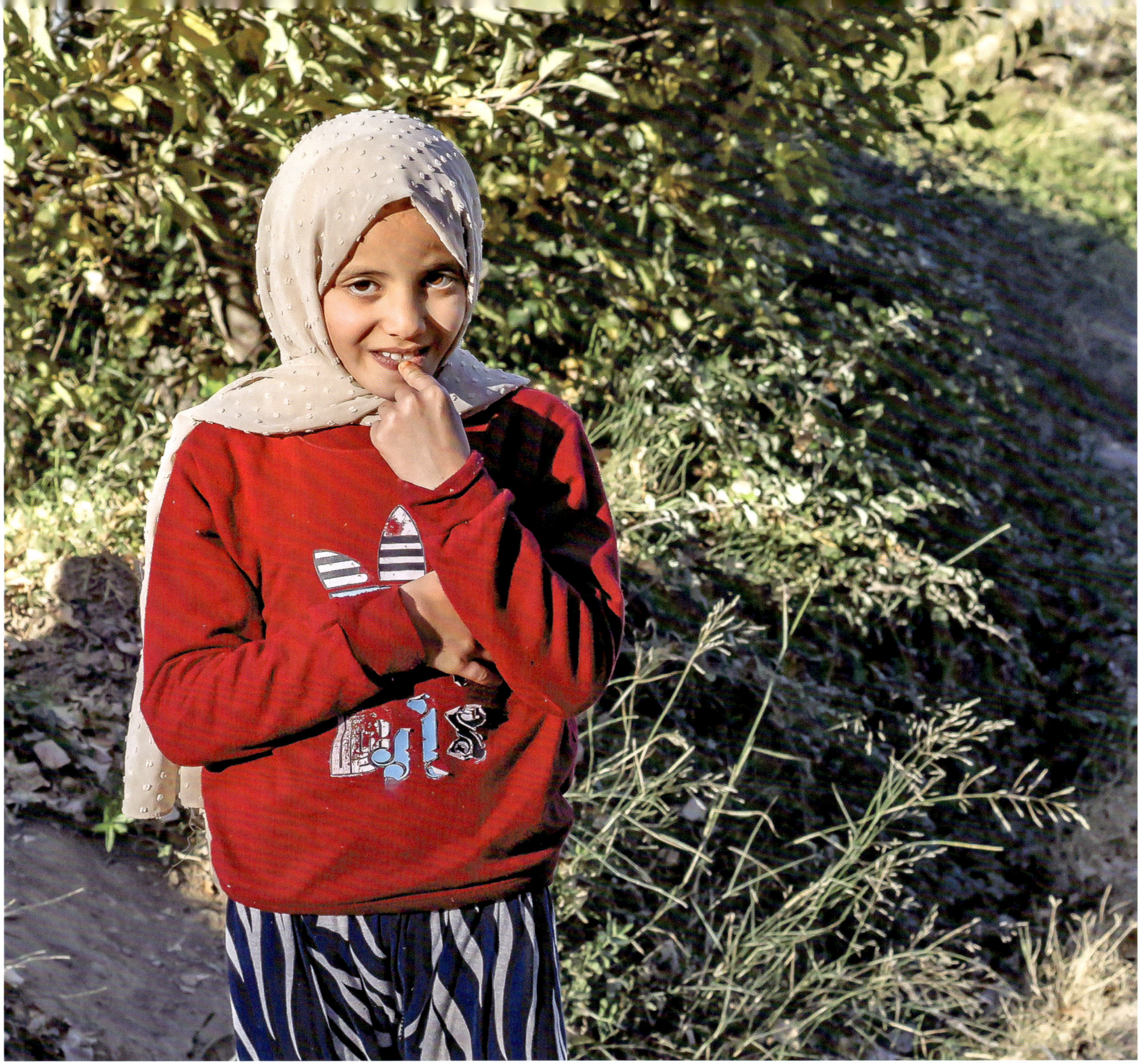
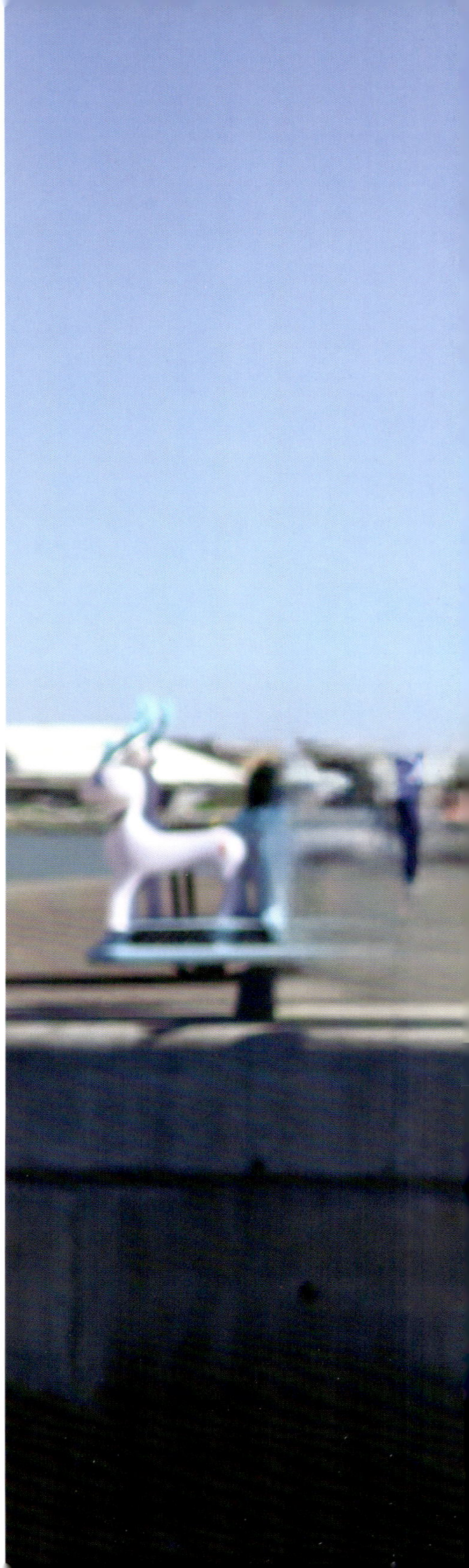

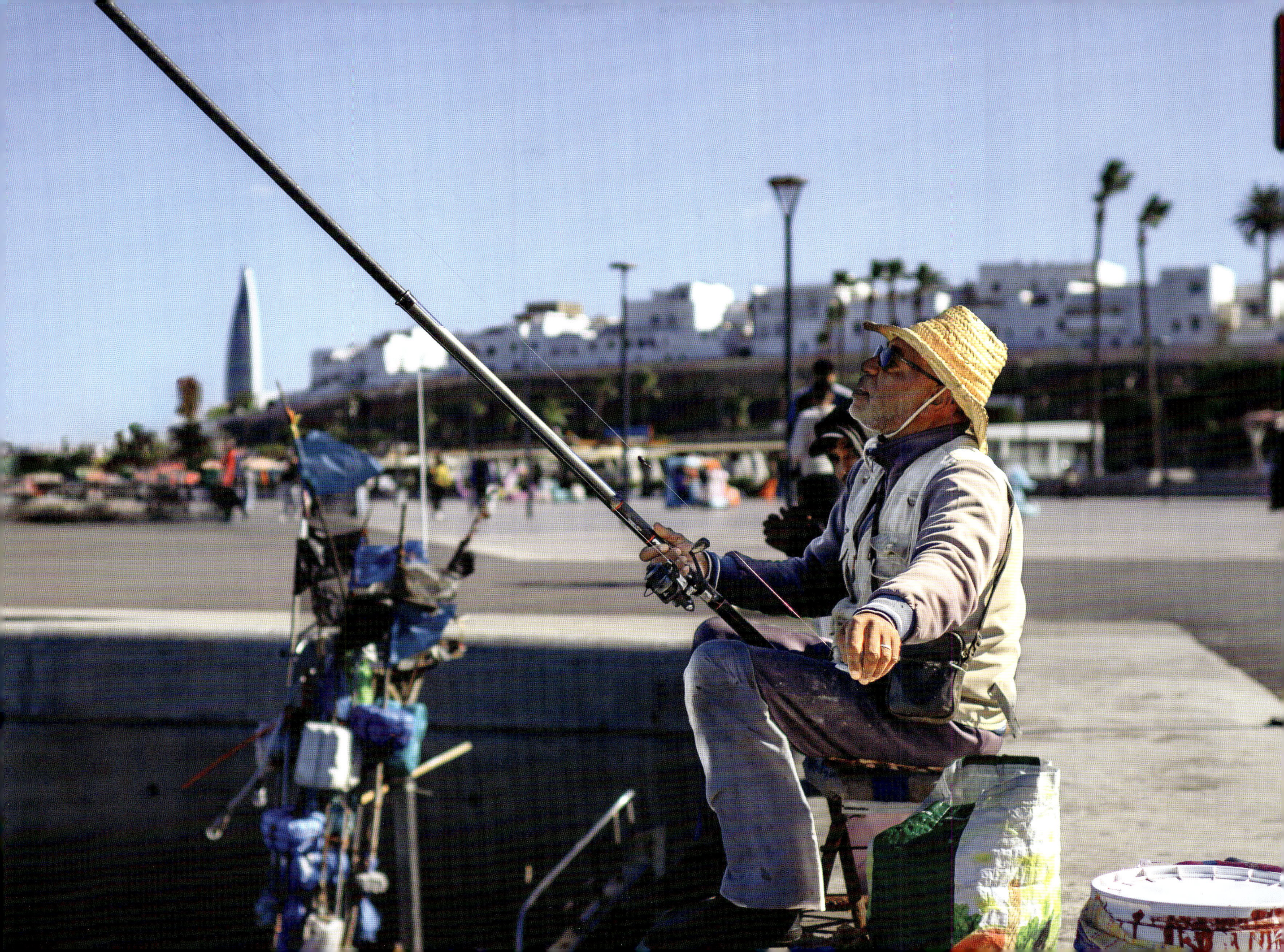

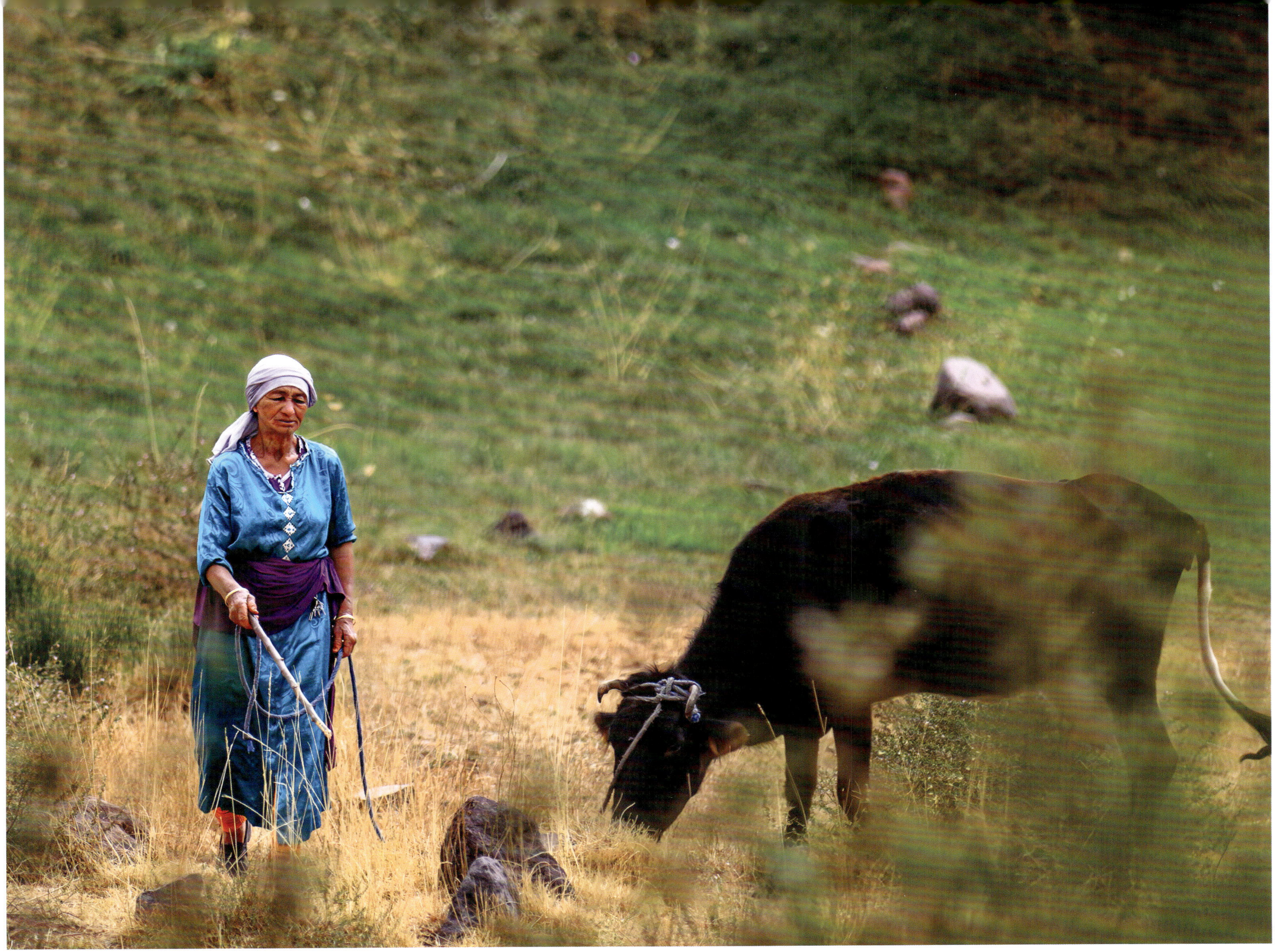

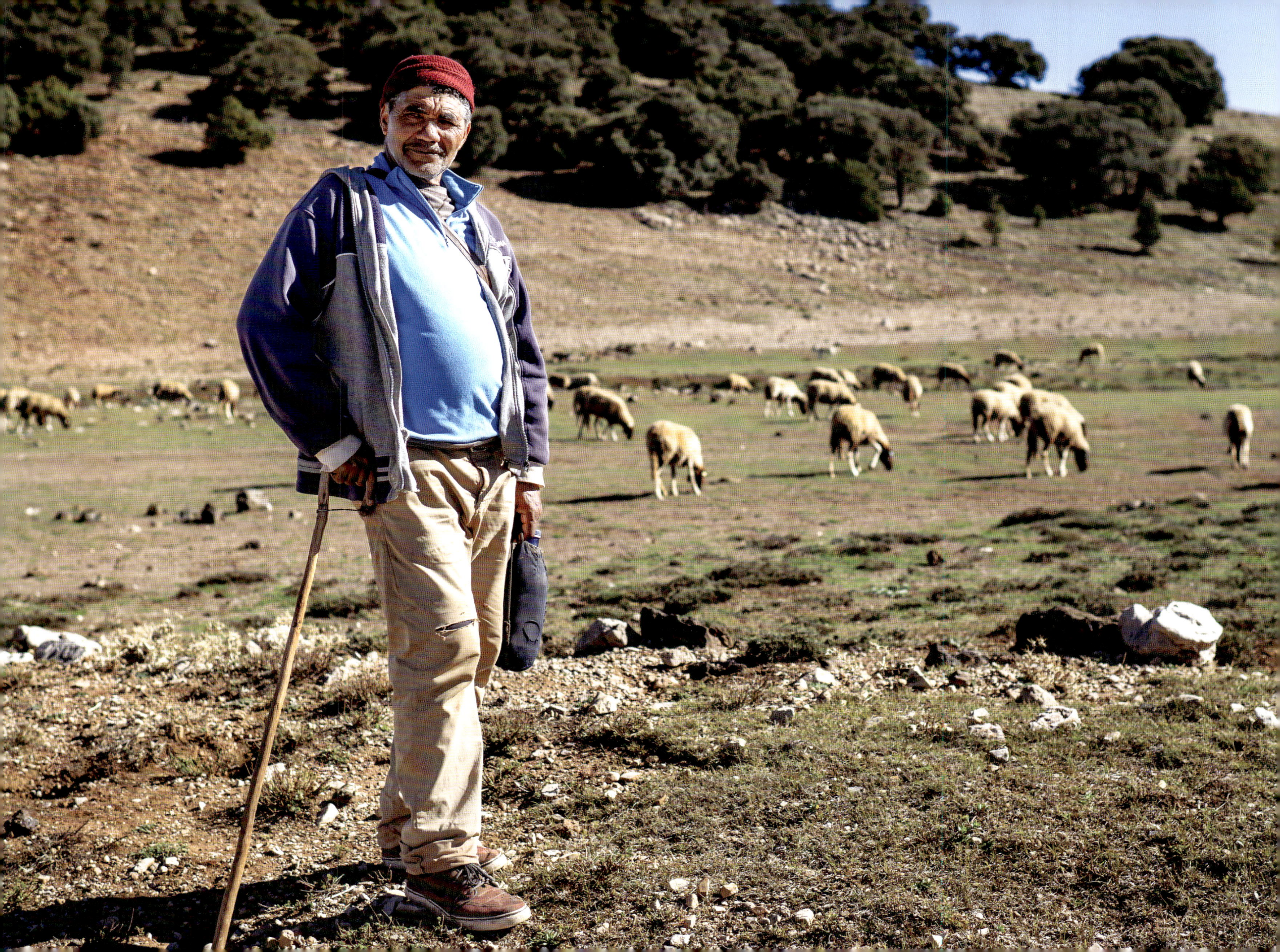

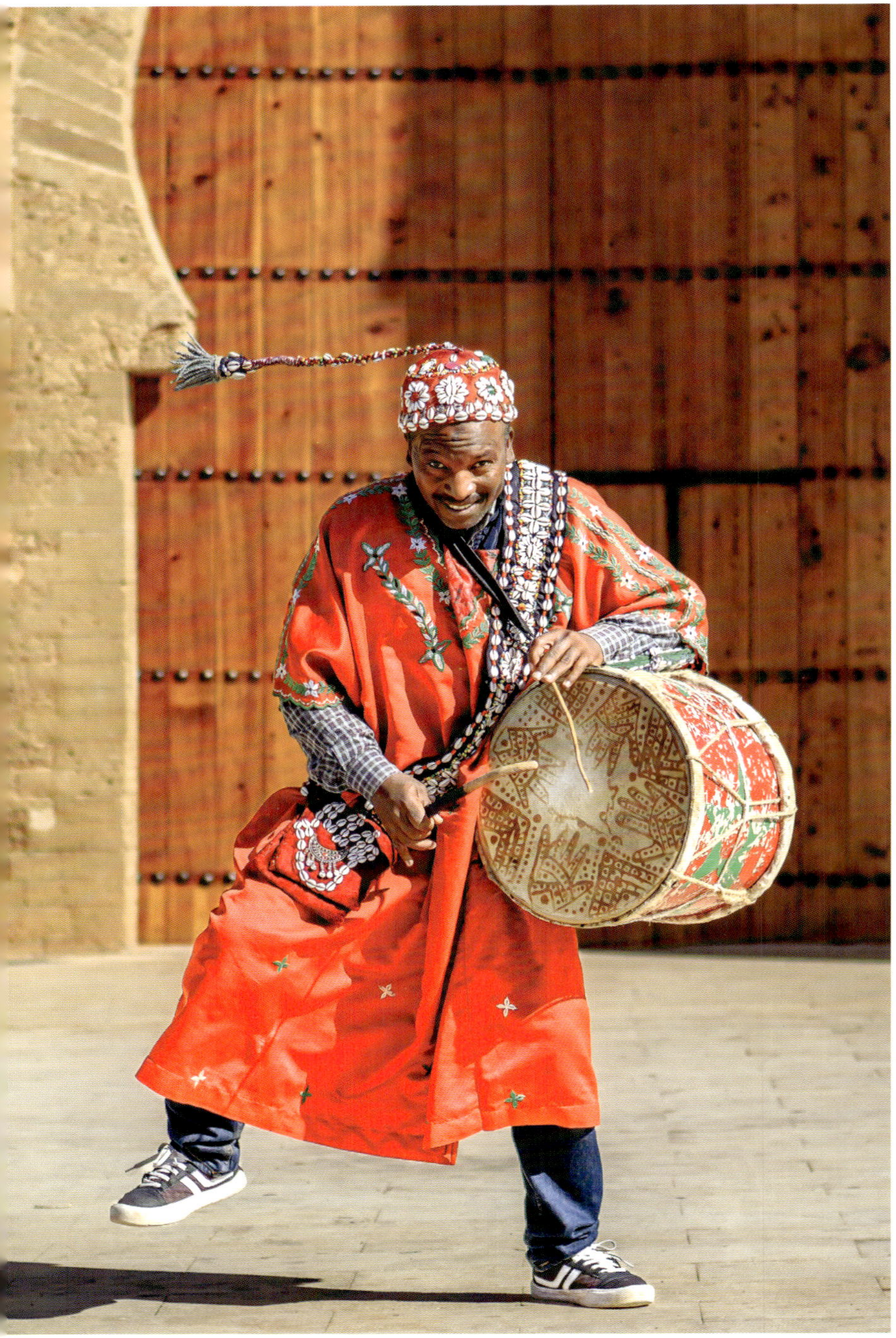

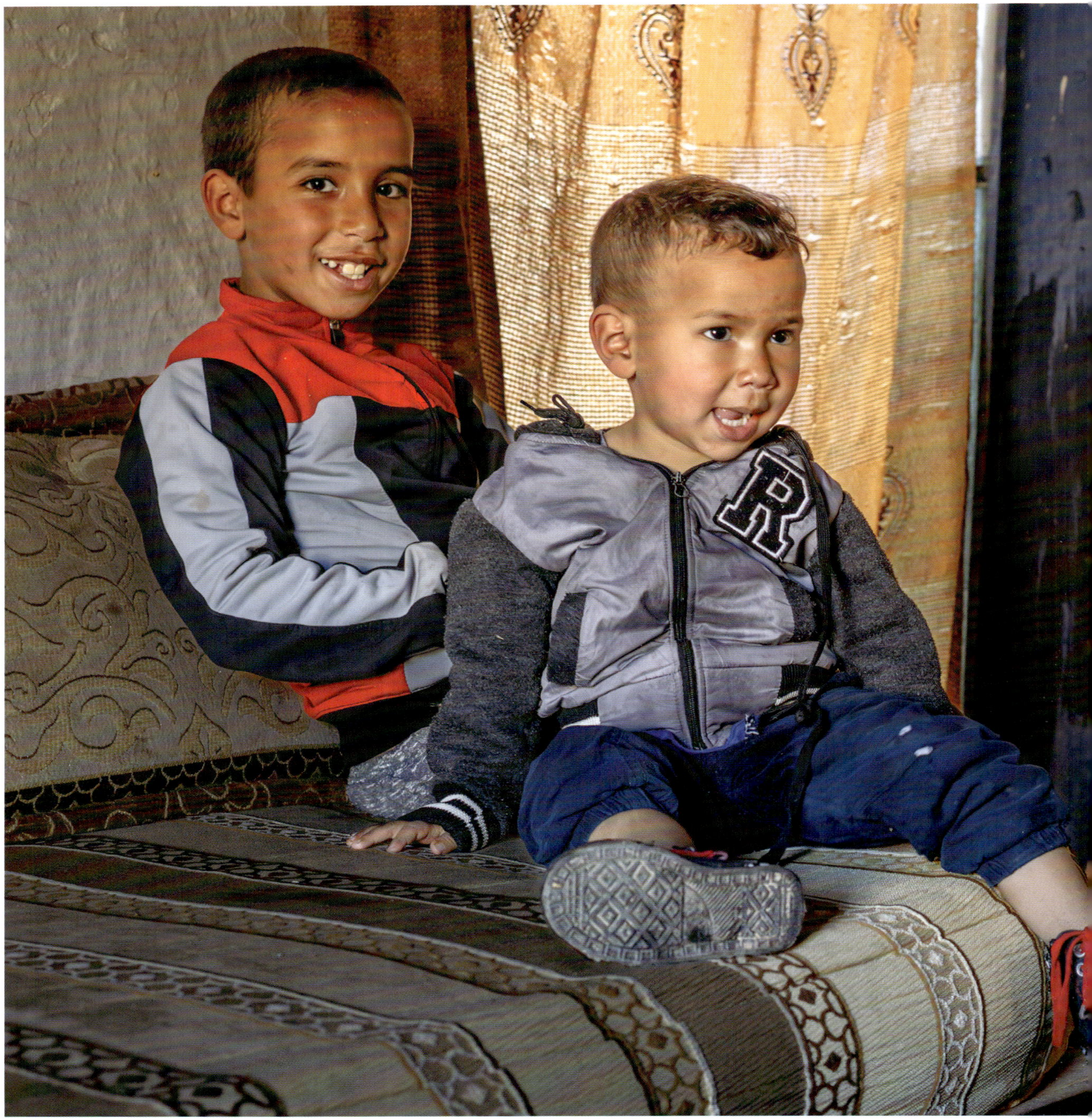

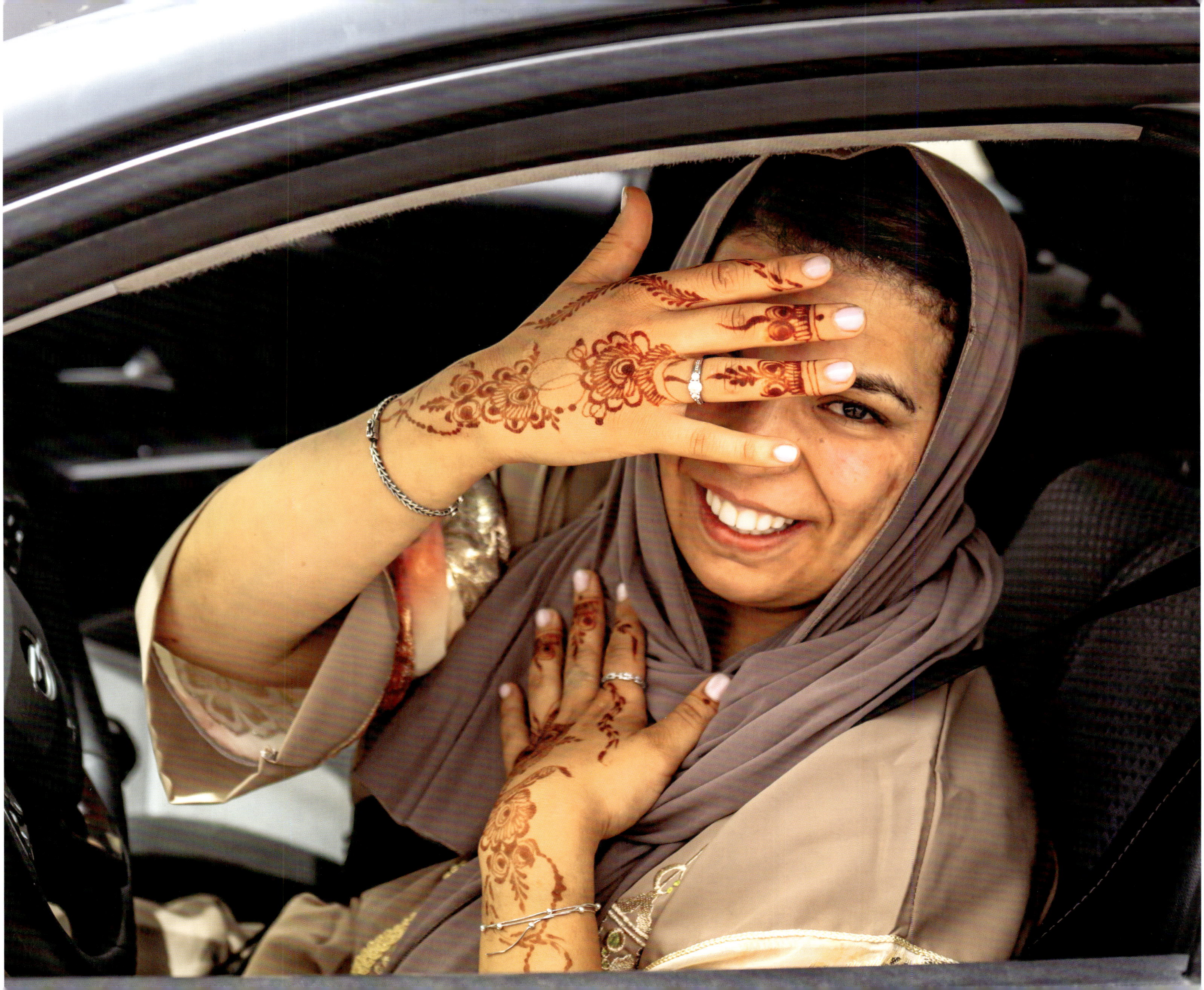

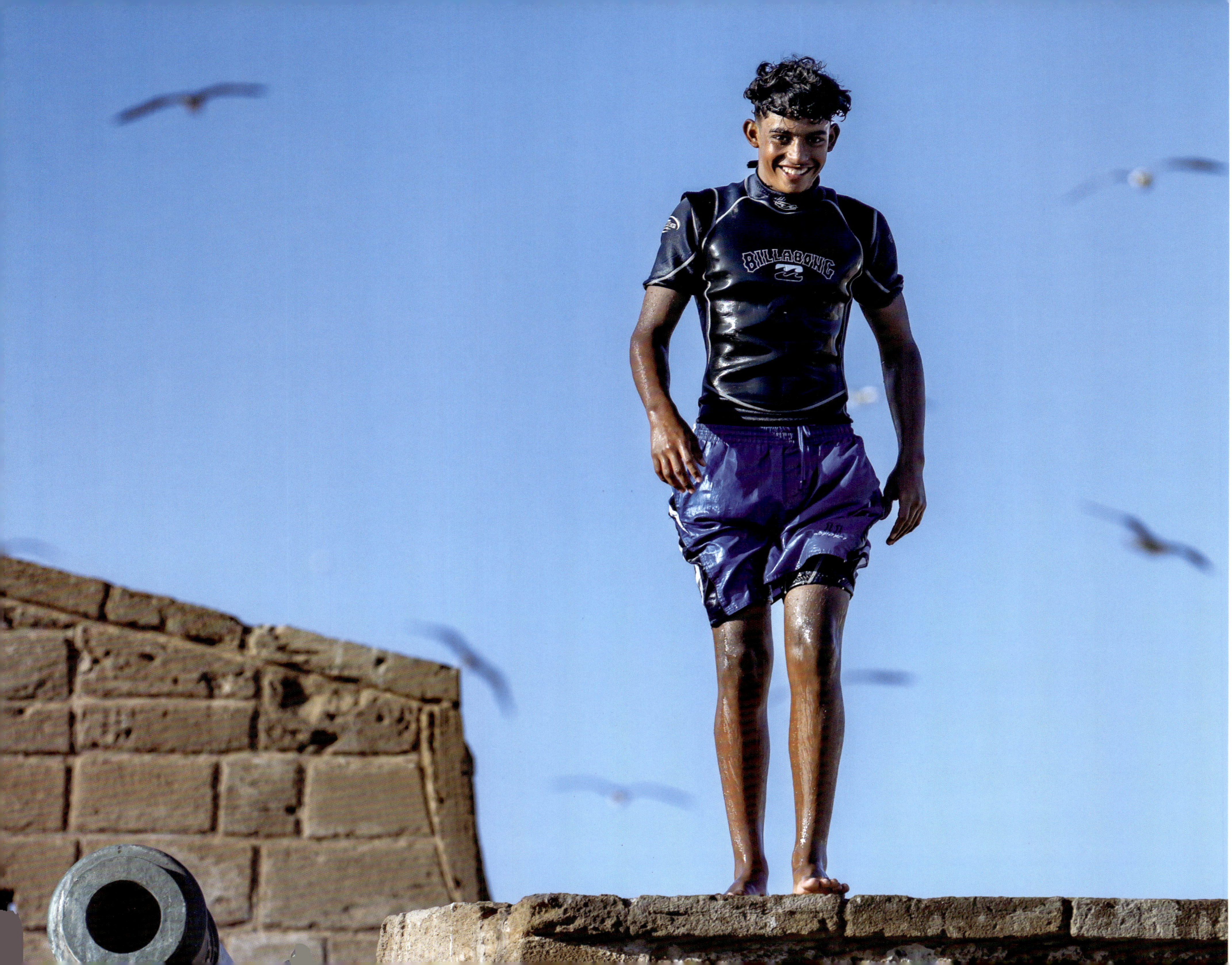
BILLABONG

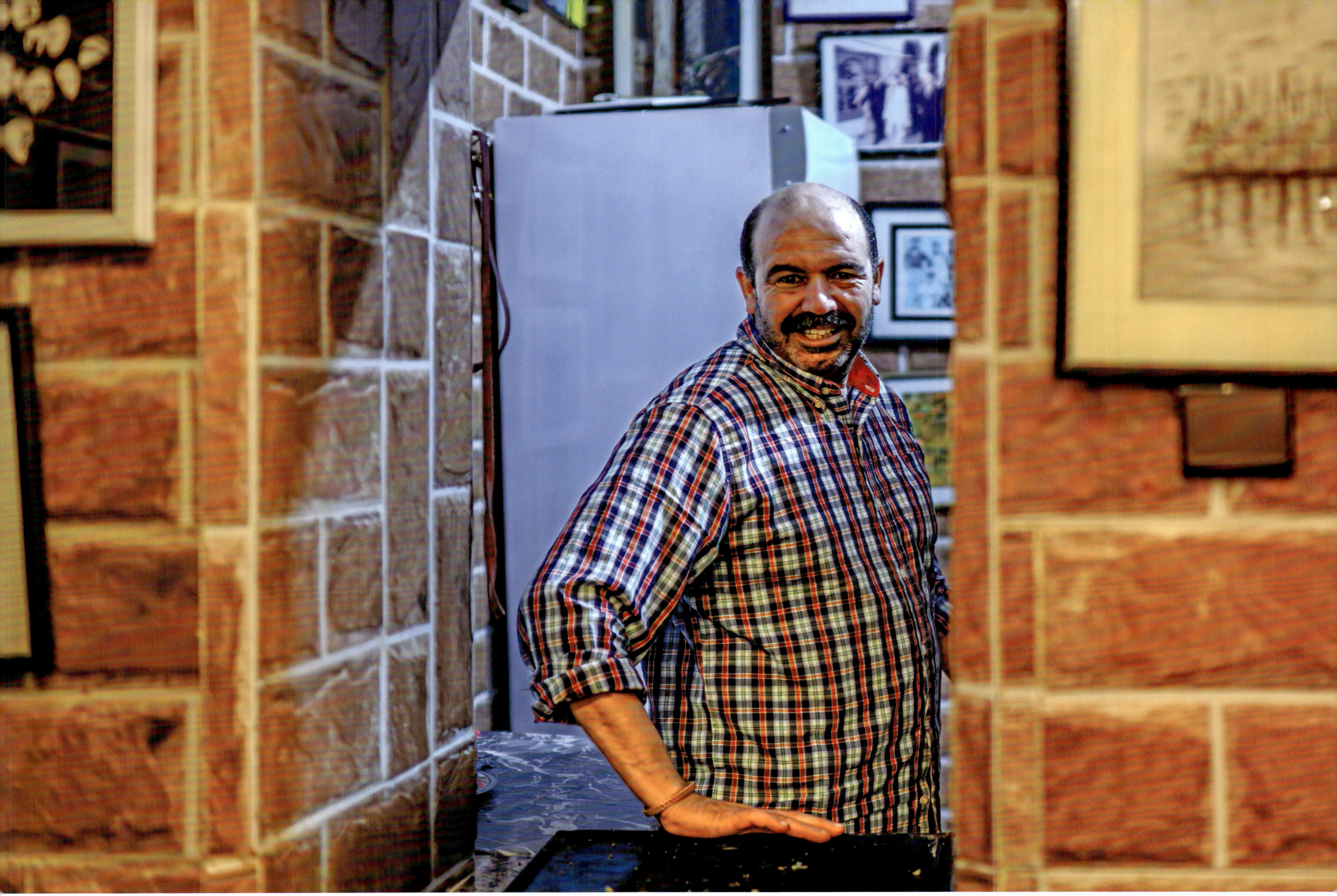

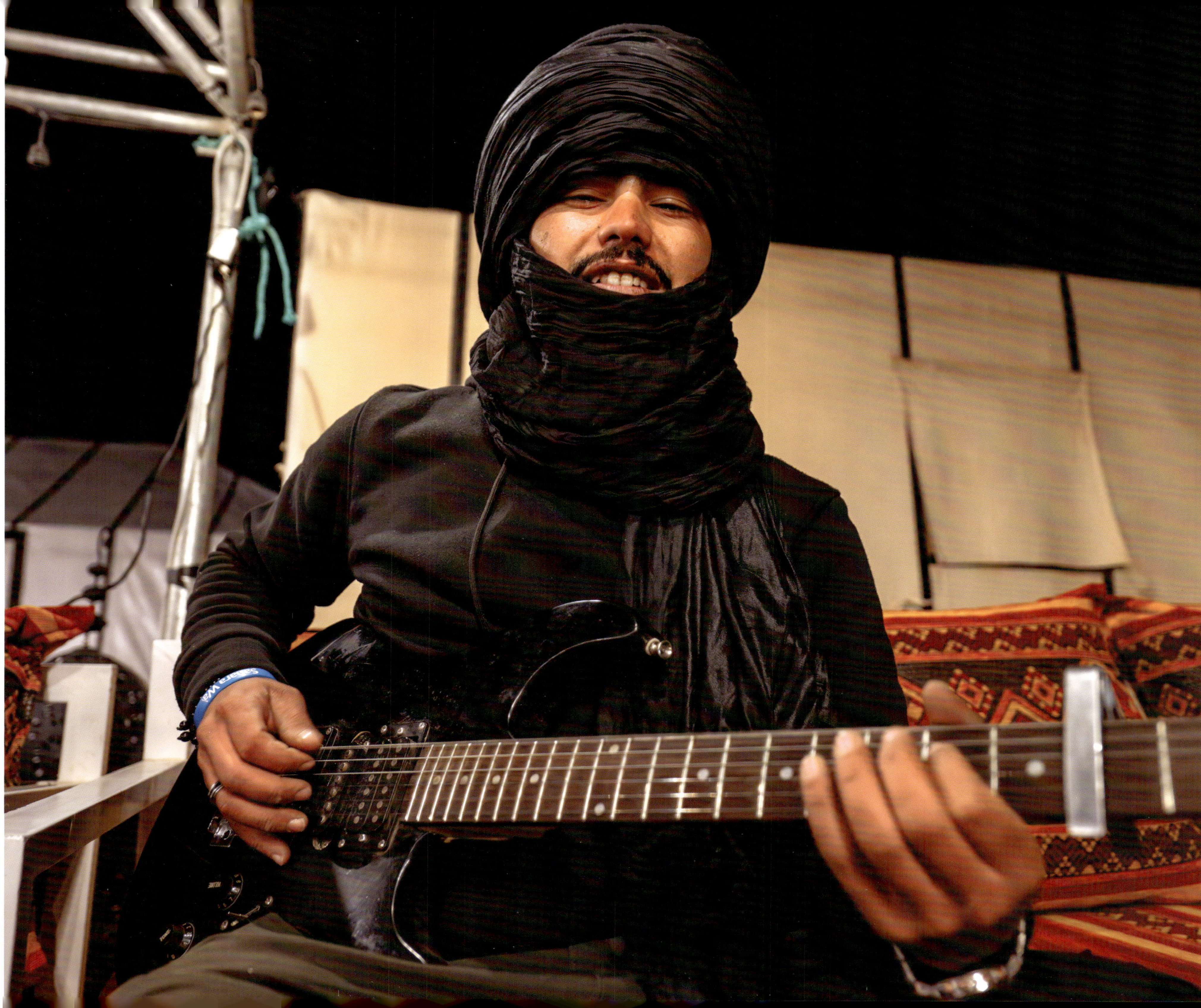

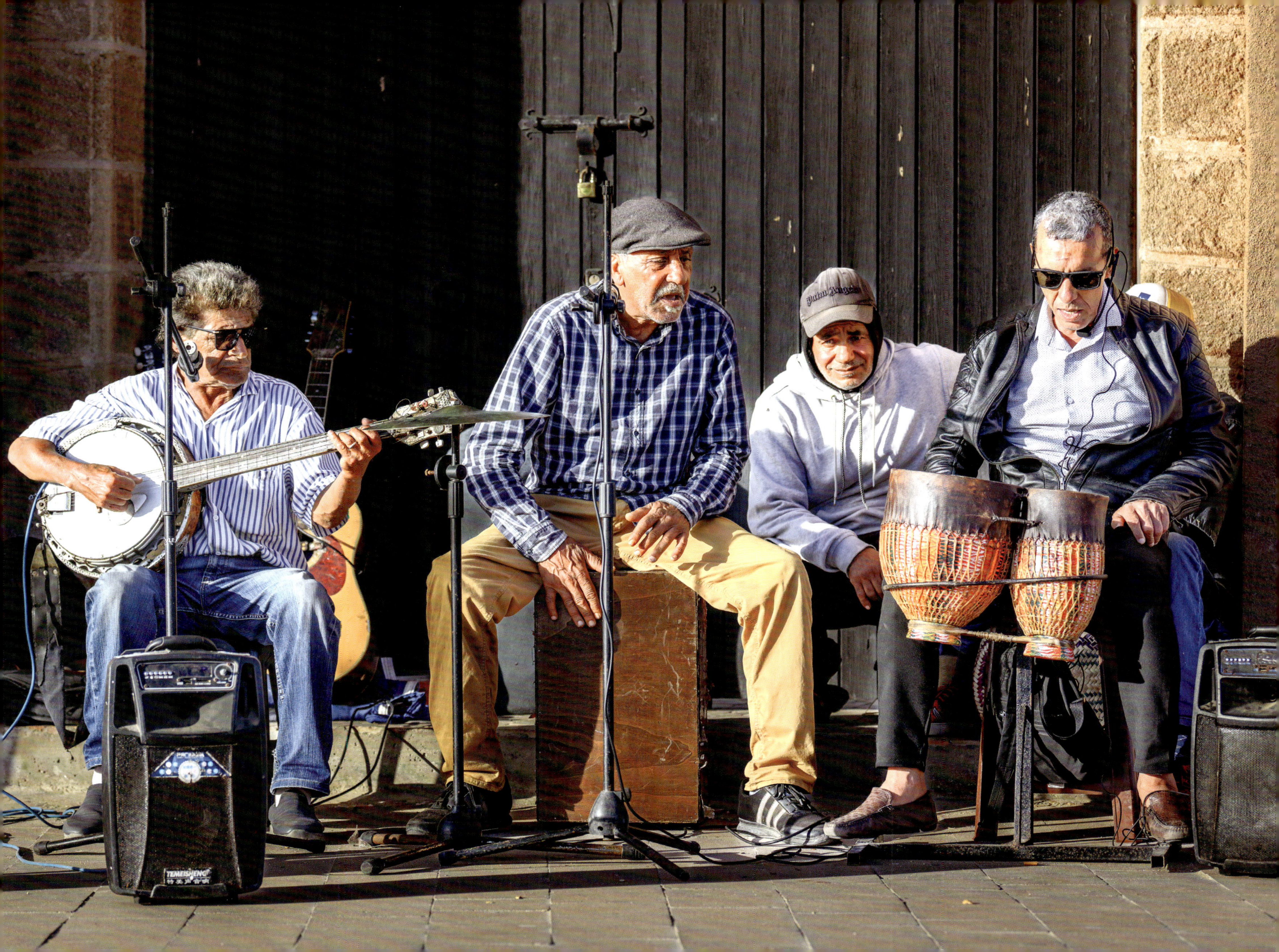
TEMEISHENG

# DEDICATION AND APPRECIATION

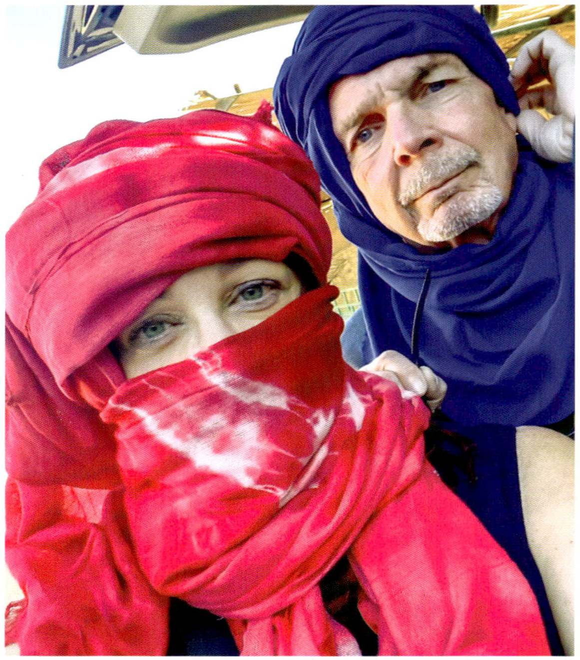

When we first visited Morocco in November 2023, it was supposed to be just a special anniversary adventure for me and my wife, Kathy. It was never intended to be the beginning of a project over a year in the making.

I was only planning on taking photos that documented our trip together and I brought one camera, two lenses, and my laptop. Just enough!

My plans for taking just vacation photos changed as soon as we walked into the Hassan II Mosque in Casablanca on the afternoon we arrived for our 15-day tour.

The mosque was breathtaking, inside and out. From Casablanca, we headed to Rabat and, well, the idea of just making vacation photos ended when Kathy looked at what I was shooting, and what she was taking on her iPhone.

"We have to do a book," Kathy said on the third day.

I've been a photographer since 2010, when I switched from a career as a newspaper reporter and sportswriter, to working as a freelance journalist covering rowing and I picked up my first camera.

What I wrote and photographed had typically been published pretty much right away. I liked it that way.

I was not thinking book. But Kathy was.

She's a lifelong career communications professional with a business MBA, and she can be very convincing. She had looked for a "coffee table" photo book about Morocco when we were planning the trip. But did not find anything more than travel books, the kind that are invaluable for planning, but are not visual keepsakes of this beautiful country and people.

And so, there is now a book of just images—this book. And without Kathy's creativity, determination, and vision, *Epic Morocco* would not exist.

Kathy drove this project from the beginning. I am grateful to have listened to her.

Morocco is stunning in its beauty, and Moroccans are warm and generous people. Working with them, photographing them, and listening as they passionately talked about their history and culture over two trips made this project a work of joy.

We would like to thank every Moroccan we encountered, but since we can't, we will dedicate a portion of the proceeds from every sale to local organizations making a difference in Morocco.

We would like to especially thank Mark Stallwood and our new friends at *Nomadic Tours* who organized our adventures, and then invested in and supported this project. A special shoutout goes to our Amazigh guide, Khalid El-Ouafy (*from the high Atlas Mountains*) who works for *Nomadic Tours*, and who greeted us each morning with a boatload of enthusiasm and a cheerful "today we will see many wonderful things." And we did.

Kathy and I hope you enjoy the images on these pages and are inspired to visit Morocco and meet its warm and generous people.

*Ed and Kathy Moran*

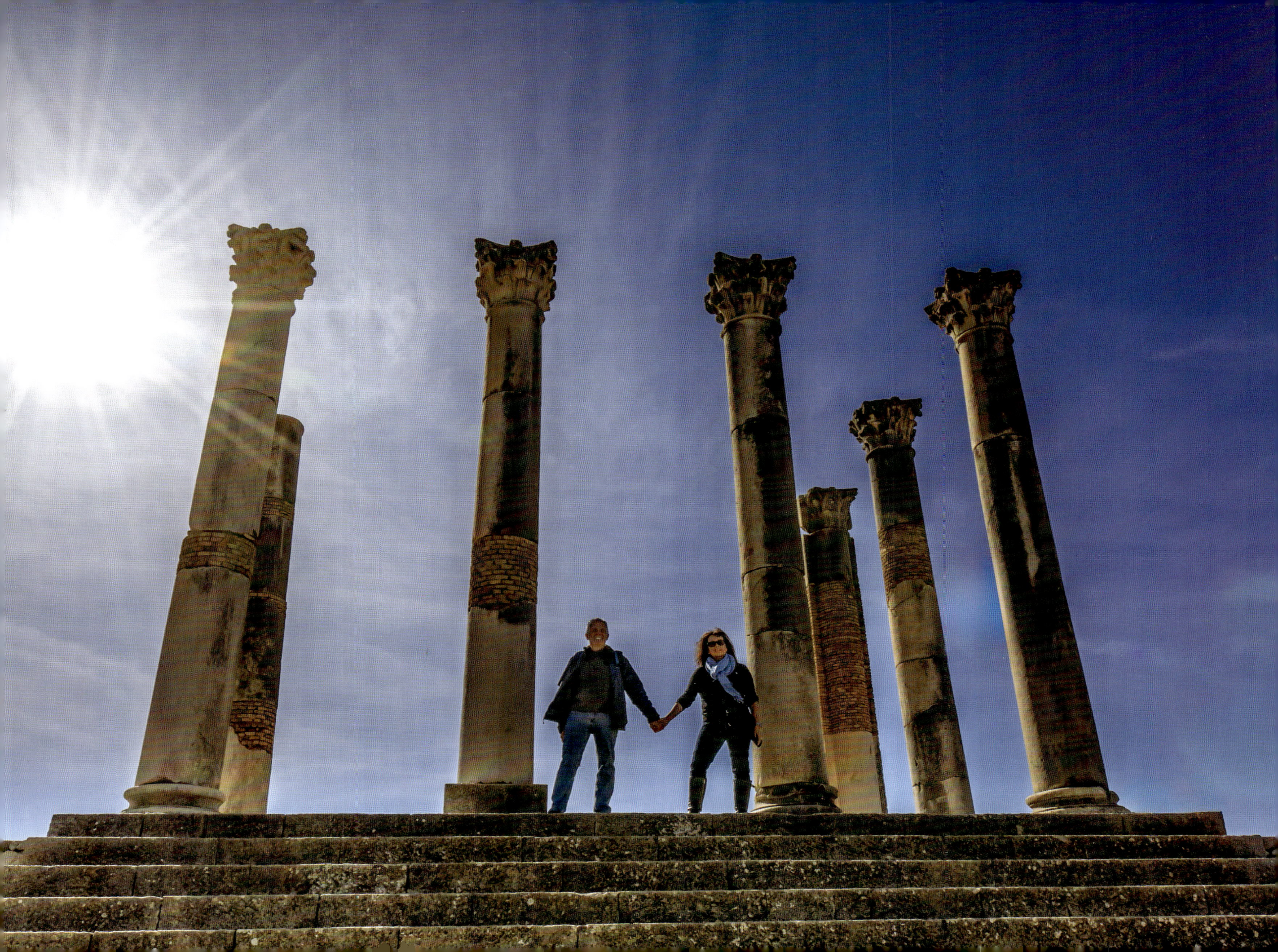

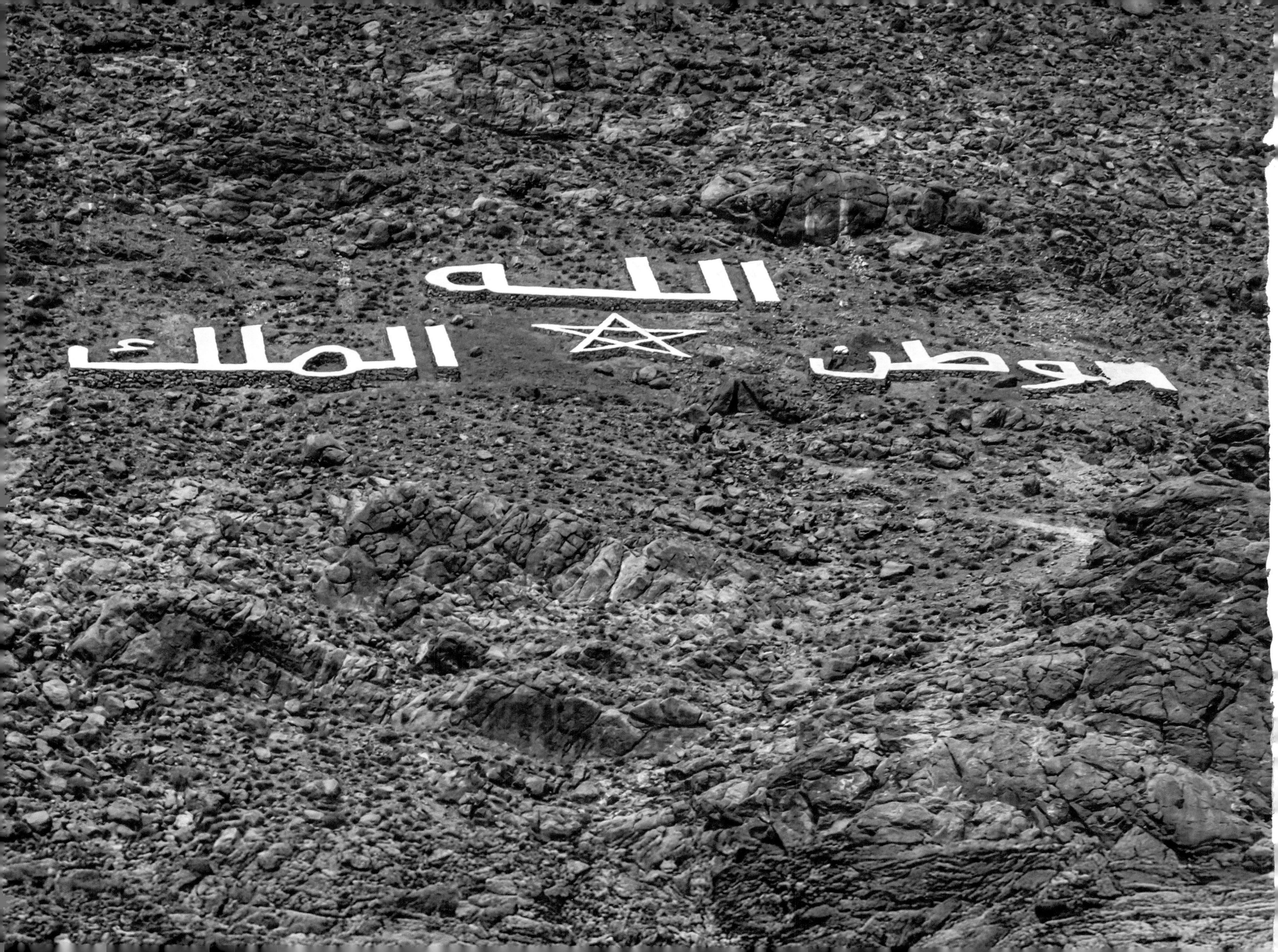
الله
الوطن
الملك

Editor:
Kathy Ridgely Moran

Photography:
Ed Moran
edmoranphotography.com

Design:
Steve Dariotis

Printed in China

Library of Congress Control Number:
2024926291

ISBN: 979-8-218-98987-3

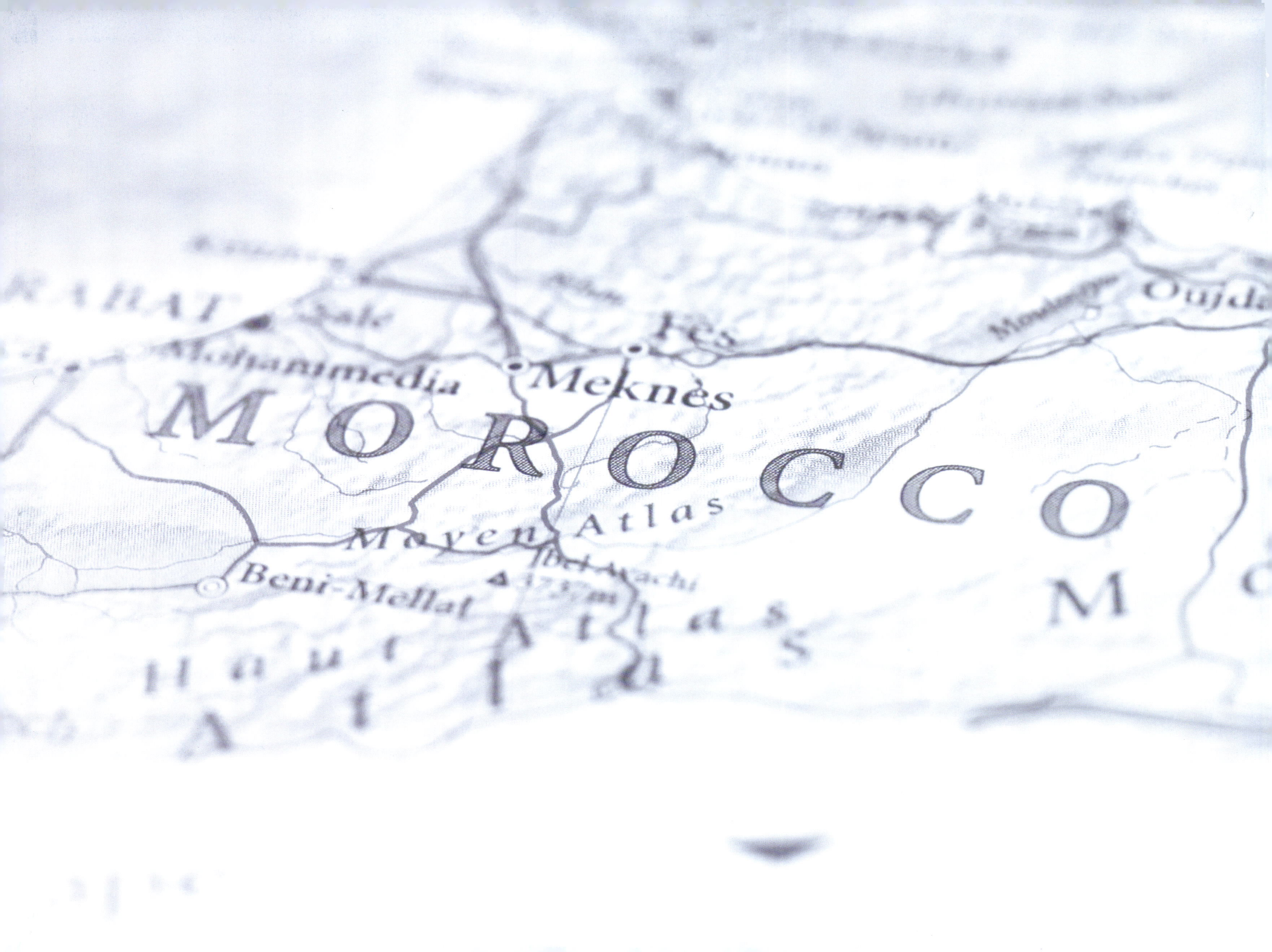
MOROCCO
Meknès
Fès
Oujda
Mohammedia
Moyen Atlas
Beni-Mellal